KU-865-508

THIRD EDITION

Theories of Development

Concepts and Applications

William Crain
*The City College
of the City University of New York*

PRENTICE H   rsey 07632

WORCESTER COLLEGE OF TECHNOLOGY

* 0 0 7 2 6 7 9 *

Library of Congress Cataloging-in-Publication Data

Crain, William C., (date)
   Theories of development: concepts and applications / William
Crain.—3rd ed.
     p.   cm.
   Includes bibliographical references and index.
   ISBN 0-13-913476-X
   1. Developmental psychology.   I. Title.
BF713.C72   1992   91-32823
155—dc20   CIP

Acquisition editor: Carol Wada
Editorial/production supervision and
   interior design: Linda B. Pawelchak
Cover design: Mike Fender Design
Prepress buyer: Kelly Behr
Manufacturing buyer: Mary Ann Gloriande

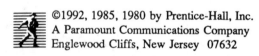 ©1992, 1985, 1980 by Prentice-Hall, Inc.
A Paramount Communications Company
Englewood Cliffs, New Jersey 07632

All rights reserved. No part of this book may be
reproduced, in any form or by any means,
without permission in writing from the publisher.

Printed in the United States of America
10 9

ISBN 0-13-913476-X

Prentice-Hall International (UK) Limited, *London*
Prentice-Hall of Australia Pty. Limited, *Sydney*
Prentice-Hall Canada Inc., *Toronto*
Prentice-Hall Hispanoamericana, S. A., *Mexico*
Prentice-Hall of India Private Limited, *New Delhi*
Prentice-Hall of Japan, Inc., *Tokyo*
Simon & Schuster Asia Pte. Ltd., *Singapore*
Editora Prentice-Hall do Brasil, Ltda., *Rio de Janeiro*

To Ellen
and to Adam, Tom, and Sally

Contents

Preface   xi

Introduction   xv

1
Early Theories: Preformationism, Locke, and Rousseau   1

Preformationism   *1*
Locke's Environmentalism   *3*
Rousseau's Romantic Naturalism   *8*

2
Gesell's Maturational Theory   16

Biographical Introduction   *16*
Principles of Development   *17*
Philosophy of Child-Rearing   *22*
Evaluation   *25*

3

Ethological Theories: Darwin, Lorenz and Tinbergen, and Bowlby 28

Darwin and the Theory of Evolution   *28*
Modern Ethology: Lorenz and Tinbergen   *31*
An Ethological View of Child
   Development: Bowlby's Theory   *38*

4

Montessori's Educational Philosophy 57

Biographical Introduction   *57*
Theory of Development   *58*
Early Education in the Home   *62*
The Montessori School   *63*
Evaluation   *72*

5

Werner's Organismic and Comparative Theory 75

Biographical Introduction   *75*
Werner's View of Development   *77*
Some Comparative Studies   *82*
Symbol Formation: An Organismic View   *89*
Theoretical Issues   *91*
Practical Applications   *95*
Evaluation   *97*

6

Piaget's Cognitive-Developmental Theory 100

Biographical Introduction   *100*
Overview of the Theory   *102*
Period I. Sensori-Motor Intelligence
   (Birth to Two Years)   *103*
Periods II and III. Preoperational
   Thought (Two to Seven)
   and Concrete Operations
   (Seven to 11)   *108*
Period IV. Formal Operations
   (11 to Adulthood)   *119*
Theoretical Issues   *121*
Implications for Education   *124*
Evaluation   *127*

7
Kohlberg's Stages of Moral Development   134

Biographical Introduction   *134*
Piaget's Stages of Moral Judgment   *135*
Kohlberg's Method   *136*
Kohlberg's Six Stages   *136*
Theoretical Issues   *141*
Implications for Education   *149*
Evaluation   *151*

8
Learning Theory: Pavlov, Watson, and Skinner   154

Pavlov and Classical Conditioning   *154*
Watson   *157*
Skinner and Operant Conditioning   *161*

9
Bandura's Social Learning Theory   175

Biographical Introduction   *175*
Basic Concepts   *176*
Socialization Studies   *178*
Abstract Modeling and Piaget's Stages   *185*
Practical Implications   *188*
Evaluation   *190*

10
Vygotsky's Social-Historical Theory of Cognitive Development   193

Biographical Introduction   *193*
Marx's Views on Human Nature   *195*
Vygotsky's Theory of Psychological Tools   *197*
Memory Aids   *200*
Speech   *201*
Schooling   *210*
Practical Applications   *215*
Evaluation   *217*

11

Freud's Psychoanalytic Theory   222

Biographical Introduction   *222*
The Stages of Psychosexual Development   *225*
The Agencies of the Mind   *236*
Practical Implications   *242*
Evaluation   *244*

12

Erikson and the Eight Stages of Life   247

Biographical Introduction   *247*
Erikson's Stage Theory   *248*
Theoretical Issues   *262*
Practical Implications   *267*
Evaluation   *268*

13

A Case Study in Psychoanalytic Treatment: Bettelheim on Autism   271

Biographical Introduction   *271*
The Autistic Syndrome   *272*
The Cause of Autism   *273*
Therapy   *274*
Evaluation   *279*

14

Schachtel on Childhood Experiences   281

Biographical Introduction   *281*
Basic Concepts   *282*
Implications for Education   *285*
Evaluation   *286*

15

Jung's Theory of Adulthood   287

Biographical Introduction   *287*
Personality Structure   *290*
Theory of Development   *293*

Practical Implications   *297*
Evaluation   *297*

16

Chomsky's Theory of Language Development   299

Biographical Introduction   *299*
Basic Concepts   *300*
Notes on the Growth of Grammar   *306*
Chomsky and Learning Theory   *309*
Chomsky and Piaget   *313*
Implications for Education   *314*
Evaluation   *315*

17

Conclusion: Humanistic Psychology and Developmental Theory   317

Humanistic Psychology   *317*
Developmentalists as Humanists   *322*
Summary   *327*
Postscript   *328*

References   331

Name Index   349

Subject Index   355

Preface

This third edition of *Theories of Development* is fundamentally similar to the first two. Its purpose, once again, is to introduce students to a variety of theorists, giving special attention to those who have contributed to that distinctly developmental perspective that began with Rousseau. The book focuses, that is, on writers who help us understand how development might arise from our inner promptings and spontaneous interests and how we might view the world differently at different stages of life.

The theorists discussed in this edition are the same as those in the second, with two notable exceptions. I have added a chapter on L. S. Vygotsky and a section on Mary Ainsworth. Vygotsky provides fresh insights into the cultural influences on development, and Ainsworth's research has done so much to advance ethological theory that it deserves special attention.

This new edition has also given me an opportunity to update certain chapters, especially those on Bandura, Erikson, Chomsky, and humanistic psychology, and to say a bit more about the educational implications of Piaget's theory.

Many people have been very helpful in the writing of this new edition. I would like to thank, first of all, the students and colleagues who gave me feedback on the earlier editions. I would also like to express my deepest thanks to my wife Ellen; her constant encouragement and insights helped move the book forward. And then there has been the contribution of our children. As I noted in the first edition, it was by watching them that I became so impressed by the nature of the growth process that I wanted to write this book about it, and they have inspired and informed the later editions as well.

Behind any book are those who played a role in the author's intellectual development. I am indebted to many fine teachers, including Robert White, George W. Goethals, Bernice Neugarten, Lawrence Kohlberg, Wilbur Hass, Daniel G. Freedman, Bruno Bettelheim, and Erik Erikson.

The previous editions were reviewed by James P. Connell, Donald J. Dickerson, Robert Liebert, Richard Rosinsky, Margaret Schadler, Douglas Kimmel, William King, and Lawrence Nyman, who made many useful suggestions, as did the reviewers for this edition: Joan B. Cannon, University of Lowell, Lowell, MA; Kathleen E. Fite, Southwest Texas State University; John C. McCullers, Oklahoma State University; and Jacquelyn Sanders, Director, The Sonia Shankman Orthogenic School of the University of Chicago. My brother Stephen Crain again helped me write the chapter on Chomsky.

I am grateful, finally, to those who have given permission to quote from various sources: W. W. Norton & Co., Inc. and The Hogarth Press Ltd. granted permission to quote from Erik H. Erikson's *Childhood and Society*, 2nd ed., 1963; Macmillan Publishing Co., Inc., and Bruno Bettelheim granted permission to quote from his book, *The Empty Fortress*, copyright © 1967 by Bruno Bettelheim; Little, Brown & Co. granted permission to quote the first stanza of "Growth of Man like growth of Nature" from *Poems by Emily Dickinson*, edited by Martha Dickinson Bianchi and Alfred Leete Hampson, © 1929 by Martha Dickinson Bianchi, © 1957 by Mary L. Hampson; and *Family Circle Magazine* granted permission to quote from Louise B. Ames's "Don't push your preschooler," in the December 1971 issue, © 1971, The Family Circle, Inc., all rights reserved. Credit for the use of illustrations and other material is given within the text.

Growth of Man like growth
Of Nature
Gravitates within,
Atmosphere and sun confirm it
But it stirs alone.

Emily Dickinson

Introduction

We all have assumptions about the nature of development. We commonly assume, for example, that children's development is in our hands—that children become what we make them. We think it is our job to teach them, to correct their mistakes, to provide good models, and to motivate them to learn.

Such a view is reasonable enough, and it is shared by many psychologists—by those called learning theorists and by many others as well. Psychologists use more scientific language, but they too assume that parents, teachers, and others structure the child's thought and behavior. When they see a child engaging in a new bit of behavior, their first guess is that it has been taught. If, for example, a two-year-old girl shows an intense interest in putting objects into place, they assume that someone taught her to do this. For she is a product of her social environment.

There is, however, another tradition in psychology—a line of theorists dating from Rousseau—that looks at development quite differently. These writers, the developmentalists, are less impressed by our efforts to teach or otherwise influence children. Instead, they are more interested in how children grow and learn on their own. The developmentalists would wonder if this two-year-old's interest in ordering objects might not be a spontaneous one—something she has begun entirely by herself. Her concern for order might even be greater than that of those around her. For just as children, at a certain stage, develop an inner urge to stand and walk, they may also develop a spontaneous need to find order in their environment.

If we follow a child around, taking the time to observe the child's natural tendencies, we find that the child has many spontaneous interests.

A 1½-year-old may become fascinated by a ball, a puddle of water, or a mound of sand—things that can be touched, felt, and acted upon. The child may examine and play with such objects for long periods of time. Such interests may be so intense and so different from our own that it is unlikely that they are the product of adult teachings. Rather, the developmentalists think, children may have an inner need to seek out certain kinds of experiences and activities at certain times in life.

The developmentalists—theorists such as Rousseau, Montessori, Gesell, Werner, and Piaget—do not agree on every point, and they have studied different aspects of development. Nevertheless, they share a fundamental orientation, which includes this interest in inner growth and spontaneous learning.

The developmentalists' concerns have been practical as well as theoretical. Montessori, for example, became dissatisfied with customary educational methods, in which teachers try to direct children's learning by rewarding their correct answers and by criticizing their mistakes. This practice, she thought, undermines children's independence, for children soon turn to the teacher, an external authority, to see if they are right. Instead, she tried to show that if we observe children's spontaneous interests, we can help provide tasks on which they will work independently and with the greatest concentration, without external direction or motivation. For, she thought, there is an inner force that prompts children to perfect their capacities at each developmental stage.

In many other ways, the developmentalists have contributed to a new understanding of childhood and later development as well. Unfortunately, however, their writings have not received the full consideration they deserve. It seems that their emphasis on spontaneous development has often struck psychologists as too romantic or too radical. Piaget, to be sure, has found a wide audience, but even he was ignored for decades.

There is one place where the developmentalists' concerns are seriously addressed. This is in modern humanistic psychology. Humanists such as Maslow have drawn heavily upon developmental ideas. However, the humanists have usually done this in a very implicit way, without recognizing how much they owe to earlier developmental contributions.

This book, then, is devoted to an appreciation of some of the outstanding developmental theorists. We will discuss some of the theorists who have followed closely in the footsteps of Rousseau, along with other theorists, including ethologists and psychoanalysts, who share a developmental outlook. We will discuss their concepts and some of the practical implications of their work. We also will review the first orientation we mentioned—that of the learning theorists, who help us understand behavior from a more environmental perspective. We will not cover learning theory in the depth it deserves, for this short book is primarily concerned with the developmental tradition. But we will try to get a flavor of the learning theorists' ideas. In the chapter on Vygotsky, in addition, we will look at a pioneering attempt to integrate strong developmental and environmental perspectives. Finally, in the Conclusion, we will discuss the ways in which both developmentalists and environmentalists have been working in the humanistic tradition for some time.

1

Early Theories:
Preformationism, Locke, and Rousseau

The two great pioneers in child psychology were Locke and Rousseau. Locke was the father of environmentalism and learning theory: his heirs are scientists such as Pavlov and B. F. Skinner. Rousseau began the developmental tradition in psychology; his followers include Gesell, Montessori, Werner, and Piaget. Both Locke and Rousseau made radical departures from an earlier outlook called preformationism.

PREFORMATIONISM

For centuries, people seem to have looked upon children as fully formed, miniature adults. Ariès (1960) described how this view was predominant during the Middle Ages. Medieval paintings, for example, routinely portrayed children—even newborns—with adult body proportions and facial characteristics. The children were distinguished only by their size. It was as if the children had arrived preformed in the adult mold (Ariès, 1960, pp. 33–34).

Socially, too, medieval children were treated like adults. By the age of six or seven, they had usually entered adult society—working, mingling, and playing with the grownups (1960, pp. 71–72, 128, 411).

Some historians argue that Ariès overstated the degree to which medieval society considered children to be little adults. But Ariès has also received a good deal of support, and he alerted us to the prevalence of preformationism during other historical epochs (see Pollock, 1983).

Why have people held preformationist views? Ariès (1960, p. 40) speculated that for a long time people were reluctant to pay much attention to children's distinctive features because of the high rates of childhood mortality. Knowing that their children might very well die, parents were hesitant to attend to and cherish their unique qualities. According to Ausubel (1958, p. 24), preformationism also may have had to do with natural adult egocentrism. Adults tend to assume that all human life has the same form and function as their own. It takes a special open-mindedness to see the unique properties of life at different periods—an open-mindedness that is not easily acquired.

In the sciences, preformationism is most evident in the early theories of embryology. For many centuries, most scientists believed that a tiny, fully formed human, or homunculus, is implanted in the sperm or the egg at conception (see Figure 1.1). They believed the human is "preformed" at the instant of creation and grows only in size and bulk until birth. Preformationism in embryology dates back at least to the fifth century B.C. and dominated scientific thinking throughout the ages. Even as late as the eighteenth century, most scientists held preformationist views. They admitted that they had no direct evidence for the existence of a fully formed homunculus, but they argued that this was only because it is transparent and too small to see (Needham, 1959, pp. 34–35, 91, 213–22; Balinsky, 1981, p. 11).

In embryology, preformationism began to give way in the last half of the eighteenth century, when microscopic investigations showed that the embryo develops through a series of stages. In European social thought, preformationism declined earlier, in the sixteenth century. Religious lead-

FIGURE 1.1
Drawing by Hartsoeker (1694) of a fully formed human in the sperm. (Reprinted in Needham, 1959, p. 206.)

1

ers and moralists began emphasizing children's special qualities. According to some, children enter the world with a God-given purity and innocence that is later corrupted. Others argued that children bear humankind's original sin. Children, they emphasized, are ignorant creatures who possess a wanton sensuality and a lack of morals (Ariès, 1960, Ch. 5).

In either case, this new interest in the distinctive nature of children was accompanied by a new concern for education. The proponents of childhood innocence wanted to preserve and strengthen children's innate goodness against the world's evil influence. They optimistically held that the right education would make the child into "the good magistrate," "the good priest," and "the good lord" (Ariès, 1960, p. 114). Those who viewed children more pessimistically were also very concerned about the need for education. Children's irrational and vile ways, they argued, must be forced out of them. We must impose stern discipline, including the frequent use of physical beatings. In either case—whether children were seen as innocent or sinful—they must be educated to become right-minded adults, and it is never too early to begin (1960, pp. 128–33).

LOCKE'S ENVIRONMENTALISM

Biographical Introduction

By the sixteenth century, then, preformationism had begun to give way to a more environmentalistic position, at least in the realm of social thought. Children, in the new view, are not born just like adults but become the adults they do because of their upbringing and education. The writers of this period, however, were not thoroughgoing environmentalists; they still recognized certain inborn traits of childhood, such as innocence or depravity. The first clear, comprehensive statement of the environmentalist position was made by the English philosopher John Locke (1632–1704). In 1690 Locke proposed that children are neither innately good or innately bad—innately, they are nothing at all. The child's mind, Locke said, is initially a *tabula rasa*, a blank slate, and whatever the mind becomes is almost completely the result of learning and experience.

Locke's theory fit well with the liberal and democratic thinking of the Enlightenment. If children are all initially empty organisms, they are all born equal. If some people become in any way better than others, this is due to more favorable circumstances. In theory at least, it is possible to educate all people to become equal as adults.

Locke was born in the small village of Somerset, England, the son of a pious and affectionate mother and a strict father. Locke's father, who had sided with the Parliament in the civil war against King Charles I, first instilled in him a belief in democracy. Locke was educated at Oxford, where he stayed on to teach Greek and moral philosophy. There he also studied medicine. As a physician, Locke successfully treated Lord Ashley, later the Earl of Shaftesbury, became Shaftesbury's friend and personal secretary, and also tutored his grandson. His association with Shaftesbury,

however, eventually proved troublesome. When Shaftesbury was impris-
oned for criticizing the king, Locke was forced to flee England and find
exile in Holland. While in Holland, Locke wrote a series of letters to his
friend Edward Clark, offering advice on the upbringing of Clark's son.
These letters inspired Locke's most important work on education, *Some
Thoughts Concerning Education* (1693). After the successful Revolution of
1688, Locke returned to England and saw the publication of two other
great books. The first was his *Essay Concerning Human Understanding* (1690),
which established him as the father of empiricism in philosophy and learning theory in psychology. His other great book was *Two Treatises on Government* (1689), which set forth many of the central ideas in the U.S. Con-
stitution (Russell, 1945, pp. 604–5; Sahakian and Sahakian, 1975, Ch. 1).

Locke's Views on Development

The starting point of Locke's theory was his refutation of the doctrine
of innate ideas. Plato, Descartes, and others had maintained that certain
ideas are innate, existing in the mind prior to experience. For example,
when we see a mathematical proof, we immediately perceive its truth.
Locke argued, however, that since children and idiots know nothing of
mathematics or logic, these ideas cannot exist from the beginning (Locke,
1690, Vol. I, Bk. 1, Ch. 2, sec. 27). Locke suggested that we consider

> the mind to be, as we say, white paper void of all characteristics, without any
> *ideas*. How comes it to be furnished? . . . Whence has it all the materials of
> reason and knowledge? To this I answer, in one word, from *experience*; in
> that all our knowledge is founded, and from that it ultimately derives itself.
> (1690, Vol. I, Bk. 2, Ch. 1, sec. 2)

Locke admitted that individuals have different temperaments, but on
the whole, the environment forms the mind (Locke, 1693, secs. 1, 32). Of
particular importance is learning during infancy. At this time the mind
is the most pliable, so we can mold it in any way we wish. And once we
do so, its basic nature is set for the rest of life (1693, secs. 1, 2).

How, then, does the environment shape the child's mind? First, many
of our thoughts and feelings develop through *associations*. Two ideas regularly occur together, so we cannot think of one without simultaneously
thinking of the other. For example, if a child has had bad experiences in
a particular room, the child cannot enter it without automatically experiencing a negative feeling (Locke, 1690, Vol. I, Bk. 2, Ch. 33, sec. 15).

Much of our behavior also develops through *repetition*. When we do
something over and over, such as brushing our teeth, the practice becomes
a natural habit, and we feel uneasy when we have failed to perform it
(Locke, 1693, sec. 66).

We also learn through *imitation*. We are prone to do what we see
others do, so models influence our character. If we are frequently exposed
to silly and quarrelsome people, we become silly and quarrelsome ourselves;
if we are exposed to more noble minds, we too become more noble (1693,
sec. 67).

Finally, and most important, we learn through *rewards* and *punishments*. We engage in behavior that brings praise, compliments, and other rewards; we refrain from those actions that produce unpleasant consequences (1693, sec. 54).

These principles, Locke believed, often work together in the development of character. For example, a little girl is likely to hang up her clothes if she sees her parents hang theirs up, through imitation. After she hangs up her clothes a few times in succession, this good trait becomes a habit, and this habit becomes all the stronger if she receives some praise or compliment for it.

The previous example illustrates how Locke's principles can be applied to child-rearing. Let us now look more closely at his views on child-rearing and education.

Locke's Educational Philosophy

Self-control. The main goal of education is self-control. "It seems plain to me," Locke said, "that the principle of all virtue and excellency lies in a power of denying ourselves the satisfaction of our own desires, where reason does not authorize them" (1693, sec. 38).

To instill self-discipline, we first should tend to the child's physical health. When the body is sick and weak, one has little ability to control its demands. Accordingly, Locke advised us to give children plenty of exercise so their bodies will become strong, and he suggested that children play outdoors in all seasons so they will learn to endure the hardships of all kinds of weather (1693, secs. 1–16, 33).

If children are to acquire discipline, we must be firm with them from the start. Many parents coddle their children and give in to their every whim; they think that such indulgence is all right because their children are still small. What they fail to realize is that early habits are difficult to break. Children who find that they can get whatever they want, simply by asking or crying out, never unlearn this bad habit. Thus, parents should never reward children when they desire things they do not need. Children should learn that they will get favorable results only when they ask for things that their parents consider appropriate (1693, secs. 38–40).

The best rewards and punishments. From the beginning, then, we should pay close attention to how we reinforce our children's behavior. We should reward only reasonable behavior, never behavior that is unreasonable or self-indulgent.

The use of rewards and punishments, however, is a tricky matter. Not all rewards and punishments produce desirable effects. Locke was especially opposed to the use of *physical punishment*. In the first place, its use establishes undesirable associations. For example, the child who has been repeatedly beaten or chastised in school cannot look upon books, teachers, or anything having to do with school without experiencing fear or anger. Further, physical punishment is often ineffective. The child submits while the rod is in sight, but just as soon as the child sees that no one is looking, the child does whatever he or she wants. Finally, when physical punishment does work, it usually works too well. It succeeds in "breaking the mind; and then, in the place of a disorderly young fellow, you have a low-spirited moped creature" (1693, sec. 51).

Similarly, not all kinds of rewards are desirable. Locke opposed the use of money or sweets as rewards because their use undermines the main goal of education: to curb desires and to submit to reason. When we reward with food or money, we only encourage children to find happiness in these things (1693, sec. 52).

The best rewards are praise and flattery, and the best punishment is disapproval. When children do well we should compliment them, making them feel proud; when they do poorly we should give them a cold glance, making them feel ashamed. Children are very sensitive to approval and disapproval, especially from their parents and those on whom they depend. So we can use these reactions to instill rational and virtuous behavior (1693, sec. 57).

We also can strengthen the effectiveness of our approval and disapproval by pairing these reactions with other consequences. For example, when a little boy asks politely for a piece of fruit, we give it to him, and we also compliment him on his politeness. In this way, he learns to associate approval with agreeable consequences and thus becomes more concerned about it. Alternatively, when he breaks something he likes, we add a look of disappointment in him, so he will come to associate our disapproval with negative consequences. Through such practices, we deepen the child's concern for the opinions of others. Locke said that if you can make children "in love with the pleasure of being well thought on, you may turn them as you please, and they will be in love with all the ways of virtue" (1693, sec. 58).

Rules. Most parents set down all kinds of rules and then punish their children when they disobey them. This practice is basically useless. Children have great difficulty comprehending and remembering rules in the abstract, and they naturally resent getting punished for failing to comply with a rule which they could barely keep in mind. As an alternative to commands, Locke suggested two procedures.

First, since children learn more from example than precept, we can teach them much by exposing them to good models. Children will eagerly model their behavior after that of a virtuous person, especially when we compliment them for doing so (1693, sec. 68).

Second, Locke suggested that, instead of issuing commands, we have children practice the desired behavior. For example, instead of instructing children to bow whenever they meet a lady, it is better to give them actual practice in bowing, complimenting them each time they bow correctly. After repeated practice, they will bow as naturally as they breathe, without any thought or reflection, which is essentially foreign to them anyway (1693, sec. 66).

Children's special characteristics. Locke's discussion of the futility of teaching rules that exceed a child's understanding introduced something new into his system. Before this, he had written as if the child's mind were a lump of clay which we could mold in any way we wished. Now, however, he was saying that children have their own cognitive capacities that set limits on what we can teach. He also suggested that children have temperaments peculiar to their age, such as a liking for noise, raucous games, and gaiety, and he added that it would be foolish to try to change their natural dispositions (1693, sec. 63). Thus, Locke seemed to admit that children are not blank slates after all. As various scholars have pointed out (e.g., Russell, 1945, p. 606; Kessen, 1965, pp. 59, 72). Locke was not above a certain amount of inconsistency. If he had insights that contradicted his basic environmentalism, the inconsistency didn't trouble him.

In an interesting discussion (Locke, 1693, secs. 118–19), Locke wrote about children's innate curiosity in a way that makes one wonder about the rest of his thesis. Children, he said, learn for the sake of learning; their minds seek knowledge like the eye seeks light. If we simply listen to their questions and answer them directly, their minds will expand beyond what we would have imagined possible. But if the child's curiosity is so powerful, why do we need to use rewards and punishments for learning? Perhaps they are necessary in the development of moral behavior, but it may be that children will develop their intellectual powers through their intrinsic curiosity alone. Locke, however, never entertained this possibility, and in the end he reverted to his main thesis. When children reason clearly, we should compliment and flatter them. In this way, we teach them to reason (1693, sec. 119).

Evaluation

As a psychologist, Locke was far ahead of his time. His principles of learning—the principles of association, repetition, modeling, and rewards and punishments—all have become cornerstones of one or another version of modern learning theory. His ideas on education, furthermore, are pretty much those of the contemporary educator. Most teachers use rewards and punishments, such as praise, grades, and criticism, to motivate children to learn. Most enlightened teachers are also aware of the influence of models and of the need for repetition and are reluctant to use physical punishment.

Most modern educators even share Locke's inconsistencies. Although they believe that it is necessary to shape or mold the child through rewards and punishments, they also recognize that such social influences are not all-powerful. They are sensitive to the child's readiness to learn different things, and they recognize that children learn best when they are spontaneously curious about a particular subject. Nevertheless, like Locke, they are not prepared to rely too heavily on children's intrinsic motivation to learn on their own. Teachers believe that it is up to them, the adults, to teach children the right things. They do not really believe that children would learn what they should without external inducements such as praise, grades, and the hope of advancing from Reading Group 2 to Reading Group 1. In general, they share Locke's view that education is essentially a socialization process. The child learns to gain our approval, and in this way the child learns what he or she needs to know to become a useful and virtuous member of society.

ROUSSEAU'S ROMANTIC NATURALISM[1]

Biographical Introduction

We have now reviewed two early conceptions of development. We have discussed the preformationist view, which considered the child as a miniature adult. We have also discussed the views of Locke, who argued that children are like empty containers that are filled in by adult teachings.

The true developmentalist position is different again. Its first force-ful expression is found in the work of Jean Jacques Rousseau (1712–1778). Rousseau agreed with Locke that children are different from adults, but he made the point more positively. They are not empty containers or blank slates but have their own modes of feeling and thinking. This is because they grow according to Nature's plan, which urges them to develop different capacities and modalities at different stages.

Rousseau believed that it is vital for us to give Nature the chance to guide the child's growth. Unlike Locke, he had no faith in the powers of the environment, especially the social environment, to form a healthy in-dividual. Well-socialized adults, he felt, are far too dependent on the opinions of others. They have forgotten how to see with their own eyes and to think with their own minds; they only see and think what society expects them to. So, instead of rushing in to teach children to think in the "correct" ways, we should allow them to perfect their own capacities and to learn in their own ways, as Nature intends. Then they will learn to trust their own powers of judgment.

Rousseau's beliefs, especially his faith in Nature as opposed to societal influences, sparked the Romantic Movement in the history of ideas. At the same time, his belief in a natural ground plan for healthy growth ushered in the developmental tradition in psychology.

Rousseau's revolt against society grew out of his personal life. He was born in Geneva, the son of a watchmaker and a beautiful, sentimental mother who died giving birth to him. For the first eight years of his life, he was raised by his father and an aunt. He said that his father was devoted to him, but he added that his father never let him forget that he had caused his mother's death (Rousseau, 1788, p. 5). His aunt also was kind, but she refused to let him play in the street with the other children. Rousseau therefore spent most of his time reading, and by the age of seven he had read every novel in his mother's library.

When Rousseau was ten, his father got into a bitter dispute and had to flee Geneva to avoid prison. For the next six years, Rousseau was shuttled through several homes. He rarely got along with his masters, who often humiliated him, intensifying his already timid and self-conscious

[1]This heading is suggested by Muuss (1975, p. 27).

nature. He told, for example, of wanting to buy some pastry but of being afraid to enter the shop because he imagined that acquaintances would spot him and laugh at him (1788, p. 36). His main relief came from fantasies, in which he imagined himself in the heroic situations he had read about. He also engaged in a good deal of stealing and cheating.

When Rousseau was 16, he began the life of a vagabond. He travelled about, trying to earn what money he could, but he was never successful. His main talent, he found, was winning the favors of older women. He was not exactly a Don Juan—he was very timid when it came to sex—but he did get several ladies to take care of him.

At the age of 33, Rousseau took up with an illiterate servant girl named Thérèse, with whom he spent the rest of his life. She gave birth to five children, but Rousseau placed them all in a state foundling home. He said that he later realized that his action was wrong, but at the time he did not have the money to raise them, and he felt that if he did they would wind up living a life as miserable as his own (1788, p. 367).

Rousseau's literary career began at the age of 37, when he entered an essay contest which asked whether the arts and sciences had contributed to the betterment of morals. Rousseau argued in the negative and won the prize (Rousseau, 1750). During the next several years, he wrote several essays and books, the most important of which are *The Social Contract* (1762a) and *Emile* (1762b). *The Social Contract* opens with the famous line, "Man is born free, and everywhere he is in chains." That is, humans are naturally good and could live happily according to their spontaneous passions, but they are enslaved by social forces. This book describes a better society. *Emile* is Rousseau's main book on child development and education. It is titled after the fictitious boy whom Rousseau proposed to tutor according to Nature's plan for healthy development.

In the course of his writings, Rousseau challenged the feudal state and Church. He considered himself a devout Christian, but he argued against uncritical conformity to religious authority. As a result, Paris tried to arrest him and Geneva barred him from the city, and he spent many of his last years in exile, paranoid and miserable. When Rousseau died, he was buried in the French countryside, where his body remained until after the French Revolution, which his writings had helped inspire. His remains were then triumphantly removed to Paris and placed in the Pantheon.

Many people have found Rousseau so deficient as a man that they have refused to take his ideas seriously, especially on education. How can a man who abandoned his own children to an orphanage have the audacity to prescribe the right upbringing for others? However, it sometimes takes one who has lived on the outside of the conventional social order to create a radical vision. Rousseau said that he was "thrown, in spite of myself, into the great world, without possessing its manners, and unable to acquire or conform to them . . . " (Rousseau, 1788, p. 379). He felt that his only legitimate response was to rail against society and to seek, in its place, a different vision of how life might unfold. He tried to show how the healthiest development might come not from society's influence, but from Nature. In so doing, Rousseau became the father of developmental psychology.

Rousseau's Theory of Development

Childhood has a special place in the sequence of human life, yet we know nothing about it. This is because we are so exclusively concerned with the child's future—with the things the child will need to know to fit into adult society. Even "the wisest writers devote themselves to what a man ought to know, without asking themselves what a child is capable of learning. They are always looking for the man in the child, without considering what he is before he becomes a man" (Rousseau, 1762b, p. 1).

When we take the time simply to observe children, we find that they are very different from us. "Childhood has its own ways of seeing, thinking, and feeling . . . " (1762b, p. 54). This is according to Nature's design. Nature is like a hidden tutor who prompts the child to develop different capacities at different stages of growth (1762b, p. 181). Her product might not be an individual well-trained to fit into a social niche, but a strong, complete person. If we wish to aid Nature in this process, we must first learn all we can about the stages of development. Rousseau believed that there are four main stages.

Stage 1: Infancy (birth to about two years). Infants experience the world directly through the senses. They know nothing of ideas or reason; they simply experience pleasure and pain (1762b, p. 29). Nevertheless, babies are active and curious and learn a great deal. They constantly try to touch everything they can, and by doing so they learn about heat, cold, hardness, softness, and other qualities of objects (1762b, p. 31). Infants also begin to acquire language, which they do almost entirely on their own. In a sense, they develop a grammar that is more perfect than ours; they employ grammatical rules without all the exceptions that plague adult speech. Pedantically, we correct their mistakes, even though children will always correct themselves in time (1762b, p. 37).

Stage 2: Childhood (about two to 12 years). This stage begins when children gain a new independence; they can now walk, talk, feed themselves, and run about. They develop these abilities, too, on their own (1762b, p. 42).

During this stage, children possess a kind of reason, But it is not the kind that deals with remote events or abstractions. Rather, it is an intuitive reason that is directly tied to body movement and the senses. For example, when a girl accurately throws a ball she demonstrates an intuitive knowledge of velocity and distance. Or when a boy digs with a stick, he reveals an intuitive knowledge of leverage. However, thinking is still extremely concrete. Rousseau told, for example, about a boy who had made a globe, with all the countries, towns, and rivers. When he was asked, "What is the world?," he replied, "A piece of cardboard" (1762b, p. 74).

Stage 3: Late Childhood (about 12 to 15 years). This third stage is a transitional one between childhood and adolescence. During this period, children gain an enormous amount of physical strength; they can plough, push carts, hoe, and do the work of adults (1762b, p. 128). They also make substantial progress in the cognitive sphere and can, for example, do relatively advanced problems in geometry and science. Still, they are not yet disposed to think about purely theoretical and verbal matters. Instead, they can best exercise their cognitive functions through concrete and useful tasks, such as farming, carpentry, and map-making.

During the first three stages, children are by nature *presocial*. That is, they are primarily concerned with what is necessary and useful to themselves and have little interest in social relationships. They enjoy working with physical things and learning from Nature; the world of books and society is foreign to them. Even as late as the third stage, between 12 and 15 years, the model for the child's life should be Robinson Crusoe, a man who lived alone on an island and who became self-sufficient by dealing effectively with the physical environment (1762b, p. 147).

Stage 4: Adolescence.   Children become distinctly social beings only at the fourth stage, which begins with puberty. Rousseau said that puberty begins at age 15, somewhat later than we would date it today. At this time, the child undergoes a second birth. The body changes and the passions well up from within. "A change of temper, frequent outbreaks of anger, a perpetual stirring of the mind, make the child almost ungovernable" (1762b, p. 172). The young person, who is neither child nor adult, begins to blush in the presence of the opposite sex, for he or she is dimly aware of sexual feelings. At this point, the youngster is no longer self-sufficient. The adolescent is attracted to and needs others.

The adolescent also develops cognitively. He or she can now deal with abstract concepts and takes an interest in theoretical matters in science and morals.

These, then, are Rousseau's four stages, which he believed unfold in an invariant sequence according to Nature's plan. His stages, especially adolescence, would seem to emerge more slowly than we would expect today, and this might partly reflect a genuine historical difference. However, Rousseau also believed that the true course of human development is slower than we ordinarily recognize. We are always looking at children as if they were already adults, whereas Nature would have children take the time to develop the capacities and interests of childhood (1762b, p. 181).

Rousseau also proposed that these stages *recapitulate* the general evolution of the human species. Infants are similar to the earliest "primitives," who dealt with the world directly through their senses and were concerned only with pleasure and pain. The next two stages of childhood parallel the "savage" era, when people learned to build huts, make tools, fish, trap, and utilize other skills. People formed loose associations with others, but they still were largely self-sufficient.

Adolescence, finally, parallels the beginning of true social life. Historically, social existence began with the division of labor. As work became specialized, people could no longer produce all they needed by themselves. Thus, they had to rely on others. As they became increasingly immersed in society, they became the slaves of conventions and social approval. Even savages, to be sure, were somewhat concerned with the opinions of others, but this concern deepened as people became embedded in social life. As a result, modern individuals no longer think for themselves. "The savage," Rousseau said, "lives within himself; the sociable man, always outside himself, knows how to live only in the opinion of others" (Rousseau, 1755, p. 179).

Rousseau's Educational Method

Rousseau thought we were most fulfilled as savages, but he realized that those days are gone forever. Still, we do not need to become the weak conformists that we presently are. Nature will still guide children's development along the road to independence. Under her urging, children will spontaneously perfect their capacities and powers of discrimination by dealing with physical things, without adult teaching. So, if one followed Nature's guidance, it should be possible to bring the child to adolescence with an independent mind. Then, when the young person did enter the social world, he or she could cope effectively with it.

Rousseau told how this would happen in the case of Emile, his imaginary pupil.

Emile's education. Rousseau would have a basic faith in Emile's capacity to learn much on his own, from Nature's inner promptings. For example, as an infant Emile would have a strong urge to explore the world through his senses. Accordingly, Rousseau would remove all harmful objects from the house and let Emile explore it. If Emile wished to inspect an object, Rousseau would bring it to him. No adult guidance would be necessary (Rousseau, 1762b, pp. 31, 35).

At the same time, Rousseau would not permit Emile to rule over him. He would bring Emile an object when Emile had a genuine need to learn about it, but never when Emile simply had a capricious desire to have his tutor do his bidding (1762b, p. 52).

Emile also would learn to walk and talk on his own. Rousseau would never push or correct his pupil. Such practices only make children timid and anxious. They begin looking to others for correction and thereby lose their independence (1762b, pp. 39–40).

As Emile moved into the second stage, that of childhood, he would have an urge to run, jump, shout, and play. Rousseau would never check these activities, for Emile would be following Nature's inner prompting to develop his body through vigorous exercise. Rousseau would not, like many adults, always be saying, "Come here, go there, stop, do this, don't do that" (1762b, p. 82). For Emile would then turn to his tutor for guidance and "his own mind would become useless" (1762b, p. 82).

Rousseau would present various lessons, but only those that fit Emile's age. Since children at this stage are developing their senses, Rousseau would suggest games such as finding one's way in a completely dark room, thus developing the sense of touch (1762b, p. 98). Since children do anything that keeps them moving freely, he would take advantage of this impulse to help Emile learn to judge heights, lengths, and distances. He would point to a cherry tree and ask Emile to select a ladder of the proper height. Or he would suggest that they cross a river, and ask Emile which plank would extend across the banks (1762b, p. 105).

In all such lessons, Emile would be able to judge his successes by himself. Emile could see for himself, for example, if he had chosen a plank that was large enough to extend across the river. He could make this judgment because the lesson corresponds to his current capacities. It requires only the use of his senses. There is nothing in the lesson that is beyond his grasp, nothing that would force him to turn to his tutor for help (1762b, p. 141).

Rousseau said that each stage "has a perfection, a ripeness, of its own" (1762b, p. 122). We are used to thinking about a "grown man," but it is no less pleasing to consider a "grown child," and to look at Emile at age 10 or 12.

> His face, his bearing, his expression speak of confidence and contentment; health shines in his countenance . . . I see him keen, eager, and full of life, . . . His manner is free and open . . . [He excels] at running, jumping, raising weights, estimating distances, inventing games . . . He will not be so stupid as to go ask other people about what he sees; he will examine it on his own account . . . His ideas are few but precise, he knows nothing by rote and much by experience . . . So do not expect set speeches or studied manners from him, but just the faithful expression of his thoughts and the conduct that springs from his inclinations. (1762b, pp. 122–26)

To most observers, Emile will be simply a rough, happy boy, but raised in concert with Nature he will have "reached the perfection of childhood" (1762b, p. 126).

During the third stage, that of late childhood, Emile's maturing cognitive powers would enable him to learn mathematics and science, but he would reason effectively in these spheres only in connection with concrete activities. Accordingly, Rousseau would encourage him to think about mathematical problems that naturally emerged in the course of activities such as farming and carpentry. Rousseau would provide only minimal guidance and, again, he would never correct Emile's mistakes. His goal would not be to teach Emile the right answers but to help him learn to solve problems on his own.

> Let him know nothing because you have told him, but because he has learned it for himself. Let him not be taught science, let him discover it. If ever you substitute authority for reason he will cease to reason; he will be a mere plaything for other people's thoughts. (1762b, p. 131)

Only at adolescence would Emile begin reading many books and receive his introduction into the larger social world. By this time he would have developed an independent nature, and with his new capacities for theoretical reasoning, he could judge society at its true worth (1762b, p. 183).

Comparison with the usual practices.   Rousseau, then, would encourage Emile to perfect his capacities at each stage, according to Nature's own schedule, and he would never present anything that Emile could not judge for himself.   His method would differ radically from that of most educators.

Most teachers are not content to treat children as children, with their own needs and ways of learning.   Instead, they try to instill adult knowledge as quickly as possible.   As a result, they present many lessons that exceed the child's understanding.   For example, they give lessons in history, geography, and mathematics that have nothing to do with the child's direct experience and assume a capacity for reasoning that the child lacks.   As children struggle with such lessons, they find learning a miserable experience.   And not only this.   Because they cannot fully comprehend what the adult is saying, they are forced to take things on faith, to accept answers simply because the adult has explained them to be true.   They have no recourse but to ask their parents or teachers, "Did I get the right answer here?"   "Is this right?"   They thereby learn to depend on others and cease to think for themselves.

When children are asked to learn things that exceed their grasp, they become lazy and unmotivated.   To motivate them, teachers use threats, bribes, disapproval, flattery, and other social reinforcers.   They try to get children to learn in order to win the adult's approval.   Such procedures only reinforce the child's dependency on the approval of others (1762b, p. 54).

Rousseau said that his own method, in contrast, would be "merely negative" (1762b, p. 57).   That is, he would exercise Emile's body and senses but keep his mind idle as long as possible.   He would shield Emile from all opinions until his capacity for reasoning had developed, at which point he could judge them for himself.   At the age of 12 or 15 years, Emile would appear ignorant in the conventional sense.   He would know nothing of society or morals and have no precocious knowledge to display.   But he would have learned to judge everything according to his own experience.   He therefore would be capable of real thinking (1762b, pp. 127, 170).

Rousseau anticipated the impatience others would have with his advice.   It seemed as if he were failing to prepare the child for the future.   How could we be certain that the child would know what was necessary when the time came?   Rousseau's reply was that societies change so rapidly that it is really impossible to predict what knowledge will be useful.   But more importantly, our obsession with the future contains the greatest of all traps; in our hurry to teach children what we think they will need, we present lessons that exceed their understanding and force them to turn to us for help.   Rousseau wanted us to slow down and give children a chance to learn in ways that come naturally to them and to learn on their own (1762b, pp. 141, 157).

Evaluation

Rousseau introduced several key ideas into developmental theory.   First, he proposed that development proceeds according to an inner, biological timetable.   For the first time, we have a picture of development unfolding fairly independently from environmental influences. Children are no longer simply shaped by external forces, such as adult teachings and social reinforcements. They grow and learn largely on their own, according to Nature's plan. Today we would call this plan biological maturation.

Second, Rousseau suggested that development unfolds in a series of stages, periods during which children experience the world in different ways. Children differ from adults not because they are blank slates that will gradually take on adult teachings; rather, at each stage, the child's patterns of thought and behavior have their own unique characteristics.

Third, Rousseau proposed a new philosophy of education, one which we would today call "child-centered." He said, "Treat your scholar according to his age" (1762b, p. 55), by which he meant we should fit our lessons to the child's particular stage. In this way, children will be able to judge matters according to their own experience and powers of understanding.

All three of these ideas have become central tenets of many developmental theories; this is shown in the following chapters. At the same time, though, many developmental theorists would disagree with parts of Rousseau's theory. Many would argue, in particular, that the child is not nearly as asocial as Rousseau suggested. For example, modern ethologists point out how babies become strongly attached to their caretakers. This attachment, they say, is genetically governed; it has evolved because proximity to parents has enhanced babies' chances for survival (see Chapter 3 in this book). Actually, Rousseau was aware of such attachments (1762b, p. 174), but he conveniently ignored them when outlining his overall theory. He wanted children to learn to reason on their own, apart from society's corrupting influences, and he therefore declared that Nature intends for them to live apart from the social world, even if he knew better.

When Rousseau argued that we should protect children from society, he had particular concerns in mind. He saw adults teaching children social manners and beliefs before children have the ability to judge them according to their own powers of reasoning. In this process, adults make children the slaves of social conventions.

Today, however, there are developmentalists (e.g., Kohlberg, Chapter 7 in this book) who prize independent thinking as much as Rousseau did, but who believe, nevertheless, that children can make their way through the social world. They believe that children will form social and moral theories on their own, fairly independent of adult teachings. Furthermore, if children think long and hard about social problems, they will reach stages that transcend conventional modes of social thought. Thus, it may be that children can live in the social world without being undone by it.

All the same, it was Rousseau who introduced the crucial question into modern developmental and humanistic thinking: Can inner growth lead to ways of experiencing and feeling that can stand up to the crushing pressure of social conformity?

2

Gesell's Maturational Theory

BIOGRAPHICAL INTRODUCTION

Rousseau, as we saw, believed that behavior unfolds according to Nature's inner plan or timetable. Today we would call this process biological maturation, and the person who did the most to initiate the study of maturation was Arnold Gesell (1880–1961).

Gesell grew up in Alma, Wisconsin, a small town on the bank of the upper Mississippi River. In an autobiographical account, he described an almost idyllic midwestern childhood, in which "hills, valley, water and climate concurred to make the seasons distinct and intense in my home town. Each season had its own challenges and keen pleasures, accentuated by the everchanging, yet enduring river" (Gesell, 1952a, p. 124). Gesell used similar language to describe the beauty he saw in the growth process, with "its seasons and sequences" (Gesell and Ilg, 1943, p. 57). This is not to say, however, that Gesell was merely a gushing romantic. He studied children's development with painstaking observation. To increase his knowledge of the underlying physiological processes, he went to medical school at the age of 30, even though he already had a Ph.D. and had been working successfully as a psychologist. In his 50 years at the Yale Clinic of Child Development, he and his colleagues engaged in incredibly extensive and detailed studies of the neuromotor development of babies and children. They developed behavior norms that are so complete that they still serve as a primary source of information for pediatricians and psychologists. Gesell also developed one of the first tests of infant intelligence (Gesell and Amatruda, 1941) and was one of the first researchers to make extensive use of film observations.

Gesell also wrote on child-rearing, advocating a child-centered approach. He was the best known "baby doctor" in the early 1940s, until Spock published his famous book (1945). Nevertheless, Spock was partly influenced by Gesell.

PRINCIPLES OF DEVELOPMENT

The Concept of Maturation

The child's growth or development, Gesell said, is influenced by two major factors. First, the child is a product of his or her environment. But more fundamentally, Gesell believed, the child's development is directed from within, by the action of the genes. Gesell called this process *maturation* (Gesell and Ilg, 1943, p. 41).

An outstanding feature of maturational development is that it always unfolds in fixed sequences. This can first be seen in the developing embryo, where, for example, the heart is always the first organ to develop and function. Soon afterward, the rapidly differentiating cells begin to form the central nervous system—the brain and the spinal cord. The development of the brain and the head, in turn, begins before the other parts, such as the arms and the legs. This order, which is directed by the genetic blueprint, is never violated.

Similarly, sequential development continues after birth. For example, just as the head develops early in the embryo, it also takes the lead in early postnatal development. Babies first have control over their lips and tongues, then gain control over their eye movements, followed by control over the neck, shoulders, arms, hands, fingers, trunk, legs, and feet. In both prenatal and postnatal development there is a head–to–foot (cephalocaudal) trend (Gesell, 1946, p. 339).

As babies grow, they learn to sit up, to stand, to walk, and to run, and these capacities, too, develop in a specific order. They emerge with the growth of the nervous system, which itself is mediated by the genes.

Children, of course, vary in their *rates* of development. They do not all stand up and walk at the same age. Nevertheless, they all proceed through the same sequences. Moreover, individual differences in growth rates, in Gesell's view, are largely controlled by the internal genetic mechanism (Gesell, 1945, p. 161).

As indicated, the effects of maturation are contrasted with those of the environment. In prenatal development, this means that maturation is distinguished from aspects of the internal environment, such as the embryo's temperature and the oxygen it receives from its mother. These environmental factors are certainly vital—they support proper growth—but they play no direct role in the sequential unfolding of structures and action patterns. This is the work of the maturational mechanism.

Once the baby is born, it enters a different kind of environment. It is not only an environment that meets its physical needs, but a social and cultural environment which tries to induce it to behave in the proper ways. Gesell said that the child clearly needs the social environment to realize his or her potentials, but he also argued that socializing forces work best when they are in tune with inner maturational principles (Gesell and Ilg, 1943, p. 41).

Gesell was particularly opposed to efforts to teach children things ahead of schedule. Children will sit up, walk, and talk when they are ready, when their nervous systems have sufficiently matured. At the right moment, they will simply begin to master a task, from their own inner urges. Until then, teaching will be of little value, and may create tensions between caretakers and children.

Some evidence for the maturational position on teaching has come from studies with identical twins. For example, Gesell and Thompson (1929) gave one twin practice at such activities as stair-climbing and the grasping and manipulation of cubes. This twin did show some skill superior to that of the other, but the untrained twin soon caught up, with much less practice. And he did so at about the age at which we would expect him to perform the various tasks. Apparently, then, there is an inner timetable that determines the readiness to do things, and the benefits of early training are relatively temporary. The question of early stimulation is controversial, but it does seem that our efforts to speed up early motor development produce only small effects (Sroufe and Cooper, 1988, pp. 162–68; Cole and Cole, 1989, pp. 186–88).

Maturation, then, refers to the process by which development is governed by intrinsic factors—principally the genes, which are chemical substances contained within the nucleus of each cell (see Figure 2.1). The genes determine the sequence, timing, and form of emerging action-patterns.

However, the precise mechanism by which the genes work, in Gesell's day as today, is still mysterious. We know that the genes do not work in isolation from one another, and they appear to receive some cues from the cytoplasm, the cellular substance outside the nucleus (Gesell, 1945, p. 22; Gilbert, 1988, pp. 10, 442; see Figure 2.1). Since the cytoplasm is, in effect, the environment of the genes, we see how difficult it becomes to draw sharp distinctions between internal and environmental factors. Nevertheless, we can still think of maturation as the process by which the genes direct development, albeit in conjunction with other factors.

So far, I have primarily been illustrating maturational growth with early motor behavior, which was Gesell's main scientific focus. However, Gesell believed that maturation governs the growth of the entire personality. He said, for example,

> [The child's] nervous system matures by stages and natural sequences. He sits before he stands; he babbles before he talks; he fabricates before he tells the truth; he draws a circle before he draws a square; he is selfish before he is altruistic; he is dependent on others before he achieves dependence on self. All his capacities, including his morals, are subject to the laws of growth. (Gesell and Ilg, 1943, p. 11)

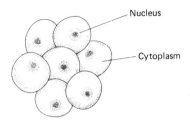

FIGURE 2.1
A group of cells. The nucleus contains chromosomes, made up of genes. (Adapted from Munn, N. L. *The Growth of Human Behavior*, 3rd ed. Boston: Houghton Mifflin Co., 1974, p. 40. By permission.)

The Study of Patterns

Gesell said that when we study growth we should not just measure things in quantitative form but should examine patterns. A pattern may be anything that has a definite shape or form—for example, an eyeblink. But what is most important is the patterning process, the process by which actions become organized (Gesell and Ilg, 1943, pp. 16–17).

We find good illustrations of the patterning process in the case of babies' vision. At birth, babies' eyes are apt to rove around aimlessly, but after a few days or even hours babies are able to stop their eyes and look at objects for brief periods. They can stop their eyes and stare "at will" because a new patterned connection has been made between the nerve impulses in the brain and the tiny muscles that move the eyes (1943, pp. 17–18).

By one month, babies can usually regard a ring that is dangled before them and then follow it through an arc of about 90°. This ability implies a new organization—that between the eye muscles and the grosser muscles that rotate the head (1943, p. 19).

Patterning continues to widen when babies organize their eye movements with their hand movements, when they look at what they hold. By four months, babies can usually hold a rattle and look at it at the same time. "This is a significant growth gain. It means that eyes and hands are doing team work, coming into more effective coordination. Mental growth cannot be measured in inches and pounds. So it is appraised by patterns" (1943, p. 19).

Still, hand-eye coordination is by no means complete at four months. For some time, the eyes will be in the lead. At four months, for example, babies can often "pick up" a one-inch cube or even a small candy pellet with their eyes; that is, they can focus intently on the cube or pellet and consider it from slightly different angles. But they cannot yet grasp it with their hands. Babies may be seen looking at the cube and then looking at their hands, as if they have an idea of grasping the cube, but they simply cannot do it. The nervous system has not yet sufficiently grown. It is not until six months that babies are usually able to pick up the cube with a crude palmar grasp, and not until 10 months that they can pick up the small candy pellet with a pincer grasp, with opposing thumb and index finger (see Figure 2.2). Thus, hand-eye coordination develops slowly—it becomes gradually more organized and comes to include more differentiated or refined movements.

(a) Four months: (b) Six months: (c) Ten months:
         sees but cannot contact.   palmar grasp.   pincer grasp.

FIGURE 2.2   Developments in hand-eye coordination. (Adapted from Vincent, E. L., and Martin, P. C., *Human Psychological Development*. Copyright © 1961. The Ronald Press, p. 130. By permission of John Wiley and Sons, Inc.)

Other Principles of Development

Gesell's observations suggested several other principles of growth. We will consider three: reciprocal interweaving, functional asymmetry, and self-regulation.

Reciprocal interweaving.   Humans are built on a bilateral basis; we have two hemispheres of the brain, two eyes, two hands, two legs, and so on.   Our actions, too, have a dualistic quality, as when we either flex or extend our limbs.   "Reciprocal interweaving" refers to the developmental process by which two tendencies gradually reach an effective organization. For example, in the development of handedness, the baby first uses one hand, then both together, then prefers the other hand, then both together again, and so on until he or she ultimately reaches one-handed dominance. This back-and-forth quality of preferences suggests the metaphor of weaving; hence the term "reciprocal interweaving."   Gesell showed how reciprocal interweaving describes the patterning of many behaviors, including visual behavior and crawling and walking (Gesell, 1946, pp. 342–49).

Gesell also believed that reciprocal interweaving characterizes the growth of the personality.   Here we see the organism integrating introverted and extraverted tendencies.   For example, the child who was self-composed at age three turns inward at three-and-a-half, becoming timid and unsettled. This period of introversion is followed by a swing to extraversion at age four, and the two tendencies finally become integrated and balanced at five.   Cycles such as this begin in infancy and continue at least until age 16.   The organism temporarily loses its equilibrium as it expands into new inner or outer realms, but it then reorganizes itself at new levels (Gesell et al., 1956, pp. 16–20).

Functional asymmetry.   Through the process of reciprocal interweaving, then, we balance the dualities of our nature.   However, we rarely achieve perfect balance or symmetry.   In fact, a degree of asymmetry is highly functional; we are most effective when we confront the world from an angle, favoring one hand, one eye, and so on.

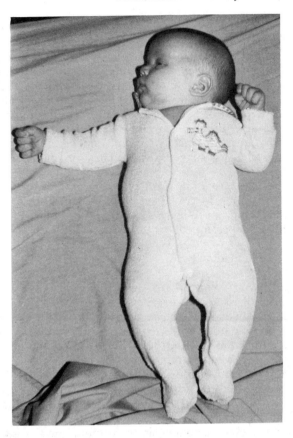

FIGURE 2.3
The tonic neck reflex.

The infant's asymmetric tendency is seen in the *tonic neck reflex*, a reflex which Gesell discovered in humans. Gesell noted that babies prefer to lie with their heads turned to one side, and when they do so they automatically assume the tonic neck reflex posture. They extend the arm on the side to which the head is turned (as if looking at the hand) and flex the other arm behind the head. The tonic neck reflex posture looks very much like the basic stance of a fencer (see Figure 2.3). The tonic neck reflex is dominant during the first three months after birth and then eclipses, with new developments in the nervous system (Gesell, 1946, pp. 349–54).

 Self-regulation. Gesell believed that intrinsic developmental mechanisms are so powerful that the organism can, to a considerable degree, regulate its own development. In one series of studies, he showed how babies can regulate their cycles of feeding, sleep, and wakefulness. When the babies were permitted to determine when they needed to nurse and sleep, they gradually required fewer feedings per day and stayed awake for longer periods during the daytime. Progress did not follow a straight line; there were many fluctuations, including regressions. But the babies did gradually work out stable schedules (1946, pp. 358–64).

Gesell also wrote about self-regulation from a slightly different angle, focusing on the organism's capacity to maintain an overall integration and equilibrium. Growth, of course, also involves disequilibrium. As we just saw, infants' sleeping and feeding patterns frequently fluctuate. We saw comparable fluctuations in the development of the personality, where periods of stability are followed by periods of instability as children enter new introverted or extraverted phases. Tensions arise when children venture into new unknowns. However self-regulatory mechanisms are always at work, ensuring that the organism never goes too far in one direction before it catches its balance, consolidating its gains before moving forward once again.

Because of intrinsic self-regulating processes, children will sometimes resist our efforts to teach them new things. It is as if something inside tells them not to learn too much too soon. The integrity of the organism must be preserved.

Individuality

We have now reviewed many of Gesell's ideas about growth. One general issue, however, needs to be discussed. This is the problem of individuality. Gesell strongly believed in the uniqueness of each child. Unfortunately, however, his position was obscured by the way in which he summarized his findings. For example, he wrote about the child at two, two-and-a-half, three, and so on as if we could expect all children at each age to behave in exactly the same way. He did warn that he was using age norms only as short-cut devices (Gesell and Ilg, 1943, pp. 60–61), but he never indicated the actual amount of individual variation that does occur at each age, so individuality did often become lost in his writings.

Gesell's actual position, as mentioned, was that normal children all go through the same *sequences*, but they vary in their *rates* of growth. He also suggested that growth rates might be related to differences in temperament and personality. In an interesting discussion (Gesell and Ilg, 1943, pp. 44–45), he presented three hypothetical children—one who grows slowly, one who grows rapidly, and one who grows irregularly—and suggested how each growth style might show up in a variety of personal dispositions. Child A, who grows slowly, might, for example, be generally slow and cautious, able to wait, even-tempered, and generally wise about life's problems. Child B, who develops rapidly, might be quick-reacting, blithe and happy, up and at it, and generally bright and clever. Child C, who develops irregularly, might sometimes be overcautious and sometimes undercautious, often moody, have trouble waiting, and show flashes of brilliance. Gesell believed that each individual temperament and growth style makes different demands on the culture, and that the culture should try to adjust to each child's uniqueness.

PHILOSOPHY OF CHILD-REARING

Gesell believed that child-rearing should begin with a recognition of the implicit wisdom of maturational laws. Babies enter the world with an inborn schedule which is the product of at least three million years of biological evolution; they are preeminently "wise" about their needs, and what they are ready and not ready to do. Thus parents should not try to force their children into any preconceived pattern, but they should take their cues from the children themselves.

On the topic of feeding, for example, Gesell strongly advocated demand feeding—feeding when the baby indicates a readiness—as opposed to feeding by any predetermined schedule. He wrote,

> There are two kinds of time—organic time and clock time. The former is based on the wisdom of the body, the latter on astronomical science and cultural conventions. A self-demand schedule takes its departure from organic time. The infant is fed when he is hungry; he is allowed to sleep when he is sleepy; he is not roused to be fed; he is "changed" if he fusses on being wet; he is granted some social play when he craves it. He is not made to live by the clock on the wall, but rather by the internal clock of his fluctuating needs. (Gesell and Ilg, 1943, p. 51)

As parents suspend their ideas about what the baby "ought" to be doing—and instead follow the baby's signals and cues—they begin to appreciate the baby's inherent capacity for self-regulated growth. They see how the baby regulates his or her own cycles of feeding, sleep, and wakefulness. A little later, they see how the baby learns to sit up, creep, and crawl on his or her own, without pushing and prodding. Parents begin to trust the child and the growth process.

Gesell emphasized that the first year is the best time for learning to respect the child's individuality (Gesell and Ilg, 1943, p. 57). Parents who are alertly responsive to the child's needs during infancy will naturally be sensitive to the child's unique interests and capacities later on. They will be less inclined to impose their own expectations and ambitions on the child and more inclined to give the child's individuality a chance to grow and find itself.

Gesell said that parents need, besides an intuitive sensitivity to the child, some theoretical knowledge of the trends and sequences of development. In particular, they need to realize that development fluctuates between periods of stability and instability. This knowledge fosters patience and understanding. For example, the parent will be helped by the knowledge that 2½-years-olds go through a troubled period during which they can be very obstinate. Knowing this, the parent will not feel an urgent need to stamp out this behavior before it is too late. Instead, the parent will be able to deal with the child more flexibly, and perhaps even enjoy this child who so intently tries to establish his or her independence (1943, pp. 197, 296).

One of Gesell's followers, Louise Bates Ames (1971), offers parents the following advice:

1. Give up the notion that how your child turns out is all up to you and there isn't a minute to waste.
2. Try to appreciate the wonder of growth. Observe and relish the fact that every week and every month brings new developments. . . .

3. Respect his immaturity. Anticipate the fact that he will, in all likelihood, need to creep before he walks, express himself with single words before he talks in sentences, say "No" before he says "Yes."
4. Try to avoid thinking always in terms of what comes next. Enjoy, and let your child enjoy each stage he reaches before he travels on. . . . (pp. 108, 125)

So far, Gesell's philosophy sounds like one of extreme indulgence and permissiveness. One might ask, "Doesn't this attitude lead to spoiling?" "Won't children start becoming bossy, always wanting their own way?"

Gesell's answer was that of course children must learn to control their impulses and get along with the demands of their culture. However, he argued that children best learn to do this when we pay attention to their own maturing ability to tolerate controls. For example, with respect to feedings, the baby at first should not be made to wait too long. "The most vital cravings of the infant have to do with food and sleep. These cravings have an individual, organic nature. They cannot be transformed or transgressed" (Gesell and Ilg, 1943, p. 56). But a little later—by four months or so—the baby's gastrointestinal tract no longer dominates life as it did before, and the baby's less intense and less frequent cries tell the parent that he or she is now able to wait for feedings.

Later on, developments in language and an increased time perspective help children delay immediate gratification. At two-and-a-half years they do not need their juice immediately because they understand when the parents says, "Pretty soon." At three they may understand "When it's time." And by four they want to help prepare the meals themselves. The culture, then, can ease children into its fabric by gearing itself to children's own maturing readiness to tolerate controls (1943, p. 54).

Thus, Gesell believed that alert caretakers can achieve a reasonable balance between maturational forces and enculturation. However, it is clear that Gesell wanted the culture to do most of the adjusting. Enculturation, he said, is necessary, but our first goal should not be to fit the child into the social mold. This is the aim of authoritarian regimes. In democracies we prize autonomy and individuality, qualities that have their deepest roots in the biological impulse toward optimal growth (1943, p. 10).

Enculturation takes place in the school as well as in the home. Schools teach children the skills and habits they will need as adult members of society. But teachers, like parents, should not think so exclusively in terms of cultural goals that they overlook the manner in which the child grows. For example, although our culture values accurate work, teachers need to recognize that children are naturally less precise at one age than another. Vigorous, unstable six-year-olds are error prone, whereas more stable seven-year-olds readily take to drills and perfectionistic work. Accordingly, the developmentally minded teacher will not force six-year-olds to learn in a way that runs counter to their nature but will save drills for the time when the child benefits from them (Gesell and Ilg, 1946, pp. 374–81).

At the same time, it is not enough to adjust techniques to each age or grade; for children also vary widely in their growth rates, as well as in their special talents. Accordingly, teachers need to gear their work to the individual child's state of readiness and special abilities. At present, most schools do not do this. They overemphasize uniform achievement standards, such as grade-level reading scores, thereby ignoring children's need to grow according to their own timing and to develop their unique potentials. Schools, of course, do need to teach standard cultural skills, but in a democracy their first task is to help children develop their full personalities. To do this, they must let children guide them, just as children themselves are guided by a biological ground plan for optimal growth (1946, pp. 388–92).

EVALUATION

In Gesell's hands, Rousseau's idea of an inner developmental force became the guiding principle behind extensive scholarship and research. Gesell showed how the maturational mechanism, while still hidden, manifests itself in intricate developmental sequences and self-regulatory processes. Gesell indicated that there are good reasons to suppose that development follows an inner plan.

Nevertheless, most contemporary psychologists would consider Gesell's maturational position too extreme. Most psychologists acknowledge the role of maturation but nevertheless believe that teaching and learning are much more important than Gesell claimed. They believe that the environment does more than merely support inner patterning; it also structures behavior. For example, although children cannot learn to throw a ball or play a piano before attaining some level of neuromotor maturation, they also acquire such behavior pattens through teaching and reinforcement. Still, it is largely because of Gesell's work that even most ardent learning theorists take some notice of inner maturational processes.

The most frequently voiced criticisms of Gesell center on his manner of presenting age norms. As mentioned, his norms imply too much uniformity and give us no idea of how much variation to expect at any given age. Moreover, Gesell's norms were based on middle-class children in a university setting (Yale) and may not apply perfectly in other cultural contexts.

In recent years, Gesell's age norms have been challenged by a new wave of research focusing on newborns (babies under one month of age). Newborns, it now seems, have many surprising capacities. Under the right conditions, they can visually follow moving objects for short distances, can reach for objects, and can discriminate among shapes, colors, sounds, tastes, and odors. They can imitate movements such as tongue-protrusions and can exhibit a walking reflex (MacFarlane, 1981; Bower, 1982; Gardner, 1982, pp. 109–32; Meltzoff and Moore, 1989). In light of such findings, the developmental picture provided by Gesell seems too slow. Newborns now seem to be "a lot smarter" and "more competent" than anyone had supposed (Lipsitt, 1971; Bower, 1977, 1989, p. 14). Indeed, researchers sometimes make it sound as if newborns are so advanced that they do not need to develop at all; they are really little adults, as the preformationists maintained.

These new findings are important, but they must be viewed with caution. In the first place, many of the newborn's advanced competencies, including visual following and hand-reaching, are very fragile and difficult to elicit. Experimenters must sometimes wait for hours and even days for babies to demonstrate them (Als, 1978; MacFarlane, 1981; Bower, 1982, p. 169).

Furthermore, some precocious abilities, including reflexive walking, reaching, and imitation, ordinarily disappear after a month or two. Some of these, to be sure, may be maintained by exercise (Bower, 1982), but they ordinarily seem to drop out as behavior comes under the control of higher cortical centers. Then, when they do reappear, they have a much more voluntary appearance (Hofer, 1981, pp. 120–23). Thus, some of the early, precocious capacities are only temporary. Perhaps they are vestiges of our evolutionary past, of a time when we developed much more rapidly than we now do.

In any case, the new research on newborns at most supplements, rather than directly contradicts the developmental picture Gesell provided. Contemporary pediatricians and infant specialists still consider Gesell's norms of great value, using them to help determine what babies should be able to do at various ages.

Gesell also provided a coherent philosophy of child-rearing. We should not, he said, try to force children into our predetermined designs, but should follow their cues as they express basic biological forces of growth. The research findings bearing on Gesell's position have often been ambiguous (Caldwell, 1964), but some interesting studies do support him (Appleton et al., 1975). In a particularly impressive study, Bell and Ainsworth (1972) asked what happens when parents respond promptly to their babies cries (rather than acting on their own ideas about when it is all right for them to cry). The clear finding was that responsiveness does not lead to spoiling. On the contrary, by the age of one year these babies, in comparison to babies of less responsive parents, cried less and were more independent. They enjoyed being held, but if the mother put them down they did not cry or protest but happily ventured off into exploratory play. They might check back on the mother's presence from time to time, as is natural at this age, but they were basically quite independent. Apparently, then, when babies' signals are heeded, they become confident that they can always get help when needed and therefore can relax and venture forth on their own.

There also is some evidence, still only impressionistic and anecdotal, that things can go very wrong when Gesell's principles are excessively violated. This evidence comes from the study of schizophrenic patients, whose childhood experiences often seem precisely the opposite of those that Gesell recommended. These patients seem to have felt, as children, that their own natural impulses and desires counted for little, or threatened others, and that they were forced to fulfill others' predetermined images and expectations (R. W. White, 1963; Laing, 1965; Bettelheim, 1967). We will discuss this matter more fully when we consider Bettelheim (Chapter 13), but here I would like to illustrate the point with a brief description of a nine-year-old boy whom I saw for a psychological evaluation. The boy found life very frightening and probably was on the verge of psychosis. The parents had not wanted a child, since they were in their 40s, and the mother had a number of physical ailments that made it taxing for her to care for him. Consequently, she wanted a good, well-disciplined boy—an adult, really—who would cause her no trouble. She tried to toilet-train him at six months of age, long before he showed any readiness to participate in the process. And when he began walking and vigorously exploring the world at one year, she became distressed; he was becoming a nuisance and "getting into things." She even perceived his behavior as abnormal. Because of her circumstances, then, she practically reversed Gesell's advice: She had a fixed image of the good child she wanted and was unable to accept and follow his natural inclinations. As a result, the boy developed an intense fear that any action he might take, unless approved by his parents beforehand, was extremely dangerous. He did not trust himself or his natural impulses.

There is some evidence, then, in support of Gesell's position—that it is desirable to respond to children's cues and inclinations as they follow an inner, biological schedule. However, there also is evidence which might argue partly against Gesell. In particular, research by Baumrind (1967) suggests that independent, self-reliant, and mature three- and four-year-olds have parents who demand a great deal of them. Baumrind thinks that these parents set tasks that are within their children's abilities, and to this extent the parents follow Gesell's recommendations. However, these parents also seem more demanding and controlling than Gesell might have thought necessary.

Perhaps philosophies such as Gesell's will never be completely proven or refuted by empirical evidence alone; too much may depend on one's own values. All the same, it would seem that we have much to gain by listening to Gesell. For while it is true that we must control, direct, and instruct our children to some extent, we usually seem to be in quite a hurry to do these things. What seems more difficult for us is to take the time to watch, enjoy, and appreciate our children as we give them a chance to do their own growing.

3

Ethological Theories:
Darwin, Lorenz and Tinbergen, and Bowlby

Ethology is the study of animal and human behavior within an evolutionary context. The person most identified with modern evolutionary theory is Darwin.

DARWIN AND THE THEORY OF EVOLUTION

Biographical Introduction

Charles Darwin (1809–1882) was born into a distinguished English family. His grandfather, Erasmus Darwin, was a renowned physician, poet, and philosopher, and his father also was a prominent physician. Young Darwin, in contrast, seemed headed for no great heights. As his father once said, "You care for nothing but shooting, dogs, and rat-catching, and you will be a disgrace to yourself and your family" (Darwin, 1887, p. 28).

Darwin studied medicine for a while, and then began studying for the Anglican clergy at Cambridge, but he was generally bored and his grades were uneven. Still, he made a favorable impression on some of his professors at Cambridge, especially those who shared his interests in nature and wildlife. One professor, John Henslow, recommended Darwin for the position of naturalist on the worldwide voyage of the *H.M.S. Beagle*, the voyage on which Darwin made observations that eventually led to his theory of evolution.

As Darwin examined fossils and variations among living species, he concluded that the various species had a common ancestor and that newer species either had died out or had changed to meet the requirements of their changing environments. If this conclusion were correct, then the common theological view on the origin of the species must be wrong; the species had not been created in a fixed and perfect form, but had evolved. Although the idea of evolution had been expressed before, its plausibility deeply distressed Darwin. It caused religious doubts in his mind and he knew it would shock others (Gruber, 1981).

Darwin wanted to make sure the evidence supported his theory, and he didn't publish it until 20 years after he first formulated it. In fact, he wouldn't have published it then had he not learned that Alfred Wallace was going to publish a similar theory. Since the theory was going to be made public anyway, Darwin wanted partial credit for it. Upon the recommendation of their colleagues, Darwin and Wallace presented their theory in 1858 under joint authorship. A year later, Darwin published his great work, *The Origin of Species*. Darwin continued developing his theory the rest of his life, and, despite the bitter reactions it produced, he became widely recognized for his monumental achievements. When Darwin died, he was buried in Westminster Abbey, next to Isaac Newton.

The Theory of Natural Selection

As mentioned, Darwin was not the first to propose a theory of evolution. In Darwin's day, biologists had been debating the views of Lamarck, who proposed that evolution occurred through the inheritance of acquired characteristics. For example, giraffes stretched their necks to reach the leaves on high trees and then passed along their lengthened necks to the next generation. Lamarck's theory, however, turned out to be wrong.

In the Darwin-Wallace theory, no new characteristics need be acquired during an individual's lifetime. In essence, Darwin's theory is as follows. Among the members of a species, there is endless variation; and among the various members, only a fraction of those who are born survive to reproduce. Thus, there is a "struggle for existence" during which the fittest members of a species live long enough to transmit their characteristics to the next generation. Over countless generations, then, Nature "selects" those who can best adapt to their surroundings—hence the term "natural selection" (Darwin, 1859, Chs. 3 and 4).

Darwin asked us to consider, for example, the situation of wolves (1859, p. 70). During seasons when prey is scarce, the swiftest and strongest wolves have the best chances for survival. They are therefore more likely than the others to live long enough to reproduce and pass on their traits—today we would say their genes—to the next generation. After many such seasons, the traits of speed and strength will become increasingly prevalent in the population of the species.

Evolution usually seems to occur extremely slowly, revealing noticeable changes only after numerous generations. Consequently, we do not usually get a chance to see evolution at work in any simple way. However, biologists did have such an opportunity in England in the mid-1800s. In Manchester, there were numerous white moths who blended in well with the white trees in the area, making it difficult for birds to spot and kill them. Among the moths, there were a small number of dark ones (the products of mutations), who were easily detected by the predators. Consequently, only a few dark moths lived and reproduced. However, with industrialization, coal smoke darkened the trees, making the white moths easy prey. Now the dark ones had the best chance of surviving long enough to reproduce, and over the next 50 years their number increased from less than 1 percent to 99 percent (Ehrlich and Holm, 1963, pp. 126–30).

Social behavior and reason. Darwin's terms "struggle for existence" and "survival of the fittest" conjure up images of individuals in violent combat. In one sense, such images accurately reflect Darwin's views; for males of various species do compete for the females, as when deer battle during the spring. Such competitions ensure that the strongest males, rather than the weak and frail ones, will transmit their characteristics to the next generation (Darwin, 1871, p. 583).[1]

In another sense, however, terms such as the "struggle for existence" are misleading. For Darwin also wrote extensively on the importance of social instincts for group survival. Those animals that evolved danger signals and aided their fellow members must have had better chances for survival than those that did not. Similarly, those groups of early humans who banded together, cooperated, and looked out for the common good probably had a better chance of surviving (Darwin, 1871, pp. 483, 500).

In humans, in addition, a crucial factor was the development of reason. Since humans are physically weaker and slower than many species, they must have relied on their intelligence and inventions (such as tools) to survive (1871, p. 444). Thus, the capacities for social behavior and reason, along with physical characteristics, must have undergone natural selection.

Evolution and embryology. Darwin (1859, p. 345) said that embryological findings fit well with the theory of evolution. In particular, he noted that the embryos of most species are highly similar in their early forms, perhaps revealing their descent from a common ancestor. The strongest argument of this kind was made by Haeckel, who in the late 1860s proposed that *ontogeny recapitulates phylogeny*. That is, the development of an individual organism (ontogeny) repeats in an abbreviated way the evolutionary history of its species (phylogeny). The recapitulation argument has always seemed somewhat fanciful, but biologists still consider it a fair working model. For example, before mammalian embryos take on their

---

[1]Darwin believed that the males often fight to the death (1871, p. 583). In most species, however, they probably do not, for they have evolved appeasement gestures which stop fights before they reach this point. Humans are a notable exception (Lorenz, 1963, pp. 129–38, 241).

distinctive shapes, they resemble the young embryos of fish, amphibians, reptiles, and birds—in that order, the same order in which the species appeared on the earth, as judged by fossil evidence (Waddington, 1962, p. 99, Balinsky, 1981, pp. 8–10).

Evaluation

Today Darwin is generally considered correct but incomplete. He was right in pointing out that there is enormous variation within species and that species change because only some members survive long enough to reproduce. However, it was only after the work of Mendel and others that we began to understand how genetic combinations and mutations produce variations and how traits are transmitted. Thus, the science of genetics is helping to round out Darwin's theory.

Darwin believed, as we have seen, that natural selection applies not only to physical characteristics (such as coloring) but also to various kinds of behavior. Thus, Darwin was the first ethologist—the name given to biologists who study animal behavior from an evolutionary perspective. We will now review some of the ideas of modern ethologists and then look at the applications of these ideas to the study of human development.

MODERN ETHOLOGY: LORENZ AND TINBERGEN

Biographical Introduction

Konrad Lorenz (1903–1989) is often called the father of modern ethology. He did not necessarily make more discoveries than other ethologists, but his bold, vivid, and often humorous writing style did much to call attention to this new field.

Lorenz was born and raised in Austria. His father was a prominent physician who wanted Lorenz to become a doctor too, so Lorenz dutifully earned a medical degree. However, he never lost his boyhood enthusiasm for the study of nature and wildlife, and he next studied zoology at the University of Vienna, earning a Ph.D. in this field. Lorenz began his studies in ethology in the early 1930s, when he became convinced that one can see the landmarks of evolution in the innate behavior patterns of animals just as surely as in their physical characteristics (Tanner and Inhelder, 1971, p. 28). He made many of his observations on his own large Austrian estate, where many species of wild animals freely roamed.

Niko Tinbergen (1907–1988) worked quietly in Lorenz's shadow. Despite this, ethologists consider his work equally substantial. Tinbergen was born in the Hague, the Netherlands, and like Lorenz was fascinated by animals and wildlife as a boy. In school, Tinbergen's work was erratic; he did well only in subjects that interested him, and he struck many of his teachers as a lazy youngster whose primary enthusiasm was for sports. Nevertheless, Tinbergen went on to earn a Ph.D. degree in biology at the University of Leiden in 1932 and began doing brilliant ethological studies.

His research was interrupted during World War II when the Germans put him in a prison camp for protesting the dismissal of Jewish professors at the university.   During his imprisonment, Tinbergen wrote on ethology as well as writing stories for children.   After the war he became a professor at Oxford.   In 1973 Tinbergen and Lorenz, along with a third eminent ethologist, Karl Von Frisch, won the Nobel Prize in physiology and medicine (Baerends et al., 1975).

Methodological Approach

Ethologists are convinced that we can understand an animal's behavior only if we study it in its natural setting.   Only in this way can we watch an animal's behavior patterns unfold and see how they serve in the adaptation of the species.   We cannot, for example, understand why birds build nests where they do unless we see how such behavior protects the species from predators in the natural environment.   Psychologists who only study animals in their laboratories miss out on a great deal.   In such captive situations, many species do not even reproduce, and one frequently has no opportunity to observe their nesting, mating, territorial, or parental behavior.

When an ethologist studies a new species, his or her first step is simply to get to know the species as well as possible.   That is, the ethologist engages in *naturalistic observations*; the ethologist observes an animal's characteristic behavior and then compares the behavior with that of other species.   Only after ethologists have gathered a great deal of descriptive material do they attempt experiments to test their ideas or try to formulate general laws.

Instinctive Behavior

Ethologists are interested in instincts.   In everyday language, we casually refer to any unlearned behavior as "instinctive" or as an "instinct," but ethologists consider instincts as a special class of unlearned behavior.

An instinct, in the first place, is *released by a specific external stimulus.* This is the case, for example, in the rescuing behavior of the chicken.   The hen appears to respond any time her chicks are in danger, but a closer examination reveals that she is actually reacting to a very specific stimulus— the chick's distress call.   This point has been demonstrated in an experiment by Brückner (cited in Tinbergen, 1951).   When chicks were tied to a post and hidden behind a screen, the mother still rescued them because she heard the distress calls.   When, however, the screen was removed and the struggling chicks were covered by a glass enclosure—so the hen could see her chicks in trouble but could not hear them call—she ignored them. She needed to hear the specific distress call.

Similarly, a specific stimulus releases the tendency to fight in the male three-pronged stickleback fish (Tinbergen, 1951, p. 28).   In the spring the adult male establishes a territory, builds a nest, and courts females.   He also develops a bright red spot on his belly.   When other sticklebacks enter his territory, he may or may not fight—depending on the sight of a specific stimulus, the red spot on the invader's belly.

If a pregnant female enters his territory, his behavior is different. When he moves toward her, she tilts her body upward, exposing her full belly, and this stimulus causes him to go into a zig-zag dance. This dance is a signal for her to approach, and when she does, he returns to the nest. Once there, his behavior signals her to enter. This intricate ritual continues until the eggs are fertilized, with each component of the ritual governed by a specific releasing stimulus (1951, pp. 48–50).

Specific releasing stimuli also determine the reactions of the young to their parents. For example, a young pheasant will rush for cover only when it hears its parent's warning call. Similarly, a young jackdaw bird will follow its parent into the air only when the parent takes off at a certain angle and speed (Lorenz, 1935, pp. 157–61).

Instincts also are *species-specific*, which means that the particular behavior patterns are found only in members of a specific species. The behaviors always include some *fixed action pattern*, some stereotyped motor component. Fighting gestures, courtship behavior, and modes of following always contain some fixed aspect.

Not every part of an instinct, however, must be of a fixed nature. For example, peregrine falcons engage in free flight when searching for prey. There is no rigid pattern to their search; they glide around in various areas where past experience has taught them to look. But once they spot their prey (e.g., a starling bird), their actions do become stereotyped. Their swoop and their manner of catching their prey constitute a fixed action pattern (Lorenz, 1952a, p. 306).

At the same time, some parts of a motor performance may be less fixed than it first appears. Bowlby (1982) points out that the falcon must be able to adjust its flight if it is to intercept moving prey. He thinks the falcon possesses, in addition to stereotyped movements, a "goal-corrected" feedback mechanism by which it alters its movements in accordance with those of the prey, much as a missle is programmed to do to intercept a moving target. Lorenz did not comment on such a mechanism, but his description of young jackdaws' following behavior suggests that after a time they develop a similar capacity to maintain contact with a parent in flight (Lorenz, 1935, p. 159).

The fixed action pattern also has an underlying *drive component*, an inner urge to engage in the instinctive behavior. Consequently, if the behavior has not been released for a long time, the drive behind it can build up to the point that less specific stimuli will suffice, as when males court females who lack the specific releasing stimuli. In some cases, the internal pressure for release builds up to such a high pitch that the fixed action pattern goes off "in a vacuum" (Lorenz, 1963, pp. 52–53).

Finally, instincts, as the products of evolution, have some *survival value for the species*. However, as Freedman (1971) observes, it is often all too easy to create plausible-sounding explanations of a behavior's adaptive value. What is really needed is research on the question. For example, Tinbergen (1965) wondered why herring gulls remove their egg shells after hatching. After all, this requires them to spend time away from the nest, endangering their young. He hypothesized that the glistening of the shells in the sun attracts predators, and he conducted an experiment to see if this were so. He scattered some egg shells in one area and found that, in fact, predators investigated this area much more than a comparable area lacking the shells.

As mentioned earlier, instincts are distinguished from other forms of unlearned behavior. An instinct seems different from a general drive such as hunger, because the hunger drive is found in many species (it is not species-specific). Instincts also seem different from reflexes. Instincts may contain reflexes, but they also may be more complex. For example, the stickleback's zig-zag dance must involve many reflexes. Also, a reflex, such as an eyeblink, can be released by many stimuli—wind, noise, dust, bright lights, and so on. There does not seem to be a specific external releaser.

Imprinting

In many instances an animal's responsiveness to specific releasers is innate or inborn. In many other instances, however, the animal is born with a gap in its knowledge. It is innately equipped with all the behavior patterns of an instinct, but it lacks some information about the releasing stimulus. This information is filled in during an early critical period in a process calling *imprinting*.

For example, many species of young birds and mammals are born without a knowledge of the stimulus that will release their following instinct. They might seem innately disposed to follow their mother, but they actually follow her because she was the first object they saw and followed during a specific time in infancy. When Greylag goslings were raised by Lorenz instead of by their own mothers, they took him for their "mother." They energetically followed him about in single file wherever he went, ignoring other geese (see Figure 3.1). They had imprinted on him (Lorenz, 1935, p. 124).

Although Lorenz was not the first to observe imprinting, he was the first to state that it occurs during a *critical period*. This means that the young animal will form an attachment to an object only if it is exposed to and follows that object during a specific time early in life. If it is exposed to an object before or after the critical period, no attachment is formed. And once the critical period has passed, it may be impossible to induce the animal to attach itself to another kind of object (1935, p. 127).

Lorenz found that species differ with respect to the range of objects on which they will imprint. Greylag goslings seem to imprint on almost anything that moves (some even have imprinted on boats). Mallard duck-lings, in contrast, are more finicky. Lorenz found that they would imprint on him only if he stooped below a certain height and made a quacking sound as he moved about. Mallards, then, have an innate schema of certain aspects of the proper parent—the parent must move, be of a certain height, and make a certain sound. Imprinting only fills in the rest of the visual pattern (Lorenz, 1935, p. 135; 1952b, pp. 42–43).

Imprinting can determine not only the following response in the young but later social behavor as well. In particular, early imprinting can affect later sexual preferences, as Lorenz also learned from personal ex-

Ethologists also have wondered about the adaptive value of imprinting. It appears to have evolved as a particularly early, strong attachment mechanism in those birds and mammals (including deer, sheep, and buffalo) that live in groups, move about soon after birth, and are under strong predator pressure. In these species, the quick formation of a following response ensures that the young will follow an escaping parent in times of danger (Freedman, 1974, p. 19).

Still, one can ask why imprinting is necessary at all. Why, that is, have the young of all vulnerable species not evolved built-in parental schemas? One suggestion is that adult appearances often vary and change over time, so the young can benefit from some opportunity to discover for themselves who their parents are (Bateson, 1966).

Although imprinting is an especially early, rapid process in some species, some form of imprinting may occur in a wide range of species, including primates such as chimpanzees. Young chimpanzees do not show much concern over whom they are with until they are about three or four months old. Then they develop a marked preference for their mother (or foster parent) and become distinctly wary of other adults. After this, they stay fairly near her, returning to her from time to time, and if she should signal that she is about to depart, they rush over and climb aboard. Thus, chimps clearly attach themselves to a particular object during a certain period in life (Bowlby, 1982, pp. 190, 196). A similar process may occur in human children, as we shall discuss presently.

Evaluation

Ethology has given us a number of new, interesting concepts and new ways of looking at behavior. At the same time, it has drawn heavy fire from many psychologists, particularly from American psychologists who have criticized it for ignoring the role of learning and experience (e.g., Riess, 1954; Schneirla, 1960). Such attacks, however, seem largely misdirected. For ethologists do not, as it is often supposed, claim that behavior is entirely innate and that learning and experience count for nothing. Imprinting, after all, is a kind of learning. It is a process by which the stimulus properties of social releasers become filled in through experience. Imprinting is not, to be sure, the kind of learning that Locke, Pavlov, or Skinner talk about. It is a remarkably permanent learning that occurs only during a maturationally determined critical period. Still, it is a kind of learning.

Some psychologists have tried to refute the concept of instinct by showing that instincts do not develop properly if animals are deprived of key experiences. For example, Riess (1954) showed that rats deprived of experiences with sticks failed to show the nest-building instinct. Such experiments, however, miss the ethologists' point. Ethologists recognize that instincts have evolved because they have been adaptive within certain environments and that instincts need the right environment to develop properly. The environment is important. All that ethologists claim is that instinctive behaviors have a large innate component and that, given the environment to which the instinct is preadapted, the instinct will emerge without elaborate conditioning or learning.

Ethology is still a very young science, so we can still debate its ultimate fruitfulness. For our purposes, the basic question is: How useful is it for understanding human development? We will now turn to a major effort to apply ethological concepts to human development—that of John Bowlby.

AN ETHOLOGICAL VIEW OF CHILD DEVELOPMENT: BOWLBY'S THEORY

Biographical Introduction

John Bowlby (1907–1990) was born in London. He taught in a progressive school for children, received medical and psychoanalytic training, and, starting in 1936, was involved in child guidance work. In 1936 Bowlby became concerned about the disturbances of children raised in institutions. Children who grow up in nurseries and orphanages, he found, frequently showed a variety of emotional problems, including an inability to form intimate and lasting relationships with others. It seemed to Bowlby that such children were unable to love because they missed the opportunity to form a solid attachment to a mother-figure early in life. Bowlby also observed similar symptoms in children who grew up in normal homes for a while but then suffered prolonged separations. These children seemed so shaken that they permanently turned away from close human ties. Such observations convinced Bowlby that one cannot understand development without paying close attention to the mother/infant bond. How is this bond formed? Why is it so important that, if disrupted, severe consequences follow? In his search for answers, Bowlby turned to ethology (Tanner and Inhelder, 1971, pp. 25–27).

Theory of Attachment: Overview

Bowlby said that we can understand human behavior only by considering its *environment of adaptedness*, the basic environment in which it evolved (1982, p. 58). Throughout most of human history, humans probably moved about in small groups, searching for food, and often risking attack by large predators. When threatened, humans, like other primate groups, probably cooperated to drive off the predators and to protect the sick and young. To gain this protection, human children needed mechanisms to keep them close to their parents. That is, they must have evolved *attachment behaviors*—gestures and signals that promote and maintain proximity to caretakers (Bowlby, 1982, p. 182).

One obvious signal is the baby's cry. The cry is a distress call; when the infant is in pain or is frightened, he or she cries and the parent is impelled to rush over to see what is wrong. Another attachment behavior is the baby's smile; when a baby smiles into a parent's eyes, the parent feels love for the baby and enjoys being close.   Other attachment behaviors include babbling, grasping, sucking, and following.

Bowlby suggested that the child's attachment develops along the following lines.   Initially, babies' social responsiveness is indiscriminate.   For example, they will smile at any face or cry for any person who leaves. However, between about three and six months of age, babies narrow their responsiveness to a few familiar people, develop a clear-cut preference for one person in particular, and then become wary of strangers.   Soon after this, they become more mobile, crawling about, and take a more active role in keeping their principal attachment-figure nearby.   They monitor this parent's whereabouts, and any sign that the parent might suddenly depart releases following on their part.   The whole process—focusing on a principal attachment-figure who then releases following—parallels imprinting in other species.   Once babies begin following, their behavior takes on a goal-corrected quality; they adjust or correct their movements in response to those of the attachment-figure.

Throughout his discussions, Bowlby spoke of attachment behaviors (such as crying, smiling, and following) as "instinctive."   However, he used the term "instinct" in a purposely loose sense.   He meant that such behaviors are basically innate, have a fairly typical pattern in almost all members of the species, and have an adaptive value for the species (1982, p. 136).   Bowlby did not try to show how each behavior pattern was released by a specific external stimulus, although he did talk about releasers when it was convenient to do so.

Let us now look more closely at the phases of attachment.

Phases of Attachment

Phase 1 (birth to three months): Indiscriminate Responsiveness to Humans.   During the first months of life, babies show various kinds of responsiveness to people, but this responsiveness is unselective; babies react to most people in fairly similar ways.

Right after birth, babies like to listen to human voices and to look at human faces (Fantz, 1961; Freedman, 1974, p. 23).   One study, for example, indicates that babies who are only 10 minutes old prefer the face to other visual stimuli; they move their heads farther to follow an accurate model of a face than to follow scrambled faces or a blank sheet (Jirari, in Freedman, 1974, p. 30).   To ethologists such as Bowlby, this preference suggests a genetic bias toward a visual pattern that will soon release one of the most powerful attachment behaviors, the *social smile*.

During the first three weeks or so, babies will sometimes emit eyes-closed smiles, usually as they are about to fall off to sleep.   These smiles are not yet social; they are not directed at people.   At about three weeks, babies begin smiling at the sound of a human voice.   These are social smiles, but they are still fleeting (Freedman, 1974, pp. 178–79).

At five or six weeks, the most intense social smiling begins.   Babies smile happily and fully at the sight of a human face, and their smiles include

FIGURE 3.2
The sight of a baby smiling into
one's eyes stirs love and fosters
attachment.

eye contact.   One can tell when such visual smiles are about to start.   About a week beforehand, the baby starts to gaze intently at faces, as if studying them.   Then the baby breaks into open smiles.   This is often an electrifying moment in a parent's life; the parent now has "proof" of the baby's love. The sight of one's baby looking deeply into one's eyes and smiling causes a feeling of love to well up from within.   (Even if you are not a parent, you might have had a similar feeling when any baby smiled at you.   You cannot help but smile back, and you think that you and the baby share a special bond.)

Actually, until three months or so, the baby's smiles show no personal preferences.   Babies will smile at any face, even a cardboard model of one. The main stipulation is that the face be presented in the full or frontal position.   A profile is far less effective.   Also a voice or a caress is a relatively weak elicitor of smiling during this stage.   It seems, then, that the baby's social smile is released by a fairly specific visual stimulus (Freedman, 1974, pp. 180–81, 187; Bowlby, 1982, pp. 282–85).

In Bowlby's view, smiling promotes attachment because it maintains the proximity of the caretaker.   When the baby smiles, the caretaker enjoys being with the baby; the caretaker "smiles back, 'talks' to him, strokes and pats him, and perhaps picks him up" (Bowlby, 1982, p. 246).   The smile itself is a releaser that promotes loving and caring interaction—behavior that increases the baby's chances for health and survival.

At about the time that babies begin smiling at faces, they also begin *babbling* (and cooing and gurgling). They babble primarily at the sound of a human voice and, especially, at the sight of a human face. As with smiling, babbling is initially unselective; babies will babble when most any person is around. The baby's babbling delights the caretaker, prompting the caretaker to talk back. "Babbling, like smiling, is a social releaser [that] has the function of maintaining a mother-figure in proximity to an infant by promoting social interaction between them" (1982, p. 289).

Crying also results in proximity between caretaker and child. It is like a distress call; it signals that the baby needs help. Babies cry when they are in pain, hungry, cold, or experience discomfort. They even cry when a person at whom they had been looking leaves their field of vision, although during the first weeks the particular person in question matters little. Babies also will permit most any person to quiet them through rocking or by attending to their needs (1982, pp. 289–96).

Proximity also is maintained by the baby's *holding on*. The newborn is equipped with two holding responses. One is the grasp reflex; when any object touches the baby's open palm, the hand automatically closes around it. The other is the Moro reflex, which occurs either when babies are startled by a loud noise or when they suddenly lose support (as when one holds their head from underneath and then suddenly lets it drop). Their response is to spread their arms and then to bring them back around the chest. The action looks as if the baby were embracing something (see Figure 3.3). In earlier times, Bowlby thought, these reflexes served the purpose of keeping hold of the parent who carried them about. If, for example, a mother saw a predator and suddenly ran, the chances were that the baby had a grasp of some part of her with the hand (see Figure 3.4). And if the baby lost hold, he or she would embrace the mother again (1982, p. 278).

Babies also are equipped with *rooting* and *sucking* reflexes. When their cheek is touched, they automatically turn their head to the side from which the stimulation came and then "root" or grope until their mouth touches something, which they then suck. The rooting and sucking reflexes obviously aid breast-feeding, but Bowlby also regards them as attachment patterns because they bring the baby into interaction with the mother (1982, p. 275).

Phase 2 (three to six months): Focusing on Familiar People. Beginning at about three months, the baby's behavior changes. For one thing, many reflexes—including the Moro, grasp, and rooting reflexes—drop out. But more importantly for Bowlby, the baby's social responses begin to become much more selective. Between three and six months, babies gradually restrict their smiles to familiar people; when they see a stranger, they simply stare (1982, pp. 287, 325). Babies also become more selective in their babbling; by the age of four or five months, they coo, gurgle, and babble only in the presence of people they recognize (1982, p. 289). Also, by this age (and perhaps long before), their crying is most readily quieted by a

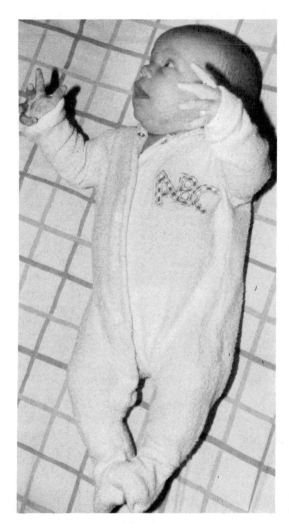

FIGURE 3.3
The Moro reflex: A startled baby
exhibits an embracing action.

preferred figure (1982, pp. 279, 300).   By five months, finally, babies begin
to reach for and grasp parts of our anatomy, particularly our hair, but they
do so only if they know us (1982, p. 279).

During this phase, then, babies narrow their responsiveness to familiar
people.   They usually prefer two or three people—and one in particular.
They most readily smile or babble, for example, when this person is near.
This principal attachment-figure is usually the mother, but it doesn't have
to be.   It can be the father or some other caretaker.   Babies seem to develop
the strongest attachment to the one person who has most alertly responded
to their signals and who has engaged in the most pleasurable interactions
with them (1982, pp. 306–16).

FIGURE 3.4
With her grasp reflex, this month-old baby has a hold on her mother's shirt.

Phase 3 (six months to three years): Intense Attachment and Active Proximity-Seeking. Beginning at about six months of age, the infant's attachment to a particular person becomes increasingly intense and exclusive. Most notably, infants *cry out* when the mother-figure leaves the room, demonstrating *separation anxiety*. Earlier, they might have protested the departure of anyone they had been looking at; now, however, it is primarily this one person's absence that upsets them. Observers have also noted the intensity with which the baby *greets* the mother after she has been away for a brief time. When she returns, the baby typically smiles, reaches to be picked up, and when in the mother's arms, hugs her and crows with delight. The mother, too, displays her happiness at the reunion (1982, pp. 295, 300).

The new exclusiveness of the baby's attachment to a parent is also evident at about seven or eight months when the baby exhibits a *fear of strangers*. This reaction ranges from a slight vigilance to outright cries at the sight of a stranger, with the stronger reactions usually occurring when the baby feels ill or is in an unfamiliar setting (1982, pp. 321–26).

But babies are not restricted to the expression of strong emotions. By eight months, they can usually *crawl* and therefore can begin to *actively follow* a departing parent. Babies will make the most concerted efforts to regain contact when a parent departs suddenly, rather than slowly, or when they are in unfamiliar surroundings (1982, pp. 256–59). (See Figure 3.5.)

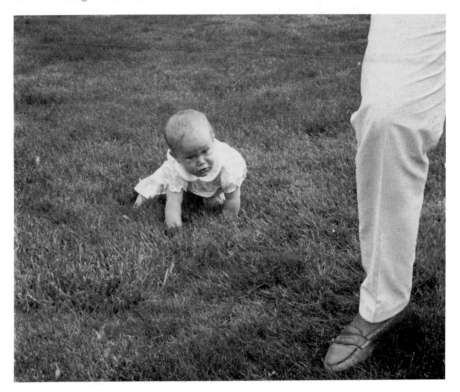

FIGURE 3.5   An eight-month-old baby struggles to follow her mother.

Once infants can actively follow a parent, their behavior begins to consolidate into a *goal-corrected system*. That is, babies monitor the parent's whereabouts, and if the parent starts to leave, they urgently follow, "correcting" or adjusting their movements until they regain proximity. When they get near the parent, they typically reach up with their arms, gesturing to be picked up. When held, they calm down again (1982, p. 252).

Babies also begin to *call out* in a new way, and calling too takes on a goal-corrected quality. That is, babies alter their calls according to their estimates of the parent's location and movements. If the parent is far or departing, they call loudly; if the parent is near or approaching, they call more quietly (1982, p. 252).

Another sign that the child's behavior is taking on the properties of an organized system is a clearer distinction between goals and means. The child's goal is proximity to the caretaker, and the child will use any and all means at his or her disposal to achieve this goal. When the child wants to move closer to a parent, "he will crawl, shuffle, walk, or run. If he is grossly deficient in locomotory equipment, for example as a result of thalidomide, he will still achieve his end, even if it means rolling. . . . The overall objective is constant; the techniques for obtaining it are flexible" (1982, p. 248).

   Babies, of course, often move away from attachment-figures as well as toward them. This is particularly evident when they use the caretaker as a *secure base from which to explore.* If a mother and her one- or two-year-old child enter a park or playground, the child will typically remain close for a moment or two and then venture off to explore. However, the child will periodically look back, exchange glances or smiles with her, and even return to her from time to time before venturing forth once again. The child initiates brief contacts "as though to assure himself that she is still there" (1982, p. 209).

   In Bowlby's view, the attachment system functions at various levels of arousal. Sometimes the child feels an intense need to be close to the mother-figure; at other times the child feels hardly any need at all. When the toddler uses the mother as a secure base from which to explore, the activation level is relatively low. The child does, to be sure, periodically monitor the mother's presence and may even return to her on occasion. But by and large, the child can comfortably explore and play at some distance from her (Bowlby, 1988, p. 62).

   Still, this situation can quickly change. If, when a toddler glances back at the mother, she seems inaccessible (or, more threatening yet, seems ready to depart), the child will hurry back to her. The child also will rush back if he or she is frightened by some event, such as a loud noise. In these circumstances, the child will want close physical contact and may require a good deal of comforting before he or she will venture away from the mother once again (Bowlby, 1982, pp. 257–59, 373).

   Attachment behavior also depends on other variables, such as the child's internal physical state. If a little child is ill or tired, the need to remain close to the mother will outweigh the need for exploration (1982, p. 258).

   By the end of the first year, an important variable is the child's general *working model* of the attachment-figure. That is, the child has begun to build up, on the basis of day-to-day interactions, a general idea of the caretaker's accessibility and responsiveness. So, for example, a one-year-old girl who has developed some general doubts about her mother's availability will tend to be anxious about exploring new situations at any distance from her. If, in contrast, the girl has basically concluded that "my mother loves me and will always be there when I really need her," she will explore the world with more courage and enthusiasm. Still, she will periodically monitor her mother's presence, for the attachment system is too vital to ever completely shut down (Bowlby, 1973, pp. 203–6; 1982, pp. 354, 373).

Phase 4 (three years to the end of childhood): Partnership Behavior. Prior to the age of two or three years, children are concerned only with their own need to maintain a certain proximity to the caretaker; they do not yet consider the caretaker's plans or goals. For the two-year-old, the knowledge that mother or father is "going next door for a moment to borrow some milk" is meaningless; the child simply wants to go too. The three-year-old, in contrast, has some understanding of such plans and can visualize the parent's behavior while he or she is away. Consequently, the child is more willing to let the parent go. The child begins acting more like a partner in the relationship.

Bowlby admitted (1982, p. 387) that little is known about phase 4 attachment behavior, and he had little to say about attachments during the rest of life. Nevertheless, he felt that they remain very important. Adolescents break away from parental dominance, but they form attachments to parental substitutes; adults consider themselves independent, but they seek proximity to loved ones in times of crisis; and older people find that they must increasingly depend on the younger generation (1982, p. 207). In general, Bowlby said that being alone is one of the great fears in human life. We might consider such a fear silly, neurotic, or immature, but there are good biological reasons behind it. Throughout human history, humans have best been able to withstand crises and face dangers with the help of companions. Thus, the need for close attachments is built into our nature (Bowlby, 1973, pp. 84, 143, 165).

Attachment as Imprinting

Now that we have examined the child's attachment in some detail, we are in a position to appreciate Bowlby's thesis that it follows a course similar to imprinting in animals. Imprinting, you will recall, is the process by which animals learn the releasing stimuli for their social instincts. In particular, young animals learn which moving objects to follow. They begin with a willingness to follow a wide range of objects, but this range quickly narrows, and at the end of the imprinting period they usually will follow only the mother. At this point the fear response limits the ability to form new attachments.

In humans we can observe a similar process, although it develops much more slowly. During the first weeks of life babies cannot actively follow objects through locomotion, but they do direct social responses toward people. They smile, babble, hold on, cry, and so on—all of which keep people close. At first babies direct these responses toward anyone. However, by six months of age they have narrowed their attachment to a few people and one in particular. They primarily want this person near. At this point they become afraid of strangers, and, as they learn to crawl, they follow their principal attachment-figure whenever she departs. Thus, they have imprinted on a particular person; it is she who releases following.

Effects of Institutional Care

Institutional deprivation. As we mentioned in the introductory remarks, Bowlby turned to ethology as a way of accounting for the damaging and seemingly irreversible effects of institutional deprivation. He was particularly struck by the inability of many institutionally reared children to form deep attachments later in life. He called these individuals "affectionless characters"; such individuals use people solely for their own ends and seem incapable of forming a loving, lasting tie to another person (Bowlby, 1953). Perhaps these people, as children, lacked the opportunity to "imprint" on any human figure—to form a loving relationship with another. Because they did not develop the capacity for intimate ties during the normal early period, their relationships remain shallow in adult life.

The conditions in many institutions do seem unfavorable for the formation of intimate human ties. In many institutions, babies receive care from several nurses who can meet their physical needs but who have little time to interact with them. Frequently, no one is around to heed the babies' cries, to return their smiles, to talk to them when they babble, or to pick them up when they desire. Consequently, it is difficult for the baby to establish a strong bond to any particular person.

If a "failure to imprint" explains the effects of institutional deprivation, there should be a critical period beyond which these effects cannot be reversed. That is, babies who lack sufficient human interaction up to a certain age might never develop appropriate social behavior. Researchers, however, have had trouble pinpointing the precise ages of any such critical period. Bowlby's discussions of imprinting (Bowlby, 1982, pp. 222–23; see also 1953, p. 58) suggest that the critical period ends with the onset of the fear response, just as it does with other species. This would place the end of the critical period at eight or nine months, the age by which almost all babies have shown some fear of separation from the mother as well as a fear of strangers. In fact, some evidence suggests that babies who lack human interaction up to this point may experience permanent difficulties with vocalization (Ainsworth, 1962). In general, however, it appears that therapeutic interventions can make up for most social deficits up to the age of 18 to 24 months. In one view, institutional deprivation puts babies in "cold storage," slowing up social growth and extending the critical or sensitive period for attachments into the second year. After this point, babies lacking in human interaction may never develop normally (Ainsworth, 1973).

Separations. Although Bowlby was interested in "failures to imprint," he was even more interested in cases where the child forms an attachment and suffers a separation. In a groundbreaking film (1952), Bowlby's co-worker James Robertson filmed the eight-day hospitalization of Laura, a normal two-year-old. As was the practice at the time, visits from Laura's family were limited, and the little girl's suffering had a profound impact on everyone who saw the film.

According to Bowlby and Robertson (Bowlby, 1982, Ch. 2), the effects of separation typically run the following course. First, children *protest*; they cry and scream and reject all forms of substitute care. Second, they go through a period of *despair*; they become quiet, withdrawn, and inactive and appear to be in a deep state of mourning. Finally, a stage of *detachment* sets in. During this period, the child is more lively and may accept the care of nurses and others. The hospital staff may think that the child has recovered. However, all is not well. When the mother returns, the child seems not to know her; the child turns away and seems to have lost all interest in her.

Fortunately, most children do reestablish their tie to the mother after a while. But this is not always the case. If the separation has been prolonged, and if the child loses other caretakers (e.g., nurses), the child may give up on people altogether. The result here, too, is an "affectionless character," a person who no longer cares for others in any deep way.

In Bowlby's (1973) view, only ethology explains why separations have such profound effects on children. Ethology suggests that the child's need to keep the parent close has enabled the species to survive and this need is as basic as other biological needs, such as feeding and sex. Thus we cannot interfere with this need without producing powerful emotional reactions.

Mary Ainsworth's Patterns of Attachment

Bowlby and Robertson alerted us to the damage that institutional placements can do to normal attachment. But ordinary child-rearing, too, might vary in the degree to which it promotes healthy attachment. The scholar who has done the most important research on this topic is Mary D. S. Ainsworth.

As a young psychologist, Ainsworth worked as Bowlby's assistant in London for four years and then journeyed with her husband to Uganda, where she studied the growth of attachment in 28 Ganda infants. Her findings (Ainsworth, 1967) had a major impact on Bowlby's thinking. In fact, he credits Ainsworth with the discovery that infants, by the age of eight months, commonly use the mother as a secure base from which to explore (Bowlby, 1988, pp. 46, 122).

After returning from Africa, Ainsworth's next project, which is our focus here, was the study of 23 middle-class babies and their mothers in Baltimore. Ainsworth and her students observed the babies and their mothers for the first year of the children's lives, visiting them for about four hours every three weeks. When the infants were 12 months old, Ainsworth wanted to see how they would behave in a new setting, so she brought them and their mothers to a playroom at Johns Hopkins University. She was particularly interested in how the babies would use the mother as a base from which to explore and how they would react to a stressful event—being left in the room with a stranger for three minutes. In this procedure, called the Strange Situation, Ainsworth and her co-workers observed three basic patterns (Ainsworth et al., 1971, 1978).

1. Securely attached infants. Soon after entering the playroom with the mother, these babies used her as a base from which to explore. When the mother left the room, however, their exploratory play diminished and they sometimes became visibly upset. When the mother returned, they actively greeted her and remained close to her for a moment or two. Once reassured, they eagerly ventured forth to explore the environment once again.

When Ainsworth examined the earlier home observations of these children, she found that the mothers had typically been rated as sensitive and promptly responsive to their babies' cries and other signals. The mothers had been lovingly available when the babies needed their comfort.

For their part, the babies cried very little at home and used the mother as a base from which to explore in the home as well.

Ainsworth believes that these infants demonstrated the healthy pattern of attachment behavior. The mother's day-in and day-out responsiveness had given them faith in her as a protector; her simple presence in the Strange Situation gave them the courage to actively explore the surroundings. At the same time, their responses to her departure and return in this new environment revealed their strong need for proximity to her—a need that has had enormous survival value throughout human evolution. This pattern has been found to characterize 65 to 70 percent of the one-year-olds evaluated in the Strange Situation in U.S. samples (Aber and Slade, 1987).

2. Insecure-avoidant infants. These infants appeared quite independent throughout the Strange Situation. As soon as they entered the room, they rushed off to inspect the toys. Although they explored, they didn't use the mother as a secure base, in the sense of checking in with her from time to time. They simply ignored her. When the mother left the room, they didn't become upset, and they didn't seek proximity to her when she returned. If she tried to pick them up, they tried to avoid her, turning their bodies away or averting their gaze. This avoidant pattern has been found in about 20 percent of the infants in U.S. samples (Aber and Slade, 1987).

Because these infants display such independence in the Strange Situation, they have struck many people as exceptionally healthy. But when Ainsworth saw their avoidant behavior, she guessed that they were suffering from some degree of emotional difficulty. Their detachment reminded her of children who had experienced painful separations.

The home observations supported Ainsworth's guess that something was wrong. The mothers had been rated as relatively insensitive, interfering, and rejecting. And the babies often seemed insecure. Although some were very independent in the home, many were anxious about the mother's whereabouts and cried intensely when the mother left the room.

Ainsworth's overall interpretation, then, is that when these babies entered the Strange Situation, they suspected that they couldn't count on their mother for support and they therefore reacted in a defensive way. They adopted an indifferent, self-contained posture to protect themselves. Having suffered so many rejections in the past, they attempted to block out their need for their mother to avoid further disappointment. And when the mother returned from the separation episodes, they refused to look at her, as if denying any feelings for her. They behaved as if they were saying, "Who are you? Am I supposed to know you?—you who won't help me when I need it" (Ainsworth et al., 1971, p. 47; 1978, pp. 241–42, 316).

It is possible that this defensive behavior will become a fixed and pervasive part of the personality. If this occurs, the child will become an adult who is overly self-reliant and detached, a person who can never let down his or her guard and trust others sufficiently to form close relationships with them (Bowlby, 1988, pp. 124–25).

3. Insecure-ambivalent infants.   In the Strange Situation, these infants were so clingy and preoccupied with the mother's whereabouts that they hardly explored at all.   They became extremely upset when the mother left the room, and they were markedly ambivalent toward her when she returned.   At one moment they reached out for her; at the next moment they angrily pushed her away.

In their homes, these mothers had typically treated their babies in an inconsistent manner.   The mothers had been warm and responsive on some occasions but not on others.   This inconsistency had apparently left the babies uncertain whether the mothers would be there for them when called upon.   As a result, they usually wanted to keep the mother close at hand—a desire that intensified greatly in the Strange Situation.   These babies became very distressed when the mother left the playroom, and they urgently tried to regain contact with her when she returned, although they also vented their anger toward her.   The ambivalent pattern usually characterizes about 10 percent of the one-year-olds in U.S. samples (Aber and Slade, 1987).

Later behavior.   If the Strange Situation taps fundamental differences among children, it should predict differences in their later behavior.   A number of studies (e.g., Sroufe and Cooper, 1988, pp. 393–97) have found that the children classified as securely attached in the Strange Situation at 12 or 18 months continued to behave differently from the others as three- to five-year-olds.   The securely attached children have consistently scored higher on measures of curiosity and persistence in their play, as well as on preschool teachers' ratings of social competence, self-esteem, and empathy.   The research has lent impressive support to Ainsworth's view that securely attached infants demonstrate the healthiest pattern of development.

Investigators have found it more difficult to distinguish between the avoidant and the ambivalent children as three- to five-year-olds.   Both groups display various kinds of emotional difficulty, ranging from mild to severe, but it takes more effort on the part of the researcher to detect the differences between the two patterns.   Perhaps these patterns have not yet become firmly established in children this young (Sroufe, 1983).

In adolescence and adulthood, the avoidant and ambivalent patterns seem to characterize many people suffering from emotional difficulties (Parkes, 1982).   Psychotherapists are very familiar with "avoidant" clients—people who are compulsively self-sufficient and have great difficulty forming close relationships with others.   Therapists are also quite familiar with the "ambivalent" clients—those who are clinging, dependent, and prone to depression.   Because these patterns are so prevalent, one hopes that research into their early roots will continue.

Other research.   Ainsworth's followers have been engaged in a wide variety of research projects.   These include efforts to expand the initial classification system and to assess the child's attachment to his or her father.   We cannot discuss the various areas of new research here (see Bretherton,

1985; Bowlby, 1988, Ch. 7 and pp. 166–71 for reviews). But I would like to call attention to one topic that many attachment researchers consider especially important: internal working models.

Bowlby, you will recall, thought of the working model of attachment as the child's expectations and feelings about the attachment-figure's availability and responsiveness. Since the working model involves thoughts and feelings, it is difficult to investigate in infancy; one cannot interview babies about such matters. But after the age of three years or so, research becomes more feasible. For example, Bretherton et al. (1990) found that three-year-olds could complete stories about attachment situations. They could provide endings, for instance, to a story about a child who fell and hurt her knee while taking a walk with her family. As predicted, the securely attached children, compared to the others, most frequently depicted the parents in their story endings as responsive and helpful (saying, for example, that a parent will put a Band-Aid on the child's knee).

Parents, too, have developed thoughts and feelings about attachment, and their attitudes undoubtedly influence the way they treat their children. Main and her associates (Main et al., 1985; Main and Goldwyn, 1987) have interviewed the parents of infants studied in the Strange Situation, asking about their own early memories. Main's focus, however, is not on the parents' early experiences per se, but on the way they talk about them. She has been especially interested in the openness and flexibility with which they discuss their past attachment experiences.

Main has found that the parents of securely attached children generally talk openly and freely about their own experiences. Apparently the parents' acceptance of their own feelings goes hand-in-hand with an acceptance of their infants' signals and needs. The parents of avoidant infants, in contrast, tend to dismiss their own attachment experiences as unimportant. They reject their own experiences, Main speculates, in much the same way that they reject their infants' proximity-seeking.

The parents of ambivalent children are still preoccupied with their own attachment needs. Inwardly or outwardly, they are still struggling to win their own parents' love and approval. Perhaps it is their own neediness that makes it so difficult for them to respond consistently to their infants' needs.

Ainsworth's attachment patterns, then, have generated a great deal of enthusiastic research. But this does not mean that everyone believes in them. Some psychologists note that the proportion of children in each pattern seems to vary across cultures, and these psychologists await plausible explanations of these variations (see Sagi et al., 1991).

In a different vein, Kagan (1984) has argued that Ainsworth ignores the role of innate temperament. Kagan says that the avoidant infants, for example, ignore the mother in the Strange Situation not because they are defending themselves against her rebuffs, but because they are innately fearless. Attachment theorists have mounted a good deal of evidence that suggests that parental responsiveness, rather than innate temperament, is the overriding factor, but some psychologists suggest that both factors are at play (Sroufe and Cooper, 1988, pp. 237–40).

Implications for Child-Rearing

Bowlby (1982, p. 356) said that both parents and professionals repeatedly asked him one basic question: Should a mother always meet her baby's demands for her presence and attention? The fear is that too much attention will lead to spoiling.

Bowlby's position was basically the same as Gesell's. Evolution has provided infants with signals and gestures that promote healthy development, and it is wisest to respond to them. As parents, we should follow our impulse to go to our babies when they cry, to return their smiles, to talk back when they babble, and so on. Infants are biologically prepared to guide us with respect to the experiences they need, and our relationships with them will develop most happily when we follow their initiatives.

Bowlby's position is strongly buttressed by Ainsworth's research. Parents who respond sensitively and promptly to their infants' signals produce babies who, at one year of age, are securely attached. In home settings, these babies cry less than other babies and they are relatively independent. They seem to have developed the feeling that they can always get the parent's attention when necessary, so they can relax and explore the world. Such infants do, to be sure, monitor the parents' whereabouts; the attachment system is too strong to ever completely shut down. But even in new settings, they do not worry excessively about the mother's presence. Instead, they use her as a secure base from which to explore. They venture away from her to investigate the surroundings, and even though they glance back at her and perhaps even return to her from time to time, it is not long before they venture forth once again. "The picture," as Bowlby put it, is "that of a happy balance between exploration and attachment" (1982, p. 338).

Parents, Bowlby said, can in fact produce a spoiled or overmothered child. But they do not accomplish this by being too sensitive and responsive to the baby's signals. If we look closely, we see that the parent is taking all the initiative. A parent might insist on being close to a child, or showering the child with love, whether the child wants it or not. The parent is not taking his or her cues from the child (1982, p. 375).

In recent years, many parents have found a new way to be intrusive. They provide their infants and toddlers with all kinds of early stimulation, from flash cards to computers, in an effort to accelerate their children's intellectual development. Ainsworth has said that she believes that such parental behavior is unhealthy because it takes too much control away from the child (quoted in Karen, 1990, p. 69).

Parents can be more helpful, Ainsworth and Bowlby say, by giving children opportunities to pursue their own interests. Parents can frequently do this by simply being available to the child, by providing the child with a secure base from which to explore. When, for example, a young girl wants to climb some large rocks, or wade into the ocean surf, the parent's presence is necessary for the sake of the child's safety, and to help out if called upon. But the child doesn't want or need the parent's supervision or instructions. All she needs is the parent's patient availability.

This alone gives her the assurance she needs to boldly try out new activities and explore the world on her own.

As children grow older, they can comfortably spend increasingly longer periods of time completely apart from their primary caretakers. Five-year-olds can go to school for a half day, or even longer, and adolescents may be able to spend weeks or even months away from home. Yet we all meet life with the greatest confidence when we know that there is a home base, provided by our family or companions, to which we can return. "All of us, from the cradle to the grave, are happiest when life is organized as a series of excursions, long or short, from a secure base provided by our attachment figure(s)" (Bowlby, 1988, p. 62).

Separations. Bowlby, as we have seen, was among the first to alert people to the potentially harmful effects of separations from parents. His work with James Robertson in the early 1950s convinced many people that placing a young child in a hospital with little parent contact caused the child great suffering, and over the years more and more hospitals have permitted mothers to room-in with their young children.

Bowlby's work also has implications for adoption and foster placements. If we must move a child from one home to another, we should consider the baby's stage of attachment. When possible, it would seem wisest to place a baby in a permanent home during the first few months of life, before the baby begins to focus his or her love onto a single person. Between six months and three or four years, separations are likely to be most painful. During this time, children are intensely forming attachments and lack the independence and cognitive capacities to deal with separations in very adaptive ways (Ainsworth, 1973).

Institutional deprivation. Bowlby, as noted, was also among the first to call attention to the potentially damaging effects of institutional upbringing. In the early 1950s he observed that many institutions provided so little contact between children and adults that the children failed to develop attachments to any adult. Bowlby's writings have had a positive impact in this area as well.

In the same tradition, in 1970 two pediatricians, Marshall Klaus and John Kennell, began arguing that the typical hospital care for the newborn baby was itself a kind of institutional deprivation. Until then, hospitals routinely kept the mother apart from her new baby for long periods of time. The baby was kept in a nursery and fed on a four-hour schedule. The practice was designed to prevent infections, but the main effect, in Klaus and Kennell's (1970) view, was to deny mothers the opportunity to begin forming a bond with their infants. This was particularly unfortunate because the first few days might constitute a "sensitive period" for the bonding process.

The work of Klaus and Kennell (1970, 1983) and their associates (e.g., Lozoff et al., 1977) is very ethological in orientation. Throughout most of human evolution, these authors say, babies began life in an environment of close physical contact with their mothers. In this "environment of adaptedness," babies evolved characteristics and responses that facilitate parental attachment right from the start. Newborns are for brief periods wide-eyed and alert; they prefer looking at a human face and hearing a human voice (to which they make subtle movements); they stop crying when lifted to an adult's shoulder; they enjoy nursing; and they strike most parents as beautiful. Such responses and characteristics immediately stir feelings of love in the mother. She loves this baby who looks at her intently, who takes comfort from her hold, who takes pleasure at her breast, who makes subtle movements in response to her voice, and who looks so beautiful. She begins to feel these things, that is, when she is in close contact with her baby, as she had been throughout human history—until the advent of the modern hospital.

To support their view, Klaus, Kennell, and their associates have marshalled a substantial amount of evidence that development proceeds along better lines when mothers and babies are permitted just a few extra hours of daily contact during their hospital stay. When extra care is permitted, babies cry less in the hospital and mothers feel more confident in their handling of them. During the next few months, the mothers continue to feel more confident and to soothe, kiss, and smile at their babies more frequently. They also are more likely to breast-feed their babies and talk to them in soothing tones. Child abuse is rare. For their part, babies smile and laugh more and cry less (Lozoff et al., 1977; Klaus and Kennell, 1983).

Not everyone has agreed that the research so clearly supports the early-bonding position (Goldberg, 1983). However, Klaus and Kennell's work has contributed to some significant changes in hospital policies, and the evidence generally suggests that these changes should continue.

Day care. As increasing numbers of U.S. mothers work outside the home, families are turning to day care for assistance, and they are placing their children in day care settings at younger and younger ages. Indeed, even day care for infants (children under 12 months of age) is already quite common, and it will undoubtedly become more common in the years to come (Clarke-Stewart, 1989).

To some extent, day care has become a political issue. Some people argue that day care supports the woman's right to pursue a career. Others lobby for day care because it enables economically disadvantaged parents to work and make more money. Nevertheless, Bowlby, Ainsworth, and other attachment theorists (e.g., Belsky, 1988) have raised questions about it. Does early day care prevent the baby from forming a bond with the parent? And what are the emotional effects of long, daily separations from the parents in the first few years of life (Ainsworth, 1973, p. 70)?

The research on such questions is still incomplete, but it is clear that even young infants who attend day care for several hours a day become primarily attached to their parents (not to their day care workers). These infants, compared to babies raised at home, do more frequently demonstrate insecure patterns of maternal attachment, but not to an enormous extent; their incidence of insecure attachment is about 7 percent higher

(Clarke-Stewart, 1989).   Moreover, the evidence thus far suggests that when children older than 12 months of age attend high-quality day care programs (in which a permanent staff is available and sensitively responsive to each child), there are no ill effects.   The trouble is that high-quality day care is difficult to find and afford (Sroufe and Cooper, 1988, pp. 230–31).

In a sense, the search for quality day care really reflects wider problems in contemporary societies, as Bowlby (1988, pp. 1–3) and Ainsworth (Karen, 1990) have tried to indicate.   In earlier, village societies, parents could take their children to work with them in the fields or in the shops, and parents received a good deal of child care assistance from grandparents, aunts and uncles, teenagers, and friends.   There was also time for leisure, for games and socializing with the children.   In today's hectic world, the situation is very different.   Parents usually live apart from their relatives and must raise their children alone, and they usually come home from work too exhausted to be very responsive to their children.   Efforts to set aside a half-hour of "quality time" for the children each evening only show how hard-pressed parents have become.   Thus, although quality day care may seem desirable, what parents really need are new occupational and social arrangements that permit them to spend considerably more relaxed and enjoyable time with their children.

Evaluation

Bowlby and the ethologists have given us a new way of looking at a great deal of childhood behavior. Before reading Bowlby, we might have regarded the infant's cries as merely childish, or the infant's smiles as merely cute. But Bowlby encourages us to see how these and other behaviors have contributed to the survival of our species. Cries are similar to the distress calls in other species; they elicit parental help in times of trouble. Smiles, too, make parents want to be near the child, generating love and care in the parents. Thus, we see how children may be innately programmed with signals and gestures that promote proximity to parents and foster loving bonds with them.

One test of a theory is its capacity to stimulate new research. On this score, Bowlby's theory has been highly successful. Most notably, it has inspired the research of Mary Ainsworth and her colleagues on patterns of attachment. This research has shown that parental responsiveness to infants' signals fosters a secure pattern of attachment and healthy social growth, whereas a lack of parental responsiveness leads to insecure patterns of attachment. Ainsworth's research has supported and enriched Bowlby's theory, and her method of assessing attachment patterns, the Strange Situation, has become one of the most widely used research tools in child psychology.

At the same time, Bowlby's theory has its limitations.   For one thing, it focuses fairly exclusively on infancy.   We would like more ethological insights into later periods of development.   To some extent, Ainsworth and her followers have begun to fill this gap.   We have seen how investigators have followed infants tested in the Strange Situation into their early childhood years and have examined parents' feelings about attachment. In addition, Ainsworth (1982) and others (e.g., Weiss, 1982) have speculated on the adult's need for attachment-figures—not just companions, but people on whom one can count for help and support when needed. Young adults, for example, may look for such a person when they consider marriage. But the insights of attachment theorists into the developmental periods after infancy are still sketchy.

A major drawback to Bowlby's own writing, I believe, was a vague and hesitant use of specific ethological concepts. This is a bit ironic, for Bowlby was the psychoanalyst who so boldly argued that the concepts of Lorenz and Tinbergen are relevant to human development. Nevertheless, he didn't always emphasize the extent to which ethological concepts might characterize human behavior. This was particularly true with respect to releasers, the specific external stimulus configurations that trigger instincts. When babies engage in early social smiling, it is the sight of a specific stimulus, the face in the frontal position, that elicits the response. Similarly, when infants start following an attachment-figure, the sight of that figure departing, especially in a sudden manner, seems to be the key stimulus. One would have expected Bowlby to stress these facts. Instead, he merely pointed to them and turned his attention to his own ideas about the formation of a goal-corrected feedback system. Perhaps he didn't want to push the parallels between humans and other species too far. Whatever the reason, a more exacting analysis of where releasers and traditional ethological concepts apply or don't apply to human behavior would have been helpful.

These criticisms notwithstanding, Bowlby and the ethologists are making us realize the importance of viewing human development in an evolutionary context. They also are inspiring a new humility when we consider children. They are making us realize that we cannot change children's behavior in any way we wish. Evolution has provided children with responses and signals that must be heeded if development is to proceed properly. If, for example, we do not attend to children's cries, smiles; and other signals, they do not form the secure attachments which seem so necessary for later social growth. Before we try to change children's behavior, then, we should first understand how it follows Nature's plan for healthy development. By asking for a respectful attitude toward Nature, the ethologists are very much in the developmental tradition.

4

Montessori's Educational Philosophy

BIOGRAPHICAL INTRODUCTION

Most of the developmentalists whom we discuss in this book had ideas on education, but only Maria Montessori dedicated herself to the actual teaching of children. Montessori (1870–1952) was born in the province of Ancona, Italy. Her father was a successful civil servant with traditional ideas on the role of women in society. Her mother, in contrast, hoped that Montessori would go as far as she could in life. It was this hope that took hold. It is said that when Montessori was seriously ill as a 10-year-old, she told her anxious mother, "Don't worry, Mother, I cannot die; I have too much to do" (Kramer, 1976, p. 28). At the age of 26, Montessori became the first woman physician in Italy's history.

Montessori's first professional interest was in mental retardation. She was impressed by the extent to which institutionalized retarded children hungered for experience; she felt that they might be teachable if the right methods were used. She read as much as she could find on the subject and found that her own intuitions had guided an earlier line of educators, including Itard, Seguin, and Froebel—men who had worked in the spirit of Rousseau. According to these men, we cannot simply begin teaching retarded children things that we think they ought to know, such as reading and writing. This will lead only to frustration; for these children are not intellectually ready to learn on this level. Instead, we must first simply observe the children and take note of their natural tendencies and spontaneous interests. Then we will be in a position to take advantage of their own natural inclinations and ways of learning. For example, Seguin found that retarded children, like normal children at younger ages, are most interested in objects that stimulate their senses and permit physical activity. Accordingly, he gave them objects to place in different-sized holes, beads to thread, pieces of cloth to button and lace, and other concrete and useful tasks (Kramer, 1976, p. 61).

Montessori followed Seguin's approach, using many of his materials and trying out new materials of her own. To her delight, this new approach worked, and she ventured to teach more difficult matters, including reading and writing, in the same way. Since the retarded children seemed to learn best by touching and feeling objects, she gave them wooden script letters that they liked to run their hands over again and again. By such methods, she taught many of these children to read and write as well as normal children of their age.

During her work with the retarded children, Montessori worked closely with another physician, Dr. Montessano, with whom she had a love affair. The result was a son, Mario. Montessori and Montessano never married, apparently because his parents objected (Kramer, 1976, p. 92). At that time in Italy, news of an illegitimate child would have ruined her career, so she followed the advice of her friends and secretly sent Mario to a wet nurse in the country. She did continue to visit her son, who later became an important educator in the Montessori movement. Nevertheless, the episode threw Montessori into a crisis, which she weathered by deepening her Catholic faith.

In 1907 Montessori took over responsibility for educating children who lived in a tenement in the slums of San Lorenzo, a section of Rome. There she established a school for over 50 extremely poor children—the sons and daughters of unemployed laborers, beggars, prostitutes, and criminals. In this school—called the Casa dei Bambini, or Children's House—Montessori continued to develop her ideas and techniques, and she was so successful that by 1913 she was one of the most famous women in the news. It seemed that her ideas were about to change the course of education throughout the world. However, her ideas apparently turned out to be too radical for the educational mainstream, and within five years she was all but forgotten except by a small band of followers. It was not until the 1960s that her work once again began to catch the attention of psychologists, educators, and the general public (Lillard, 1972; Kramer, 1976).

THEORY OF DEVELOPMENT

Although Montessori's interests were more practical than theoretical, she did develop a definite theoretical position, one that owed much to Rousseau. She argued that we are wrong to assume that children are whatever we make them, for children also learn on their own, from their own maturational promptings (Montessori, 1936a, p. 22; 1949, pp. 17, 223). And, like Rousseau, she argued that children often think and learn quite differently from adults (Montessori, 1936b, p. 69).

A central component of Montessori's theory is the concept of *sensitive periods*. Sensitive periods are similar to critical periods; they are genetically programmed blocks of time during which the child is especially eager and able to master certain tasks. For example, there are sensitive periods for the acquisition of language and for the beginning use of the hand. During these periods, the child works with all his or her might at perfecting these abilities. And, "if the child is prevented from enjoying these experiences at the very time when nature has planned for him to do so, the special sensitivity which draws him to them will vanish, with a disturbing effect on development . . . " (Montessori, 1949, p. 95).

The Sensitive Period for Order

During the first sensitive period, which takes place primarily during the first three years, the child has a strong need for order.[1] As soon as children can move about, they like to put objects where they belong; if a book or a pen is out of place, they resolutely put it back. And even before this, they often become upset at the sight of something out of order. Montessori told, for example, of a six-month-old girl who cried when a visitor put an umbrella on the table. The girl looked at the table and cried for some time. She became calm only when the mother, with a flash of insight, put the umbrella on the rack where it belonged (Montessori, 1936b, p. 50).

To us, such reactions, which are quite common, seem silly. This is because the adult need for order is on a different plane. For the adult, order provides a certain measure of external pleasure, but for the young child, it is essential. "It is like the land upon which animals walk or the water in which fish swim. In their first year [infants] derive their principles of orientation from their environment which they must later master" (1936b, p. 53).

The Sensitive Period for Details

Between one and two years of age, children fix their attention on minute details. For example, they detect small insects that escape our notice. Or, if we show them pictures, they seem to disregard the main objects, which we consider important, and focus instead on tiny objects in the background. This concern for details signals a change in children's psychic development. Whereas they were at first attracted to gaudy objects and brilliant lights and colors, they are now trying to fill in their experience as completely as possible. To adults, the small child's concern for the minutest details is perplexing. It is further evidence that a child's "psychic personality is far different from our own, and it is different in kind and not simply in degree" (1936b, p. 69).

---

[1]Montessori was rather vague about the ages of her sensitive periods, so the ages listed in this chapter are not definite.

The Sensitive Period for the Use of Hands

A third sensitive period involves the use of the hands.   Between about 18 months and three years of age, children are constantly grasping objects. They particularly enjoy opening and shutting things, putting objects into containers and pouring them out, and piling objects up (1936b, p. 83). During the next two years or so, they refine their movements and their sense of touch.   For example, four-year-olds enjoy identifying objects by touching them with their eyes closed—a game that has far greater interest for the child than the adult (Montessori, 1948, pp. 127, 229).

The Sensitive Period for Walking

The most readily visible sensitive period is for walking.   Learning to walk, Montessori said, is a kind of second birth; the child passes from a helpless to an active being (Montessori, 1936b, p. 77).   Children are driven by an irresistible impulse in their attempts to walk and they walk about with the greatest pride as they learn how.

We frequently fail to realize that walking, like other behaviors, means something different to the child than it does to us.   When we walk, we have a destination in mind; we wish to get somewhere.   The toddler, in contrast, walks for the sake of walking.   For example, the child may walk up and down the staircase, over and over.   The child does not walk to get somewhere, but to "perfect his own functions, and consequently his goal is something creative within himself" (1936b, p. 78).

The Sensitive Period for Language

A fifth sensitive period—and perhaps the most remarkable one of all—involves the acquisition of language.   What is remarkable is the speed with which children learn such a complex process.   To learn a language, children must learn not just words and their meanings, but a grammar, a system of rules that tells them where to place the various parts of speech. If, for example, we say, "The tumbler is on the table," the meaning we give those words derives from the order in which we say them.   If we had said, "On tumbler the is table the," our meaning would have been hard to grasp (Montessori, 1949, p. 25).   The rules underlying grammars are so elusive and abstract that linguistic scholars are still trying to understand them in a formal way.   Yet children master them without much thinking about it.   If a child is exposed to two languages, the child masters them both (1949, p. 111).

Because the child's ability to grasp language is so great, Montessori concluded that the child must be endowed with a special kind of language receptivity or "mechanism" (1949, p. 113).   This mechanism is very different from anything in the mental life of the older child or the adult. Whereas we learn a second language with great deliberation, consciously struggling to memorize rules regarding tenses, prefixes, modifiers, and so on, the child absorbs language *unconsciously*.

From Montessori's descriptions, the child's language acquisition sounds very much like a kind of imprinting. At a certain critical time—from the first few months of life until two-and-a-half or three years—children are innately prepared to absorb sounds, words, and grammar from the environment. "The child *absorbs* these impressions not with his mind, but with his life itself" (1949, p. 24). Sounds create impressions of incredible intensity and emotion; they must set in motion invisible fibers in the child's body, fibers that start vibrating in the effort to reproduce those sounds (1949, p. 24). We adults can hardly imagine what this experience is like, except perhaps by recalling the feeling we get when we are profoundly moved by a symphony, and then imagining a similar feeling that is several times stronger. This particular sensitivity for language comes into play during the first three years or so, and then is gone.

Montessori suggested that because language acquisition is governed by innate, maturational factors, children develop language in the same stages no matter where they grow up (1949, p. 111). For example, they all proceed from a stage of babbling to a stage where they begin speaking words. Next, they enter a stage in which they put two-word sentences together (e.g., "Boy go"), and there follows a period in which they master increasingly complex sentence structures.

These stages, Montessori emphasized, do not emerge in a gradual, continuous manner. Instead, there are several times during which the child seems to be making no progress, and then new achievements come in explosions. For example, the child bursts out with a number of new words, or suddenly masters a set of rules for forming parts of speech, such as suffixes and prefixes, in a sudden explosion (1949, p. 114).

Between the ages of about three and six years, children no longer absorb words and grammar unconsciously, but they still are in the general sensitive period for language. During this time they are more conscious of learning new grammatical forms and take great delight in doing so (see Figure 4.1).

By the time the child is five or six, then, and is ready for the traditional school, the child has already learned to talk. "And all this happens without a teacher. It is a spontaneous acquisition. And we, after he has done all this by himself, send him to school and offer as a great treat, to teach him

FIGURE 4.1 Some early sensitive periods.

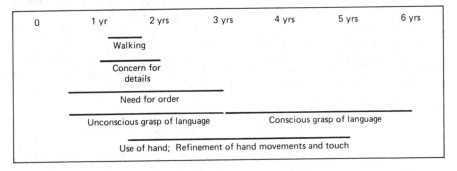

the alphabet!" (1949, p. 115).   We are also so presumptuous as to focus on the child's defects, which are trivial in comparison to the child's remarkable achievements.   We see how adults assume that what they teach the child amounts to everything and how they grossly underestimate the child's capacity to learn on his or her own.

EARLY EDUCATION IN THE HOME

At various sensitive periods, then, children are driven by an inner impulse to independently master certain experiences.   The goal of education is to assist this process.   Since children do not ordinarily enter nursery or Montessori schools until they are two or three years old, parents and caretakers are really the first educators.

To be of help, we do not necessarily need a formal knowledge of child psychology.   What we need is a certain attitude.   We need to realize that it is not our job to direct our children's learning, for we must, above all, respect their efforts at independent mastery.   We must have faith in their powers of inner construction.   At the same time, we do not have to simply ignore or neglect our children.   What we can do is give them the opportunities to learn what is most vital to them.   We can watch for their spontaneous interests and give them the chance to pursue them.

For example, Montessori (1936b, p. 49) told about a nurse who pushed her five-month-old girl in the carriage through the garden.   Each day, the girl was delighted to see a white marble stone cemented to an old gray wall. Apparently the girl took pleasure in her discovery that the stone was in the same place; she was developing her sense of order in the world.   In any case, the nurse, noting the girl's interest, stopped each day to permit the child to look at the sight.   The nurse did not just push the girl along at her own pace, but let the infant's spontaneous interest guide her.   She was not teaching the child in the ordinary sense, but she was behaving like the ideal teacher.   She was giving the baby the opportunity to make whatever spontaneous connection she was working on.

To take another example, parents can help their children during the sensitive period for walking.   Some parents enjoy following their child about as he or she masters this new skill.   They follow their children as they travel amazingly long distances, and stop with their children when they stop to examine new sights.   They also give their children time to master new aspects of walking, such as stair-climbing.   They follow their children's own rhythms and enjoy watching the pride children take in mastering this new skill (1936b, Ch. 11).

Other parents, however, fail to give their children full opportunities to master walking on their own and in their own way.   Some try to teach the child to walk—a practice that probably gives the child the sense that his or her own efforts are inadequate.   Or parents fail to realize what walking means to the child; they assume that the child, like them, wants to get somewhere.   So they pick up their children and carry them, or push them in strollers, so as to reach their destination more rapidly.   Or parents become afraid of where the child's walking may lead, so they surround the child with safeguards, such as playpens (1936b, Ch. 11).

All normal children, of course, do eventually learn to walk, but the parental reactions affect the children's feelings about their inner rhythms and independence. In the one case, they gain the feelings of freedom and pride that come from mastering an important skill on one's own. In the other case, they find that their own efforts at mastery produce negative reactions. The result may be a lingering inhibition with respect to one's inner promptings. It is possible that later athletic ability and physical grace are related to the manner in which children first learn to walk.

THE MONTESSORI SCHOOL

When children are about two-and-a-half years old, they can enter a Montessori school. There they learn in the same class with children up to age six or so—approximately the same age range as in Montessori's Children's House. Increasingly, Montessorians are opening schools so that children can continue with Montessori's more advanced methods—sometimes even through high school. But the ages are still mixed (e.g., six to nine) because Montessori found that children enjoy this arrangement.

Independence and Concentration

The goal of education in the school is the same as that in the home. The teacher does not try to direct, instruct, drill, or otherwise take charge of the child; instead, the teacher tries to give the child opportunities for *independent* mastery. The assumption is that if the school environment contains the right materials—those that correspond to the children's inner needs at various sensitive periods—the children will enthusiastically work on them on their own, without adult supervision.

To create the right environment, Montessori first spent considerable time simply observing children's behavior with respect to various materials. She then retained those that the children themselves told her were the most valuable to them. They told her this in a rather dramatic way; when they came across materials that met deep, inner needs, they worked on them with amazing *concentration*.

Montessori first became aware of the child's capacity for concentrated effort when she saw a four-year-old girl in the Children's House working on cylinders. That is, the girl was placing different-sized cylinders in the holes of a wooden frame until she had them all in place (see Figure 4.2). Then she would take them out again, mix them up, and start over. All the while she was oblivious to the world around her. After she had repeated this exercise 14 times, Montessori decided to test her concentration. She had the rest of the class sing and march loudly, but the girl simply continued with her work. Montessori then lifted the girl's chair—with the child in it—onto a table. But the girl merely gathered up her cylinders in her lap and kept on working, hardly aware of the disturbance. Finally, after 42 repetitions, the child stopped on her own, as if coming out of a dream, and smiled happily (Montessori, 1936b, p. 119).

After that, Montessori observed the same phenomenon on countless occasions. When given tasks that met inner needs at sensitive periods, the

FIGURE 4.2   A boy works on wooden cylinders.   (St. Michael's Montessori School, New York City, Haledjian photo.)

children worked on them over and over.   And when they finished, they were rested and joyful; they seemed to possess an inner peace.   It seemed that children were achieving, through intense work, their true or normal state; Montessori therefore called this processs *normalization* (1949, p. 206). She then made it her goal to create the most favorable environment for this kind of concerted effort.

Free Choice

In preparing her environment, Montessori tried to suspend her own ideas about what children should learn and to see what they selected when given a free choice.   Their free choices, she learned, usually led to work on the tasks that most deeply engrossed them.   For example, she noticed that the two-year-olds, when free to move around in the room, were constantly straightening things up and putting them in order.   If, for example, a glass of water slipped from a child's hands, the others would run up to collect the broken pieces and wipe the floor (Montessori, 1936b, p. 121). What she observed was their need for order.   Accordingly, she altered the environment so they could fulfill this need.   She made small washbasins so the children could wash their hands and brushes; she made small tables and chairs, so they could arrange them just right; and she lowered the cupboards, so they could put their materials away where they belonged. In this way, activities of daily living became part of the curriculum.   All the children enjoyed these activities, but the two-year-olds took them the most seriously.   They constantly inspected the room to see if anything was out of place.   For them, ordering the environment met the deepest inner need (Montessori, 1948, p. 88).

Today, the core Montessori materials are largely set, but the teacher still relies heavily on the principle of free choice.   Each child goes to the cupboard and selects the apparatus that he or she wants to work on.   The teacher has the faith that the children will freely choose the tasks that meet their inner needs at the moment.

Although the teacher permits free choice, the teacher will from time to time introduce a child to a new task that he or she seems ready for. This is done most delicately.   The teacher presents the material clearly and simply and then steps back to observe the child's behavior.   The teacher watches for concentration and repetition.   If the child does not seem ready for the new task, it is put aside for another day.   The teacher must be careful to avoid giving the impression that the child "ought" to learn a particular task; this would undermine the child's ability to follow his or her tendencies.   If the child does begin to work actively on the material, the teacher moves away and lets the child work independently (Lillard, 1972, pp. 65–68).

The teacher's attitude, Montessori said, is essentially a passive one—that of an observer (Montessori, 1936a, p. 39).   He or she spends most of the time simply watching the children, trying to guess each one's particular needs and state of readiness.

Rewards and Punishments

The Montessori teacher, then, is not so much a director, but a follower. It is the child who leads the way, revealing what he or she most needs to work on.   In this, the Montessori teacher behaves very differently from the typical teacher, who has set goals for the children and tries to take charge of their education.

The typical teacher often finds that children lack enthusiasm for the things they are asked to learn.   The teacher therefore relies heavily on external rewards and punishments—praise, grades, threats, and criticism. Yet these external inducements often seem to backfire.   Quite often children become so concerned with external evaluations—so afraid of getting wrong answers and looking stupid—that they cannot concentrate deeply on their work.   Driven by such pressure, they will learn a certain amount of material, but they can easily come to dislike school and the learning process (Montessori, 1948, p. 14; Holt, 1964).

Equally damaging, external evaluations rob children of their independence.   Children soon begin looking to external authorities, such as the teacher, to know what they should do and say.   Montessori felt that authorities use rewards and punishments primarily to make the child submissive to their will.   Like Rousseau, she wondered how a child who becomes anxious about external approval will ever learn to think independently or will ever dare to criticize the conventional social order (Montessori, 1948, pp. 14–18).

Thus, rewards and punishments have no place in the Montessori classroom. Montessori teachers trust that if they pay attention to children's spontaneous tendencies, they can find the materials on which children will work intently on their own. The children will do so out of an inherent drive to perfect their capacities, and external inducements will become superfluous.

The traditional teacher often justifies reward and criticism as necessary because children need to know when they are right or wrong. Montessori agreed that children need to learn from their errors, but she did not want the children to have to turn to adults for this information. Accordingly, she developed many materials with a built-in *control of error*. For example, the cylinders, which teach spatial dimensions, have this control. If a child has not put each cylinder in the proper hole, there will be one cylinder left over. When children see this, their interest is heightened. They then figure out how to correct the matter on their own. Thus, control of error enables them to correct their own mistakes, without relying on adults for criticism or advice.

Gradual Preparation

Montessori found that children cannot learn many skills all at once. For example, four-year-olds often desperately want to learn to button their coats and tie their own shoes, as a consequence of their natural urge toward independence, but these tasks are too difficult for them. They lack the fine motor skills.

To deal with such problems, Montessori developed materials that would enable the children to learn skills in steps, at levels they could master. In the case of shoe-tying, she developed a large tying frame (Figure 4.3) so the children could practice the correct tying pattern with grosser muscle movements (1948, p. 93). She also utilized the principle of indirect preparation (1948, p. 224). That is, she gave them unrelated tasks, such as cutting vegetables (Figure 4.3) and holding a pencil, through which they could simultaneously perfect their dexterity. Then, when the children decided to attempt to tie their own shoes, they could readily do so, for they had gradually mastered all the necessary subskills.

Reading and Writing

I have mentioned, by way of illustration, some of the tasks that are part of the Montessori method (e.g., the cylinders and the exercises of daily living). We cannot review every component of the Montessori curriculum in this book, but I will indicate how Montessori approached one important area—reading and writing.[2]

---

[2]For a summary of the method for teaching arithmetic, see Montessori, 1948, Chs. 18 and 19.

FIGURE 4.3 Children at work on a tying frame and an exercise of daily living. (St. Michael's Montessori School, New York City, Haledjian photo.)

Montessori found that if one begins at the age of about four years, children will learn to read and write with great enthusiasm. This is because they are still in the general sensitive period for language. They have just mastered language unconsciously and are now eager to learn all about it on a more conscious level, which reading and writing permit them to do. If, in contrast, one waits until the age of six or seven years to teach written language, as schools usually do, the task is more difficult because the sensitive period for language has already passed (1948, p. 276).

Four-year-olds will usually master writing before reading. This is because writing is the more concrete and sensory activity and therefore better suits the young child's style of learning (1948, p. 233). Still, one cannot teach writing all at once. If one asks four-year-olds to make a sound and write it, they will be unable to do so; one must introduce writing through a series of separate preparatory exercises.

First, the child is shown how to hold a pencil and then practices drawing by staying within outlines. Children love to practice drawing as precisely as posssible, for they are in the sensitive period for precise hand

FIGURE 4.4 A girl works on sandpaper letters. (St. Michael's Montessori School, New York City, Haledjian photo.)

movements. They also have been mastering precise hand-eye coordination through exercises of daily living, such as cutting vegetables, pouring, and polishing silver.

In another exercise, children trace their fingers over sandpaper letters that are pasted onto blocks of wood (see Figure 4.4). For example, they make the "m" sound and trace it as they do so. The letters are written in script, rather than print, because children find the movements of script freer and more natural. Through this exercise, then, they learn to make the movements of the letters. They love repeating this exercise, for they are still in the sensitive periods for learning about sounds and refining their sense of touch. Frequently they like to close their eyes and trace the letters with their fingers alone. Six-year-olds, in contrast, derive no particular pleasure from the sandpaper letters, for they have already moved out of the sensitive period for touch. The letters, incidentally, have a built-in control of error, since the child can tell when his or her finger has strayed off the letter and onto the wood because the wood feels different (1948, p. 229).

In a third exercise, children are given a moveable alphabet that permits them to form the letters of words. For example, they look at a picture of a cat, sound out the letters, and then make the word with the letters. This, too, they repeat endlessly, out of their spontaneous interest in the elements of spoken language (1948, pp. 234–37).

Through these and other separate exercises, then, children learn the various skills involved in writing. When they finally put these skills together and begin to write letters, there usually follows an "explosion of writing." They will write all day long (1948, p. 239).

Writing paves the way for reading. Through writing, children form a muscular and visual memory of the letters and words and therefore can recognize them. Consequently, the five- or six-year-old who has learned to write can usually learn to read with very little help from the teacher (Lillard, 1972, p. 122). Children often say that nobody taught them to read at all. Montessori did aid the process, though. Her essential method was to show a word printed on a card, ask the child to sound it out, and then ask the child to sound it out more quickly. In most cases, children rapidly catch on and begin reading words on their own.

During the entire preparatory period for writing and reading, the children do not even look at a book. Then, when they first pick a book up, they can usually begin reading it immediately. Consequently, they avoid all the frustrating experiences that children so often associate with books. There follows an "explosion of reading." Children delight in reading everything they see (1948, p. 253).

The sensitive care with which Montessori prepared each small step is impressive. The exercises are arranged so that each comes easily to the child, for each corresponds to the child's natural way of learning. The method contrasts sharply with that of most teachers, who simply give children lessons and then spend most of their time criticizing them for their mistakes. Criticism, Montessori felt, is humiliating and pointless. Instead of criticizing, which only tears down, the teacher should figure out ways of helping children build their skills (Montessori, 1949, p. 245).

Misbehavior

We have emphasized how Montessori teachers prize the child's independence—how they avoid imposing expectations on the child, or even praising or criticizing the child. This is true with respect to *intellectual* work. *Moral* misconduct is another matter. Children are not permitted to abuse the materials or their classmates.

In the Montessori school, respect for the materials and for others usually develops quite naturally. The children know how important the work is for themselves, so they respect the work of the other children. If they do bother a child who is in deep concentration, the child usually insists on being left alone in such a way that they automatically respect this wish. Sometimes, though, the teacher must intervene. Montessori (1948, p. 62) recommended isolating the child for a moment. In this way, the child has a chance to see the value of the work for others and to sense what he or she is missing. The child will then begin constructive work without any further prompting.

In general, the Montessori view of discipline is different from that of most teachers, who think that it is their job to gain control over the class. They shout: "I want everyone in their seats!" "Didn't you hear what I just told you?" "If you don't behave this instant you won't go out for recess!" The Montessori teacher is not interested in such obedience. Real discipline is not something imposed from without, from threats or rewards, but something that comes from within, from the children themselves as they "pass

---

BOX 4.1   *TWO SIX-YEAR-OLD BOYS' VIEWS ON SCHOOL MATTERS*

Note the differences in the role of the teacher in the minds of these two children.

1. Who taught you to read?
   Regular School Child: "My teacher."
   Montessori Child: "Nobody, I just read the book, and to see if I could read it."

2. Do you get to work on anything you want?
   Regular School Child: "No. But we can go to the bathroom anytime we want. But we're not allowed to go to the bathroom more than four times."
   Montessori Child: "You can work on anything you want."

3. What would happen if you bothered another kid who was working?
   Regular School Child: "I'd get in trouble from the teacher."
   Montessori Child: "He'll just say, 'Please go away, I'm busy.'" (What would you do?) "I'd just go away, 'cause I don't want to bother someone working."

from their first disordered movements to those that are spontaneously regulated" (1948, p. 56).

Misbehavior, in Montessori's view, usually indicates that the children are unfulfilled in their work. Accordingly, one's task is not to impose one's authority on the children but to observe each child more closely, so one will be in a better position to introduce materials that will meet his or her inner developmental needs. The teacher expects a certain amount of restlessness and distracted behavior during the first days of the year, but once the children settle into their work they become so absorbed in it that discipline is rarely a problem.

Fantasy

Montessori was critical of attempts to enrich children's fantasy lives through fairy tales, fables, and other fanciful stories. She saw fantasy as the product of a mind that has lost its tie to reality (Montessori, 1917, p. 255). The insane lose their ability to deal with the real world and therefore turn to inner imaginings.

Montessori's position on fantasy would appear to contradict one of her most basic tenets: that we should follow children's natural inclinations. For children, she acknowledged, do have a natural bent toward fantasy. As she put it, the child's "mentality differs from ours; he escapes from our strongly marked and restricted limits, and loves to wander in the fascinating worlds of unreality . . ." (1917, p. 255). But our task is to help the child overcome these tendencies. When we read children fairy tales or tell them about Santa Claus, we only encourage their credulity. When they hear these stories, furthermore, their basic attitude is passive; they simply take in the impressions we give them. They believe fantastic things because they have not yet developed their powers of discrimination and judgment. And it is just these powers that they need to build.

Montessori did recognize the uses of a creative imagination, such as that possessed by the artist. But the artist's creativity, she maintained, is always tied to reality. In fact, the artist sees things more clearly than we do. The artist is more sensitive to forms, colors, harmonies, and contrasts. And "it is by refining his powers of observation that the artist perfects himself and creates a masterpiece" (1917, pp. 250–51). If we wish to help children become creative, then, we need to help them develop their powers of observation and discrimination with respect to the real world, and not encourage them to drift off into an unreal one.

Summary

We ordinarily assume that it is our task to mold or shape our children, to teach them to learn and to think, but we are mistaken. Children learn on their own, from their inner need to develop their capacities. We assist children's development by preparing the right environment, an environment which contains materials that correspond to their inner needs at various sensitive periods. For example, since young children have a need for order, furniture and other objects should be built in such a way that they can arrange them. In this way, they can actively develop their sense of order and orientation in the world. To a considerable extent, children can be trusted to choose freely the materials that they most need, and they will work on them with the greatest concentration. From time to time, though, teachers can introduce new tasks, based on their guesses about the individual child's sensitive period. For example, when a child shows an interest in written language, the teacher can introduce an appropriate preparatory task, such as the sandpaper letters. The teacher then watches for concentration and repetition. If the sandpaper letters do in fact correspond to the child's sensitive period, the child will become deeply absorbed in tracing them. In this situation, praise and criticism are unnecessary. Even worse, praise and criticism can undermine concentration and independence by creating a concern for external evaluation. It is far better for children to correct their own mistakes, which the proper materials enable them to do.

Although the Montessori teacher would never criticize, let alone punish, a child for an intellectual error, certain misbehavior is not tolerated. Children must respect the materials and the work of others. Misbehavior, however, usually indicates that a child is unfulfilled in his or her work. Instead of commanding obedience, the teacher looks for ways to get the child absorbed in work. The Montessori school, finally, does not encourage fantasy. Children develop themselves by mastering the real world.

EVALUATION

In my experience, those who visit a Montessori school usually come away impressed. They are especially struck by the quiet dignity of the classroom; the atmosphere is almost that of a monastery, with everyone seriously at work. There is no teacher shouting, and the children show respect for one another.

Psychologists would want to know, however, about the empirical research on the effectiveness of Montessori education. Good studies are scarce, and they are not terribly conclusive, but they generally indicate that Montessori preschools advance children's test scores about as well or better than other preschool programs. Montessori children may read and spell particularly well. But researchers have been more impressed by the attitudes that Montessori schools foster—concentration, confidence, and independence (Evans, 1975, pp. 270–75; Miller and Dyer, 1975; Chattin-McNichols, 1992).

If Montessori were to hear of this pattern of results, she probably would be pleased. For her primary goal was not high scores on achievement tests, but inner attitudes. If children in Montessori schools typically learn to read and write at an early age, this is fine, but in terms of her overall philosophy, it is just a fortunate happenstance. Montessori chose to teach writing and reading to four-year-olds only because they revealed an inner urge to write at this young age. If she had found no such urge until, say, age 10, she would not have taught it until then. She did not want to impose tasks on children just because adults are anxious that they learn them as soon as possible. She cared little about how rapidly children learn standard skills or about advancing them along the ladder of achievement tests. Rather, she was concerned with children's attitudes toward learning. She wanted to unharness their natural love for learning and their capacities for concerted and independent work, which unfold according to an inner timetable. As she once said:

> My vision of the future is no longer of people taking exams and proceeding on that certificate from the secondary school to the University, but of individuals passing from one stage of independence to a higher, by means of their own activity, through their own effort of will, which constitutes the inner evolution of the individual. (1936, cited in Montessori, 1970, p. 42)

Although Montessori is well known as a teacher, she is underestimated as an innovative theoretician. She anticipated much that is current in developmental thinking. For one thing, she was among the first to argue for the possibility of sensitive or critical periods in intellectual development. Even more impressive were her insights into language acquisition. Early on, she suggested that children unconsciously master complex grammatical rules and suggested that they must possess an innate mechanism that enables them to do this—suggestions that anticipated the work of Chomsky (see Chapter 16 in this book).

What are the criticisms of Montessori? Dewey (Dewey and Dewey, 1915) thought the Montessori teacher sometimes limits the child's freedom and creativity. When, in particular, a child finds an apparatus too difficult and therefore plays with it in some new way (e.g., rolling cylinders), the teacher will suggest working on something else. The child is not allowed to innovate. Montessori teachers respond that children inwardly feel inadequate with respect to such tasks and will feel far more creative working on tasks for which they are ready. Still, the teachers hope the times they must intervene are few.

A more fundamental criticism is that Montessori emphasized cognitive development to the exclusion of the child's social and emotional life. In the Montessori classroom, the children work primarily with physical objects and do not interact much either with other children or the teacher. The teacher tries, as far as possible, to stay in the background, allowing the child to work on his or her own. In the Montessori view, things, not people, are the best teachers (Kramer, 1976, p. 21). This method fosters independence, but it also leaves a great deal out; " . . . it seems to leave out a whole dimension of being human—the emotional" (Kramer, 1976, p. 21). Montessori, of course, was justifiably suspicious of learning based on emotional involvements with others. It is all too easy for children to become trapped in the process of learning to please grown-ups rather than learning for its own sake. Nevertheless, many people believe the Montessori went too far in the opposite direction, making learning too impersonal.

Montessori's attitude toward the child's inner emotional life is exemplified by her view toward fantasy and fairy tales. She admitted that children possess a natural bent toward fantasy and enjoy fairy tales, but she discouraged them anyway. Imaginary stories only encourage children to depart from reality. Further, when children listen to fairy tales, they passively receive impressions from adults. They do not think on their own (Montessori, 1917, p. 259).

It is not clear, however, that Montessori was right. Bettelheim (1976) pointed out that fairy tales do not really teach children to believe in imaginary happenings, for children know that the fairy tale is make-believe. The stories themselves make this point with their opening lines—"Once upon a time," "In days of yore and times and tides long ago," and so on (Bettelheim, 1976, p. 117). Children intuitively understand that the story addresses itself not to real, external events, but to the inner realm of secret hopes and anxieties. For example, "Hansel and Gretel" deals with the child's fear of separation and does so in a way that points to a solution. It indirectly encourages children to become independent and use their own intelligence.

Furthermore, the process of listening to a fairy tale may be much more active than Montessori realized. When children listen to a story, they interpret it in their own way and fill in the scenes with their own images.[3] When a story speaks to an issue with which the child is inwardly struggling, the child wants to hear it over and over, much as Montessori children work repeatedly on external exercises. And, finally, children often emerge from the story in a state of calm and peace, as if they have resolved some issue (Bettelheim, 1976, p. 18).

Montessori, then, may have been too quick to dismiss the child's inner world of fantasy and the value of fairy tales. Nevertheless, such oversights seem minor in comparison to her contributions. Montessori demonstrated, as much or more than anyone else, how the developmental philosophies of Rousseau, Gesell, Piaget, and others can be put into effective practice. She showed how it is possible to follow children's spontaneous tendencies and to provide materials that will permit them to learn on their own. Montessori must be regarded as one of history's greatest educators.

[3]The process of listening to a fairy tale seems much more active, for example, than most television watching. Television itself usually supplies the child with all the images (Singer and Singer, 1979).

__5__

Werner's Organismic and Comparative Theory

BIOGRAPHICAL INTRODUCTION

Heinz Werner (1890–1964) was born and grew up in Vienna, Austria. He was a studious boy who also loved music, taking up the violin when he was seven years old. After completing the Gymnasium (roughly the equivalent to our high school), Werner thought briefly about becoming an engineer, but he changed his mind and entered the University of Vienna hoping to become a composer and a music historian. At the university, however, his interests quickly broadened to include philosophy and psychology. This change began one day when he mistakenly went to the wrong lecture hall. He had thought he was attending a music class but found himself listening to a lecture on the philosophy of Kant. Since he felt it would be too embarrassing to walk out, he stayed, and he became so engrossed in the topic that he soon decided to major in philosophy and psychology (the two fields were still combined). Still, Werner's interest in music remained, and he wrote his doctoral dissertation on the psychology of esthetic enjoyment.

In 1917 Werner joined the Psychological Institute at Hamburg, which was later incorporated into the University of Hamburg. There he was influenced by several great scholars, including the psychologist William Stern and the ethologist Jacob Von Uexküll.

A new theoretical movement that was enthusiastically discussed at Hamburg was Gestalt psychology. Gestalt psychologists argued that when we perceive things, we perceive whole forms, *gestalts*, and these forms cannot be analyzed into separate elements. In Figure 5.1, for example, we directly perceive circles, and it does not matter whether the circles are comprised of dots or dashes. There is a sense in which the circle is a whole pattern that is more than its parts.

Gestalt psychologists went on to assert that our experience of forms is governed by organizing forces in the central nervous system, and they tried to show the principles by which these forces work. One principle is closure, a tendency to complete patterns. Figure 5.2, for example, is not perceived merely as two lines, but as a triangle with pieces missing. We tend to perceive it as a whole meaningful pattern.

Werner was strongly influenced by Gestalt psychology, but not the Gestalt psychology with which we are familiar. That form was brought here by Wertheimer, Koffka, and Kohler, who gave us examples like those above. These psychologists were sometimes called the Berlin School. Werner identified more closely with the Leipzig School of Krueger, Sander, and others—people who are still hardly known to us. The Leipzig School agreed with the general Gestalt principles, but it felt that the Berlin orientation was not genuinely wholistic because it focused too narrowly on perception instead of the whole, acting, feeling organism. The Leipzig School was also more developmentally oriented. As we shall see, the Leipzig viewpoint had a strong influence on Werner's organismic-developmental writings.

Werner's years at Hamburg were extremely productive, and it was there that he published the first edition of his famous book, *Comparative Psychology of Mental Development* (1926). This book was a bold, sweeping venture. In it, Werner tried to show how the concept of development, properly defined, could be used to compare patterns found in humans across various cultures and even between humans and other species.

In 1933 Werner was dismissed from Hamburg by the Nazis because he was Jewish. He spent a few months in Holland and then came to the United States, where he held a number of positions, including that of research psychologist at the Wayne County Training School in Michigan.

FIGURE 5.1   An example of Gestalt perception: We perceive both forms as circles despite their different elements.

FIGURE 5.2
The Gestalt principle of closure: We tend to close or complete figures into whole patterns.

There, between 1936 and 1943, he did a great deal of research on retarded and brain-injured children.   In 1943 Brooklyn College gave him his first full-time teaching position in the United States, assigning him to what we would now consider the ridiculously low rank of instructor.   Werner was simply not recognized here as the great theorist he was.

Nevertheless, he continued with his work, and in 1947 Clark University hired him as a professor of psychology and education.   At Clark he found a true intellectual home, working with sympathetic colleagues and inspired students.   Former students remember Werner as a short, formal, but kindly man who was extremely open-minded and had a rare ability to draw out the best in his students.[1]

WERNER'S VIEW OF DEVELOPMENT

Werner wanted to tie development to both an organismic and a comparative orientation.   We will first review his conception of development and then relate it to these two orientations.

Psychologists usually talk about development in loose ways, but Werner believed the concept needed a precise definition.   Development, he argued, refers to more than the passage of time; we may grow older but without developing.   Furthermore, development refers to more than increases in size; we may grow taller or fatter, but such growth is not necessarily developmental.   Development involves changes in structure, which may be defined according to the *orthogenic principle:*

> Whenever development occurs, it proceeds from a state of relative lack of differentiation to a state of increasing differentiation and hierarchic integration. (Werner and Kaplan, 1956, p. 866)

Let us look at these two concepts—differentiation and hierarchic integration—more closely.   *Differentiation* occurs when a global whole separates into parts with different forms or functions.   For example, the embryo begins as a global unit that separates into different organs, such

---

[1]Most of this biographical material is from Witkin, 1965.   In addition, Margery Franklin and Joseph Glick provided helpful comments and recollections.

as the brain, heart, liver, and kidney. Similarly, the fetus' motor activity becomes more differentiated when its limbs and trunk no longer all move together in one "mass action" but move separately.

As behavior becomes differentiated, it also becomes *hierarchically integrated*. That is, behaviors come under the control of higher regulating centers. In the fetus, for example, limb and trunk movements become not only more differentiated but also more fluid and coordinated as they come under the control of higher organizing circuits in the central nervous system (Hofer, 1981, pp. 97–100).

Similarly, the orthogenic principle describes motor development after birth. Grasping, for example, starts off as a stereotyped reflex; babies grasp whatever touches their palms with the same motion. Beginning at about five months of age, however, their grasping becomes more differentiated; they begin to grasp different-sized objects in different ways. Hierarchic integration is also involved because their grasping is coming under control of the cerebral cortex. This is why babies can now more purposefully and skillfully reach out and grasp the things they see (Peiper, 1963, pp. 254–56).

The orthogenic principle describes development in many spheres, even where we cannot pinpoint any underlying neurological mechanisms. In the area of personality development, for example, adolescents try to differentiate between the goals they want to pursue in life and those they do not. The goals they select then assume hierarchical control over much of their daily behavior. A girl who decides to become a doctor, for example, will organize many of her daily activities with this goal in mind. Until young people do settle on their goals, they often feel that their lives lack coherence and structure. They complain that they cannot find themselves. They need a guiding plan.

A Major Theme: Self-Object Differentiation

Werner wrote extensively on the many applications of the orthogenic principle, as we will discuss below. However, he was particularly interested in the process of self-object differentiation, the gradual process by which children separate themselves from the environment. This process often seems to progress through three levels. These levels roughly correspond to infancy, childhood, and adolescence, but Werner was not concerned with ages; he was interested only in differing developmental patterns.

Initially, at the *sensori-motor-affective* level, infants hardly experience an outside world apart from (differentiated from) their own immediate actions, sensations, and feelings. They know objects only insofar as they are sucking them, touching them, grasping them, and so on. If, as Piaget (1936b) showed, a young baby loses hold of a toy, the baby will act as if the toy no longer exists. There is little sense of objects existing apart from oneself.

Gradually, children come to function on a more purely *perceptual* level, perceiving things "out there," apart from themselves. They stand back and look at objects, point to them, ask their names, and describe them. They gain a measure of objectivity. Still, their perceptions remain strongly bound up with their actions and feelings. For example, Katz and Katz (cited in Werner, 1948, p. 383) observed that preschool children take a great interest in furniture that can be used for climbing and jumping and houses in which acquaintances live, whereas other furniture and houses hardly seem to enter into their awareness.

The extent to which children's perceptions are colored by their personal needs and actions is sometimes revealed by the words they use. For example, four-year-old Laura called a certain tree the "resting tree" because she often sat under its cool branches on the way home from school. She called the yard where the "resting tree" was located the "resting place," and the family who lived there "the resting people." Her perceptions were still bound up with her personal needs and activities (Smart and Smart, 1978, p. 89).

To gain the most impersonal, objective view of the world we must rise to a *conceptual level* of thought. That is, we must begin to think in very general and abstract dimensions, such as height, volume, and velocity, which lend themselves to precise measurement. For example, the rule "area = height × width" enables us to quantify space objectively, without any reference to our personal feelings about it. Such detached, impersonal analysis has long been the goal of Western science.

With development, then, we gradually form perceptual and conceptual ways of knowing the outer world apart from (differentiated from) our immediate needs, feelings, and actions. And as these specifically mental operations emerge, they gain hierarchical control over our behavior. This is seen when spontaneous actions give way to behavior governed by mental plans. For example, when children first draw, they often just scribble lines and circles and decide afterward what they have drawn. Drawing becomes more organized when it is governed from the outset by a plan, a perceptual image of an object, which guides the hand movements.

At an advanced level, perceptions themselves are subordinated to a conceptual mode of thought. Scientific psychologists, for example, observe an animal's behavior, but they are not primarily interested in forming vivid perceptual images or pictures of the animal. Rather, they classify and quantify their observations in line with abstract concepts such as "stimuli" and "rates of responding."

Returning to Primitive Levels

Werner believed that development is teleological, which means that it directs itself toward mature end-states. Humans, therefore, naturally progress toward abstract, conceptual modes of thought. This does not mean, however, that once we develop these intellectual operations, we must rely on them alone. If we did, our lives would become empty, abstract, and barren. The world would become, in Whitehead's words, "a dull affair, soundless, scentless, colorless . . . " (1929, p. 88). We would long for the kinds of thinking that characterized earlier levels, in which images were tied to feelings, sensations, and actions.

Thus, Werner wanted to specify the ways in which we, as rational adults, preserve the richness and vitality that characterize earlier levels.

To an extent, the concept of hierarchic integration serves this purpose. It implies that abstract thinking does not work in a vacuum but organizes and integrates sensations, actions, and feelings. The intellect imposes order upon "the confusing multiplicity of sensuous impressions by means of judgments and interpretations" (Werner, 1948, p. 52).

Still, do we have access to genuinely primitive modes of thought, before they become differentiated and hierarchically integrated? Werner believed we do. In his earlier writing (e.g., 1948, p. 82), he observed that we regress to primitive levels during dreams or in states produced by hallucinogenic drugs. In his later writings, however, Werner (1957; Werner and Kaplan, 1963) increasingly emphasized a new concept—*microgenesis*. Microgenesis refers to the developmental process that occurs each time we confront a task, such as perceiving an object or figuring out a problem. In each instance, our mental process goes through the same sequences that characterize development during the lifespan. That is, we begin with vague, global impressions that are fused with feelings and bodily sensations. These impressions give way to more differentiated perceptions, which finally become integrated into a coherent whole. Microgenesis, then, is a self-renewing process in which we continually begin at undifferentiated levels.

Microgenesis often occurs so rapidly that we are unaware of the process, but we may become aware of it at times, as when we find ourselves in new, unfamiliar settings. Imagine, for example, that we enter a foreign city. At first our perception is likely to be global, diffuse, and heavily colored by feelings. We are struck by the strange sounds, lights, odors, shapes, and colors. We feel disoriented, vaguely wondering if we are safe and how we are going to find anything. Soon, however, our picture of the city becomes more differentiated; we identify a hotel, a restaurant, a bus route to the Capitol. And finally we may begin to see how the various parts of the city are interrelated; we form a more conceptual map of the city. Thus, within a fairly short time, our knowledge of the city goes through a developmental process similar to that which characterizes development during childhood.

Werner suggested that people differ in the extent to which they engage in the microgenetic process. Some people have greater *microgenetic mobility*; they can regress farther back and fully utilize both primitive and advanced forms of thinking. Above all, this ability to regress characterizes the creative person, the person who is willing to start anew. Many creative scientists, for example, have admitted that they begin thinking about problems on a preconceptual level, starting out with vague intuitions, hunches, dreamlike images, and gut-level feelings (Dubos, 1961). As a group, the ethologists make a special point of forming rich perceptions of animals with whom they feel a certain empathy before detaching themselves and moving on to a formal, conceptual plane (Tinbergen, 1977; Lorenz, 1981).

Some thinking, in contrast, is distinctly lacking in microgenetic mobility. Schizophrenic patients regress to primitive forms of thought, but they get stuck there and their thinking remains disorganized. Conversely, many of us seem to shift too quickly to conventional, rational modalities, so our thinking lacks richness and creativity. In general, Werner said,

"[T]he more creative the person, the wider his range of operations in terms of developmental level, or in other words, the greater his capacity to utilize primitive as well as advanced operations" (1957, p. 145).

The Organismic Orientation

We have seen how mental processes such as perception and cognition emerge from contexts in which they are fused with actions, sensations, and feelings. This occurs in the development of the child, and it keeps re-curring, microgenetically, in us as adults. For Werner, this conception of development coincided with a position to which he was deeply committed— the organismic position. Essentially, this position maintains that we should, as far as possible, study psychological processes as they occur within the whole, acting, feeling, striving organism. We should not, for example, study perceptual activities in isolation, but as they emerge from the more primitive matrices of action and feeling in which they are embedded.

Despite Werner's appeals, the organismic orientation has been more the exception than the rule in psychology. Reserchers usually study pro-cesses such as perception, cognition, language, and memory as if they were self-contained activities. This compartmentalized approach, Werner noted (1948, p. 49), is convenient, and it does not strike us as too inappropriate when studying adults because adult functioning has become fairly differ-entiated. As adults we can usually distinguish between our thoughts and our feelings, so we believe it is all right to study thinking as an isolated activity. Yet, even as adults we do not become disembodied minds. We still need to know how cognitive processes are related to the rest of the organism. Here the concepts of microgenesis and hierarchic integration are helpful, for they indicate how cognitive processes emerge from and integrate physical, emotional, and sensory experiences.

Compartmentalized research becomes most problematic when we turn to children. In children, as we have seen, the various psychological pro-cesses are far less differentiated than in adults. The child's perception, for example, is strongly fused with motoric action and emotion. A child, upon seeing a wooden triangle, does not see it as we do, as simply a geo-metric form. Because it looks sharp, it is something one might dig with, or something that is threatening. When, therefore, we examine and meas-ure the child's "form perception" as an isolated activity, as is usually done, we miss out on the chance to see how it is distinctive in the child's experience. We examine form perception as if it were already differentiated from action and emotion, which it is not (see Wapner et al., 1973).

The Comparative Approach

Werner wanted to study development not only from an organismic viewpoint, but from a comparative viewpoint as well. That is, he wanted to show how the orthogenic principle enables us to compare developmental patterns across many diverse areas, including various cultures, species, and pathological states.

Werner was particularly interested in parallels between humans and cultures in their early phases of development. In many ways, he argued, the mental life of children and preliterate people has underlying similarities. He noted, for example, that the thought of both children and preliterate people is characterized by a lack of differentiation between the self and the external world. Both may, for example, perceive trees, clouds, and wind expressing emotions like those they themselves experience. We will discuss such parallels below, but as Baldwin (1980) has demonstrated, it is first useful to point to some misunderstandings concerning Werner's purpose.

First, Werner was not trying to show that children and preliterate people think in completely identical ways. The thought of children in industrialized cultures, for example, is not nearly as rich, complex, and fully formed as that of adults in small tribal cultures. Children may have some impressions of the emotions and forces expressed by the natural elements, but they have nothing resembling the complex mythologies of preliterate peoples.

Second, Werner was not advancing a theory of recapitulation (such as that proposed by Rousseau or Haeckel). That is, he did not believe that children resemble preliterate peoples because children are repeating the evolutionary history of the species. He felt that the recapitulation theory takes the similarities between children and people in early tribal societies too literally, ignoring the differences between them.

Werner, moreover, was not interested in evolutionary history itself. That is, he was not interested in *when* behavior appeared, but in its developmental status in a *formal* sense, as defined by the orthogenic principle. In some instances, the thinking of extinct cultures may have been more differentiated than that found in some contemporary cultures. In any event, when Werner used terms such as "primitive," "early," or "advanced," he was referring to developmental status in terms of a formal, theoretical model.

For many people, the greatest problem with Werner's comparative theory is that it seems to have political overtones. When Werner describes preliterate peoples as primitive and compares them to children, he seems to be implying that they are inferior.

But Werner wanted to avoid such value judgments. He noted (1948, p. 34) that in earlier stable environments, primitive modes of thought were highly adaptive. And, as we saw in our discussion of microgenesis, even Western adults may need to return to primitive levels to think in creative ways. Furthermore, as we shall later see, artists still develop primitive forms of experience and thereby enrich our lives. Thus, the term "primitive" hardly need carry any negative connotations.

SOME COMPARATIVE STUDIES

In Werner's comparative writings, he often phrased the orthogenic principle in terms of more specific dimensions. One dimension is *syncretic vs.*

discrete.[2] This is the dimension Werner most frequently used, and I have already been referring to it without calling it by its name. Syncretic functioning means that processes that become separate are still fused together. Whenever, for example, children's perceptions of external events are fused with their needs and actions, their perceptions are syncretic. Werner illustrated syncretic functioning with respect to such topics as time and space.

Time

Western adults conceive of time as an abstract, quantitative system that exists apart from their own actions. We refer to 5 o'clock, 6 o'clock, and so on. Children, however, initially consider time not in this impersonal way but in terms of personally meaningful events, such as "breakfast," "nap time," "when mommy comes home," and "suppertime." When a father began taking his three-year-old daughter to nursery school, he found it pointless to tell her that he would pick her up at 12 o'clock. She told him, "You go and pick me up after lunch."

In a similar way, preliterate peoples commonly viewed time in terms of meaningful activities. Cattle-raising Uganda tribesmen, for example, divided the day into "milking time," "watering time," "home-coming time for the cattle," and so on. They also divided time into lucky and unlucky, and holy and unholy periods. In Werner's terms, their conception of time, like the child's, was syncretically fused with personal activities and emotions.

Even in industrialized societies, of course, adults recognize that certain time periods are more personally meaningful than others and that time can take on various emotional dimensions. However, we consider it most accurate to think of time in an abstract, scientifically measurable manner (Werner, 1948, Ch. 6 and p. 418).

Space

Children conceive of space, like time, not as something that exists impersonally and objectively, apart from themselves. Rather, it is a "space of personal action." When a 3½-year-old boy was asked where his bedroom was, he described how he got to it: "First you go through the playroom, then the steps go down, and then you're there. And then you go all the way down to the living room . . . " (1948, pp. 173–74). The child's space, moreover, is a "lived space," fused with emotion. Places are safe or dangerous and familiar or mysterious long before they are abstractly considered as mere areas subject to formal measurement.

Preliterate peoples, too, seem to have perceived space in terms of actions, bodily orientations, and emotions. Their spatial terms often varied completely according to the direction they were facing. Moreover, there was hardly any space that did not carry some emotional or spiritual mean-

---

[2]The other dimensions, which we will not consider, are diffuse vs. articulated, rigid vs. flexible, and labile vs. stable. The interested reader can refer to Baldwin (1980) and to Werner (1948, especially Chs. 3 and 6).

ing. Places were holy or unholy or identified with particular people, myths, or magic (1948, pp. 168–72).

Contemporary adults also recognize that space is not just impersonal; we value and cherish some places and care little about others. However, when we are most scientific, we strip space of emotional meaning and consider it in a neutral, objective, quantitative manner (1948, Ch. 5).

Werner observed that in industrialized societies some adult mental patients, such as those suffering from brain damage or from schizophrenia, may lose their objective, impersonal conceptions of time and space. Schizophrenics, for example, may feel that certain time periods or places are mysteriously dangerous. In such cases, time and space are again fused with emotion, but the schizophrenic's experience is not exactly like that of the child or the tribesman. The latter organize time and space in a way that coincides with the social system in which they live. Mental patients, in contrast, feel themselves losing their hold on the stable, objective world (1948, pp. 417–18).

Pictorial Imagery

Primitive experiences of time and space, then, are fused with personal activities and feelings. For time and space to become objective and impersonal, they must be grasped more abstractly. But this is what children cannot do. They are initially incapable of purely conceptual thought. Instead, they often perceive the world concretely, as pictures of particular things.

Children's picturelike thinking may be seen when they are asked to define words. If a five-year-old is asked to define the word "girl," he may say, "She has long hair and a dress. She's pretty." The boy's definition is based on a specific pictorial image.

According to Werner, this definition is syncretic because the concept is not yet freed from a particular perception. To think on a purely conceptual level, we must use categories that are general and abstract. We might define "girl" as "a young female member of the human species."

Werner observed that pictorial imagery is so dominant in young children that many possess *eidetic* imagery, or what we commonly call photographic memory. Children can describe a scene in such vivid detail that one is amazed to find that they are no longer looking at it. Strong forms of eidetic imagery seem to be present in only a minority of children, but many children possess some form of it, and it is very rare in adults (Werner, 1948, p. 143; Haber, 1969).

Werner believed that preliterate peoples commonly had eidetic imagery, but this is difficult to document. In any case, their languages indicate that they seemed to have thought much more in pictorial images than in general categories. They had few general terms, but many words which evoke specific images. In one Bantu language, for example, there is no general term "to go," but many specialized words for different kinds of walking. There is a word that means "to walk along slowly and carefully with a convalescent man" and another one that means "to hop across earth seared by great heat" (Werner, 1948, p. 267). One anthropologist observed that the Solomon Islanders would never say anything so general and abstract as, "Five people arrived." They might say, "A man with a large nose, an old man, a child, a man with a skin disease, and a little fellow are waiting outside" (1948, p. 288).

Social scientists still debate the capacity of preliterate peoples to think in abstract terms. Perhaps they had the capacity but rarely exercised it. In any case, they seemed to consider broad, impersonal categories as meaningless. For them the goal was to describe specific objects and events in precise detail. They used words like artists, trying to depict the world in vivid, picturelike images.

Werner noted, finally, that in our culture mental patients frequently lose the ability to think abstractly and resort to specific, pictorial imagery. Schizophrenic patients, for example, have reported that since their disorders began, "The single ideas are much more picture-like than before," and "It is no more thinking, it is somehow more like seeing many things one after the other" (1948, pp. 331–32).

Physiognomic Perception

If there was a single topic on which Werner wrote with the deepest feeling, it was physiognomic perception. We perceive stimuli physiognomically when we react to their dynamic, emotional, expressive qualities. For example, we might perceive a person as happy and energetic or sad and tired. Werner called this perceptual mode physiognomic because it is the physiognomy—the face—that most directly conveys emotion to us, although we may also perceive emotion in other ways—for instance, through a person's posture.

Physiognomic perception is contrasted with *geometric-technical* perception. Here we perceive objects in terms of shape, length, hue, width, and other objective, measurable properties. Geometric-technical perception is more realistic and matter-of-fact. It is the perceptual modality of the scientist and technician.

As rational adults, we believe that physiognomic perception is appropriate only when stimuli are animate. We feel it is silly to perceive emotions in rocks, sticks, cups, and other inanimate objects. Occasionally, of course, we wax poetic and respond to the physical environment physiognomically, as when we say a landscape is majestic or subdued. Usually, however, we perceive the physical environment in a more impersonal, matter-of-fact manner (Werner, 1956).

For children the situation is very different. Children, lacking clear self/environment boundaries, perceive the whole world as full of life and emotion. A child, seeing a cup lying on its side, might say the cup is tired. Watching a stick broken in two, the child might feel that the stick is being hurt. Or, looking at the number 5, the child might say the number is angry or mean, finding a facial expression in it. Children, Werner argued, quite naturally experience the inanimate world in terms of the same forces and emotions that they feel within themselves (1948, pp. 67–82).

Like children, preliterate peoples felt a strong unity with the rest of the world, and they too displayed a greater degree of physiognomic per-

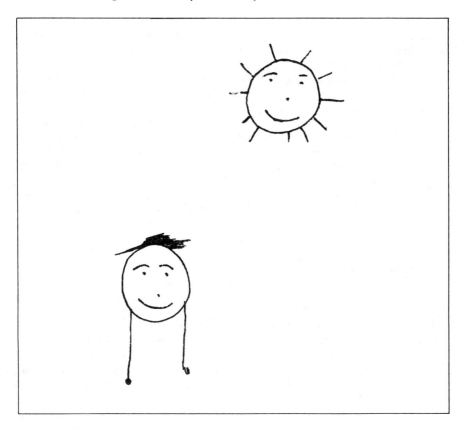

FIGURE 5.3   A five-year-old's drawing reveals physiognomic perception (the sun is smiling).

ception than adults in modern society. Native Americans, for example, typically grew up feeling that they were one with nature and that everything around them—the wind, the trees, even the stones—possessed life and feeling (Lee, 1959, p. 61). Consequently, they were often shocked at the white people's indifference toward the environment. As an old Wintu woman said:

> We don't chop down the trees. We only use dead wood. But the White people plow up the ground, pull up the trees, kill everything. The tree says, "Don't. I am sore. Don't hurt me." But they chop it down and cut it up. The spirit of the land hates them. . . . The White people destroy all. They blast rocks and scatter them on the ground. The rock says, "Don't. You are hurting me." But White people pay no attention. . . . Everywhere the White man has touched it, the earth is sore. (Lee, 1959, pp. 163–64)

This old woman's attitude is completely different from the geometric-technical approach of the engineer or surveyor. She perceives the environment physiognomically, as teeming with life and emotion.

In advanced cultures, dramatic examples of physiognomic perception may be found in the reports of schizophrenic patients who regress to primitive mental states. These patients may lose their sense of detachment from physical objects and experience them as dangerously alive. One patient, for example, looked fearfully at some swinging doors and exclaimed, "The door is devouring me!" (Werner, 1948, p. 81).

So far I have probably managed to convey the impression that physiognomic perception is something fairly strange and unusual—something that most of us have long overcome. And to an extent this is true. As we develop, Werner (1956) said, physiognomic perception is superseded by a geometric-technical outlook. We increasingly come to view the world through the eyes of the engineer or technician. We evaluate things in terms of their measurable properties and practical uses. Even people become categorized in terms of impersonal, quantifiable dimensions. We define them in terms of their IQ, age, income, property holdings, number of dependents, and so on.

Nevertheless, we never lose our capacity for physiognomic perception, and it too develops within us, if at a slower rate than geometric-technical perception. Werner and others have devised some simple demonstrations to show that we can still perceive physiognomic properties in supposedly impersonal forms. Figure 5.4 shows two lines; which is happy and which is sad? Most adults will immediately report that the upwardly moving line expresses gaiety and the downward sloping line conveys sadness. We can see that simple lines—which, of course, are merely inanimate figures—do express feelings through their dynamic patterns.

Most of all, we are aware of physiognomic qualities when we perceive them esthetically, through the eyes of the *artist*. For in modern industrial cultures, it is primarily painters, poets, musicians, and others who alert us to the expressive features of forms, colors, sounds, and movements. They help us experience the sad posture of a willow tree, the anger of thunder, the caress of a tonal pattern, the smile of a sunny sky, the upward striving of a geometric column (Werner, 1956; Arnheim, 1954).

FIGURE 5.4   Lines express feelings.   Which is happy and which is sad?

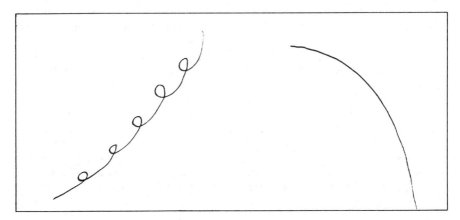

The extent to which artists develop physiognomic sensitivities is suggested by the painter Kandinsky:

> On my palette sit high, round rain-drops, puckishly flirting with each other, swaying and trembling. Unexpectedly they unite and suddenly become thin, sly threads which disappear in amongst the colors, and roguishly slip about and creep up the sleeves of my coat. . . . It is not only the stars which show me faces. The stub of a cigarette lying in an ash-tray, a patient, staring white button lying a midst the litter of the street, a willing, pliable bit of bark—all these have physiognomies for me. (Werner, 1948, p. 71)

Because artists like Kandinsky have developed physiognomic capacities, our world is a richer place.

The Unity of the Senses

Physiognomic perception, as we have noted, is based on a syncretic unity between oneself and objects. That is, we perceive objects as full of the same dynamic forces we feel within ourselves. Physiognomic perception is also based on *synesthesia*, the syncretic unity of the senses. Sounds, for example, may simultaneously involve several of our senses. A sad tone may seem dark and heavy. A cheerful tone may strike us as bright, clear, and light.

Werner believed that intersensory experiences are developmentally primitive; they exist prior to the differentiation of the senses into separate modalities. If this is so, synesthesia might be especially prominent in children, and Werner offered several anecdotes to this effect. For example, a four-year-old girl says, "Father talks . . . boom boom boom! As dark as night . . . ! But we talk light, like the daytime . . . bim bim bim!" (1948, p. 262). There is also some experimental evidence that synesthesia, especially color hearing, is more common in children than in adults (Werner, 1948, pp. 89–91; Marks, 1975).

Intersensory modes of experience were often well developed among preliterate peoples. In West African languages, for example, a *high pitch* may express something that is fine, pointed, alert, fresh, energetic, loud of color, sharp of taste, quick, or agile. A *low pitch* may express something big, plump, awkward, muggy, dull, colorless, stupid, or slow (Werner, 1948, pp. 259–60).

Intersensory experiences also become prominent in contemporary Western adults who regress to primitive states in psychosis or under the influence of hallucinogens. One subject experimenting with mescaline said, "I think that I hear noises and see faces, and yet everything is one and the same. I cannot tell whether I am seeing or hearing. I feel, taste, and smell the sound. It's all one. I, myself, am the tone" (1948, p. 92).

Intersensory experiences, finally, are the special domain of the artist. The painter Kandinsky, for example, wrote that for him even geometric shapes have "inner tones" and "their own inimitable fragrances" (Werner, 1956, p. 4). And through his great paintings, colors affect us as warm or cold, sharp or soft, and so on. Fine music, too, affects us through many senses, as when tones seem golden or pale, bright or dull, sweet or harsh, sharp or soft, light or heavy.

When we have truly intersensory experiences, Werner added, we do not experience colors or sounds objectively, as "out there," but feel them within our bodies. Colors or sounds invade us or envelop us or fill us up. Werner believed that the various senses influence one another through general bodily feelings because "they develop out of a common primitive level . . . that is bodily, motoric, and affective" (Werner, 1934, p. 164).

SYMBOL FORMATION: AN ORGANISMIC VIEW

Although Werner wrote many articles, he published only two books. The first was the *Comparative Psychology of Mental Development* (1948), which I have been summarizing. The other, *Symbol Formation* (Werner and Kaplan, 1963), was on language.

The study of language has mushroomed in recent years, but from Werner's perspective the general approach has been nonorganismic. That is, researchers have focused on the elements of speech and grammar as if these developed in a vacuum, unrelated to a living, acting, feeling organism. Werner believed, in contrast, that language initially emerges out of an undifferentiated matrix that includes bodily, gestural, and affective (emotional) processes. Language does eventually become a relatively separate activity, but it never completely loses touch with its rich organismic grounding.

As the title *Symbol Formation* suggests, Werner's focus was on the formation of symbols. A symbol is a word, image, or action that represents something else—some other object, concept, or event. For example, the word "tree" symbolizes a tree. When we use symbols, we implicitly recognize that the symbol is different from its referent (e.g., the word "tree" is different from the tree itself).

How are symbols formed? Probably the most common view is what might be called the label theory. We simply learn our culture's labels for things. We learn that the word "tree" goes with trees, "cup" with cups, and so on. In this view, the connections between symbols and things are purely arbitrary. They are mere conventions handed down to us by our culture.

Werner viewed the process quite differently. He acknowledged, of course, that children do learn the culture's labels, but he argued that symbolic activities initially emerge out of *bodily-organismic* activities—motoric actions, physical and vocal gestures, and feelings. The process of referring to things, for example, begins with the physical act of *pointing*. The child points to an object of interest and says something like "da," inviting the mother to look at it too (Werner and Kaplan, 1963, pp. 70–71).

Many of the child's first "natural" symbols are *motoric imitations*. Children might flutter their eyelids to depict the flickering of lights, or they might tremble their hands to portray the agitation of water stirred by a boat (1963, p. 89).

Most of the child's early symbols are vocalizations—sounds that represent things. Vocalization, too, emerges out of bodily-emotional patterns, such as cries, calls, and expressions of pleasure, and vocalization retains a motoric component (action of the mouth organs) even in adults.

The child's early "baby talk" words are also physically expressive and oriented toward the action in the world. A child might refer to a dog as "wfff," a hammer as "boom," and a coffee grinder as "rrr," creating words to imitate the sounds that objects make (1963, p. 46).

A bit later, children use expressive intonation to capture other qualities of objects. A girl might speak of tiny objects in a high peeping voice and large objects in a deep gruff voice. Or she might say something rapidly or slowly to indicate how fast an object is moving. Werner called such speech *physiognomic* because it depicts the active, expressive aspects of things.

It is clear that children do not feel that their natural symbols are related to objects in an arbitrary manner. The symbol "wfff," for instance, conveys the most striking property of a dog.

When, however, children begin using conventional language, the connection between symbols and referents would seem to dissolve. What, after all, is the inner relationship between the word "hammer" and a hammer? For a while, children may preserve the tie by using combinations of their own natural symbols and conventional words, as when they say "boom-hammer" or "bah-sheep." But with the shift to purely conventional speech, any felt similarity between symbol and referent would seem to disappear.

But Werner believed that the tie is never completely broken. In his studies, he found that adults can still respond to words as physiognomic forms that directly express the dynamic, expressive qualities of objects. One man reported that when he said the word "hammer," the short "ha" seemed to come down sharply on the "mmm," evoking the sensation of hammering (1963, p. 130). Another subject, looking at the German word "Wolle" (wool), spoke of the dull, stringy quality of the "ll" (1963, p. 209).

Readers might wonder if these subjects weren't simply giving Werner the responses he wanted to hear. However, writers and poets have also tried to get us to see that words have physiognomic properties. Balzac, for instance, asked us to consider how the sound of an abstract word like "vrai" (true) expresses the feeling-tone of truth itself. Is there not, he asked, in the word

> a fantastic strength of honesty? Does one not find in the short sound which it commands a vague image of modest nakedness, of the inherence of the truth in everything? This syllable breathes forth an indefinable freshness. (Werner, 1948, pp. 257–58)

According to Werner, we may perceive words physiognomically more frequently than we realize. We may do so whenever we first try to recognize them (during the early microgenetic phases of word perception). To investigate this possibility, Werner presented words for a very short time, without giving subjects a chance to recognize them fully, and he found that their impressions were dominated by feelings and bodily reactions. Subjects said that although they couldn't make a word out, it felt "warm," "heavy," "distressing," and so on—qualities that they later said corresponded to the word's meaning for them (Werner and Kaplan, 1963, p. 215).

In summary, then, Werner argued that even conventional words are not merely empty, arbitrary labels. They seem to be such only when we examine their external structure in a purely objective manner. Inwardly, we may perceive words as expressive forms that resonate with life and feeling, evoking the same emotional and bodily reactions as their referents. An inner, organismic tie between symbol and referent is maintained.

THEORETICAL ISSUES

We have now reviewed Werner's writing on several topics, including primitive conceptions of space and time, physiognomic perception, and the development of language. But Werner was never just interested in particular topics; he was also concerned with the larger theoretical issues that the topics addressed.

The Multilinear Nature of Development

One theoretical concern was whether development is unilinear or multilinear, whether it proceeds along a single line or along many separate lines (Werner, 1957). A consideration of physiognomic perception helped him answer this question.

Physiognomic perception, as we have seen, is attuned to the dynamic and expressive qualities of things. It is an early form of perception, dominant in children, and in our culture is superseded by a more geometrical-technical outlook. We may sometimes revert to physiognomic modes, as in moments of creative regression, but we generally rely on more logical, rational modes of thought.

If this were the whole story, we could conclude that development is unilinear; one cognitive mode follows another. Yet physiognomic perception itself develops. In most of us, to be sure, it develops only modestly, since we do not nurture it, but in artists it becomes quite advanced. Thus, we must conceive of development as a multilinear branching-out process, with separate lines following their own course. Figure 5.5 attempts to diagram this conception of development.

The Discontinuity Issue

An even more fundamental issue is whether development is continuous or discontinuous. Basically, when we say change is continuous we are proposing that we can measure it along a single *quantitative* dimension. Just as we can measure a child's height with a tape measure, we can measure a child's vocabulary, attention span, memory capacity, and a host of other psychological variables along one quantitative scale. A vast amount of research in developmental psychology has assumed that change is measurable in this manner. To many, the concept of continuous, quantifiable measurement seems to be the essence of science.

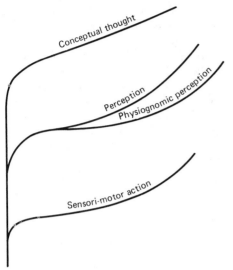

FIGURE 5.5
Werner thought that different lines of development branch out.   (Adapted from Langer, J., *Theories of Development*. New York: Holt, Rinehart & Winston, 1969, p. 153.)

Actually, biologists in particular have long recognized that many changes are discontinuous, involving *qualitative* transformations.   Early forms emerge into new forms that are different in kind; they have different patterns and modes of functioning.   Particularly dramatic examples of qualitative changes are metamorphoses, such as the emergence of a caterpillar into a butterfly.   In such cases, many quantitative comparisons become meaningless.   It makes no sense, for instance, to measure the speed with which caterpillars can fly.   They have their own mode of locomotion.

Since Rousseau, developmentalists have been more like the biologists who emphasize qualitative change.   The transformations from childhood to adulthood may not be as dramatic as the metamorphoses, but, as Rousseau argued, "Childhood has its own way of seeing, thinking, and feeling" (1762b, p. 54).   If this position is correct, one cannot measure children in terms of an adult yardstick without missing what is unique to the child.

Werner, taking the broadest possible perspective, noted that both quantitative and qualitative changes occur.   Like Rousseau, however, he really believed that the most important changes are qualitative.   The adult's abstract thought, for example, differs *in kind* from the child's perceptual-motor-affective thinking.

In many respects, comparing the child to the adult is like comparing the artist to the scientist.   The child, like the artist, approaches the world through a physiognomic, intersensory, vividly pictorial style.   This seems particularly true between the ages of two and seven or so, when children love to draw, act, and sing; and they exhibit so much life, energy, and imagination in their activities.   Their drawings, for example, achieve a special kind of perfection.   Beginning at about four years, they draw tadpole figures which, while missing many details, nevertheless capture the essence of the human figure in a few simple lines (see the person in Figure 5.3, accompanied by the smiling sun).   During the next two or three years, their drawings are routinely fresh, lively, and beautifully formed; they express gaiety, playfulness, and a strong sense of life. After the age of eight or so, their drawings lose this flavor, becoming more precise, realistic, and geometric (Gardner, 1980, Ch. 6). It seems that geometric-technical thinking is taking over (see Figures 5.6 and 5.7). It is hardly surprising that many great artists say that they struggle to recapture the attitude they had as young children (Gardner, 1973, p. 20).

Young children do, to be sure, also demonstrate the beginnings of scientific skills. There is continuity with later orientations. But their dominant outlook seems more naturally artistic, and it seems almost beside the point to persist in evaluating them in terms of the logical, rational skills of adults, although this is what researchers usually do.

6-year-old

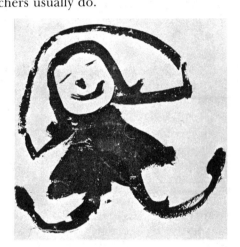

FIGURE 5.6
Young children's drawings are often freer and livelier than those of older children which tend to be geometric. (The six-year-old's drawing is reprinted from H. Gardner, *Artful Scribbles*, New York: Basic Books, 1980, p. 5 by permission.)

10-year-old

Andy, age 6   Andy, age 9

FIGURE 5.7
Andy's drawings illustrate the shift from a livelier to a more geometric style.

It might be objected that I am overemphasing discontinuity. Isn't it also true that adults think like children, especially in the early phases of microgenesis? Isn't this continuity between adults and children? In a sense, this is correct, but microgenesis itself involves qualitative changes. The early phases are qualitatively different from the highly articulated, formal organizations that characterize later phases.

Discontinuity, then, refers to qualitative changes. Such changes need not be sudden. The emergence of abstract thought may occur gradually, as do many other qualitative changes, such as the transition from crawling to walking. Discontinuity only means that the change involves a qualitative shift; the suddenness of the change is another matter (Werner, 1957).

Phenomenology

A school of thought with which Werner was very familiar was phenomenology. Phenomenologists believe that the first thing we should do when studying children (or anyone else) is abandon our preconceptions about them. We cannot assume that children think as we do; we need to take a fresh look at children themselves. Above all, we need to learn about children's subjective experiences of things. We need to explore their *phenomenal* world—how it appears to them.

Most developmentalists have been phenomenological only up to a point (see Chapter 17). They have believed that we should suspend any preconceptions that the child thinks as we do, but they have generally analyzed the child's thinking from the outside instead of trying to see things through the child's eyes.   Werner, too, usually described thinking from an external viewpoint (e.g., as syncretic or concrete).   Still, he provided some fine insights into children's subjective experiences, suggesting, for instance, that they perceive objects very physiognomically.

Werner (1948, Ch. 12) also wrote enthusiastically about the phenomenological research of his colleagues Jacob von Uexküll and Martha Muchow.   Von Uexküll was an ethologist who tried to show how different the environment looks to different species.   By analyzing the reactions of a fly, for example, he indicated how a room must look very different to it than it does to us.   Muchow, following von Uexküll's lead, thought everyday scenes might appear different to children from the way they do to adults. She therefore observed children and adults in some everyday settings, including a canal dock in Hamburg, and inferred how these settings might appear to them (Wohlwill, 1984).

The dock was at the bottom of a steep slope, and to get to it one could walk down a narrow path that was fenced in.   This is what adults did. Children, however, ignored the path.   Instead, they spent their time climbing and swinging on the fence and rolling and sliding down the grassy slopes beside it.   Because the children were so much more motorically inclined, they seemed to perceive the entire scene very differently from the adults.   To them the fence and the slopes—mere background elements for the adults—were the main features.

A second setting was a large new department store in the city.   The youngest children (ages six to nine) did not approach the store as we do. They paid little attention to the merchandise, rushing instead to areas that provided opportunities for action and games.   They were particularly attracted to the stairs, elevators, and escalators, on which they liked to run up and down in the wrong direction.   Here again, Muchow inferred, young children experienced the setting very differently from adults.

Muchow, who died at an early age, did not develop her research as fully as we might like.   She inferred children's perceptions from their behavior alone; we would like other evidence, such as drawings, to show how they viewed the scenes.   Still, she made a beginning effort to depict the child's phenomenal world.

PRACTICAL APPLICATIONS

Werner was first and foremost a theoretician, and he wrote very little on the practical applications of his work.   He offered scant advice on child-rearing, education, or therapy.   Nevertheless, some important practitioners have incorporated his thinking into their work.

In the treatment of schizophrenia, psychoanalysts such as Searles (1965) have found Werner's concepts to be of great value.   Searles believes that one cannot understand most schizophrenic patients without appreciating the undifferentiated quality of their experience.   These patients have little sense of themselves as separate from inanimate objects or other people. They may feel that they are actually part of a room or the therapist.   The therapist's recognition of this can in itself be beneficial, because one thing that helps patients is their sense that someone else understands what life is like for them.   Searles discusses such points and many specific ways in which Werner's concepts guide his therapeutic interventions.

Werner's own work with patients was limited to diagnostic research with children suffering from brain injuries.   Between 1937 and 1945, he and Alfred Strauss carried out a number of studies comparing the cognitive behavior of these children to that of retarded children (Barten and Franklin, 1978, Pt. III).   They found that whereas retarded children often behaved in ways that seemed simple, vague, and global, brain-injured children exhibited special kinds of disorganization.   When copying designs, for example, they were often unable to concentrate on the main figure because they were so distracted by background details.   They were, in Werner's terms, stimulus-bound; everything jumped out at them.   They could not stand back from a design and differentiate between the main figure and the background details.   Such findings impressed many workers in the field, who have found it useful to keep rooms and background settings bare and uncluttered to help the children focus on the tasks at hand (White and Watt, 1973, p. 527).

Werner composed no treatises on the education of normal children, but his brief comments (e.g., Werner, 1948, p. 100; Werner and Kaplan, 1963, p. 112) indicate that he believed, like Rousseau, Montessori, and the developmentalists, that instruction should be tailored to the child's own ways of learning.   For Werner, this meant that children need opportunities to learn through sensori-motor activities and emotionally meaningful tasks. Werner, one guesses, would have liked Montessori's use of sandpaper letters, for these allow children to become familiar with letters motorically and through several senses at once.   He also would have liked Dewey's learning-through-doing approach, in which children study topics such as history not just through books, but by making tools and fabrics and performing the daily activities of earlier peoples.   With regard to reading itself, Werner undoubtedly would have agreed with Bettelheim and Zelan (1981), who argue that children need reading materials that strike them as emotionally and personally meaningful.   And Werner's theory would suggest the importance of artistic activities, for these provide opportunities for physical and emotional expression.   Werner's theory, in short, implies that education should not restrict itself to the child's intellect but should appeal to the child organismically as someone who is active, sensual, expressive, and emotionally alive.

Since Werner himself wrote so little about education, it is ironic that he offered one of the few developmental concepts that has direct relevance for the *education of adults*.   This is the concept of *microgenetic mobility*.   Werner, you will recall, proposed that the most creative thinking does not restrict itself to advanced, rational analysis, but it begins with the full use of preconceptual processes—global impressions fused with bodily sensations, intuitions, and so on.   If so, educators in many fields, including the arts and sciences, medicine, and architecture, may wish to broaden the range of the thinking they try to nurture and enhance in their students.

A case in point is the education of physicians, where there is a growing effort to teach strictly rational problem-solving skills. Young doctors are encouraged to make diagnostic evaluations in a purely logical, step-by-step fashion, often employing decision trees, flow charts, and other devices derived from computer-based theories of cognition. Werner's concept of microgenetic mobility, however, suggests that doctors make fuller clinical judgments when they begin at preconceptual levels, with the impressions, sensations, and feelings that patients arouse in them.

Following Werner's lead, my wife (a pediatrician) and I (Crain and Crain, 1987) asked pediatricians at different levels of competence to report their thoughts and impressions as they examined infants with fevers who had come to the emergency room of a large urban hospital. Analyses of the tape recordings revealed that the beginning doctors tried to think about the patients in a purely objective, logical manner throughout the examination. In contrast, the most experienced and esteemed pediatricians initially engaged the babies in informal interactions, trying to get a global sense of the baby's health through the sensations and feelings the baby evoked in them. Their approach demonstrated greater microgenetic mobility; they initially engaged in more primitive, intuitive processes before advancing to a conceptual approach. Thus, educators who stress a purely rational approach to medical decision-making may be overlooking the rich preconceptual ground from which the most mature clinical judgments emerge.

EVALUATION

Today Werner is frequently considered a historical relic. Many people vaguely remember him as someone who constructed a theory similar to Piaget's—both began writing in the 1920s—but it was Piaget, not Werner, who became the dominant figure in developmental psychology. Werner, to be sure, did contribute his well-known definition of development (the orthogenic principle), and he did influence some important people. But by and large he has receded into the background.

Let us look first at some possible reasons for this neglect and then consider the need to take him seriously once again.

Werner has been overlooked partly because his theory is so abstract and difficult. Moreover, on major issues he was often vague and noncommittal. One thing we would like to know of any developmental theorist is his or her view of developmental change. To what extent does the writer see change as an innate maturational process? Or as a product of environmental influences? Werner's biological model is that of a maturationist (Baldwin, 1980), but if one looks to Werner for a clear statement, one looks in vain. Instead, one finds statements such as, "[D]evelopmental psychology directs its efforts not toward the solution of the tricky problems of innate versus acquired function, but only the establishment and description of . . . types of mental activity" (Werner, 1948, p. 18). Thus, he tried to avoid the issue.

In a similar vein, one might like to know the extent to which Werner believed that the child spontaneously creates his or her ideas, as opposed to absorbing the ideas of adults. Again, Werner was surprisingly noncommital. *Symbol Formation* (1963), for example, extensively describes early symbols that are so different from ours that they must be spontaneous creations, yet Werner and Kaplan said, "In our opinion the problem of free 'inventions' has been unduly stressed in the literature" (p. 102). Here again Werner took no stand, saying that he was interested only in the pattern of the child's thought.

Werner may seem noncommittal partly because he was a tolerant man who tried to see the value in all points of view. He also believed that a degree of theoretical looseness was a good thing. He wanted to keep his concepts general and tentative so others would feel free to specify the details in their particular areas of investigation (Glick, 1983). So, for example, he never committed himself to any single set of levels or stages. He proposed some levels (sensori-motor, perceptual, and conceptual), but he hoped others would feel at liberty to find their own.

Complaints about Werner's vagueness, then, may be unfair because they ignore his purpose. Still, the fact remains that Werner has been generally neglected, and a major reason may be that he frequently failed to give us anything we could sink our teeth into. If he had proposed a set of clear-cut stages, as Piaget did, researchers could test them and try to prove him right or wrong. But this he didn't do.

But no matter how vague and difficult, Werner's theory may become increasingly important. The reason has to do with broad trends in our culture, of which psychology is a part.

If social critics such as Roszak (1972) are correct, our culture has steadily become dominated by science and technology. That is, we have come to view the world almost exclusively through the mental categories of logic, number, and mechanistic connection. Taking the computer as our model, we have translated mental life into flow charts and decision trees, and we have made precision, objectivity, and rationality our ultimate goals. The problem in all this, Roszak says, is that we have glorified intellectual goals to such an extent that we have lost touch with nonrational modes of experience. We have cut ourselves off from the fluid world of dreams, emotions, and intuitions and the organic rhythms of the body. Simultaneously, we have lost our feeling for nature, reducing her to mere physical matter to be exploited and controlled. Employing our great technological powers, we have turned the organic world into an artificial environment "as lifeless and gleamingly sterile as the glass and aluminum, stainless steel and plastic of the high-rise architecture and its interiors that now fill the urban-industrial world" (Roszak, 1972, p. 89). We have, Roszak says, pressed technology forward against the natural world to such an extent that we are startled when anxious ecologists remind us that our survival still depends on air, water, soil, plants, and animals (1972, p. 10).

Roszak calls his critique Rousseauist and Romantic (1972, p. 12). He is upset by contemporary trends and would like us to recover more primitive modes of experience. He would like us to get back in touch with our bodies and with nature, to become more like he imagines children to be.

Yet Roszak would find little sympathy for his vision in contemporary child psychology.   Instead, he would find our research journals full of studies on how children acquire rational problem-solving skills, studies that increasingly model cognition on the programs of high-speed digital computers.

For those who share Roszak's concerns, Werner is a rewarding theorist.   Not that Werner was a thoroughgoing Romantic.   He saw the great value of advanced, scientific thinking.   But Werner also recognized the distinctive contributions of primitive forms of thinking, those that are fused with bodily and emotional processes and are in tune with dynamic forces of nature.   He tried to show how these primitive modalities are involved in artistic expression and in the early phases of all creative thinking.   Thus, he helped us appreciate the contributions of the primitive as well as the advanced forms of mental life.

6

Piaget's Cognitive-Developmental Theory

BIOGRAPHICAL INTRODUCTION

In all psychology, few theorists are as important as Jean Piaget (1896–1980), who forged the single most comprehensive and compelling theory of intellectual development.

Piaget was born in Neuchâtel, a small college town in Switzerland where his father was a medieval historian at the university. Piaget (1952) described his father as a careful and systematic thinker. His mother, in contrast, was highly emotional, and her behavior created tensions within the family. Piaget adopted his father's studious ways and found refuge from the family's conflicts in solitary research.

Piaget showed promise as a scientist from the start. At the age of 10 he published an article on an albino sparrow he had seen in the park. While he was still in high school, his research on mollusks brought invitations to meet with foreign colleagues and a job offer to become the curator of a museum—all of which he turned down because of his age.

At 15, Piaget experienced an intellectual crisis when he realized that his religious and philosophical convictions lacked a scientific foundation. He therefore set out to find some way of bridging philosophy with science. He read widely and worked out his new ideas in writing, even though the writing was intended for no one but himself. This search did not occupy all his time—he still managed to earn his doctorate in the natural sciences at the age of 21—but Piaget's broader quest did at times leave him confused and exhausted. Finally, at the age of 23, he settled on a plan. He would first do scientific research in child psychology, studying the development of the mind. He then would use his findings to answer broader questions in epistemology, philosophical questions concerning the origin of knowledge. He called this new enterprise "genetic epistemology" (Piaget, 1952, pp. 239–44; Ginsburg and Opper, 1988, pp. 2–3).

Piaget decided to study children in 1920 while working in the Binet Laboratory in Paris. There his assignment was to construct an intelligence test for children. At first he found this work very boring; he had little interest in scoring children's answers right and wrong, as intelligence testing requires. However, Piaget soon became interested in the younger children's responses, especially their *wrong* answers. Their mistakes, he found, fit a consistent pattern that suggested that their thinking might have a character all its own. Young children, Piaget speculated, might not simply be "dumber" than older children or adults, but might think in an entirely different way (Ginsburg and Opper, 1988, p. 3).

In order to learn about children's potentially unique ideas, Piaget abandoned the standardized tests, which forced children's responses into "artificial channels of set question and answer," and devised a more open-ended clinical interview which "encourages the flow of spontaneous tendencies" (Piaget, 1926, p. 4). He also spent many hours observing children's spontaneous activities. The point was to suspend his own adult preconceptions about children's thinking and to learn from the children themselves.

While in Paris, Piaget published two studies based on his new approach, but he did most of this new research at the Rousseau Institute in Geneva, where he settled in 1921. He primarily interviewed children between the ages of four and 12 years, and he found that the younger children, before the age of seven or so, do indeed think in a qualitatively different way about dreams, morals, and many other topics.

In 1925 Piaget's first child, Jacqueline, was born—an event that initiated an important series of studies on the cognitive behavior of infants. Piaget and his wife, Valentine Châtenay, made very careful observations of Jacqueline's behavior, as they also did of their next two babies, Lucienne and Laurent.

Beginning about 1940 Piaget returned to the study of children, and adolescents as well, but he changed his research focus. Whereas his earlier investigations covered such topics as dreams, morality, and other matters of everyday interest to the child, his new studies focused on the child's understanding of mathematical and scientific concepts—a focus that dominated his work till the end of his life (Ginsburg and Opper, 1988, pp. 15–16).

In the 1950s Piaget finally turned to philosophical questions in epistemology, although he continued to study children's cognitive development. In this book we will say little about Piaget's epistemological theory; our task will be to gain some understanding of his developmental theory.

Piaget's research has evoked different responses from psychologists at different times. His first work caught the attention of psychologists in many parts of the world.   After this initial enthusiasm, however, interest in Piaget declined, especially in the United States.   For one thing, psychologists had difficulty understanding his orientation.   They also objected to his methodology.   Piaget sometimes changed his questions during an interview if he thought this might help him understand a particular child's thinking; this, many psychologists pointed out, violates the canon of standardized interviewing.   Piaget also ignored such matters as reports on his sample sizes and statistical summaries of his results.   He seemed to regard such matters as less important than rich, detailed examples of children's thinking (Flavell, 1963, pp. 10–11, 431; Ginsburg and Opper, 1988, p. 6).

By and large, Piaget's research has suffered from the same methodological shortcomings throughout his career, but the 1960s saw a remarkable revival of interest in his work.   Psychologists began to realize that his theory, no matter how difficult and how casually documented, is of tremendous importance.   Today, there is hardly a study of children's thinking that does not refer to Piaget.

OVERVIEW OF THE THEORY

Although Piaget's research changed over the years, each part of it contributes to a single, integrated stage theory.   The most general stages, or periods, are listed in Table 6.1.

Before we examine these stages in detail, it is important to note two theoretical points.   First, Piaget recognized that children pass through his stages at different rates, and he therefore attached little importance to the ages associated with them.   He did maintain, however, that children move through the stages in an *invariant sequence*—in the same order.

Second, as we discuss the stages, it is important to bear in mind Piaget's general view of the nature of *developmental change*.   Because he proposed an invariant stage sequence, some scholars (e.g., Bandura and McDonald, 1963) have assumed that he was a maturationist.   He was not.   Maturationists believe that stage sequences are wired into the genes and that stages

TABLE 6.1   The General Periods of Development

Period I.	Sensori-Motor Intelligence (birth to two years). Babies organize their physical action schemes, such as sucking, grasping, and hitting, for dealing with the immediate world.
Period II.	Preoperational Thought (two to seven years). Children learn to think—to use symbols and internal images—but their thinking is unsystematic and illogical. It is very different from that of adults.
Period III.	Concrete Operations (seven to 11 years). Children develop the capacity to think systematically, but only when they can refer to concrete objects and activities.
Period IV.	Formal Operations (11 to adulthood). Young people develop the capacity to think systematically on a purely abstract and hypothetical plane.

unfold according to an inner timetable. Piaget, however, did not think that his stages are genetically determined. They simply represent increasingly comprehensive ways of thinking. Children are constantly exploring, manipulating, and trying to make sense out of the environment, and in this process they actively construct new and more elaborate structures for dealing with it (Kohlberg, 1968).

Piaget did make use of biological concepts, but only in a limited way. He observed that infants inherit reflexes, such as the sucking reflex. Reflexes are important in the first month of life but have much less bearing on development after this.

In addition, Piaget sometimes characterized children's activities in terms of biological tendencies that are found in all organisms. These tendencies are assimilation, accommodation, and organization. *Assimilation* means taking in, as in eating or digestion. In the intellectual sphere, we have a need to assimilate objects or information into our cognitive structures. For example, adults assimilate information by reading books. Much earlier, a baby might try to assimilate an object by grasping it, trying to take it into his or her grasping scheme.

Some objects do not quite fit into existing structures, so we must make *accommodations*, or changes in our structures. For example, a baby girl might find that she can grasp a block only by first removing an obstacle. Through such accommodations, infants begin constructing increasingly efficient and elaborate means for dealing with the world.

The third tendency is *organization*. For example, a four-month-old boy might have the capacity to look at objects and to grasp them. Soon he will try to combine these two actions by grasping the same objects he looks at. On a more mental plane, we build theories. We seem to be constantly trying to organize our ideas into coherent systems.

Thus, even though Piaget did not believe that stages are wired into the genetic code, but constructed by children themselves, he did discuss the construction process in terms of biological tendencies (Ginsburg and Opper, 1988, pp. 16–19).

If Piaget was not a maturationist, he was even less a learning theorist. He did not believe that children's thinking is shaped by adult teachings or other environmental influences. Children must interact with the environment to develop, but it is they, not the external environment, who build new cognitive structures.

Development, then, is not governed by internal maturation or external teachings. It is an *active construction process*, in which children, through their own activities, build increasingly differentiated and comprehensive cognitive structures.

PERIOD I. SENSORI-MOTOR INTELLIGENCE (BIRTH TO TWO YEARS)

Piaget's first developmental period consists of six stages.

Stage 1 (birth to one month).[1]   The Use of Reflexes

When Piaget talked about the infant's action-structures, he used the term *scheme* or *schema* (e.g., 1936a, p. 34). A scheme can be any action pattern for dealing with the environment, such as looking, grasping, hitting, or kicking. As mentioned, although infants construct their schemes and later structures through their own activities, their first schemes consist primarily of inborn reflexes. The most prominent reflex is the sucking reflex; babies automatically suck whenever their lips are touched.

Reflexes imply a certain passivity. The organism lies inactive until something comes along to stimulate it. Piaget, however, showed that even a reflex like sucking quickly becomes part of the human infant's self-initiated activity. For example, when his son Laurent was only two days old, he began making sucking movements when nothing released them. Since he did this between meals, when he wasn't hungry, he seemed to suck simply for the sake of sucking. Piaget said that once we have a scheme, we also have a need to put it to active use (1936a, pp. 25–26, 35).

Furthermore, when babies are hungry, they do not just passively wait for the mother to put the nipple into their mouth. When Laurent was three days old, he searched for the nipple as soon as his lips touched part of the breast. He groped, mouth open, across the breast until he found it (1936a, p. 26).

Babies do not confine themselves to sucking on nipples. Piaget's children sucked on clothes, pillows, blankets, their own fingers—on anything they chanced upon. In Piaget's terms, they assimilated all kinds of objects into the sucking scheme (1936a, pp. 26, 32, 34).

Although assimilation is the most prominent activity during stage 1, we also can detect the beginnings of accommodation. For example, babies must learn to adjust their head and lip movements to find the breast and nurse. Such adjustments also demonstrate the beginnings of organization; babies organize their movements so that nursing becomes increasingly smooth, rapid, and efficient (1936a, pp. 29–31, 39).

Stage 2 (one to four months).   Primary Circular Reactions

A circular reaction occurs when the baby chances upon a new experience and tries to repeat it (1936a, p. 55). A prime example is thumb-sucking. By chance, the hand comes into contact with the mouth, and when the hand falls the baby tries to bring it back. For some time, however, babies cannot do this. They hit the face with the hand but cannot catch it; or they fling their arms wildly; or they chase the hand with the mouth but cannot catch it because the whole body, including the arms and hands, moves as a unit in the same direction (1936a, pp. 51–53). In Piaget's language, they are unable to make the accommodations necessary to assim-

---

[1]The age norms for this period are those suggested by Ginsburg and Opper (1988) in their excellent review of Piaget's theory.

ilate the hand to the sucking scheme.   After repeated failures, they organize sucking and hand movements and master the art of thumb-sucking.

As with thumb-sucking, most of the primary circular reactions involve the organization of two previously separate body schemes or movements. For example, when we see a baby girl repeatedly bring her hand next to her face and look at it, she is exercising a primary circular reaction.   She is coordinating looking with hand movements (1936a, pp. 96–97).

These circular reactions provide a good illustration of what Piaget means by intellectual development as a "construction process."   The baby actively "puts together" different movements and schemes.   It is important to emphasize the amount of work involved; the baby manages to coordinate separate movements only after repeated failures.

Stage 3 (four to 10 months).   Secondary Circular Reactions

The developments of the second stage are called *primary* circular re-actions because they involve the coordination of parts of the baby's own body.   *Secondary* circular reactions occur when the baby discovers and re-produces an interesting event *outside* himself or herself (1936a, p. 154). For example, one day when Piaget's daughter Lucienne was lying in her bassinet, she made a movement with her legs which stirred the dolls hanging overhead.   She stared at the dolls a moment and then moved her legs again, watching the dolls move again.   In the next few days, she repeated this scene many times, kicking her legs and watching the dolls shake, and she often would squeal with laughter at the sight of the moving dolls (1936a, pp. 157–59).

Piaget sometimes referred to secondary circular reactions as "making interesting sights last" (1936a, p. 196).   He speculated that infants smile and laugh at the recognition of a moderately novel event (1936a, p. 197). At the same time, it seems that they are enjoying their own power, their ability to make an event happen again and again.

Stage 4 (10 to 12 months).   The Coordination of Secondary Schemes

In stage 3, the infant performs a single action to get a result—for example, kicking to move some dangling dolls.   In stage 4, the infant's actions become more differentiated; he or she learns to coordinate two separate schemes to get a result.   This new accomplishment is most ap-parent when infants deal with obstacles.   For example, one day Laurent wanted to grab a matchbox, but Piaget put his hand in the way.   At first, Laurent tried to ignore the hand; he tried to pass over it or around it, but he did not attempt to displace it.   When Piaget kept his hand in the way, Laurent resorted to "storming the box while waving his hand, shaking himself, [and] wagging his head from side to side"—various "magical" gestures (1936a, p. 217).   Finally, several days later, Laurent succeeded in removing the obstacle by striking the hand out of the way before he grabbed the box.   Thus, Laurent coordinated two separate schemes—striking and grabbing—to obtain the goal. One scheme, striking, became a means to an end, grabbing the box.

Such simple observations are very important for our understanding of how children develop the basic categories of experience, of space and time. We cannot talk to babies and ask them about their experiences of space and time, but we can see how these categories are developing through their actions. When Laurent learned to move the hand to get the box, he showed a sense that some objects are *in front of* others in space, and that some events must *precede* others in time (Ginsburg and Opper, 1988, p. 52).

Stage 5 (12 to 18 months). Tertiary Circular Reactions

At stage 3, infants perform a single action to obtain a single result—to make an interesting sight last. At stage 4, they perform two separate actions to obtain a single result. Now, at stage 5, they experiment with different actions to observe the different outcomes.

For example, one day Laurent became interested in a new table. He hit it with his fist several times, sometimes harder, sometimes more gently, in order to hear the different sounds that his actions produced (Piaget, 1936a, p. 270).

Similarly, a 12-month-old boy was sitting in the bathtub, watching the water pour down from the faucet. He put his hand under the faucet and noticed how the water sprayed outward. He repeated this action twice, making the interesting sight last (stage 3). But he then shifted the position of his hand, sometimes nearer, sometimes farther away from the faucet, observing how the water sprayed out at different angles. He varied his actions to see what new, different results would follow.

It is worth pausing to note that the infants were learning entirely on their own, without any adult teaching. They were developing their schemes solely out of an intrinsic curiosity about the world.

Stage 6 (18 months to two years). The Beginnings of Thought

At stage 5, children are little scientists, varying their actions and observing the results. However, their discoveries all occur through direct physical actions. At stage 6, children seem to think out situations more internally, before they act.

The most widely known example of stage 6 behavior involves Lucienne and a matchbox. Piaget placed a chain in the box, which Lucienne immediately tried to recover. She possessed two schemes for getting the chain: turning the box over and sticking her finger in the box's slit. However, neither scheme worked. She then did something very curious. She stopped her actions and looked at the slit with great attention. Then, several times in succession, she opened and shut her mouth, wider and wider (1936a, p. 338). After this, she promptly opened the box and obtained the chain.

Piaget (1936a, p. 344) noted that at stage 5 the child probably would have obtained the chain through a slow, trial-and-error process of experimenting with different actions. Because Lucienne stopped acting and thought out the situation, she was able to achieve the result much more quickly. She did not yet have a good grasp of language, so she used motor movements (her mouth) to symbolize the action she needed to perform.

Children's progress at stage 6 can also be seen in their efforts at imitation. Piaget observed that for some time children cannot imitate new models at all; they can only reproduce actions that already exist in their behavioral repertoires. By stage 5, though, they can make the necessary accommodations to imitate new behavior through experimental trial-and-error. But it is only at stage 6 that children are capable of *deferred imitation*—the imitation of absent models. For example, at 16 months of age Jacqueline

> had a visit from a little boy . . . whom she used to see from time to time, and who, in the course of the afternoon, got into a terrible temper. He screamed as he tried to get out of a play-pen and pushed it backwards, stamping his feet. J. stood watching him in amazement, never having witnessed such a scene before. The next day, she herself screamed in her play-pen and tried to move it, stamping her foot lightly several times in succession. The imitation of the whole scene was most striking. (Piaget, 1946, p. 63)

Piaget argued that because Jacqueline's imitation came an entire day later, she must have carried within her some internal representation of the model. Since she lacked the vocabulary to represent his actions in words, she probably used some form of motoric representation. She may have imitated his behavior with very brief muscle movements when she saw it, and these movements served as the basis for her later imitation (1946, Ch. 3).

The Development of Object Permanence

We have so far described only some of the main features of the six sensori-motor stages. Piaget studied other developments during this period; he showed how infants construct concepts of permanent objects, time, space, and causality, and how they develop capacities for play. Because of space limitations, we will briefly review only one important development—that of object permanence.

During stages 1 and 2, babies have no conception of objects existing outside themselves. If a person or an object leaves their field of vision, the most they do is to continue to look for a moment to where they last saw it. If the object does not reappear, they go on to something else. They make no attempt to search for it. For the baby, out of sight is out of mind (Piaget, 1936b, pp. 1–12).

At stage 3, new progress is made. As we mentioned earlier, babies are now becoming interested in the external world (e.g., in making interesting sights last). Consequently, they have been gaining a better sense of the permanence of external things. If objects are dropped from their line of vision, they now look to the place where the object has fallen. They can also find partly hidden objects. If they temporarily put an object aside (for example, behind their backs), they can, after a brief interruption, recover it. They can do so when the object was related to their own actions. However, infants at this stage cannot find objects that are completely hidden by others (1936b, pp. 13–48).

Stage 4 marks the beginning of a genuine sense of object permanence. Babies can now find completely hidden objects. If we completely cover a toy with a blanket, the baby will lift the blanket and find it (1936b, p. 51).

However, Piaget found an interesting limitation at this stage. When he hid an object at point A, his children could find it, but when he then hid the same object at point B, they again tried to find it at point A—the place of their prior success. In Piaget's terms, they could not follow a series of displacements (movements from hiding place to hiding place) (1936b, p. 54).

At stage 5, children can follow a series of displacements, so long as they can see us making them. It is only at stage 6 that infants can follow invisible displacements. For example, it was only at the sixth stage that Jacqueline could recover a ball that rolled under the sofa by making a detour around the sofa. She could do this because she now had the ability to visualize to herself, internally, the ball's trajectory path even when it was invisible (1936b, p. 231).

For Piaget, such detour behavior is very important. It shows that the child has constructed a sense of space that has the characteristics of a mathematical model called a *group*. For example, Jacqueline's detours demonstrate the principle of *associativity*, that one can reach a point through different interconnected paths. She also demonstrates the group principle of *reversibility* by bringing the ball back. Similarly, detour behavior reveals the other principles that define a coherent group structure (Piaget and Inhelder, 1966, pp. 15–17).

Less technically, we can note the tremendous progress that infants make when they achieve object permanence. At the beginning of life, they have no sense of objects existing in their own right, independent of their sight or actions. By the end of the sensori-motor period, objects are separate and permanent. Thus, children develop a universe containing independent objects, in which they are only one object among many. Along with object permanence, then, they develop a clear sense of themselves as independent beings (Piaget, 1936b, pp. 108–9).

PERIODS II AND III.
PREOPERATIONAL THOUGHT (TWO TO SEVEN)
AND CONCRETE OPERATIONS (SEVEN TO 11)

By the end of the sensori-motor period, the child has developed efficient and well-organized actions for dealing with the immediate environment. The child continues to use sensori-motor skills throughout life, but the next period, that of preoperational thought, is marked by a major change. The child's mind rapidly advances to a new plane, that of symbols (including images and words). As a result, the child must organize his or her thinking all over again. This cannot be done at once. For some time, during the entire preoperational period, the child's thinking is basically unsystematic and illogical. It is not until the age of seven or so, the beginning of concrete operations, that thinking becomes organized on a mental plane (Piaget, 1964a, p. 22).

The Growth of Symbolic Activity

Children begin to use symbols when they use one object or action to represent an absent one (Ginsburg and Opper, 1988, p. 70). Actually, as we have seen, children begin to do this during the sixth stage of sensori-motor development. For example, when Lucienne opened her mouth before opening the matchbox, she used her mouth to represent an action she had not yet performed. Similarly, deferred imitation involves some kind of internal representation—of past events. Piaget believed that deferred imitation also initially involves motoric images, and he emphasized that the first symbols are motoric, not linguistic.

We also find examples of nonlinguistic symbols in children's play. One day Jacqueline pretended that a piece of cloth was her pillow. She put her head on the cloth and, laughing, pretended to go to sleep. Her play was symbolic because she used one object, a piece of cloth, to represent an absent one, the pillow (Piaget, 1946, p. 96). Make-believe play also begins during the sixth sensori-motor stage and becomes pronounced during the next few years.

A major source of symbols, of course, is language, which develops rapidly during the early preoperational years (from about two to four). One of Jacqueline's first symbolic uses of language came when she was almost two years old, after she had visited a pond. When she returned home, she told her father about the experience, saying, "Robert cry, duck swim in lake, gone away" (1946, p. 222). She thus used words to reconstruct an absent event, one from the past.

Language vastly widens the child's horizons. Through language, the child can relive the past, anticipate the future, and communicate events to others. But precisely because the young child's mind is so rapidly expanding, it initially lacks the properties of a coherent logic. This is apparent in the young child's use of words. He or she does not use words to stand for true classes of objects, but merely as *preconcepts*. For example, when Jacqueline was three years old, she said that a daddy is a man who "has lots of Luciennes and lots of Jacquelines" (1946, p. 255). She did not yet possess the concept of a general class, children, within which those with the names Lucienne and Jacqueline comprise only a small subset.

Because children lack general classes, their reasoning is frequently *transductive*, shifting from the particular to the particular. At four-and-a-half years Lucienne said, "I haven't had my nap yet so it isn't afternoon" (1946, p. 232). She did not yet understand that afternoons are general time periods that contain many particular events, of which her nap was only one.

Some psychologists believe that children learn to think more logically as they master language. In this view, language provides us with our conceptual categories (see Brown, 1965). Piaget, however, disagreed. Although language is tremendously important—it provides us with a source of shared symbols for communicating with others—it does not itself provide the structure of logical thinking. Logic, instead, stems from actions. Infants develop logically coherent action systems during the sensori-motor period, before they talk, and later logic is simply organized actions of a more internal kind (Piaget and Inhelder, 1966, pp. 86–90). To study how internal actions form logical systems, Piaget gave children various scientific tasks. He usually began such experiments with children at age four, because they could now sit down, focus on the tasks, and communicate with the examiner.

Scientific Reasoning

Conservation of continuous quantities (liquids). This is Piaget's most famous experiment. In one version (Piaget and Szeminska, 1941, p. 17), the child is shown two glasses, A1 and A2, which are filled to the same height (see Figure 6.1). The child is asked if the two glasses contain the same amount of liquid, and the child almost always agrees that they do. Next, the experimenter (or the child) pours the liquid from A2 to glass P, which is lower and wider. The child is asked if the amount of liquid is still the same. At the *preoperational* level, the responses fall into two substages.

At the first substage, the children clearly fail to conserve—that is, they fail to realize that the quantity is the same. Usually, they say that A1 now has more because it is taller. Occasionally, the child says that P now has more because it is wider. In either case, the child "centers" on only one dimension, the height or the width. The child is so struck by a single perceptual dimension—the way it looks—that he or she fails to understand that logically the liquid must remain the same.

At the second substage, the child takes steps toward conservation but does not achieve it. A boy might at one moment say that A1 has more because it is taller, then change his mind and say that P has more because it is wider, and then become confused. The boy is showing "intuitive regulations"; he is beginning to consider *two* perceptual dimensions, but he does not yet reason about the two dimensions simultaneously and recognize that a change in one dimension cancels out a change in the other. His confusion, however, means that he is becoming aware that he is contradicting himself, and it is a good bet that he will soon resolve the contradiction and move on to the stage of conservation.

Children generally achieve conservation of liquids at about age seven. When they do so, they are entering the stage of *concrete operations*. Basically, children achieve conservation by using three arguments. First, the child might say, "You haven't added any or taken any away, so it has to be the same." This is the *identity* argument. Second, the child might say, "This glass is taller here, but the other one is wider here, so they're still the same." This is the argument of *compensation*—that the changes cancel each other out. The child assumes that the changes are part of an organized system— that a change in one dimension is necessarily related to a compensating

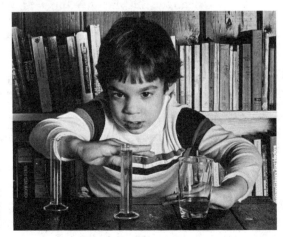

FIGURE 6.1
Conservation-of-liquid experiment. Child sees that beakers A1 and A2 contain the same amount of liquid. He then pours A2 into P and claims that now A1 has more because it is taller.

change in another dimension. Third, the child might say, "They are still the same because you can pour this one back to what it was before." This is the argument of *inversion* (Piaget and Inhelder, 1966, p. 98). Piaget believed that the concrete operational child can use all three arguments, although the child might not spontaneously do so on any given task.

Underlying these arguments are logical *operations, mental actions* that are *reversible* (Piaget and Inhelder, 1966, p. 96). When the child argues that a change in one glass is cancelled out by a change in the other, the child understands that the end result is a return, or reversal, to the original amount. Similarly, when arguing that we can pour the water back, the child is suggesting that we reverse the process.

Operations, it is important to note, are mental actions. The child is carrying out compensations or reversals in his or her mind. The child has not actually performed or seen the transformations that he or she is talking about. The transformations (e.g., reversibility) are similar to those of the infant but are now on a more internalized plane.

People sometimes wonder if young children might fail to conserve simply because of their difficulties with language. They might think that what the experimenter means by "more" is "taller," and therefore they point to the taller glass. One can get around such difficulties by changing one's wording—for example, by asking, "Which one would give you more to drink?" Usually we find that the young child still fails to conserve (Peill, 1975, p. 7, Ch. 2).

How does the child learn conservation? The most ready answer is that conservation is taught. However, as we shall see, the teaching of conservation frequently meets with unexpected resistance. The preoperational child does not genuinely believe the adult's explanations.

Piaget argued that children master conservation *spontaneously*. The crucial moment comes at the second substage, when the child first says that one glass has more because it is taller, then says the other has more because it is wider, and then becomes confused. The child is in a state of *internal contradiction*, which he or she resolves by moving on to a higher stage. Sometimes we can see this change happen before our very eyes. The child says, "This has more . . . no, that one is wider, no, wait. They're both the same. This looks taller, but you've poured it into a wider glass."

Conservation of number.

In one of his experiments on the conservation of number (Piaget and Szeminska, 1941, pp. 49–56), Piaget gave children a row of egg cups and a bunch of eggs. He then asked them to take just enough eggs to fill the cups. Again, the responses at the preoperational period fell into two substages.

At the first substage, the children simply made the rows equal in length, ignoring the number of eggs in the row. When Piaget then asked them to actually put the eggs in the cups, they were surprised to find that they had too many or too few eggs.

At the second preoperational stage, the children spontaneously created a one-to-one correspondence, placing one egg beneath each cup (see Figure 6.2). According to Piaget, they have used an intuitive approach to achieve a precise perceptual order. However, their success was limited to

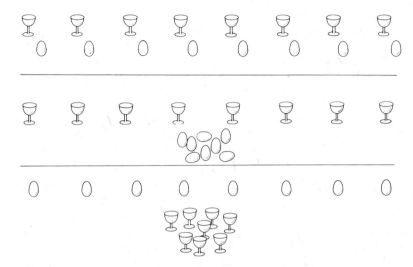

FIGURE 6.2   Conservation-of-number experiment.   Young children can often create two rows of equal number, but if we lengthen or shorten one row, they think that the number has changed.   (Adapted from Inhelder B., *The criteria of the stages of mental development.*   In J. M. Tanner and B. Inhelder (Eds.), *Discussions of Child Development.*   New York: International Universities Press, Inc., p. 79.   Copyright © 1971 by Tavistock Publications Ltd.   By permission of the publishers.)

this simple perceptual arrangement.   When Piaget then bunched up (or, sometimes, spread out) one of the rows, the children claimed that now one had more.   As with conservation of liquids, the children failed to conserve because they were more influenced by their immediate perceptions than by logic.   Because one row now looked so much longer, they failed to reason that the number must remain the same.

At this stage, in addition, children sometimes begin to waver in their answers.   One moment they say that one row has more because it is longer, but the next moment they think that the other row has more because it is denser.   This state of conflict marks the transition to concrete operations.

At the stage of concrete operations, children realize that the number in each row is the same despite the different appearances in length.   They reason that the two rows are the same because "you haven't taken any away or added any" (identity), because "one row is longer here but this one is more bunched in" (compensation), or because "you could make this row long again and make them equal" (inversion).

Other conservation experiments.   Piaget has studied several other kinds of conservation, such as the conservation of substance, weight, volume, and length.   For example, in a conservation-of-substance experiment, the child is shown two equal balls of plasticine or play dough and then watches as one ball is rolled into a longer, thinner shape, like that of a hot dog.   At the preoperational level, the child thinks that the two balls now have different amounts of play dough.

We will not describe the various kinds of conservation here, but simply note that they all are thought to involve the mastery of the same logical concepts—identity, inversion, and compensation. Nevertheless, some kinds of conservation appear more difficult than others and are mastered later.[2] Thus, the attainment of conservation is a gradual process within the concrete operational period.

Classification. In a typical classification experiment, Piaget (Piaget and Szeminska, 1941, pp. 161–81) presented children with 20 wooden beads, of which 18 were brown and two were white. Piaget made sure that the children understood that although most beads were brown and two were white, they all were made of wood. He then asked the children, "Are there more brown beads or more wooden beads?" At the preoperational level, the children said that there were more brown beads. Apparently they were so struck by the many brown beads in comparison to the two white ones that they failed to realize that both brown and white beads are parts of a larger whole—the class of wooden beads. As with conservation, children master such classification tasks during the period of concrete operations, and the same logical operations appear to be involved (1941, p. 178).

Social Thinking

Egocentrism. Piaget believed that at each period there is a general correspondence between scientific and social thinking. For example, just as preoperational children fail to consider two dimensions on conservation tasks, they also fail to consider more than one perspective in their interactions with others. Preoperational children are frequently egocentric, considering everything from their own single viewpoint. This is apparent from young children's conversations (Piaget, 1923). For example, a little girl might tell her friend, "I'm putting this here," oblivious to the fact that the place to which she is pointing is blocked from her friend's vision.

One of Piaget's most widely quoted studies on egocentrism dealt with the child's perception of space. In this study (Piaget and Inhelder, 1948) the child was taken for a walk around a model of three mountains so he or she could see how the model looked from different angles. After the walk, the child was seated on one side of the model, facing a doll that looked at the model from the opposite side. The child was then asked to select from among several photographs the picture that best showed what he or she saw and the picture that showed what the doll saw. All the children could pick the picture that represented their own view, but the youngest children (from about four to six years) frequently chose the same picture to show the doll's view. Apparently, they did not understand that the doll's perspective differed from their own.

Egocentrism, then, refers to the inability to distinguish one's own perspective from that of others. Egocentrism does not, however, neces-

---

[2]In fact, the mastery of one series—conservation of substance, weight, and volume— may always occur in the same invariant sequence (Piaget and Inhelder, 1966, p. 99; Ginsburg and Opper, 1988, pp. 151–53).

sarily imply selfishness or conceit. This point can be clarified by an example. One day two boys went shopping with their aunt for a birthday present for their mother. The older boy, who was seven, picked out a piece of jewelry. The younger boy, who was three-and-a-half, selected a model car. The younger child's behavior was not selfish or greedy; he carefully wrapped the present and gave it to his mother with an expression that clearly showed that he expected her to love it. However, his behavior was egocentric; he did not consider the fact that his mother's interests were different from his own.

As long as children are egocentric, they tend simply to play alongside one another. For example, two children in the sandbox will build their own structures. As they overcome egocentrism, they learn to coordinate their actions in joint endeavors. Each might dig a tunnel so that the tunnels eventually connect. This requires considering each other's perspective. Such cooperative play occurs at the stage of concrete operations.

Egocentrism also may influence young children's speech, as when they engage in "collective monologues." Two little girls may appear to be holding a conversation while they play, but each girl is actually just talking about what is on her own mind. One girl might talk about a toy house she is building, while the other talks about a trip she took, and no connection is ever made. As children overcome egocentrism, they consider the reactions and viewpoints of their listeners.

Much peer interaction, then, is initially egocentric. Nevertheless, Piaget (1923, p. 101; 1932, p.94) speculated, children overcome egocentrism as they interact less exclusively with adults, and more with other children. They discover that whereas grown-ups seem to understand whatever is on their minds, their peers do not. Consequently, they learn to consider others' viewpoints in order to make themselves understood.

Furthermore, children are less impressed by the authority of other children and feel freer to engage in conflicts with them. They argue with their peers and sometimes reach compromises and cooperate with them. Thus, they begin to coordinate alternative viewpoints and interests (Piaget, 1924, p. 205).

Whether children overcome egocentrism primarily through peer interaction or not, the most crucial point for Piaget's theory is that children themselves play an active role in grasping the fact of alternative viewpoints. On this point, I recall an instance in which one of our sons, then five years old, seemed actually to make this discovery. He was riding alone in the car with me when, after a few minutes of silence, he said, "You know, Dad, you're not remembering what I'm remembering." I asked him what he meant, and he replied, "Like I was remembering about my shoes, but you can't see what I'm remembering; you can't be remembering what I'm remembering." Thus, at that moment he seemed actually to discover, by himself, that others' perspectives differ from his own. He might not have completely surmounted his egocentrism at that instant, but the point is that whatever step he took, he took on his own.

Moral judgment. Piaget investigated children's social thought in many areas, including morals. In his classic work, *The Moral Judgment of the Child*

(1932), he paid particular attention to how children understood the rules of the game of marbles.

Piaget first observed how children actually played the game, and he found that between the ages of four and seven children typically played in an egocentric manner. If two boys were playing, each would play in his own way. They had little sense of winning; one might exclaim, "I won and you won too!" After the age of about seven years, children tried to follow common rules and win according to them (1932, pp. 29–46).

Piaget next investigated children's *thinking* about the rules. He was particularly interested in whether children thought the rules could be changed. Here he found that children for several years—up to the age of 10 or so—believed that the rules were fixed and unchangeable. They said that the rules came from some prestigious authority, from the government or from God. The rules could not be changed, they asserted, because then it wouldn't be the real game.

After the age of 10 or so, the children were more relativistic. Rules were seen simply as mutually agreed-upon ways of playing the game. Children no longer considered the rules as fixed or absolute; they said the rules probably had changed over the years, as children invented new rules. And they said they too could change them, as long as everyone in the game agreed (1932, pp. 50–76).

These different conceptions of rules, Piaget said, reveal two basic moral attitudes. The first, characteristic of the younger children, is moral *heteronomy*, a blind obedience to rules imposed by adults. Children assume that there is one powerful law which they must always follow. The second morality, that of the older children, is *autonomy*. This morality considers rules as human devices produced by equals for the sake of cooperation (1932, pp. 401–6).

Piaget believed that moral heteronomy is tied to egocentrism; children view rules from a single perspective, that of powerful adults. As a form of egocentrism, moral heteronomy is overcome quite late, at the age of 10 or so, compared to egocentric play, which is usually overcome by age seven. Here Piaget reminded us that heteronomy is a form of egocentric *thought* and said that thought often lags behind action. Children may need to engage in a good deal of genuinely cooperative play with peers, in which they actually change rules to meet everyone's satisfaction, before they can discuss the relativity of rules on a conscious plane (1932, pp. 94–95).

Animism. Piaget described other ways in which young children's thinking differs from that of older children and adults. Like Werner, Piaget observed that young children do not make the same distinctions between living and nonliving things that we do. As Werner said, they perceive everything, including physical objects, physiognomically, as full of life and feeling. A loud truck may seem angry and a single cloud lonely. Piaget called this view of the physical world *animistic*.

Although Piaget and Werner were struck by a similar attitude in young children, they studied it somewhat differently. Werner was concerned with children's direct perceptions of objects; Piaget was more interested in their concepts and definitions of life.

At first, Piaget found, children equate life with any kind of activity. For example, one boy was asked,

> Is the sun alive?—*Yes.*—Why?—*It gives light.*—Is a candle alive?—*Yes because it gives light. It is alive when it is giving light, but it isn't alive when it is not giving light.* . . . Is the play-bell alive?—*Yes, it rings.* (Piaget, 1926, p. 196)

Such thinking is common between the ages of four and six.

A bit later, between the ages of about six and eight, children restrict life to things that move. For example,

> Is a stone alive?—*Yes.*—Why?—*It moves.* . . . How does it move?—*By rolling.*—Is the table alive?—*No, it can't move.* . . . Is a bicycle alive?—*Yes.*—Why?—*It goes.* (1926, p. 196)

Only after eight years or so do children restrict life to objects that move on their own and, later, to plants and animals.

Piaget found roughly similar stages in thinking about the kinds of objects that have feelings and consciousness. At first children believe that an object has feelings if it reacts in any way. For example, a stick feels fire because it gets burnt. A bit later children restrict feelings and consciousness to objects that move, then to objects that move on their own, and finally to animals.

Thus, children gradually abandon their animism and come to make the distinctions characteristic of most adults. The fate of animism in Piaget's theory, we might note, differs from that of physiognomic perception in Werner's. For Werner physiognomic perception, while less dominant in most adults than in young children, nevertheless remains with us and contributes to our artistic and poetic outlooks. For Piaget animism is simply overcome.

Dreams. One of Piaget's earliest studies examined children's conceptions of dreams (1926, Ch. 3). As with conceptions of life, young children's understanding of dreams seems to follow a specific stage sequence. Since Piaget's first study, others (especially Kohlberg, 1966a) have refined Piaget's dream sequence.

At first children seem to believe that dreams are real. For example, when a four-year-old girl was asked if the giant in her dream was really there, she answered, "It was really there but it left when I woke up. I saw its footprint on the floor" (Kohlberg, 1966a, p. 6). Soon afterward, children discover that dreams are not real, but they still view dreams quite differently from the way older children or adults view them. They think that their dreams are visible to others and that dreams come from the outside (from the night or the sky, or through the window from the lights outside). They also think that dreams remain outside themselves while they are dreaming. It is as if they were watching a movie, with the action taking place in their rooms in front of their eyes. Gradually, stage by stage, children realize that dreams not only are unreal but are invisible, of internal origin, of internal location, and possess the other characteristics that adults assign to them.   They usually complete their discoveries by the age of six or seven years, at the beginning of concrete operations.

How do children learn about dreams?   Our first assumption probably is that they learn about them from adults.   When children have nightmares, parents reassure them, saying, "Don't worry, it was only a dream.   It wasn't real; it was only in your mind."   Piagetians, however, maintain that children actually discover the various properties of dreams on their own.   Kohlberg (1966a), for example, argued that because children master the dream sequence in an invariant six-stage sequence, it is unlikely that their thinking is the product of adult teachings; adults do not take the trouble to teach children about dreams in such a detailed, precise order.   Instead, children arrive at different conceptualizations on their own, in an order of increasing difficulty.

To gather additional information on the role of adult teaching, Kohlberg (1966a) administered the dream interview to children in an aboriginal society in which the adults believe that dreams are real (the Atayal on Formosa).   Despite the adults' beliefs, these children seem to progress through the stages in the same order as American or Swiss children.   That is, they first discover that dreams are unreal, then that they are invisible, and so on.   Finally, when they reach the last stage, they feel the impact of the adult views and change their minds, adopting the view that dreams are real after all.   Still, they initially progress through the dream sequence in opposition to any adult beliefs, so adult views cannot be the sole determinants of their learnings.

Summary and Conclusion

Piaget argued that children's thinking during the preoperational period is very different from that of older children and adults.   Preoperational thinking is characterized by egocentrism, animism, moral heteronomy, a view of dreams as external events, a lack of classification, a lack of conservation, as well as other attributes that we have not had the space to cover.

The list is a long one, and one might ask, "What do all these characteristics have in common?"   The question is central to Piaget's theory, for it maintains that each developmental stage has a basic unity.   Unfortunately, Piaget did not give as much attention to this question as we would like, but most often (e.g., 1964a, pp. 41–60), he tried to link the various preoperational characteristics to the concept of egocentrism.

In speech, children are egocentric when they consider matters only from their own perspective.   Animism—the attribution of life to physical objects—also stems from egocentrism; children assume that everything functions just as they do.   Similarly, Piaget tried to show that young children's conceptions of dreams are related to egocentrism.   As long as children are egocentric, they fail to realize the extent to which each person has private, subjective experiences such as dreams.   In the realm of morals, furthermore, egocentrism goes hand-in-hand with moral heteronomy. Young children regard rules from only one perspective, as absolutes handed down from above.   They do not yet see how rules are based on the mutual agreements of two or more actors attempting to coordinate their different objectives in a cooperative way.

There is also a link between egocentrism and children's performances on scientific tasks, such as the experiments on conservation. Just as the egocentric child views things from a single perspective, the child who fails to conserve focuses on only one aspect of the problem. For example, when water is poured from one glass into a shorter, broader one, the child "centers" on a single striking dimension—the difference in height. The child cannot "decenter" and consider two aspects of the situation at once.

Children at the level of concrete operations are able to consider two aspects of a problem simultaneously. In their social interactions, they consider not only what they are saying, but the needs of the listener. When they perform conservation experiments, they consider not only the most visible change but compensating changes. Thus, the ability to simultaneously coordinate two perspectives forms the basis of both social and scientific thinking (Piaget, 1947, pp. 156–66).

PERIOD IV. FORMAL OPERATIONS (11 TO ADULTHOOD)

At concrete operations, children can think systematically in terms of "mental actions." For example, when water is poured into a new glass, they can tell us about the implications of reversing the process, without actually performing the activity. However, there is a limit to such abilities. They can think logically and systematically only as long as they refer to tangible objects that can be subjected to real activity (Piaget, 1964a, p. 62).

During formal operations, in contrast, thinking soars into the realm of the purely abstract and hypothetical. The capacity for abstract reasoning can be seen in responses to questions such as the following: If Joe is shorter than Bob, and Joe is taller than Alex, who is the tallest? At the level of concrete operations, children can handle this problem only if they actually place people in order and compare their heights; beyond this, they simply guess. At the level of formal operations, however, adolescents can order their thoughts in their minds alone (1964a, p. 62).

Piaget was most concerned with the capacity to reason with respect to hypothetical possibilities. In one experiment (Inhelder and Piaget, 1955, pp. 107–22), children were given four flasks containing colorless liquids, labeled 1, 2, 3, and 4. They also were given a small container of colorless liquid, labeled g. Their task was to mix these liquids to make the color yellow.

At the level of preoperational intelligence, children typically made a mess. They poured the liquids in and out of the bottles in a haphazard way.

At the level of concrete operations, children's actions showed more organization. A typical strategy was to pour g into each flask: g into 1, g into 2, g into 3, and g into 4. However, they then gave up. When questioned, these children usually said that there wasn't anything more they could do. Thus, their actions revealed some organization, as we could have expected from their systematic behavior on conservation tasks, on which they can think in terms of two dimensions at once. But they entertained only a limited range of possibilities.

At the level of formal operations, the adolescents worked systematically in terms of *all possibilities.* Some started out by trying various combinations and then realized that they had better make sure that they would include all possible combinations, so they wrote them down before acting any further.

When adolescents think about the various possibilities inherent in a situation beforehand and then systematically test them, they are working like true scientists. For example, a teenage girl might decide to test the effects of a new soil for plants. At the level of formal operations, she does not just put new soil into one plant and old soil into the other and watch them grow; she considers other possibilities. Perhaps these two plants would have grown to different heights anyway, because of individual differences, so she obtains several plants and examines the average effects of the different soils. Perhaps the sunlight also has an effect—so she makes sure that all plants have the same lighting. Perhaps the amount of water is also important—so she controls for this variable too. The essence of such reasoning is that one is systematically thinking about hypotheses. One is not just entertaining a new possibility but is isolating one hypothesis by controlling for the effects of other possible variables.

As with the other periods, Piaget introduced logico-mathematical models to describe formal operational thinking. These models are in some respects similar to those that apply to earlier developmental levels, but they also go beyond them. The models are very complex, and we will not attempt to cover them here. It is important to note, however, that at the level of formal operations, thinking reaches its highest degree of equilibrium. This means, among other things, that the various operations are more tightly interrelated and that they apply to the widest possible field of application—the realm of hypothetical possibilities.

Although Piaget limited most of his research on adolescents to mathematical and scientific reasoning, he did speculate on the role of formal operations in the adolescent's social life (Inhelder and Piaget, 1955, Ch. 18). Unlike the concrete-operational child, who lives primarily in the here and now, adolescents begin to think about more far-reaching problems— about their futures and the nature of the society they will enter. In this process, their new cognitive powers can lead to a striking idealism and utopianism. They can now grasp abstract principles and ideals, such as liberty, justice, and love, and they envision hypothetical societies very different from any that presently exist. Thus, the adolescent becomes a dreamer, constructing theories about a better world.

Piaget believed that such idealistic and utopian thinking carries with it a new kind of egocentrism. To fully appreciate this new egocentrism, we must review how egocentrism appears whenever the child enters a new realm of intellectual life. At first, infants are egocentric in the sense that they have no conception of the world apart from their own actions. External objects have no permanent existence of their own. Only at the end of the sensori-motor period do children decenter and situate themselves in a world of permanent objects, of which they are only one.

At the next level—that of preoperational thought—children enter a new, vastly enlarged world—one that includes language, symbolic representation, and communication with others. Children once again become egocentric and have difficulty considering more than their own immediate perspective. Gradually, they decenter and learn to consider alternative perspectives—as long as they are thinking about concrete objects immediately before them.

Finally, adolescents enter a broader world yet—the world of possibilities—and egocentrism reappears. This time egocentrism is seen when adolescents attribute unlimited power to their own thoughts. They dream of "a glorious future or of transforming the world through Ideas" (1955, p. 346), without attempting to test out their thoughts in reality. The final decentering comes about, in Piaget's view, when adolescents actually take up adult roles. They then learn the limits and resistances to their own thoughts. They learn that a theoretical construction or a utopian vision has value only in relation to how it works out in reality.

THEORETICAL ISSUES

The Stage Concept

Many psychologists use the term *stage* loosely, as merely a convenient device for summarizing their findings. This, however, is not the case with Piaget. As Kohlberg (1968) stressed, the Piagetian stage concept implies several strong positions on the nature of development.

First, in a rigorous stage theory, the stage sequence should be invariant. People will proceed through the stages at different rates, and some may not reach the highest of Piaget's stages; but to the extent that they move through them, they will proceed in order.

Second, stages imply that growth is divided into qualitatively different periods. If intellectual development were a continuous, quantitative process, any division into separate stages would be arbitrary (Flavell, 1963, p. 19). For example, if knowledge can be scored from 0 to 100, then any division into stages at 40, 50, and 70 makes no more sense than any other series of cut-off points. Piaget, however, believed that thinking at different times is organized along qualitatively different lines. Thinking at concrete operations, for instance, is qualitatively different from that at formal operations (it is logical insofar as it refers to concrete objects and activities, but it is not yet truly abstract and hypothetical). Consequently, there is a natural, valid distinction between the two periods.

Third, stages refer to general characteristics. Kohlberg liked to discuss this point by asking the following question: At the age of four, a child cannot copy a diamond. At the age of five, the child can. Has the child reached the diamond-copying stage? Kohlberg explained that this proposal sounds somewhat silly because diamond-copying is too specific to be called a stage. If we were to call each particular achievement a stage, we would have thousands of stages. It is more appropriate to say that the child has reached a new *general* stage of perceptual-motor coordination that permits him or her to do many new things. Similarly, Piaget's stages refer to general patterns of thought, and if we know that a child is in a particular stage, we should be able to predict behavior across a wide variety of tasks. This is not completely true, for children may be at somewhat different stages in different areas (e.g., in scientific versus social reasoning). Piaget called such irregularities *decalages*. However, there should be a substantial unity in performances at each general period.

Fourth, Piaget (Inhelder and Piaget, 1955) believed that his own stages represent hierarchic integrations. That is, the lower stages do not disappear but become integrated into, and in a sense dominated by, new broader frameworks. For example, a teenage boy who begins using formal operations can still use concrete operations—he can still reason systematically about concrete, visible events. However, he now realizes that these events are only a part of a wider range of theoretical possibilities, and he will prefer to approach difficult problems with this wider range in mind.[3]

Fifth, Piaget, like other rigorous stage theorists, claimed that his stages unfold in the same sequence in all cultures. This proposal frequently puzzles readers. Don't different cultures teach different beliefs, particularly with regard to morals? We will take up this issue in the next chapter, but in general the Piagetian answer is that the theory is not concerned with specific beliefs but with underlying cognitive capacities. Thus, young children, regardless of their cultural beliefs on matters such as sex or fighting, will base their views on what they think authority condones or punishes. It is not until adolescence, when young people acquire formal operations, that they will give abstract, theoretical treatises on moral matters, whatever their specific beliefs.

In summary, then, Piaget advanced a rigorous stage theory, which means that he believed his stages (a) unfold in an invariant sequence, (b) describe qualitatively different patterns, (c) refer to general properties of thought, (d) represent hierarchic integrations, and (e) are culturally universal.

Movement from Stage to Stage

Piaget devoted a great deal of attention to the structures of his stages and far less attention to the problem of movement through them. Nevertheless, he had definite views on this topic.

He acknowledged (1964b) that biological maturation plays some role in development. For example, children probably cannot attain concrete operations without some minimal maturation of the nervous system. However, Piaget said that maturation alone cannot play the dominant role because rates of development depend so much upon where children live.

---

[3]Piagetians imply that successive hierarchic integrations characterize development for all the periods except for preoperational thought. The illogical features of this period do not seem to be retained and integrated into any higher structures; they are simply overcome (see Inhelder, 1971).

Children who grow up in impoverished rural areas frequently develop at slow rates, apparently because they lack intellectual stimulation. Thus, the environment is also important.

However, it is easy to exaggerate the role of the environment, as learning theorists do. Generally speaking, learning theorists believe that the child's mind is primarily a product of external reinforcements and teaching. Piagetian concepts, they assume, must be taught by parents, teachers, and others. However, it is not at all clear that this is the case, as we will discuss in the last section of this chapter.

In Piaget's view, the environment is important, but only partly so. The environment nourishes, stimulates, and challenges the child, but children themselves build cognitive structures. As children seek out the environment, they encounter events that capture their *interest*. They are particularly intrigued by events that are moderately novel, events that do not quite correspond to their past experience. Children then adjust their actions to learn about these events, and in the process they build new ways for dealing with the world. For example, we saw how a little boy was struck by the way water sprayed outward when he placed his hand under it. He then adjusted his hand up and down to learn more about it, and as he did so, he probably learned a little about the efficacy of actively experimenting with different actions to see different results (stage 5 of sensori-motor development). In such behavior, it is not the environment that structures the child's mind, but the child who develops new schemes.

Experiences that promote cognitive development, in addition, are not only interesting, but usually place the child in a state of *conflict*. For example, an infant might be unable to grasp an object because an obstacle is in the way. The child needs to invent a new structure—a means-ends relationship—to obtain the object. The child assimilates new objects by making accommodations that build new cognitive structures.

The concept of conflict is involved in a fairly recent model of developmental change that Piaget called *equilibration* (1964b). We already have discussed the essence of this model, without using its name, when we described how children achieve conservation. For example, a little girl sees a ball of clay elongated and initially thinks that the amount has increased. After a while, however, she considers the clay's narrow width and thinks the clay has shrunk. Thus, she perceives something that *contradicts* her initial view. When she thinks about both the length and the width, she becomes confused. This conflict motivates the child to realize that one change cancels out the other, leading to the discovery of conservation. Piaget's equilibration model tries to assign numerical probabilities to the chances that the child will consider one dimension, then the other, and finally both.

In philosophy, Piaget's equilibration model would be called a dialectical theory. *Dialectical theory* holds that change occurs when our ideas meet with counterevidence that motivates us to formulate new and better ideas.

Another source of new, conflicting information is the social environment. For example, preoperational children overcome egocentrism when they interact with peers, with whom they get into arguments and conflicts. In such interchanges, they learn that others have views different from their own, and they also learn to coordinate different interests to behave in a cooperative fashion. This ability to coordinate viewpoints may aid in the growth of scientific thinking, where the coordination of dimensions is also important (Piaget, 1947, pp. 156–66).

Piaget, then, tried to indicate different ways in which interesting and conflicting pieces of information lead children to develop new cognitive structures. It is important to emphasize that development is always a spontaneous process. It is the children themselves who assimilate new information, resolve contradictions, and construct new cognitive structures.

IMPLICATIONS FOR EDUCATION

Piaget did not write extensively on education, but he did have some recommendations. Essentially, his overall educational philosophy is similar to that of Rousseau and Montessori. For Piaget, too, true learning is not something handed down by the teacher, but something that comes from the child. It is a process of spontaneous invention and discovery. This is clearly true of infants, who make incredible intellectual progress simply by exploring and manipulating the environment on their own, and it can be true of older children as well. Accordingly, the teacher should not try to impose knowledge on the child, but he or she should find materials that will interest and challenge the child and then permit the child to solve problems on his or her own (Piaget, 1969, pp. 151–53, 160).

Like Rousseau and Montessori, Piaget also stressed the importance of gearing instruction to the child's particular level. He did not agree with Montessori's maturational view of stages, but the general principle still holds: The educator must appreciate the extent to which children's interests and modes of learning are different at different times.

Say, for example, a boy is just entering the stage of concrete operations. He is beginning to think logically, but his thinking is still partly tied to concrete objects and activities. Accordingly, lessons should give him opportunities to deal actively with real things. If, for example, we wish to teach him about fractions, we should not draw diagrams, give him lectures, or engage him in verbal discussions. We should allow him to divide concrete objects into parts (Flavell, 1963, p. 368). When we assume that he will learn on a verbal plane, we are being egocentric; we are assuming that he learns just as we do. The result will be a lesson that sails over his head and seems unnatural to him.

It might appear that this principle—tailoring education to the child's own stage—is self-evident. Unfortunately, this is not always so. A case in point was the wave of curricular reforms that the nation initiated in the late 1950s and 1960s in response to the Soviet Union's launching of Sputnik. To try to catch up with the Russians, educators introduced the "new math," "new science," and other studies designed to teach children abstract, theoretical reasoning at very young ages. Initially, this seemed to be a great idea, but the new curriculum was not very successful. The reason, according to Kohlberg and Gilligan (1971), was that it attempted to teach young children, largely at the level of concrete operations and lower, ideas that assume capacities that are only attained at formal operations. The curricular reforms began with an adult conception of what children should learn and ignored children's own cognitive levels.

Beginning in the late 1970s and early 1980s, we witnessed a similar trend—a trend that continues today. Our nation's leaders, worried that the United States was losing its technological leadership to the Japanese, began calling for a new excellence in education. Parents, too, became anxious about their children's future and wanted to give them an early academic start. One result has been more and more academic instruction at younger and younger ages—all the way down to kindergarten and even earlier. David Elkind (1981, 1986), a Piagetian, has led a small but growing protest against this trend. Five-year-olds, Elkind points out, learn primarily through play and direct sensory contact with the environment; formal instruction, including workbooks, worksheets, and papers, does not coincide with the young child's natural modes of learning. Early formal instruction, Elkind argues, primarily teaches young children that learning is stressful and unnatural.

It is not always easy to find the educational experiences that are most natural for a given child. A knowledge of cognitive stages can help, but children are sometimes at different stages in different areas (Piaget, 1969, p. 171). What is needed is sensitivity and flexibility on the teacher's part— a willingness to look closely at the child's actions, to learn from the child, and to be guided by the child's spontaneous interests (Ginsburg and Opper, 1988, p. 239). For active learning always presupposes interest (Piaget, 1969, p. 152).

Like Rousseau and Montessori, then, Piaget believed learning should be a process of active discovery and should be geared to the child's stage. However, Piaget disagreed with Rousseau and Montessori on one point. Piaget saw much greater educational value in social interactions. Children begin to think logically—to coordinate two dimensions simultaneously— partly by learning to consider two or more perspectives in their dealings with others. Thus, interactions should be encouraged, and the most beneficial ones are those in which children feel a basic equality, as they most often do with peers. As long as children feel dominated by an authority who knows the "right" answer, they will have difficulty appreciating differences in perspectives. In group discussions with other children, in contrast, they have a better opportunity to deal with different viewpoints as stimulating challenges to their own thinking (1969, pp. 173–80).

Kamii's Constructivism

There have been several attempts to bring Piaget's ideas into the classroom, particularly the preschool and the early grades (DeVries and Kohlberg, 1987, Ch. 3). Some educators have focused on Piaget's tasks, attempting to teach conservation, classification, and so on. Others have been more concerned with the spirit of Piaget's theory. An inspired proponent of this approach is Constance Kamii (Kamii and DeVries, 1977; Kamii, 1985).

Kamii begins with the Piagetian premise that real cognitive growth only occurs when children construct their own knowledge. Children need opportunities to figure things out on their own. They will not do this, Kamii has found, if teachers use worksheets and tests. These practices make children so worried about getting the "right answers," the answers that the teacher will mark as correct, that they don't think problems out for themselves. Instead of worksheets and tests, then, teachers need to provide experiences that children will find so interesting and meaningful that they will work on them for their own sake. Such problems, Kamii says, can be found throughout children's daily lives. For example, first graders will enthusiastically work on arithmetic problems as they come up during card games, keeping score during outdoor games, voting on class decisions, and taking attendance. During such activities, the teacher can ask questions that further stimulate the child's interest in arithmetic. If children are playing softball, the teacher might ask: How many points do you need to reach 11? If a child brings pudding for the class, the teacher might ask: Are there just enough cups for all the children? The teacher's questions set the children's minds in motion, but the teacher always leaves the problem-solving to the children themselves. The teacher should even respect the children's "wrong answers." For it is better for children to come up with a wrong answer that is their own than to feel that they must turn to an adult to know what is correct (Kamii and DeVries, 1977; Kamii, 1985, pp. 46–49, 119–21, 161–65).

Kamii applies her approach to nearly every aspect of school life, including "discipline problems." If some children get into an argument during a card game, the teacher should resist the impulse to step in and solve the problem for them. Instead, the teacher might ask: Can you think of a way that would be fair to everybody? (Kamii, 1985, p. 48). In this way, the teacher prompts the children themselves to work on a question of justice.

Piagetian teaching, Kamii (1973) says, often means giving children more time to work on problems than schools usually do. Kamii tells, for example, about lessons in specific gravity. Children in the elementary grades are usually surprised to see that a pin sinks in water whereas a block of wood (which is larger) floats. And it usually takes children some time to figure out why this is so. Teachers are therefore tempted to explain the answer to their pupils, especially when the teacher wants to move on to a new lesson. But Kamii urges the teacher to wait. It is far better, she says, for the children to keep thinking and wondering about the matter than "to be told the answer and to learn incidentally that the answer always comes from the teacher's head" (1973, p. 225).

Kamii has done some preliminary evaluation research on her method of teaching arithmetic to first graders. She has found that on tests her children do about the same as those taught by conventional methods, but her children are much more independent minded. When a teacher tried to help a girl with a hint, the girl said, "Wait, I have to think it in my own head" (1985, p. 235). To Kamii, such responses are very encouraging. Like Montessori, Kamii is less interested in the amount of knowledge children gain than in their desire to think for themselves.

EVALUATION

Since about 1960 Piaget has stimulated a vast amount of research and theoretical discussion. We cannot summarize all of it here, but we can look at some trends and issues. I will organize this section around some basic questions.

Has Research Supported Piaget on His Tasks?

As mentioned in the Introduction, Piaget's own research has been criticized for its scientific shortcomings. For example, he based some conclusions only upon observations of his own three children—hardly a representative sample. Consequently, when Piaget was rediscovered in the early 1960s, many people wanted to see if they could replicate his findings.

Stage sequences. On the whole, the replication research using Piaget's own tasks has supported his stage sequence. That is, children do seem to move through the substages, stages, and periods in the order in which Piaget initially found. His stages have held up particularly well for the sensori-motor period and for scientific and mathematical reasoning with respect to the later stages (Almy et al., 1966; Lovell, 1968; Corman and Escalona, 1969; E. Evans, 1975; Neimark, 1975). The results have been somewhat less clear-cut for Piaget's stages of social thought, such as animism (Looft and Bartz, 1969), moral judgment (Kohlberg, 1964), and egocentrism (Damon, 1983, pp. 120–21), but in general younger children do differ from older children as Piaget found. This replication research, it should be noted, has typically used Piaget's own tasks. A bit later we will mention some studies that have questioned Piaget's conclusions by modifying his tasks.

Stage generality. Although Piaget's sequences have received support, his position that stages are general modes of thought has fared less well. That is, researchers have found rather low correlations among tasks that should tap the same general stages of thinking (Flavell, 1977, p. 248; Gelman and Baillargeon, 1983, pp. 169–72). For example, a child who demonstrates conservation of liquid might not exhibit the grasp of class inclusion that would seem to go along with it. Piaget himself recognized that children will master different tasks at different rates—he called such unevenness *decalage*—but he implied more consistency than has been found. On a more promising note, there is some evidence that correlations across tasks are higher when children are firmly within a general period than when they are in a transitional state (Uzgiris, 1964).

Pointing to these largely negative findings, many contemporary psychologists say we should abandon Piaget's stages altogether (see Flavell, 1985, pp. 75–93). Children, these psychologists say, do not go through any general periods during which their thinking reflects broad mental structures. Instead, they simply learn a variety of task-specific skills and strategies. Children learn arithmetic skills, reading skills, communication skills, and so on, and there are no general mental structures underlying them.

This rejection of Piagetian stages has become very popular in psychology, especially among those who study cognition with computer models. Nevertheless, such a rejection is very premature.

Consider the child during the ages five to seven. Sheldon White (1965, 1970) and others (e.g., Kegan, 1985) have accumulated a wealth of evidence that suggests that children undergo important psychological changes during this period. The changes involved in this *five-to-seven transition* go far beyond responses to Piagetian tasks; they include behavior in a variety of learning and social contexts. Prior to this shift, children are generally impulsive, distractable, and full of fantasy. Afterward, they are much more rational, logical, and self-contained. Thus, there seems to be a general, stagelike transition occurring at this time. And, as White observes, Piaget's theory is one that can help explain it: Children may begin to approach life in a more rational, conceptual manner because they are developing concrete operational thought.

We see, then, that Piaget's stage of concrete operations has great potential value. It does, to be sure, require some reworking (on the matter of internal consistency within Piagetian tasks). But it is too valuable to dismiss. In our chapter on Erikson, we will again discuss how Piagetian stages may help us understand very general changes at different points in life.

Do People Reach the Highest Stages?

A rather surprising finding is that most adults do not regularly demonstrate the highest stages of formal operations on Piaget's standard tasks. Most middle-class adults employ formal operations only some of the time (Neimark, 1975; Kuhn et al., 1977), and in many small village and tribal communities, many adults barely use any formal operations at all (Dasen, 1972; Cole and Cole, 1989, p. 566). These findings do not necessarily contradict Piaget. There is no theoretical reason why all people must reach his highest stages; perhaps their thinking has not been sufficiently challenged to move up to this level. Nevertheless, the findings are puzzling.

Piaget (1972) attempted to account for these findings. It is likely, he said, that most people attain some degree of formal operational thinking, but they employ formal operations primarily in areas of special interest or ability. An automobile mechanic may not think in a formal, theoretical manner about philosophy or physics but does use formal operations when trouble-shooting a car. An eager young law student might not employ formal operations when faced with a problem in chemistry but does so when discussing constitutional issues. Similarly, Tulkin and Konner (1973) suggest that adults in small, tribal societies might fail to demonstrate formal operations on Piagetian tasks of mathematical and scientific reasoning, but they employ them when working on problems of vital importance to them. For example, when Kalahari bush people discuss animal tracking, they advance and weigh hypotheses in ways "that tax the best inferential and analytic capacities of the human mind" (Tulkin and Konner, 1973, p. 35).

Piaget conceded, then, that at the highest stages people will not demonstrate a great deal of consistency across intellectual tasks—certainly not the same degree of consistency that one expects at the earlier stages. Instead, people employ the highest stages of thinking primarily in their areas of strongest interest.

Do Children Really Learn on Their Own?

Perhaps Piaget's most controversial claim is that cognitive development is a spontaneous process. Children, he says, develop cognitive structures on their own, without direct teaching from adults. The most incontestable evidence for spontaneous learning comes from Piaget's observations on infants, who make enormous intellectual progress simply by exploring the environment, before anyone takes the trouble to educate them. Once we begin teaching, in fact, we often seem to stifle the child's natural curiosity. In school, children become distinterested, lazy, rebellious, and frightened of failure. The major task of education, it would seem, would be to liberate the bold curiosity with which children enter life.

When Piaget said children learn on their own, he did not mean that they learn in a vacuum. Other children can stimulate and challenge the child's thinking, and it would seem that adults can do the same. As we have seen, Kamii asks children stimulating questions that start them thinking. But Piaget did not believe that it is particularly productive to try to teach children right answers or procedures. Instead, real learning comes from experiences that arouse children's curiosity and give them the chances to work out their solutions on their own.

Nevertheless, many psychologists, particularly American psychologists in the learning-theory tradition, believe that adult teaching is more important than Piaget thought. To demonstrate this, they have devised a number of "training studies," most of which have tried to teach conservation to four- and five-year olds.

A major finding is that conservation is surprisingly difficult to teach (Flavell, 1963, p. 377; E. Evans, 1975; Liebert et al., 1977, pp. 176–79). It is difficult, for example, to teach conservation by simply explaining and reinforcing the right answers. And if one does succeed on one task, the ability does not always generalize to new tasks. Further, the teaching does not always cut very deep. People have told me how they had apparently taught a child to conserve liquids; however, when they then offered the child a choice between liquids he or she liked to drink (e.g., a soft drink), the child insisted on taking the larger glass.

Nevertheless, it does seem that conservation can be taught. In the first quite successful experiment, Gelman (1969) taught children to conserve number and length by reinforcing them for attending to the most relevant stimuli—for example, the number of objects in a row rather than the row's length. The training worked, and, furthermore, 60 percent of the children showed an immediate new ability to conserve substance and liquid. However, Gelman's training procedure was laborious. The training lasted two days and consisted of 192 trials. One wonders whether such methods accurately reflect the ways in which the children master conservation in their daily lives. One also can wonder about the effect of such training on children's feelings. When children solve problems on their own, they gain confidence in their abilities to make discoveries. When they undergo an intensive training program, in which they are consistently reinforced for responding in a manner in which they would not ordinarily respond, they might learn to mistrust their own powers of thought.

Piaget (1970) added some additional thoughts that are relevant here. We frequently assume that spontaneous development is undesirable because it is slow; direct teaching seems good because it can speed things up. Piaget, however, pointed out that when Gruber examined the development of object permanence in kittens, he found that they progressed through the sequences at a much faster rate than human infants. Yet kittens "do not progress any further and one may wonder whether the slower rate of progress does not . . . make for greater progress ultimately" (p. 111). Piaget also observed that it took Darwin a remarkably long time to formulate his basic ideas, and Piaget wondered whether slowness may sometimes be one of the conditions of fruitful invention. Thus Piaget questioned the assumption that slowness is undesirable, and he further speculated that each child might have his or her own optimal rate for making the transitions through the stages.

Does Piaget Make the Young Child Appear Cognitively Inept?

During the last two decades a number of psychologists, many of whom had conducted training studies (e.g., Gelman, 1979; Bryant, 1974), have mounted another attack. Piaget, they charge, makes the young child appear cognitively inept. Piaget's description of preoperational thought, in particular, focuses on the child's shortcomings; the young child fails to conserve, cannot classify objects, is egocentric, and so forth. This picture, the critics contend, is far too negative and pessimistic. They believe that if we simplify Piaget's tasks, or render them more familiar to children, or give children various kinds of pretraining, young children will demonstrate many of the rational capacities of older children and adults.

For example, Borke (1975) suggests that young children are not as egocentric as Piaget implied. Her research indicates that although three- and four-year-olds have difficulty on Piaget's mountain task, they can perform less egocentrically on simpler versions of the task. Other researchers have produced similar findings. It seems, for example, that even many two-year-olds know that the side of a cube they see is different from the side a person facing them sees (see Gelman and Baillargeon, 1983; and Sroufe and Cooper, 1988, pp. 358–59 for summaries of this research).

Investigators have also tried to demonstrate that young children can think rationally on mathematical and scientific tasks. Gelman (1972), for example, suggests that young children have some capacity to conserve number. Piaget, you will recall, showed that when we shorten or lengthen a row of objects, preoperational children believe the number is changed.

They seem more influenced by the perceptual configuration—the way the row looks—than by logic or number. In Piaget's studies, however, the rows often contained as many as eight objects. Gelman, in contrast, presented three- to five-year-olds with smaller sets of objects—two, three, or four objects—and found that children ignored changes in length and continued to base their judgments on number alone. Thus, they displayed conservation with these small sets.

Gelman's findings, we might note, do not necessarily contradict Piaget. It may be that changing such small rows produces very little perceptual change, so we do not know if young children can ignore perceptual changes in favor of logic or number. Still, Gelman has shown that young children are beginning to think in numerical terms. They are not, she says, as incompetent as Piaget claimed.

In another kind of experiment, Bryant and Trabasso (Bryant, 1974) tried to show that the young child's difficulties with logical inferences are really problems with memory. Piaget had shown that even though the child sees that stick A is shorter than stick B, and that B is shorter than C, the child cannot logically infer that A must be shorter than C. Bryant and Trabasso, however, hypothesized that the young child simply forgets the earlier comparisons. They therefore trained children to remember them, and they found that the children did subsequently seem capable of logical inference. Once again, then, the young child seems less illogical than Piaget suggested.

These are a few of the studies that question Piaget's characterization of the young child's mind. These and many other studies suggest that children as young as three or four years already possess some of the capacities of adults. The research, it should be noted, has met with some criticism, and the findings generally seem more convincing in some areas than in others. The findings do indicate that young children are not invariably egocentric. They may be generally more egocentric than older children or adults, but their egocentrism varies from task to task. The findings with respect to conservation and other kinds of scientific reasoning, in contrast, are often less convincing. On these tasks the young child's rational capacities seem, as Gelman (1979) herself admits, fragile and difficult to elicit. Nevertheless, she and others contend that young children can exhibit the beginnings of rational thought, and Piaget was therefore wrong to portray them as cognitively inept.

Late in his career Piaget responded briefly to this charge that he had characterized young children too negatively. He pointed out (1970) that preoperational thinking also contains some positive components. For example, children during this period recognize qualitative identities, such as the fact that they are the same person as when they were babies. Nevertheless, Piaget continued to maintain that preoperational thought is, on the whole, prelogical, static and perception-bound, irreversible, full of errors, and so on. Thus, he never really made a strong reply to the charge that his view of preoperational thought was negative and pessimistic.

What I would like to do in the following paragraphs is consider this problem from a broadly developmental perspective, as I imagine Rousseau or Werner might have done. First of all, we may note that Piaget's critics seem to equate a "positive" and "optimistic" view of childhood with early and rapid development. We might ask, as Rousseau did, why it is necessarily pessimistic to observe that the development of logical structures takes time. Piaget himself made this point in response to the training studies, and he might have repeated it here.

Furthermore, Piaget's critics assume that thinking is good insofar as it is as rational and logical as ours. They never seriously consider the possibility that the child's thought is *qualitatively different*. Piaget began his research with this possibility in mind, and he provided a compelling picture of how preoperational thought is different. It is governed by perception rather than logic, it is animistic, and so on. Thus, Piaget might have pointed out that preoperational thought is not so much inferior to adult logic as it is a qualitatively different way of viewing the world.

However, Piaget never developed this point. Instead, he became so concerned with comparing preoperational thought to adult logic that he did focus on its deficiencies. In his writings the young child consistently "fails to grasp" basic notions, "continues to make the same mistake," and so on (Piaget and Szeminska, 1941, pp. 142, 13). Piaget did not fully consider preoperational thought on its own terms and appreciate its unique virtues. In particular, he overlooked Werner's insight that a perceptual and animistic (physiognomic) orientation goes hand in hand with an artistic outlook, and it may be this that the young child is developing. As indicated in the preceding chapter, there is evidence (Gardner, 1980) that young children become amazingly good artists. By the age of six or seven years they consistently produce drawings that are fresh, vital, and beautifully organized. After this age their work becomes more geometric, wooden, and lifeless. It seems that logical intelligence is taking over. Moreover, the young child's rich fantasy life and theatrical playfulness also correspond to a mental organization that is more akin to the arts than to logic.

What Piaget might have said, then, is that each period has its own kind of perfection and must be considered in its own terms. The young child may not be much of a logician, but this may not be what the child is primarily about. Young children are developing more of an artistic orientation, and the orientation they develop is so naturally graceful and lively that many great artists have said that they constantly try to recapture it (Gardner, 1973, p. 21). Scientists, too, may implicitly recognize the special qualities of preoperational thought. As Werner observed, scientific inspiration may begin with a return to perceptions and intuitions that are filled with feelings, fantasy, and imagination. Unfortunately, Piaget became so preoccupied with formal logic that he neglected such possibilities.

In summary, then, Piaget did portray preoperational children too negatively, focusing on their logical deficiencies. However, the best way to balance the picture is not necessarily to follow his critics' lead and try to show that young children's thinking is nearly as logical as ours. Instead, we need to consider the possibility that young children's thinking has its own qualities and distinctive virtues.

Conclusion

We see, then, that there are many criticisms of Piaget's theory.   In later chapters we will discuss the debates that other major theorists—Bandura, Vygotsky, and Chomsky—have had with Piaget.   For the present, though, it is worth noting that nearly everyone pits his or her ideas against Piaget's.   This in itself is a testament to the stature of Piaget's theory.   And it is a good bet that when all the dust clears, Piaget's theory will still stand. For whatever its weaknesses, it captures essential aspects of cognitive development.

7

Kohlberg's Stages of Moral Development

BIOGRAPHICAL INTRODUCTION[1]

An outstanding example of research in the Piagetian tradition is the work of Lawrence Kohlberg (1927–1987). Kohlberg focused on moral development and provided a stage theory of moral thinking that goes well beyond Piaget's initial formulations.

Kohlberg grew up in Bronxville, New York, and attended Andover Academy in Massachusetts, an academically demanding private high school. He did not go straight to college but instead went to help the Israeli cause, serving as the second engineer on an old freighter carrying European refugees through British blockades to Israel. After this, in 1948, Kohlberg enrolled at the University of Chicago, where he scored so high on admission tests that he only had to take a limited number of courses to earn his bachelor's degree. This he did in one year. He stayed on at Chicago for graduate work in psychology, at first thinking he would become a clinical psychologist. But he soon became interested in Piaget and began interviewing children and adolescents on moral issues. The result was his doctoral dissertation (1958a), the first rendition of his new stage theory. Kohlberg taught at the University of Chicago from 1962 to 1968 and at Harvard University from 1968 until his death in 1987.

[1]I would like to thank David F. Ricks for his help with this introductory section.

Kohlberg was an informal, unassuming man. When he taught, he frequently came to class dressed in a flannel shirt and baggy pants—as if he had thought it was his day off. He usually began asking questions in an off-the-cuff manner. In the first days of the school year, students didn't always know what to make of him. But they soon saw that they were in the presence of a true scholar, a man who had thought long and deeply about critical issues in philosophy and psychology, and Kohlberg was inviting them to ponder these issues with him. In his lectures and writings, he did much to help others appreciate the wisdom of the "old psychologists," writers such as Rousseau, John Dewey, and James Mark Baldwin.

Unfortunately, Kohlberg suffered from a tropical disease and bouts of depression that caused him intense pain during the last 20 years of his life. At the age of 59, he ended his life by drowning.

PIAGET'S STAGES OF MORAL JUDGMENT

While he was in graduate school, Kohlberg became deeply impressed by Piaget's studies of moral judgment. Piaget, Kohlberg saw, was talking to children about fundamental matters in moral philosophy and was drawing out their real thinking. At the same time, Piaget's work seemed incomplete.

Essentially, Piaget's findings on moral judgment fit into a two-stage theory. Children younger than 10 or 11 years think about moral dilemmas one way; older children consider them differently. As we have seen, younger children regard rules as fixed and absolute. They believe that rules are handed down by adults or by God and that one cannot change them. The older child's view is more relativistic. He or she understands that it is permissible to change rules if everyone agrees. Rules are not sacred and absolute but are devices that humans use to get along cooperatively.

At approximately the same time—10 or 11 years—children's moral thinking undergoes other shifts. Younger children base their moral judgments more on consequences, whereas older children base their judgments on intentions. When, for example, the young child hears about one boy who broke 15 cups trying to help his mother and another boy who broke only one cup trying to steal cookies, the young child thinks that the first boy did worse. The child primarily considers the amount of damage—the consequences—whereas the older child is more likely to judge wrongness in terms of the motives underlying the act (Piaget, 1932, p. 137).

There are many more details to Piaget's work on moral judgment, but he essentially found a series of changes that occur between the ages of 10 and 12, just when the child begins to enter the general stage of formal operations.

Intellectual development, however, does not stop at this point. This is just the beginning of formal operations, which continue to develop at least until age 16. Accordingly, one might expect thinking about moral issues to continue to develop throughout adolescence. Kohlberg therefore interviewed both children and adolescents about moral dilemmas, and he did find stages that go well beyond Piaget's. He uncovered six stages, only the first three of which share many features with Piaget's stages.

KOHLBERG'S METHOD

Kohlberg's (1958a) core sample was comprised of 72 boys from both middle- and lower-class families in Chicago. They were ages 10, 13, and 16. He later added to his sample younger children, delinquents, and boys and girls from other American cities and from other countries (1963, 1970).

The basic interview consists of a series of dilemmas such as the following:

> Heinz Steals the Drug
>
> In Europe, a woman was near death from a special kind of cancer. There was one drug that the doctors thought might save her. It was a form of radium that a druggist in the same town had recently discovered. The drug was expensive to make, but the druggist was charging ten times what the drug cost him to make. He paid $200 for the radium and charged $2,000 for a small dose of the drug. The sick woman's husband, Heinz, went to everyone he knew to borrow the money, but he could only get together about $1,000 which is half of what it cost. He told the druggist that his wife was dying and asked him to sell it cheaper or let him pay later. But the druggist said: "No, I discovered the drug and I'm going to make money from it." So Heinz got desperate and broke into the man's store to steal the drug for his wife. Should the husband have done that? (Kohlberg, 1963, p. 19)

Kohlberg was not really interested in whether the subject said "yes" or "no" to this dilemma but in the reasoning behind the answer. The interviewer wants to know *why* the subject thinks Heinz should or should not have stolen the drug. The interview schedule then asks new questions that help one understand the child's reasoning. For example, children are asked if Heinz had a right to steal the drug, if he was violating the druggist's rights, and what sentence the judge should give him once he was caught. Once again, the main concern is with the reasoning behind the answers. The interview then goes on to give more dilemmas in order to get a good sampling of a subject's moral thinking.

Once Kohlberg had classified the various responses into stages, he wanted to know whether his classification was *reliable*. In particular, he wanted to know if others would score the protocols in the same way. Other judges independently scored a sample of responses, and he calculated the degree to which all raters agreed. This procedure is called *interrater reliability*. Kohlberg found these agreements to be high, as he did in his subsequent work, but whenever investigators use Kohlberg's interview, they should also check for interrater reliability before scoring the entire sample.[2]

KOHLBERG'S SIX STAGES

Level I.   Preconventional Morality

Stage 1.   Obedience and Punishment Orientation.   Kohlberg's stage 1 is similar to Piaget's first stage of moral thought. The child assumes that

---

[2]For a discussion of other forms of reliability, see Colby et al., 1983.

powerful authorities hand down a fixed set of rules which he or she must unquestioningly obey.   To the Heinz dilemma, the child typically says that Heinz was wrong to steal the drug because "It's against the law," or "It's bad to steal," as if this were all there were to it.   When asked to elaborate, the child usually responds in terms of the consequences involved, explaining that stealing is bad "because you'll get punished" (Kohlberg, 1958b).

Although the vast majority of children at stage 1 oppose Heinz's theft, it is still possible for a child to support the action and still employ stage 1 reasoning.   A child might say, "Heinz can steal it because he asked first and it's not like he stole something big; he won't get punished" (see Rest, 1973).   Even though the child agrees with Heinz's action, the reasoning is still stage 1; the concern is with what authorities permit and punish.

Kohlberg calls stage 1 thinking *preconventional* because children do not yet speak as members of society.   Instead, they see morality as something external to themselves—something the big people say they must do (Colby et al., 1987a, p. 16).

Stage 2.   *Individualism and Exchange.*

At this stage children recognize that there is not just one right view that is handed down by the authorities.   Different individuals have different viewpoints.   "Heinz," they might point out, "might think it's right to take the drug, the druggist would not."   Since everything is *relative*, each person is free to pursue his or her *individual* interests.   One boy said that Heinz might steal the drug if he wanted his wife to live, but that he doesn't have to if he wants to marry someone younger and better-looking (Kohlberg, 1963, p. 24).   Another boy said Heinz might steal it because

> maybe they had children and he might need someone at home to look after them.   But maybe he shouldn't steal it because they might put him in prison for more years than he could stand.   (Colby et al., 1987b, p. 208)

What is right for Heinz, then, is what meets his own self-interests.

You might have noticed that children at both stages 1 and 2 talk about punishment.   However, they perceive it differently.   At stage 1 punishment is tied up in the child's mind with wrongness; punishment "proves" that disobedience is wrong.   At stage 2, in contrast, punishment is simply a risk that one naturally wants to avoid.

Although stage 2 respondents sometimes sound amoral, they do have some sense of right action.   There is a notion of *fair exchange* or fair deals.   The philosophy is one of returning favors—"If you scratch my back, I'll scratch yours."   To the Heinz story, subjects often say that Heinz was right to steal the drug because the druggist was unwilling to make a fair deal; he was "trying to rip Heinz off."   Or they might say that he should steal for his wife "because she might return the favor some day" (Colby et al., 1987c, pp. 16–17).

Respondents at stage 2 are still said to reason at the preconventional level because they speak as isolated individuals rather than as members of society.   They see individuals exchanging favors, but there is still no identification with the values of the family or community.

Level II. Conventional Morality

Stage 3. Good Interpersonal Relationships. At this stage children—who are by now usually entering their teens—see morality as more than simple deals. They believe that people should live up to the expectations of the family and community and behave in "good" ways. Good behavior means having good motives and interpersonal feelings such as love, empathy, trust, and concern for others. Heinz, they typically argue, was right to steal the drug because "He was a good man for wanting to save her," and "His intentions were good, that of saving the life of someone he loves." Even if Heinz doesn't love his wife, these subjects often say, he should steal the drug because "I don't think any husband should sit back and watch his wife die" (Kohlberg, 1958b; Colby et al., 1987c, pp. 27–29).

If Heinz's motives were good, the druggist's were bad. The druggist, stage 3 subjects emphasize, was "selfish," "greedy," and "only interested in himself, not another life." Sometimes the respondents become so angry with the druggist that they say that he ought to be put in jail (Colby et al., 1987c, pp. 20–33). A typical stage 3 response is that of Don, age 13:

> It was really the druggist's fault, he was unfair, trying to overcharge and letting someone die. Heinz loved his wife and wanted to save her. I think anyone would. I don't think they would put him in jail. The judge would look at all sides, and see that the druggist was charging too much. (Kohlberg, 1963, p. 25)

We see that Don defines the issue in terms of the actors' character traits and motives. He talks about the loving husband, the unfair druggist, and the understanding judge. His answer deserves the label "conventional morality" because it assumes that the attitude expressed would be shared by the entire community—"anyone" would be right to do what Heinz did (Kohlberg, 1963, p. 25).

As mentioned earlier, there are similarities between Kohlberg's first three stages and Piaget's two stages. In both sequences there is a shift from unquestioning obedience to a relativistic outlook and to a concern for good motives. For Kohlberg, however, these shifts occur in three stages rather than two.

Stage 4. Maintaining the Social Order. Stage 3 reasoning works best in two-person relationships with family members or close friends, where one can make a real effort to get to know the other's feelings and needs and try to help. At stage 4, in contrast, the respondent becomes more broadly concerned with *society as a whole*. Now the emphasis is on obeying laws, respecting authority, and performing one's duties so that the social order is maintained. In response to the Heinz story, many subjects say they understand that Heinz's motives were good, but they cannot condone the theft. What would happen if we all started breaking the laws whenever we felt we had a good reason? The result would be chaos; society couldn't function. As one subject explained,

I don't want to sound like Spiro Agnew, law and order and wave the flag, but if everybody did as he wanted to do, set up his own beliefs as to right and wrong, then I think you would have chaos. The only thing I think we have in civilization nowadays is some sort of legal structure which people are sort of bound to follow. [Society needs] a centralizing framework. (Colby et al., 1987c, p. 89)

Because stage 4 subjects make moral decisions from the perspective of society as a whole, they think from a full-fledged member-of-society perspective (Colby et al., 1987a, p. 17).

You will recall that stage 1 children also generally oppose stealing because it breaks the law. Superficially, stage 1 and stage 4 subjects are giving the same response, so we see here why Kohlberg insisted that we must probe into the reasoning behind the overt response. Stage 1 children say, "It's wrong to steal" and "It's against the law," but they cannot elaborate any further, except to say that stealing can get a person jailed. Stage 4 respondents, in contrast, have a conception of the function of laws for society as a whole—a conception that far exceeds the grasp of the younger child.

Level III.   Postconventional Morality

Stage 5.   Social Contract and Individual Rights.   At stage 4, people want to keep society functioning. However, a smoothly functioning society is not necessarily a good one. A totalitarian society might be well organized, but it is hardly the moral ideal. At stage 5, people begin to ask, What makes for a good society? They begin to think about society in a very theoretical way, stepping back from their own society and considering the rights and values that a society ought to uphold. They then evaluate existing societies in terms of these prior considerations. They are said to take a "prior-to-society" perspective (Colby et al., 1987a, p. 20).

Stage 5 respondents basically believe that a good society is best conceived as a social contract into which people freely enter to work toward the benefit of all. They recognize that different social groups within a society will have different values, but they believe that all rational people would agree on two points. First, they would all want certain basic *rights*, such as liberty and life, to be protected. Second, they would want some *democratic* procedures for changing unfair laws and for improving society.

In response to the Heinz dilemma, stage 5 respondents make it clear that they do not generally favor breaking laws; laws are social contracts that we agree to uphold until we can change them by democratic means. Nevertheless, the wife's right to live is a moral right that must be protected. Thus, stage 5 respondents sometimes defend Heinz's theft in strong language:

It is the husband's duty to save his wife. The fact that her life is in danger transcends every other standard you might use to judge his action. Life is more important than property.

This young man went on to say that "from a moral standpoint," Heinz should save the life of even a stranger, since to be consistent, the value of a life means any life.   When asked if the judge should punish Heinz, he replied:

> Usually the moral and legal standpoints coincide.   Here they conflict.   The judge should weight the moral standpoint more heavily but preserve the legal law in punishing Heinz lightly.   (Kohlberg, 1976, p. 38)

Stage 5 subjects, then, talk about "morality" and "rights" that take some priority over particular laws.   Kohlberg insisted, however, that we do not judge people to be at stage 5 merely from their verbal labels.   We need to look at their social perspective and mode of reasoning.   At stage 4, too, subjects frequently talk about the "right to life," but for them this right is legitimized by the authority of their social or religious group (e.g., by the Bible).   Presumably, if their group valued property over life, they would too.   At stage 5, in contrast, people are making more of an independent effort to think out what any society ought to value.   They often reason, for example, that property has little meaning without life.   They are trying to determine logically what a society ought to be like (Kohlberg, 1981, pp. 21–22; Colby et al., 1987c, pp. 53–55).

Stage 6.   Universal Principles.

Stage 5 respondents are working toward a conception of the good society.   They suggest that we need to (a) protect certain individual rights and (b) settle disputes through democratic processes.   However, democratic processes alone do not always result in outcomes that we intuitively sense are just.   A majority, for example, may vote for a law that hinders a minority.   Thus, Kohlberg believed that there must be a higher stage—stage 6—which defines the principles by which we achieve justice.

Kohlberg's conception of justice followed that of the philosophers Kant and Rawls, as well as great moral leaders such as Gandhi and Martin Luther King.   According to these people, the principles of justice require us to treat the claims of all parties in an impartial manner, respecting the basic dignity of all people as individuals.   The principles of justice are therefore universal; they apply to all.   Thus, we would not vote for a law that aids some people but hurts others.   The principles of justice guide us toward decisions based on an equal respect for all.

In actual practice, Kohlberg said, we can reach just decisions by looking at a situation through one another's eyes.   In the Heinz dilemma, this would mean that all parties—the druggist, Heinz, and his wife—take the roles of the others.   To do this in an impartial manner, people can assume a "veil of ignorance" (Rawls, 1971), acting as if they do not know which role they would eventually occupy.   If the druggist did this, even he would recognize that life must take priority over property; for he wouldn't want to risk finding himself in the wife's shoes with property valued over life.   Thus, they would all agree that the wife must be saved—this would be the fair solution.   Such a solution, we must note, requires not only impartiality, but the principle that everyone is given full and equal respect.   If the wife were considered of less value than the others, a just solution could not be reached.

Until 1975 Kohlberg had been scoring some of his subjects at stage 6, but he then stopped doing so.   One reason was that he and other researchers had found very few subjects who consistently reasoned at this stage. Also, Kohlberg concluded that his interview dilemmas did not draw out differences between stage 5 and stage 6 thinking. Theoretically, stage 6 has a clearer and broader conception of universal principles (including justice as well as individual rights), but the interview did not draw out this broader understanding. So he dropped stage 6 from his manual, calling it a "theoretical stage" and scoring all postconventional responses at stage 5 (Colby et al., 1987a, pp. 35–40).

One issue that would distinguish stage 5 from stage 6 is civil disobedience. Stage 5 would be more hesitant to endorse civil disobedience because of its commitment to the social contract and to changing laws through democratic agreements. Only when an individual right is clearly at stake does violating the law seem justified. At stage 6, in contrast, a commitment to justice makes the rationale for civil disobedience stronger and broader. Martin Luther King argued that laws are only valid insofar as they are grounded in justice, and that a commitment to justice carries with it an obligation to disobey unjust laws. King also recognized, of course, the general need for laws and democratic processes (stages 4 and 5), and he was therefore willing to accept the penalties for his actions. Nevertheless, he believed that the higher principle of justice required civil disobedience (Kohlberg, 1981, p. 43).

Summary

At stage 1 children think of what is right as what authority says is right. Doing the right thing is obeying authority and avoiding punishment. At stage 2 children are no longer so impressed by any single authority; they see that there are different sides to any issue. Since everything is relative, one is free to pursue one's own interests, although it is often useful to make deals and exchange favors with others.

At stages 3 and 4 young people think as members of the conventional society, with its values, norms, and expectations. At stage 3 they emphasize being a good person, which basically means having helpful motives toward people close to one. At stage 4 the concern shifts toward obeying laws to maintain society as a whole.

At stages 5 and 6 people are less concerned with maintaining society for its own sake, and more concerned with the principles and values that make for a good society. At stage 5 they emphasize basic rights and the democratic processes that give everyone a say, and at stage 6 they define the principles by which agreements will be most just.

THEORETICAL ISSUES

How Development Occurs

Kohlberg, it is important to remember, was a close follower of Piaget. Accordingly, Kohlberg's theoretical positions, including that on developmental change, reflected those of his mentor.

Kohlberg (e.g., 1968; 1981, Ch. 3) said that his stages are not the product of maturation. That is, the stage structures and sequences do not simply unfold according to a genetic blueprint.

Neither, Kohlberg maintained, are his stages the product of socialization. That is, socializing agents (e.g., parents and teachers) do not directly teach new forms of thinking. Indeed, it is difficult to imagine them systematically teaching each new stage structure in its particular place in the sequence.

The stages emerge, instead, from our own thinking about moral problems. Social experiences do promote development, but they do so by stimulating our mental processes. As we get into discussions and debates with others, we find our views questioned and challenged and are therefore motivated to come up with new, more comprehensive positions. The stages reflect these broader viewpoints (Kohlberg et al., 1975).

We might imagine, for example, a young man and woman discussing a new law. The man says that everyone should obey it, like it or not, because laws are vital to social organization (stage 4). The woman notes, however, that some well-organized societies, such as Nazi Germany, were not particularly moral. The man therefore sees that some evidence contradicts his view. He experiences some cognitive conflict and is motivated to think about the matter more fully, perhaps moving a bit toward stage 5.

Kohlberg also sometimes spoke of change occurring through role-taking opportunities, opportunities to consider others' viewpoints (e.g., Kohlberg, 1976). As children interact with others, they learn how viewpoints differ and how to coordinate them in cooperative activities. As they discuss their problems and work out their differences, they develop their conceptions of what is fair and just.

Whatever the interactions are specifically like, they work best, Kohlberg said, when they are open and democratic. The less children feel pressured simply to conform to authority, the freer they are to settle their own differences and formulate their own ideas. We will discuss Kohlberg's efforts to induce developmental change in the section on implications for education.

The Stage Concept

Piaget, you will recall, proposed that true mental stages meet several criteria. They (1) are qualitatively different ways of thinking, (2) are structured wholes, (3) progress in an invariant sequence, (4) can be characterized as hierarchic integrations, and (5) are cross-cultural universals. Kohlberg took these criteria very seriously, trying to show how his stages meet them all. Let us consider these points one at a time.

1. Qualitative differences. It seems fairly clear that Kohlberg's stages are qualitatively different from one another. For example, stage 1 responses, which focus on obedience to authority, sound very different from stage 2 responses, which argue that each person is free to behave as he or she wishes. The two stages do not seem to differ along any quantitative dimension; they seem qualitatively different.

2. Structured wholes. By *structured wholes*, Kohlberg means that the stages are not just isolated responses but are *general* patterns of thought that will consistently show up across many different kinds of issues. One gets a sense that this is true by reading through his scoring manual; one finds the same kinds of thinking reappearing on diverse items. For example, one item asks: Why should a promise be kept? As on the Heinz dilemma, children at stage 1 again speak in terms of obedience to rules, whereas those at stage 2 focus on exchanging favors that are in one's self-interest (e.g., "You never know when you're going to need that person to do something for you"). Similarly, as children proceed through the stages, they keep giving responses that are similar to those to the Heinz dilemma (Colby et al., 1987c, pp. 802–54).

In addition, Kohlberg and his co-workers (Colby et al., 1983) have obtained quantitative estimates of the extent to which subjects respond in terms of one particular stage. Since some subjects might be in transition between stages, one does not expect perfect consistency. Nevertheless, Kohlberg found that subjects scored at their dominant stage across nine dilemmas about two-thirds of the time. This seems to be a fair degree of consistency, suggesting the stages may reflect general modes of thought.

3. Invariant sequence. Kohlberg believed that his stages unfolded in an invariant sequence. Children always go from stage 1 to stage 2 to stage 3 and so forth. They do not skip stages or move through them in mixed-up orders. Not all children necessarily reach the highest stages; they might lack intellectual stimulation. But to the extent they do go through the stages, they proceed in order.

Most of Kohlberg's evidence on his stage sequence came from *cross-sectional* data. That is, he interviewed different children at various ages to see if the younger ones were at lower stages than the older ones. Figure 7.1 summarizes this data from his first studies. As you can see, stages 1 and 2 are primarily found at the youngest age, whereas the higher stages become more prevalent as age increases. Thus, the data support the stage sequence.

Cross-sectional findings, however, are inconclusive. In a cross-sectional study, different children are interviewed at each age, so there is no guarantee that any individual child actually moves through the stages in order. For example, there is no guarantee that a boy who is coded at stage 3 at age 13 actually passed through stages 1 and 2 in order when he was younger. More conclusive evidence must come from *longitudinal* studies, in which the same children are followed over time.

The first two major longitudinal studies (Kohlberg and Kramer, 1969; Holstein, 1973) began with samples of teenagers and then tested them at three-year intervals. These studies produced ambiguous results. In both, most subjects either remained at the same stage or moved up one stage, but there were also some who might have skipped a stage. Furthermore, these studies indicated that some subjects had regressed, and this finding also bothered Kohlberg, because he believed that movement through his stages should always be forward.

Kohlberg's response to these troublesome findings was to revise his

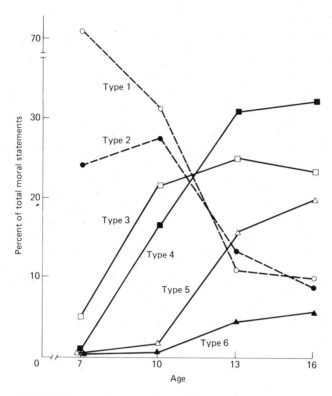

FIGURE 7.1   Use of six types of moral judgments at four ages.   (From Kohlberg, L., The development of children's orientations toward a moral order; I.   Sequence in the development of moral thought.   *Human Development, 6*, 1963, p. 16.   By permission of the publisher.)

scoring method.   He had already become uncomfortable with his first (1958b) scoring manual, believing that it relied too heavily on the *content* of subjects' answers rather than their underlying *reasoning*, and he had made some improvements on it.   So in 1975, after these longitudinal findings emerged, he decided to develop a much more precise and adequate scoring system and, to some extent, to revise his definitions of the stages.

To create the latest scoring manual, Kohlberg and his co-workers (Colby et al., 1983) worked with seven boys from his original (1958) sample who had been retested every three or four years for 20 years.   It was during this work that Kohlberg decided to drop stage 6.

Kohlberg then examined the hypothesis of invariant sequence for 51 other boys from this original sample, who had also been retested at least twice (every three or four years) over the 20-year period.   This time, Kohlberg and his colleagues (Colby et al., 1983) found no stage-skipping, and only about 6 percent of the subjects showed signs of regressing.   Four other longitudinal studies have obtained similar results, although two have found somewhat more regression (up to 15 percent) (see Colby et al., 1983). In general, then, the new longitudinal studies seem to support the invariant-sequence hypothesis.

Kohlberg's new, longitudinal study changed the earlier picture of moral development in other ways. If we look again at Figure 7.1, which depicts the age changes found in Kohlberg's first studies, we see that stage 4 had become the dominant stage by age 16. In the new scoring system, however, it is more difficult to achieve the higher stages—the reasoning must be more clearly demonstrated—and Kohlberg found that stage 4 did not become dominant until the boys were in their 20s and 30s (Figure 7.2). Stage 5, too, only appears in the mid-20s and never becomes very prevalent.

4. *Hierarchic integration.* When Kohlberg said that his stages were hierarchically integrated, he meant that people do not lose the insights gained at earlier stages but integrate them into new, broader frameworks. For example, people at stage 4 can still understand stage 3 arguments, but they now subordinate them to wider considerations. They understand that Heinz had good motives for stealing, but they point out that if we all stole whenever we had a good motive, the social structure would break down. Thus stage 4 subordinates a concern for motives to a wider concern for the society as a whole.

FIGURE 7.2 Mean percentage of moral reasoning at each stage for each age group. (From Colby et al., A longitudinal study of moral judgment. *Monographs of the Society for Research in Child Development*, Serial No. 200, 1983, p. 46. By permission.)

The concept of hierarchic integration was very important for Kohlberg because it enabled him to explain the direction of his stage sequence. Since he was not a maturationist, he could not simply say that the sequence is wired into the genes. So he wanted to show how each new stage provides a broader framework for dealing with moral issues. Stage 4, as mentioned, transcends the limitations of stage 3 and becomes more broadly concerned with social organization. Stage 5, in turn, sees the weakness of stage 4; a well-organized society is not necessarily a moral one. Stage 5 therefore considers the rights and orderly processes that make for a moral society. Each new stage retains the insights of the prior stage, but it recasts them into a broader framework. In this sense, each new stage is more cognitively adequate than the prior stage.

If Kohlberg was right about the hierarchic nature of his stages, we would expect that people would still be able to understand earlier stages but consider them inferior. In fact, when Rest (Rest et al., 1969; Rest, 1973) presented adolescents with arguments from different stages, this is what he found. They understood lower-stage reasoning, but they disliked it. What they preferred was the highest stage they heard, whether they fully understood it or not. This finding suggests, perhaps, that they had some intuitive sense of the greater adequacy of the higher stages.

Werner, we remember from Chapter 4, described hierarchic integration as a process that occurs alongside *differentiation*, and Kohlberg believed his stages represented increasingly differentiated structures as well. Kohlberg pointed out that the stage 5 value on life, for example, has become differentiated from other considerations. Stage 5 respondents say that we ought to value life for its own sake, regardless of its value to authorities (stage 1), its usefulness to oneself (stage 2), the affection it arouses in us (stage 3), or its value within a particular social order (stage 4). Stage 5 subjects have abstracted this value from other considerations and now treat it as a purely moral ideal. Their thinking, Kohlberg said, is becoming like that of the moral philosophers in the Kantian tradition (1981, p. 171).

5. Universal sequence.   Kohlberg, like all stage theorists, maintained that his stage sequence is universal; it is the same in all cultures. At first glance, this proposal might be surprising. Don't different cultures socialize their children differently, teaching them very different moral beliefs?

Kohlberg's response was that different cultures do teach different beliefs, but his stages refer not to specific beliefs but to underlying modes of reasoning (Kohlberg and Gilligan, 1971). For example, one culture might discourage physical fighting, while another encourages it more. As a result, children will have different beliefs about fighting, but they will still reason about it in the same way at the same stage. At stage 1, for example, one child might say that it is wrong to fight when insulted "because you will get punished for it," while another says that "it is all right to fight; you won't get punished." The beliefs differ, but both children reason about them in the same underlying way—in terms of the physical consequences (punishment). They do so because this is what they can cognitively grasp. Later on, the first child might argue that fighting is bad "because if everyone fought all the time there would be anarchy," while the second child argues that "people must defend their honor, because if they don't everyone will be insulting everyone, and the whole society will break down." Once again, the specific beliefs differ, reflecting different cultural teachings, but the underlying reasoning is the same—in this case it is stage 4, where people can consider something as abstract as the social order. Children, regardless of their beliefs, will always move to stage 4 thinking some time after stage 1 thinking because it is cognitively so much more sophisticated.

Kohlberg, then, proposed that his stage sequence is the same in all cultures, for each stage is conceptually more advanced than the next. He and other researchers have given his interview to children and adults in a variety of cultures, including Mexico, Taiwan, Turkey, Israel, the Yucatan, Kenya, the Bahamas, and India. Most of the studies have been cross-sectional, but a few have been longitudinal. The studies have supported Kohlberg's stage sequence. To the extent that children in different cultures move through the stages, they appear to move in order (Edwards, 1981).

At the same time, people in different cultures seem to move through the sequence at different rates and to reach different end-points. In the United States most urban middle-class adults reach stage 4, with a small percentage using some stage 5 reasoning. The picture is fairly similar in urban areas of other countries. In the isolated villages and tribal communities of many countries, however, it is rare to find any adult beyond stage 3 (Edwards, 1981; Cole and Cole, 1989, p. 581).

Kohlberg (Nisan and Kohlberg, 1982) suggested that one can understand these findings in terms of Piagetian theory. Cultural factors, in this theory, do not directly shape the child's moral thought, but they do stimulate thinking. Social experiences can challenge children's ideas, motivating them to come up with new ones. In traditional villages, however, there may be little to challenge a stage 3 morality; the norms of care and empathy work very well in governing the face-to-face interactions of the group. Thus, there is little to stimulate thinking beyond this stage.

When, in contrast, young people leave the village and go off to the city, they witness the breakdown of interpersonal ties. They see that group norms of care and empathy have little impact on the impersonal interactions of city life, and they see the need for a formal legal structure to ensure moral conduct. They begin to think in terms of stage 4 morality. Furthermore, as Keniston (1971) notes, if young people attend the universities, they may take classes in which the teachers deliberately question the unexamined assumptions of their childhoods and adolescences. Thus, they are stimulated to think about moral matters in new ways.

Moral Thought and Moral Behavior

Kohlberg's scale has to do with moral thinking, not moral action. As everyone knows, people who can talk at a high moral level may not behave accordingly. Consequently, we would not expect perfect correlations between moral judgment and moral action. Still, Kohlberg thought that there should be some relationship.

As a general hypothesis, he proposed that moral behavior is more consistent, predictable, and responsible at the higher stages (Kohlberg et al., 1975) because the stages themselves increasingly employ more stable and general standards.   For example, stage 3 bases decisions on others' approval, which can vary, but stage 4 refers to set rules and laws.   Thus, we can expect that moral behavior, too, will become more consistent as people move up the sequence.   Generally speaking, there is some research support for this hypothesis (e.g., with respect to cheating), but the evidence is not clear-cut (Brown and Herrnstein, 1975; Blasi, 1980; Kohlberg and Candee, 1984).

Some research has focused on the relationships between particular stages and specific kinds of behavior.   For example, one might expect that juvenile delinquents or criminals would typically reason at stages 1 or 2, viewing morality as something imposed from without (stage 1) or as a matter of self-interest (stage 2), rather than identifying with society's conventional expectations (stages 3 and 4).   Again, some research supports this hypothesis, but there also are some ambiguous results (Blasi, 1980).

Several studies have examined the relationship between postconventional thinking and student protest.   In a landmark study, Haan et al. (1968) examined the moral reasoning of those who participated in the Berkeley Free Speech Movement in 1964.   Haan found that their thinking was more strongly postconventional than that of a matched sample of nonparticipants, but this finding was not replicated for some other protests, apparently because moral principles were not at stake (Keniston, 1971, pp. 260–61).

Blasi (1980), after reviewing 75 studies, concluded that overall there is a relationship between moral thought and action, but he suggested that we need to introduce other variables to clarify this relationship.   One variable may simply be the extent to which individuals themselves feel the need to maintain consistency between their moral thoughts and actions (Blasi, 1980; Kohlberg and Candee, 1984).

Moral Thought and Other Forms of Cognition

Kohlberg also tried to relate his moral stages to other forms of cognition.   He first analyzed his stages in terms of their underlying cognitive structures and then looked for parallels in purely logical and social thought. For this purpose, he analyzed his own stages in terms of implicit *role-taking capacities*, capacities to consider others' viewpoints (Kohlberg, 1976; see also Selman, 1976; Rest, 1983).

At first, at stage 1 children hardly seem to recognize that viewpoints differ.   They assume that there is only one right view, that of authorities. At stage 2, in contrast, they recognize that people have different interests and viewpoints.   They seem to be overcoming egocentrism; they see that perspectives are relative to the individual.   They also begin to consider how individuals might coordinate their interests in terms of mutually beneficial deals.

At stage 3 people conceptualize role-taking as a deeper, more empathic process; one becomes concerned with the other's feelings.   Stage 4, in turn, has a broader, society-wide conception of how people coordinate their roles through the legal system.

Stages 5 and 6, finally, take a more idealized look at how people might coordinate their interests. Stage 5 emphasizes democratic processes, and stage 6 considers how all parties take one another's perspectives according to the principles of justice.

The moral stages, then, reflect expanded insights into how perspectives differ and might be coordinated. As such, the moral stages might be related to stages of logical and social thought that contain similar insights. So far, the empirical evidence suggests that advances in moral thinking may *rest upon* prior achievements in these other realms (Colby et al., 1987a, pp. 12–15). For example, children seem to advance to stage 2, overcoming their egocentrism in the moral sphere, only after they have made equivalent progress in their logical and social thought. If this pattern is correct, we can expect to find many individuals who are logical and even socially insightful but still underdeveloped in their moral judgment.

IMPLICATIONS FOR EDUCATION

Kohlberg wanted to see people advance to the highest possible stage of moral thought. The best possible society would contain individuals who not only understand the need for social order (stage 4) but can entertain visions of universal principles, such as justice and liberty (stage 6) (Kohlberg, 1970).

How, then, can one promote moral development? Turiel (1966) found that when children listened to adults' moral judgments, the resulting change was slight. This is what Kohlberg might have expected, for he believed that if children are to reorganize their thinking, they must be more active.

Accordingly, Kohlberg encouraged another student, Moshe Blatt, to lead discussion groups in which children had a chance to grapple actively with moral issues (Blatt and Kohlberg, 1975). Blatt presented moral dilemmas that engaged the classes in a good deal of heated debate. He tried to leave much of the discussion to the children themselves, stepping in only to summarize, clarify, and sometimes present a view himself (1975, p. 133). He encouraged arguments that were one stage above those of most of the class. In general, he tried to implement one of Kohlberg's main ideas on how children move through the stages. They do so by encountering views that challenge their thinking and stimulate them to formulate better arguments (Kohlberg et al., 1975).

Blatt began a typical discussion by telling a story about a man named Mr. Jones who had a seriously injured son and wanted to rush him to the hospital. Mr. Jones had no car, so he approached a stranger, told him about the situation, and asked to borrow his car. The stranger, however, refused, saying he had an important appointment to keep. So Mr. Jones took the car by force. Blatt then asked whether Mr. Jones should have done that.

In the discussion that followed, one child, Student B, felt that Mr. Jones had a good cause for taking the car and also believed that the stranger could be charged with murder if the son died. Student C pointed out that the stranger violated no law. Student B still felt that the stranger's behavior was somehow wrong, even though he now realized that it was not legally wrong. Thus, Student B was in a kind of conflict. He had a sense of the wrongness of the stranger's behavior, but he could not articulate this sense in terms that would meet the objection. He was challenged to think about the problem more deeply.

In the end, Blatt gave him the answer. The stranger's behavior, Blatt said, was not legally wrong, but morally wrong—wrong according to God's law (this was a Sunday School class). At this point, Blatt was an authority teaching the "correct" view. In so doing, he might have robbed Student B of the chance to formulate spontaneously his own position. He might have done better to ask a question or to simply clarify the student's conflict (e.g., "So it's not legally wrong, but you still have a sense that it's somehow wrong . . ."). In any case, it seems clear that part of this discussion was valuable for this student. Because he himself struggled to formulate a distinction that could handle the objection, he could fully appreciate and assimilate a new view that he was seeking.

The Kohlberg-Blatt method of inducing cognitive conflict exemplifies Piaget's equilibration model. The child takes one view, becomes confused by discrepant information, and then resolves the confusion by forming a more advanced and comprehensive position. The method is also the dialectic process of Socratic teaching. The students give a view, the teacher asks questions that get them to see the inadequacies of their views, and they are then motivated to formulate better positions.

In Blatt's first experiment, the students (sixth graders) participated in 12 weekly discussion groups. Blatt found that over half the students moved up one full stage after the 12 weeks. Blatt and others have tried to replicate these findings, sometimes using other age groups and lengthier series of classes. As often happens with replications, the results have not been quite so successful; upward changes have been smaller—usually a third of a stage or less. Still, it generally seems that Socratic classroom discussions held over several months can produce changes that, although small, are significantly greater than those found in control groups that do not receive these experiences (Rest, 1983).

One of Blatt's supplementary findings was that those students who reported that they were most "interested" in the discussions made the greatest amount of change. This finding is in keeping with Piagetian theory. Children develop not because they are shaped through external reinforcements but because their curiosity is aroused. They become interested in information that does not quite fit into their existing cognitive structures and are thereby motivated to revise their thinking. Other investigators (Berkowitz and Gibbs, 1985) have begun examining actual dialogues to see if those who become most challenged and involved in the tensions of moral debates are also those who move forward. So far the evidence suggests that this is the case.

Although Kohlberg was committed to the cognitive-conflict model of change, he also developed another strategy—the *just community* approach. Here the focus is not on individuals but on groups. Kohlberg and some of his colleagues (Power and Reimer, 1979) set up a special high school group of about 180 students and encouraged them to function as a de-

mocracy and to think of themselves as a community.   Initially, little community feeling was present.   The group's dominant orientation was stage
2; it treated problems such as stealing as purely individual matters.   If a
boy had something stolen, it was too bad for him.   After a year, however,
the group norms advanced to stage 3; the students now considered stealing
to be a community issue that reflected on the degree of trust and care in
the group.   As a result, stealing and other behavior problems sharply
declined and the students began helping one another in many ways.   Similar projects have produced similar results (Power et al., 1989).

Still, the just community approach has aroused some uneasiness among
Kohlberg's followers.   Although the students are encouraged to participate
in a good deal of democratic decision-making, the adults in the program
actively state their own positions.   When Kohlberg participated, he forcefully urged the students to behave like a true community.   Thus Reimer
and his co-workers (1983) wondered if the adults were not practicing a
kind of indoctrination.   But after discussing the matter with Kohlberg,
they seem convinced that the moral programs are not "indoctrinative . . .
because their particpants are encouraged to think critically, to discuss assumptions, and, when they feel it is necessary, to challenge the teacher's
suggestions" (Reimer et al., 1983, p. 252).

Although the just community approach focuses on the moral orientations of groups, researchers have wondered if the programs produce
changes in individuals.   Power et al. (1989) found that students who participated in the programs for two or three years, compared to similar
students in ordinary high schools, showed greater advances in their moral
judgment scores, but their progress was still modest.   Most advanced from
stage 2 to stage 3.   The researchers advise those who primarily want to
promote moral development in individuals to concentrate on academic
discussions of hypothetical moral dilemmas.   This intervention is easier
than trying to change an entire group.

EVALUATION

Kohlberg, a follower of Piaget, has offered a new, more detailed stage
sequence for moral thinking.   Piaget basically found two stages of moral
thinking, the second of which emerges in early adolescence; Kohlberg
uncovered additional stages that develop well into adolescence and adulthood.   He suggested that some people even reach a postconventional
level of moral thinking where they no longer accept their own society as
given but think reflectively and autonomously about what a good society
should be.

The suggestion of a postconventional morality is unusual in the social
sciences.   Perhaps it took a cognitive-developmentalist to suggest such a
thing.   Although most social scientists have been impressed by the ways in
which societies mold and shape children's thinking, cognitive-developmentalists are more impressed by the capacities for independent thought.
If children engage in enough independent thinking, Kohlberg suggested,
they will eventually begin to formulate conceptions of rights, values, and

principles by which they evaluate existing social arrangements.   Perhaps some will even advance to the kinds of thinking that characterize some of the great moral leaders and philosophers who have at times advocated civil disobedience in the name of universal ethical principles.

Kohlberg's theory has provoked a good deal of criticism.   Not everyone, first of all, is enthusiastic about the concept of a postconventional morality.   Hogan (1973, 1975), for example, feels that it is dangerous for people to place their own principles above society and the law.   It may be that many psychologists react to Kohlberg in a similar way, and that this reaction underlies many of the debates over the scientific merits of his research.

Others have argued that Kohlberg's stages are culturally biased. Simpson (1974), for example, says that Kohlberg has developed a stage model based on the Western philosophical tradition and has then applied this model to non-Western cultures without considering the extent to which they have different moral outlooks.

This criticism may have merit.   One wonders how well Kohlberg's stages apply to the great Eastern philosophies.   One also wonders if his stages do justice to moral development in many traditional village cultures. Researchers find that villagers stop at stage 3, but perhaps they continue to develop moralities in directions that Kohlberg's stages fail to capture.

Another criticism is that Kohlberg's theory is sex-biased, a view that has been thoughtfully expressed by one of Kohlberg's associates and co-authors, Carol Gilligan (1982).   Gilligan observes that Kohlberg's stages were derived exclusively from interviews with males, and she charges that the stages reflect a decidedly male orientation.   For males, advanced moral thought revolves around rules, rights, and abstract principles.   The ideal is formal justice, in which all parties evaluate one another's claims in an impartial manner.   This conception of morality, Gilligan argues, fails to capture the distinctly female voice on moral matters.

For women, Gilligan says, morality centers not on rights and rules but on interpersonal relationships and the ethics of compassion and care.   The ideal is not impersonal justice but more affiliative ways of living.   Women's morality, in addition, is more contextualized; it is tied to real, ongoing relationships rather than abstract solutions to hypothetical dilemmas.

Because of these sex differences, Gilligan says, men and women frequently score at different stages on Kohlberg's scale.   Women typically score at stage 3, with its focus on interpersonal feelings, whereas men more commonly score at stages 4 and 5, which reflect more abstract conceptions of social organization.   Thus, women score lower than men.   If, however, Kohlberg's scale were more sensitive to women's distinctly interpersonal orientations, it would show that women also continue to develop their thinking beyond stage 3.

Gilligan has made an initial effort to trace women's moral development.   Since she believes that women's conceptions of care and affiliation are embedded in real-life situations, she has interviewed women facing a personal crisis—the decision to have an abortion.   Through these interviews, Gilligan has tried to show that women move from a conventional to a postconventional mode of thinking.   That is, they no longer consider their responsibilities in terms of what is conventionally expected of them but in terms of their own insights into the ethics of care and responsibility.

Not everyone agrees with Gilligan's critique. Rest (1983), in particular, argues that Gilligan has exaggerated the extent of the sex differences found on Kohlberg's scale. An evaluation of this question, however, must await closer reviews of the literature.[3]

In the meantime, Gilligan has raised an interesting theoretical possibility. Like Werner, she is suggesting that development may proceed along more than one line. One line of moral thought focuses on logic, justice, and social organization, the other on interpersonal relationships. If this is so, there is the further possibility that these two lines at some point become integrated within each sex. That is, each sex might become more responsive to the dominant orientation of the other. Perhaps, as Gilligan briefly suggests (1982, Ch. 6), this integration is a major task of the adult years. (For further thoughts in this vein, see Chapter 15 on Jung's theory of adult development.)

There are other criticisms of Kohlberg's work. Many of these have to do with empirical matters, such as the problem of invariant sequence, the prevalence of regression, and the relationships between thought and action. Since I have mentioned these earlier, I would like to conclude with a more general question. Kohlberg wrote in a forceful manner and he promoted stage 6 as if it provided the decision-making tools we need for the toughest ethical dilemmas. However, there may be issues that the principles of justice frequently fail to resolve. One such issue is abortion. Stage 6 would ask us to consider the physical life of the fetus as well as all the parties' right to fulfilling lives, but does stage 6 routinely lead to decisions that we feel are right? Kohlberg's students, Reimer et al. (1983, pp. 46–47, 88–89) discuss a stage 6 approach to a hypothetical abortion decision without reaching much of a conclusion. The decision, they say, will have to vary with the situation.[4] Stage 6, of course, is not intended to provide a set of answers—it is a mode of decision-making. Still, Kohlberg sometimes seemed to skim over the incredible difficulty that some ethical problems present—a difficulty that is more directly expressed in the writing of Kant (1788).

But whatever criticisms and questions we might have, there is no doubt that Kohlberg's accomplishment was great. He not only expanded on Piaget's stages of moral judgment, but he did so in an inspiring way. He studied the development of moral reasoning as it might work its way toward the thinking of the great moral philosophers. Few people, to be sure, will grapple with moral issues so long and intently that they will come to think about them in the manner of Socrates, Kant, Gandhi, and Martin Luther King. Nevertheless, Kohlberg's stages provide us with an inspiring vision of where moral development might lead.

[3]While Rest's review of the literature indicates that large sex differences are fairly infrequent, smaller differences may appear with some consistency.

[4]Gilligan's postconventional subjects also fail to reach very satisfactory solutions to this dilemma.

8

Learning Theory:
Pavlov, Watson, and Skinner

We have discussed theorists in the developmental tradition. These theorists believe that key developments are governed by internal forces—by biological maturation or by the individual's own structuring of experience. In this and the following chapter, we will describe the work of some of the theorists in the opposing, Lockean tradition—learning theorists who emphasize the processes by which behavior is formed from the outside, by the external environment.

PAVLOV AND CLASSICAL CONDITIONING

Biographical Introduction

The father of modern learning theory is Ivan Petrovich Pavlov (1849–1936). Pavlov was born in Ryazan, Russia, the son of a poor village priest. Pavlov himself planned to become a priest until the age of 21, when he decided he was more interested in a scientific career. For many years he devoted his attention to physiological investigations, and in 1904 he won the Nobel prize for his work on the digestive system. It was just a little before this time, when Pavlov was 50 years old, that he began his famous work on conditioned reflexes. This new interest came about through an accidental discovery about the nature of salivation in dogs. Ordinarily dogs salivate when food touches their tongues; this is an innate reflex. But Pavlov noticed that his dogs also salivated *before* the food was in their mouths; they salivated when they saw the food coming, or even when they heard approaching footsteps. What had happened was that the reflex had become conditioned to new, formerly neutral stimuli.

For a while Pavlov could not decide whether to pursue the implications of his new discovery or to continue with his earlier research. Finally, after a long struggle with himself, he began studying the conditioning process. Still, Pavlov believed that he was working as a physiologist, not a psychologist. In fact, Pavlov required that everyone in his laboratory use only physiological terms. If his assistants were caught using psychological language—referring, for example, to a dog's feelings or knowledge—they were fined (R. Watson, 1968, pp. 408–12).

Basic Concepts

The classical conditioning paradigm.   In a typical experiment (Pavlov, 1928, p. 104), a dog was placed in a restraining harness in a dark room and a light was turned on. After 30 seconds some food was placed in the dog's mouth, eliciting the salivation reflex. This procedure was repeated several times—each time the presentation of food was paired with the light. After a while the light, which initially had no relationship to salivation, elicited the response by itself. The dog had been conditioned to respond to the light.

In Pavlov's terms (1927, Lectures 2 and 3), the presentation of food was an *unconditioned stimulus* (US); Pavlov did not need to condition the animal to salivate to the food. The light, in contrast, was a *conditioned stimulus* (CS); its effect required conditioning.[1] Salivation to the food was called an *unconditioned reflex* (UR), salivation to the light a *conditioned reflex* (CR). The process itself is called *classical conditioning*.

You might have noticed in this experiment that the CS appeared *before* the US; Pavlov turned on the light before he presented the food. One of the questions he asked was whether this is the best order for establishing conditioning. He and his students discovered that it is. It is very difficult to obtain conditioning when the CS follows the US (Pavlov, 1927, pp. 27–28). Other studies have suggested that conditioning often occurs most rapidly when the CS is presented about one-half second prior to the US (see Schwartz, 1984, p. 71).

Pavlov discovered several other principles of conditioning, some of which we will briefly describe.

Extinction.   A conditioned stimulus, once established, does not continue to work forever. Pavlov found that even though he could make a light a CS for salivation, if he flashed the light alone over several trials, it began to lose its effect. Drops of saliva became fewer and fewer until there

---

[1]Pavlov actually used the terms *conditional* and *unconditional*; they were translated *conditioned* and *unconditioned*, the terms psychologists now generally use.

were none at all.   At this point, extinction had occurred (Pavlov, 1928, p. 297).

Pavlov also discovered that although a conditioned reflex appears to be extinguished, it usually shows some *spontaneous recovery*.   In one experiment (1927, p. 58), a dog was trained to salivate to the mere sight of food — the CS.   (Previously, the dog would salivate only when food was in its mouth.)   Next, the CS alone was presented at three-minute intervals for six trials, and by the sixth trial, the dog no longer salivated.   Thus, the response appeared to have been extinguished.   However, after a two-hour break in the experiment, the presentation of the CS alone once again produced a moderate amount of salivation.   Thus, the response showed some spontaneous recovery.   If one were to continue to extinguish the response, without periodically re-pairing the CS to the US, the spontaneous recovery effect would also disappear.

Stimulus generalization.   Although a reflex has been conditioned to only one stimulus, it is not just that particular stimulus that elicits it.   The response seems to generalize over a range of similar stimuli without any further conditioning (Pavlov, 1928, p. 157).   For example, a dog that has been conditioned to salivate to a bell of a certain tone will also salivate to bells of differing tones.   The ability of the neighboring stimuli to produce the response varies with the degree of similarity to the original CS.   Pavlov believed that we observe stimulus generalization because of an underlying physiological process he called *irradiation*.   The initial stimulus excites a certain part of the brain that then irradiates, or spreads, over other regions of the cerebrum (1928, p. 157).

Discrimination.   Initial generalization gradually gives way to a process of differentiation.   If one continues to ring bells of different tones (without presenting food), the dog begins to respond more selectively, restricting its responses to the tones that most closely resemble the original CS.   One can also actively produce differentiation by pairing one tone with food while presenting another tone without food.   This would be called an experiment in stimulus discrimination (Pavlov, 1927, pp. 118–30).

Higher-order conditioning.   Pavlov showed, finally, that once he had solidly conditioned a dog to a CS, he could then use the CS alone to establish a connection to yet another neutral stimulus.   In one experiment (1927, pp. 33–34), Pavlov's student trained a dog to salivate to a bell and then paired the bell alone with a black square.   After a number of trials, the black square alone produced salivation.   This is called second-order conditioning.   Pavlov found that in some cases he could also establish third-order conditioning, but he could not go beyond this point (1927, p. 34).

Evaluation

In a sense, Pavlov's basic idea was not new.   In the seventeenth century Locke had proposed that knowledge is based on associations.   However, Pavlov went beyond Locke and uncovered several principles of association through empirical experiments.   He took the theory of learning out of the realm of pure speculation. Pavlov, as we shall see, did not discover every-thing there is to know about conditioning; in particular, his brand of con-ditioning seems restricted to a certain range of innate responses. Never-theless, he was the first to put learning theory on a firm scientific footing.

WATSON

Biographical Introduction

The man most responsible for making Pavlovian principles a part of the psychological mainstream was John B. Watson (1878–1958). Watson was born on a farm near Greenville, South Carolina. He said that in school "I was lazy, somewhat insubordinate, and so far as I know, I never made above a passing grade" (1936, p. 271). Nevertheless, he went to college at Furman University and graduate school at the University of Chicago, where he began doing psychological research with animals. After earning his doctorate degree, he took a position at Johns Hopkins University in Baltimore, where he did his most productive work.

In 1913 Watson made a great impact on psychology by issuing a manifesto, "Psychology as the Behaviorist Views It." In this article he argued that the study of consciousness through introspection has no place in psychology as a science. Psychology should abandon "the terms con-sciousness, mental states, mind, content, introspectively verifiable, imagery and the like" (1913, p. 166). Instead, its goal should be "the prediction and control of behavior" (1913, p. 158). In particular, it should only study stimuli, responses, and the formation of habits. In this way psychology could become a science like the other natural sciences.

A year later he read the works of Pavlov and the Russians on con-ditioned reflexes and made Pavlovian conditioning the cornerstone of his thinking. Then, in 1916, Watson began research on young children, be-coming the first major psychologist to apply principles of learning to the problems of development.

In 1929 Watson's academic career came to an abrupt end. He was divorced from his wife, an event that became so widely and sensationally publicized that Johns Hopkins fired him. Watson remarried (Rosalie Ray-nor, a co-worker) and entered the business world. In order to get a good sense of business, he worked for a while as a coffee salesman and a clerk at Macy's. He continued to write, but now for magazines such as *Cosmo-politan*, *Harper's*, and *McCall's* in which he advanced his ideas on child development.

Basic Concepts

Environmentalism. Watson was a behaviorist; he said we should study only overt behavior. He also was an environmentalist and made this famous proposal:

> Give me a dozen healthy infants, well-formed, and my own specified world to bring them up in and I'll guarantee to take any one at random and train

him to become any type of specialist I might select—doctor, laywer, artist, merchant, chief, and yes, even begger-man and thief, regardless of his talents, penchants, tendencies, abilities, vocations, and race of his ancestors. (1924, p. 104)

In the next sentence Watson added that "I am going beyond my facts, and I admit it, but so have the advocates of the contrary and they have been doing it for many thousands of years" (p. 104).

   Study of emotions.   One of Watson's major interests was the conditioning of emotions.   He claimed that at birth there are only three unlearned emotional reactions—fear, rage, and love.   Actually, all we observe are three different physical responses, but for the sake of simplicity we can call them emotions.
   Fear, Watson said (1924, pp. 152–54), is observed when infants suddenly jump or start, breathe rapidly, clutch their hands, close their eyes, fall, and cry.   There are only two unconditioned stimuli that elicit fear. One is a sudden noise; the other is loss of support (as when the baby's head is dropped).   Yet older children are afraid of all kinds of things—strange people, rats, dogs, the dark, and so on.   Therefore it must be that the stimuli evoking most fear reactions are learned.   For example, a little boy is afraid of snakes because he was frightened by a loud scream when he saw one.   The snake became a conditioned stimulus.
   Rage is initially an unlearned response to the restriction of body movement.   If we grab a two-year-old girl, preventing her from going where she wants, she begins to scream and stiffens her body.   She lies down stiff as a rod in the middle of the street and yells until she becomes blue in the face (1924, p. 154).   Although rage is initially a reaction to one situation—being forcibly held—it later is expressed in a variety of situations; children become angry when told to wash their faces, sit on the toilet, get undressed, take a bath, and so on.   Such commands elicit rage because they have been associated with physical restraint in these situations.   The child becomes angry when told to get undressed because this order was initially associated with being forcibly held.
   Love is initially a response that is automatically elicited by the stroking of the skin, tickling, gentle rocking, and patting.   The baby responds by smiling, laughing, gurgling and cooing, and other responses that we call affectionate, good-natured, and kindly (1924, p. 155).   Although Watson had no use for Freud, he noted that such responses "are essentially easy to bring about by the stimulation of what, for lack of a better term, we may call the erogenous zones, such as the nipples, the lips, and the sex organs" (1924, p. 155).
   Infants initially do not love specific people, but they are conditioned to do so.   The mother's face frequently appears along with patting, rocking, and stroking, so it becomes a conditioned stimulus which alone elicits the good feelings toward her.   Later, other people associated with the mother in some way also elicit the same responses.   Thus, tender or positive feelings toward others are learned through second-order conditioning.
   Actually, much of Watson's writing on the emotions was speculation—

and unsystematic speculation at that. He said that the three basic emotions become attached to a variety of stimuli and that "we get marked additions to the responses and other modifications of them" (1924, p. 165), but he said little about how these further developments occur. Where Watson did become specific was in his experimental work. His major experiment was on the conditioning of fear in an 11-month-old infant he called Albert B.

Conditioning fear in Little Albert. Watson and Raynor (Watson, 1924, pp. 159–64) wanted to see if they could condition Albert to fear a white rat. At the beginning of the experiment Albert showed no such fear. Next, the experimenter on four occasions presented the rat and simultaneously pounded a bar behind Albert's head, producing a startle response. On the fifth trial Albert was shown the rat alone, and he puckered his face, whimpered, and withdrew. He had been conditioned to fear the rat. For good measure, the experimenter combined the rat and the pounding twice more, and on the next trial, when the rat was again presented alone, Albert cried and tried to crawl away as rapidly as he could.

A few days later, Watson and Raynor tested for stimulus generalization. They found that although Albert played with many objects, he feared anything furry. He cried or fretted whenever he saw a rabbit, dog, fur coat, cotton wool, or a Santa Claus mask, even though he previously had not been afraid of these things. Thus Albert's fear had generalized to all furry objects.

Practical Applications

One of Watson's major practical innovations was a method for deconditioning fears. He was not able to decondition Albert of his new fears, because Albert was an orphan who was adopted and taken out of town before this could be attempted. But Watson advised one of his colleagues, Mary Cover Jones, on procedures for eliminating the fears of another little boy, a three-year-old called Peter.

Peter seemed active and healthy in every respect except for his fears. He was scared of white rats, rabbits, fur coats, feathers, cotton wool, frogs, fish, and mechanical toys. As Watson noted, "One might well think that Peter was merely Albert B. grown up, but Peter was a different child whose fears were 'home grown' " (1924, p. 173).

Jones tried a variety of methods, including having Peter watch other children play with a rabbit. But the procedure that she and Watson highlighted was the following. Peter was placed in his highchair and given a mid-afternoon snack. Then a caged white rabbit was displayed at a distance that did not disturb him. The next day, the rabbit was brought increasingly closer, until he showed a slight disturbance. That ended the day's treatment. The same thing was done day after day; the rabbit was brought closer and closer, with the experimenter taking care never to disturb Peter very much. Finally, Peter was able to eat with one hand while playing with the rabbit with the other. By similar means, Jones eliminated most of Peter's other fears as well.

In contemporary terms, Jones's technique is known as a form of *be-*

havior modification called *systematic desensitization* (see Wolpe, 1969). The subject is relaxed and gradually introduced to the feared stimulus. The experimenter makes sure that the subject is at no time made to feel too anxious. Gradually, then, the subject learns to associate relaxed feelings, rather than fear, to the object or situation.

Watson did not confine his advice to therapeutic procedures for eliminating fears. He also had much to say on child-rearing, which he wanted to turn into a scientific enterprise. Watson recommended, among other things, that parents place babies on rigid schedules, and he insisted that they refrain from hugging, kissing, or caressing their babies. For when they do so, their children soon associate the very sight of the parent with indulgent responses and never learn to turn away from the parent and explore the world on their own (Watson, 1928, p. 81). Watson's advice was quite influential in the 1930s, but it was too extreme to last; under the influence of Spock, Bowlby, and others, parents relaxed their schedules and became more affectionate with their children. Nevertheless, Watson's more general goal—that of placing child-training on the firm foundation of scientific learning principles—remains a vital part of child care in the United States.

Evaluation

Largely because of Watson's efforts, the classical conditioning paradigm became a cornerstone of psychological theory. It would seem that many of our reactions to objects and people develop through this conditioning process (see Liebert et al., 1977).

At the same time, we need to note that the model has certain limitations. For one thing, researchers have found it much more difficult to condition infants' responses than Watson implied. This seems particularly true during the first month of life (Sameroff and Cavanaugh, 1979; Lamb and Campos, 1982). Perhaps classical conditioning becomes easier once infants have developed what Piaget calls primary circular reactions. Once they can coordinate sensori-motor actions (e.g., look at what they hear), they might more readily learn to make various associations.

There also seem to be limitations to the kinds of conditioned stimuli humans will learn. When, for example, researchers attempted to classically condition infants to fear objects such as curtains and wooden blocks instead of rats, they had great difficulty. Perhaps humans are innately disposed to fear certain stimuli. There may be biological constraints on the kinds of stimuli we will associate with different responses (Seligman, 1972; Harris and Liebert, 1984, pp. 108–9).

From a learning theory perspective, finally, classical conditioning seems limited to certain kinds of responses. It seems to apply best to the conditioning of reflexes and innate responses (which may include many emotional reactions). It is questionable whether this kind of conditioning can also explain how we learn such active and complex skills as talking, using tools, dancing, or playing chess. When we master such skills, we are not limited to inborn reactions to stimuli, but we engage in a great deal of free, trial-and-error behavior, finding out what works best. Accordingly, learning theorists have developed other models of conditioning, the most influential of which is that of B. F. Skinner.

SKINNER AND OPERANT CONDITIONING

Biographical Introduction

B. F. Skinner (1905–1990) grew up in the small town of Susquehanna, Pennsylvania. As a boy, he liked school and enjoyed building things, such as sleds, rafts, and wagons. He also wrote stories and poetry. After graduating from high school, he want to Hamilton College in New York. There he felt somewhat out of place, but he graduated Phi Beta Kappa with a major in English literature.

Skinner spent the next two years trying to become a writer, but he eventually decided that he could not succeed because "I had nothing important to say" (1967, p. 395). Because he was interested in human and animal behavior, he enrolled in the graduate psychology department at Harvard, where he began doing research and formulating his ideas on learning. Skinner taught at the University of Minnesota (1936–1945), Indiana University (1945–1947), and Harvard (1947 until his death in 1990).

Despite his successful career as a scientist, Skinner never completely abandoned his earlier interests. For one thing, he continued to display his boyhood enthusiasm for building things. When his first child was born, he decided to make a new, improved crib. This crib, which is sometimes called his "baby box," is a pleasantly heated place that does away with the necessity of excessive clothing and permits freer movement. It is not, as is sometimes thought, an apparatus for training babies. It is simply a more comfortable crib. Skinner's literary interests also reemerged. In 1948 he published a novel, *Walden Two*, which describes a utopian community based on his principles of conditioning.

The Operant Model

Like Watson, Skinner was a strict behaviorist. He believed that psychology should dispense with any references to intangible mental states (such as goals, desires, or purposes); instead, it should confine itself to the study of overt behavior. Like Watson, in addition, Skinner was an environmentalist; although Skinner recognized that organisms enter the world with genetic endowments, he was primarily concerned with how environments control behavior.

In contrast to Watson, however, Skinner's primary model of conditioning was not Pavlovian. The responses that Pavlov studied, Skinner said, are best thought of as *respondents*. These are responses that are automatically "elicited" by known stimuli. For example, the ingestion of food automatically elicits salivation, and a loud noise automatically elicits a startle response. Most respondents are probably simple reflexes.

A second class of behavior, which most interested Skinner, is called *operant.* In operant behavior, the animal is not harnessed in, like Pavlov's dogs, but moves freely about and "operates" on the environment. For example, in early experiments by Thorndike (1905), cats in a puzzle box would sniff, claw, and jump about until they hit upon the response—pulling a latch—that enabled them to get food. The successful response would then be more likely to recur. In such cases, we cannot always identify any prior stimulus that automatically elicits the responses. Rather, animals emit responses, some of which become more likely in the future because they have led to favorable *consequences.* Behavior, in Skinner's terms, is controlled by the reinforcing stimuli that follow it (Skinner, 1938, pp. 20–21; 1953, pp. 65–66). The two models, respondent and operant, are diagrammed in Figure 8.1.

To study operant conditioning, Skinner constructed an apparatus that is commonly referred to as a "Skinner box." This is a fairly small box in which an animal is free to roam about (see Figure 8.2). At one end there is a bar (lever) which, when pressed, automatically releases a pellet of food or water. The animal, such as a rat, at first pokes around until it eventually presses the bar, and then it gets the reward. As time goes on, it presses the bar more frequently. The most important measure of learning, for Skinner, is the *rate* of responding; when responses are reinforced, their rates of occurrence increase. In Skinner's apparatus, the bar-presses are automatically registered on a graph, so the experimenter need not be present much of the time. The data are presented as a learning curve, illustrated in Figure 8.3.

Skinner believed that operant behavior, in comparison to respondent behavior, plays a much greater role in human life. When we brush our teeth, drive a car, or read a book, our behavior is not automatically elicited by a specific stimulus. The mere sight of a book, for instance, does not elicit reading in the same way a bright light automatically elicits an eyeblink. We may or may not read the book, depending upon the consequences that have followed in the past. If reading books has brought us rewards, such as high grades, we are likely to engage in this behavior. Behavior is determined by its consequences (Munn et al., 1974, p. 208).

Principles of Conditioning

Reinforcement and extinction. Skinnerians have performed numerous experiments showing that human behavior, beginning in infancy, can be controlled by reinforcing stimuli. For example, infants increase their

FIGURE 8.1   Respondent and Operant Conditioning. In respondent (Pavlovian) conditioning, stimuli precede responses and automatically elicit them. In operant conditioning, the initial stimuli are not always known; the organism simply emits responses that are controlled by reinforcing stimuli (S_RS) that follow.

Respondent conditioning   Operant conditioning

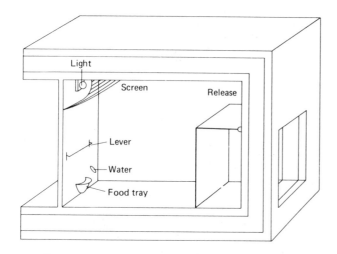

FIGURE 8.2 A Skinner Box. One side has been cut away to show the part occupied by the animal. (From Skinner, B. F., *The Behavior of Organisms*, p. 49. Copyright 1938, renewed 1966. Reprinted by permission of Prentice-Hall, Inc.)

rates of sucking when sucking results in sweet, as opposed to nonsweet, liquid (Lipsitt, 1975). Similarly, infants' rates of smiling and vocalizations can be increased by making the behavior contingent upon rewards, such as the experimenter's smiles, caresses, and attention (Brackbill, 1958; Rheingold et al., 1959).

In such experiments, one is dealing with different kinds of reinforcers. Some reinforcers, such as food or the removal of pain, are *primary reinforcers*; they have "natural" reinforcing properties. Other reinforcing stimuli, such as an adult's smiles, praise, or attention, are probably *conditioned reinforcers*; their effectiveness stems from their frequent association with primary reinforcers (Skinner, 1953, p. 78).

Operant behavior, like respondent behavior, is also subject to *extinction* (1953, p. 69). For example, because children do things "just to get attention" (1953, p. 78), one can extinguish undesirable behaviors, such as excessive crying or temper tantrums, by consistently withdrawing one's attention whenever they occur (Williams, 1959; Etzel and Gewirtz, 1967).

Operant behavior that has apparently been extinguished may also show *spontaneous recovery*. For example, a little boy whose temper tantrums had been extinguished through the withdrawal of attention began having tantrums once again when placed in a new situation (Williams, 1959). The behavior had to be extinguished further.

FIGURE 8.3
A Typical Learning Curve. (From Skinner, B. F. *The Behavior of Organisms*, Copyright 1938. Renewed 1966. Reprinted by permission of Prentice-Hall, Inc.)

Immediacy of reinforcement.   Skinner (1953, p. 101; 1959, p. 133) found that he could initially establish responses at the highest rates when he reinforced them promptly.   A rat will begin pressing a bar at a high rate only if it has promptly received a food pellet each time it has done so. As Bijou and Baer (1961, p. 44) point out, this principle has importance for child-rearing.   If a father shows pleasure immediately after his son brings him the newspaper, the boy is likely to repeat the behavior the next evening.   If, however, the father is so engrossed in something else that he delays reinforcing his son's behavior for a few minutes, the boy's behavior will not be strengthened.   In fact, what gets strengthened is the boy's behavior at the moment of reinforcement.   If he is building blocks at that moment, it is block-building, not newspaper-fetching, that gets reinforced.

Discriminative stimuli.   We have said that operant conditioning may be described without any reference to initiating stimuli.   This is true, but it does not mean that such stimuli are unimportant.   Stimuli that precede responses may gain considerable control over them.

For example, Skinner (1953, pp. 107–8) reinforced a pigeon each time it stretched its neck.   At this point Skinner had no knowledge of any initial stimulus; he simply waited for the pigeon to emit the response and then reinforced it.   Next, however, he reinforced the response only when a signal light was on.   After a few trials, the pigeon stretched its neck much more frequently when the light was flashing than when it was off.   The flashing light had become a *discriminative stimulus*.   The light controlled the behavior because it set the occasion upon which the behavior was likely to be reinforced.

Skinner (1953, pp. 108–9) listed numerous examples to show how everyday behavior becomes attached to discriminative stimuli.   In an or-chard in which red apples are sweet and all others are sour, redness becomes a stimulus that sets the occasion upon which picking and eating will produce favorable outcomes.   Similarly, we learn that a smile is an occasion upon which approaching another will meet with a positive response.   When others frown, the same approach meets with aversive consequences, such as rebuffs.   Insofar as this is true, the facial expressions of others become discriminative stimuli that control the likelihood that we will approach them.

Although discriminative stimuli do exert considerable control, it must be emphasized that this control is not automatic, as in the case of respondent conditioning.   In Pavlov's experiments, prior stimuli automatically elicit responses; in operant conditioning, such stimuli only make responses more *likely*.

Generalization.   In operant conditioning, as in respondent condi-tioning, there is a process of *stimulus generalization* (Skinner, 1953, p. 132). Suppose a little girl has been reinforced for saying "Da da" at the sight of her father, but not when she is looking at her mother or siblings.   The father has become a discriminative stimulus.   It is not unusual, however, to find the girl saying "Da da" when she sees any man at all, such as strangers on the street.   The stimulus has generalized.   Her parents must now teach her to make a finer discrimination. They might say, "That's right," when she utters "Da da" in the presence of her father, but not when she looks at any other man.

Similarly, we can observe *response generalization*. It has been shown, for example, that when children are reinforced for using one part of speech, such as plurals, they begin uttering new plurals—even though they haven't received reinforcement for those particular words. Reinforcement influences not only particular responses but those of the same general class (Lovaas, 1977, pp. 112–13).

Shaping. Operant behavior is not acquired in all-or-nothing packages. It is usually learned gradually, little by little. Even teaching a pigeon to peck a spot on the wall, Skinner (1953, p. 92) showed, must be gradually shaped. If we place a pigeon in a box and wait for it to peck the spot, we may have to wait days or even weeks. Much of the time, the pigeon doesn't even approach the spot. So we must shape its behavior. First, we give the bird food when it turns in the direction of the spot. This increases the frequency of this behavior. Next, we withhold food until it makes a slight movement in the right direction. We then keep reinforcing positions closer and closer to the spot, until the bird is facing it. At this point we can reinforce head movements, first giving food for any forward movement and finally reinforcing the bird only when it actually pecks the spot. Through this procedure we gradually shape the desired response. Shaping is also called the "method of approximations," because reinforcement is made contingent upon better and better approximations of the desired response.

We probably teach many human skills in this bit-by-bit shaping process. When we teach a boy to swing a baseball bat, we first say "Good" when he gets his hands into the right grip. We then say "Right" when he lifts his bat in the correct position over his shoulder. We then work on his stance, a level swing, and so on—gradually shaping the complete behavior.

Behavior chains. Although behavior may be shaped bit by bit, it also develops into longer, integrated response-chains. For example, batting in baseball involves picking up the bat, getting the right grip and stance, watching for the right pitch, swinging, running the bases, and so on. Skinnerians attempt to examine each step in terms of reinforcements and stimuli. Reaching for the bat is reinforced by obtaining it, which also serves as a stimulus for the next act, getting the right grip. Once the hands are placed on the bat, one gets a certain "feel" which one recognizes as the proper grip. This "feel" is a reinforcement, and it also signals the next action, pulling the bat over the shoulder. A little later, the sensation of the bat squarely striking the ball is a reinforcement for the swing, and it also signals the next action, running the bases. When a boy or girl has become a good hitter, the entire sequence is often performed in a smooth, integrated fashion (see Reynolds, 1968, pp. 53–56; Munn et al., 1974, pp. 220–24; and Schwartz, 1984, for accounts of chaining sequences).

Schedules of reinforcement. Skinner (1953, p. 99) observed that our everyday behavior is rarely reinforced *continuously*, every time; instead, it is reinforced *intermittently*. We do not find good snow every time we go skiing or have fun every time we go to a party. Accordingly, Skinner studied the effects of different schedules of intermittent reinforcement.

Intermittent reinforcement may be set up on a *fixed-interval* schedule, such that the organism receives a reward for the first response after a specified period of time. For instance, a pigeon receives food after pecking a disc, but must wait three minutes before its next peck is rewarded, then three more minutes, and so on. The rate of responding on this schedule is generally low. Higher rates are produced by *fixed-ratio* schedules, as when the pigeon gets food after every fifth peck. On both schedules, however, there is a lull in responding immediately after reinforcement. It is as if the organism knows it has a long way to go before the next reinforcement (Skinner, 1953, p. 103). Students often experience this effect immediately after completing a long term paper—it is difficult to get started on another assignment.

The lulls produced by fixed schedules can be avoided by varying reinforcement in unpredictable ways. On *variable-interval* schedules, reinforcement is administered after an average length of time, but the intervals are mixed up. With *variable-ratio* schedules, we vary the number of responses needed to produce a reward. When put on these two schedules, organisms consistently respond at high rates, especially on variable-ratio schedules. They keep responding because a reward might come at any time.

One of Skinner's most important findings is that intermittently reinforced behavior, in comparison to that which is continuously reinforced, is much more difficult to extinguish. This is why many of our children's undesirable behaviors are so difficult to stop. We might be able to resist a child's nagging or demanding behavior most of the time, but if we yield every once in a while, the child will persist with it (Bijou and Baer, 1961, p. 62).

If we wish to begin teaching a desirable form of behavior, it is usually best to begin with continuous reinforcement; this is the most efficient way to get the behavior started. However, if we also wish to make the behavior last, we might at some point switch to an intermittent schedule (Bijou and Baer, 1961, p. 62).

Negative reinforcement and punishment.   So far we have been focusing on positive reinforcement. Reinforcement means strengthening a response (increasing its rate), and positive reinforcements strengthen responses by adding positive consequences such as food, praise, or attention. Responses may also be strengthened through *negative reinforcement*, by removing unpleasant or aversive stimuli. Basically, what is strengthened in this way is the tendency to escape, as when a girl standing on a diving board learns to escape the taunts of her peers by diving into the water (Skinner, 1953, pp. 73, 173).

When we *punish*, on the other hand, we do not try to strengthen behavior but to eliminate it. Punishment, Skinner said, is "the commonest technique of control in modern life. The pattern is familiar: if a man does not behave as you wish, knock him down; if a child misbehaves, spank him; if the people of a country misbehave, bomb them" (1953, p. 182).

Punishment, however, does not always work. In an early experiment, Skinner (1938) found that when he punished rats for bar-pressing (by having the bar swing back and smack them on the legs), he only temporarily suppressed the response. In the long run, punishment did not eliminate the response any faster than did extinction. Other studies (e.g., Estes, 1944) have obtained similar results, and the findings conform to everyday experience. Parents who hit their children get them to behave for a while, but the parents find that the misconduct reappears later on.

Skinner also objected to punishment because it produces unwanted side effects. A child who is scolded in school may soon appear inhibited and conflicted. The child seems torn between working and avoiding work because of the feared consequences. The boy or girl may start and stop, become distracted, and behave in other awkward ways (Skinner, 1953, pp. 190–91).

Some researchers believe that Skinner overstated the case against punishment. In some instances punishment will in fact completely eliminate responses. This is especially true when the punishment is extremely painful. Also, punishment can be effective when it is promptly administered, and when the organism can make alternative responses that are then rewarded (Liebert et al., 1977, pp. 138–41). Nevertheless, the effects of punishment are often puzzling and undesirable.

Skinner recommended that instead of punishing children, we try extinction. "If the child's behavior is strong only because it has been reinforced by 'getting a rise out of' the parent, it will disappear when this consequence is no longer forthcoming" (1953, p. 192). Skinnerians often suggest that we combine extinction for undesirable behavior with positive reinforcement for desirable behavior. In one study, teachers simply ignored nursery school children whenever they were aggressive and gave them praise and attention whenever they were peaceful or cooperative. The result was a quieter classroom (P. Brown and Elliot, 1965).

Internal Events: Thoughts, Feelings, and Drives

Thoughts. It is sometimes said that Skinner proposed an "empty organism" theory. He examines only overt responses and ignores internal states. This characterization is accurate but slightly oversimplified. Skinner did not deny that an inner world exists. We do have inner sensations, such as the pain from a toothache. We also can be said to think. Thinking is merely a weaker or more covert form of behavior. For example, we may talk to ourselves silently instead of out loud, or we may think out our moves silently in a chess game. However, such private events have no place in scientific psychology unless we can find ways of making them public and measuring them (Skinner, 1974, pp. 16–17, and Ch. 7).

Skinner was particularly distressed by our tendency to treat thoughts as the causes of behavior. We say that we went to the store because "we got an idea to do so" or that a pigeon pecked a disc because it "anticipated" food.   However, we are in error when we speak in this way.   We go to stores, and pigeons peck discs, only because these actions have led to past reinforcements.   Any discussion of goals or expectations is superfluous. Worse, it diverts us from the true explanation of behavior—the controlling effect of the environment (Skinner, 1969, pp. 240–41; 1974, pp. 68–71).

Feelings.   Skinner acknowledged that we have emotions, just as we have thoughts.   However, feelings do not cause behavior any more than thoughts do.   We might say we are going to the movies because "we want to" or because "we feel like it," but such statements explain nothing.   If we go to the movies, it is because this behavior has been reinforced in the past (Skinner, 1971, p. 10).

Emotional responses themselves can be explained according to learning-theory principles.   In our discussion of Watson, we saw how emotional reactions might be learned through classical conditioning.   Skinner believes that an operant analysis is also useful.   Many emotions are the by-products of different reinforcement contingencies.   Confidence, for example, is a by-product of frequent positive reinforcement.   When we learn to hit a baseball sharply and consistently, we develop a sense of confidence and mastery (Skinner, 1974, p. 58).   Conversely, we become depressed and lethargic when reinforcements are no longer forthcoming.   On certain fixed-ratio or fixed-interval schedules we find it difficult to get going after receiving a reward because further rewards will not be coming for some time (1974, p. 59).

An operant analysis also helps us understand why various patterns of emotional behavior persist.   If a little girl persistently behaves in an aggressive manner, it is important to know the consequences of this behavior. Do her actions succeed in getting attention or other children's toys?   If so, her aggressiveness is likely to continue.   Similarly, if displays of happiness, meekness, sympathy, fearfulness, and other emotional responses persist, it is because they have produced positive consequences (Bijou and Baer, 1961, pp. 73–74; Skinner, 1969, pp. 129–30).

Skinner believed, then, that we can understand emotions if we look at them as the products of environmental control.   It is useless to consider emotions as intrapsychic causes of behavior, as the Freudians do.   For example, a Freudian might talk about a man who fears sex because of anticipated punishment from an internal agency, the superego.   To Skinner, such discussions get us nowhere.   If we wish to understand why a person avoids sex, we must look at the past consequences of his sexual behavior (Skinner, 1974, Ch. 10).

Drives.   Skinner's refusal to look for causes of behavior within the organism led to certain difficulties.   In particular, he had trouble with the concept of drive.   Drives, such as hunger or thrist, would seem to refer to internal states that motivate behavior, and Skinner himself deprived his animals of food and water in order to make reinforcements effective.

Skinner argued that we do not need to conceive of drives as inner states, either mental or physiological.   We simply specify the hours we deprive an animal of food or water and examine the effect of this operation on response rates (Skinner, 1953, p. 149).

Still, the drive concept has remained a thorn in the side of Skinnerians, and they have therefore searched for ways of conceptualizing reinforcement without reference to this concept. One interesting proposal has been made by Premack (1961), who suggests that we think of reinforcement simply as the momentary probability of a response. Behavior that has a high probability of occurrence at the moment can serve as a reinforcer for behavior with a lower probability. If children are supposed to be eating their dinner but are busy playing instead, playing can be used as a reinforcer for eating. We simply say, "Eat some dinner and then play some more" (Homme and Totsi, 1969). Conceptualized in this way, eating and drinking have no special status as reinforcers. Eating and drinking, like any other actions, may or may not be good reinforcers, depending on their probabilities of occurrence at a particular time.

Species-Specific Behavior

Skinner argued, then, that we need not look inside the organism for the causes of behavior. Behavior is controlled by the external environment. There do seem to be, however, certain limitations to environmental control. As we briefly mentioned in our evaluation of Watson, each species has a particular genetic endowment that makes it easier to teach it some things rather than other things. Operant research has found, for example, that it is hard to teach a rat to let go of objects, and it is hard to shape vocal behavior in nonhuman species (Skinner, 1969, p. 201). There are, as learning theorists increasingly say, biological "constraints" on what a species can learn.

In practice, Skinnerians often deal with species-specific behavior as the *topography* of a response. That is, the experimenter maps out a description of the behavior he or she can work with—for example, vocal behavior in humans. The topography is merely a description and does not constitute the most important part of the analysis, which is the way reinforcements shape and maintain behavior. Nevertheless, the topography is essential (Skinner, 1969, pp. 199–209).

In a larger sense, Skinner argued, even species-specific behavior is a product of environmental contingencies. For such behavior has become, in the course of evolution, part of the species' repertoire because it has helped that species survive in a certain environment. Thus, environments selectively reinforce all behavior—not only that in an animal's lifetime, but that in its species' evolutionary past (Skinner, 1969, pp. 199–209).

Practical Applications

Behavior modification. Skinner's research readily lends itself to practical applications, as we have seen in many of our illustrations. We mentioned how Skinnerians might extinguish temper tantrums or get an unruly class to behave. The use of operant techniques to correct behavior problems is a branch of behavior modification. Operant techniques supplement the systematic desensitization procedures first employed by Watson and Jones.

Mental health workers have used operant techniques to treat a variety of behavior problems, from temper tantrums and bedwetting to phobias and shyness (Schwartz, 1984, Ch. 7). An impressive example is Lovaas's (1973) work with autistic children. Autistic children, as we shall see in Chapter 13, are extremely isolated and engage in bizarre behaviors such as self-stimulation (e.g., spinning an ashtray for hours on end). Many are mute, and others are echolalic—they merely echo what one says. Some engage in self-injurious behavior, such as biting themselves.

Lovaas uses operant techniques to gain control over the children's behavior so he can change it. He tries to eliminate socially inappropriate behavior and reinforce socially appropriate behavior (Lovaas et al., 1973). If a child engages in echolalia, self-stimulation, or self-injurious behavior, Lovaas punishes the child or withdraws attention. If the child does something more appropriate, such as emitting correct speech, Lovaas gives the child a reward. In the case of speech, the autistic children often talk so little and poorly that their behavior must be very gradually shaped. At first they are rewarded for sounds that only roughly resemble words, and then they are gradually reinforced for better and better approximations.

In Chapter 13, we will consider Bettelheim's psychoanalytic treatment of autistic children. Bettelheim's therapy was very different. He didn't try to control the children's behavior, but he put his faith in intrinsic growth forces, letting the children take the lead. He tried to create a loving environment and allowed the children to take their own steps toward health. Thus the Bettelheim chapter will illustrate how the two theoretical approaches—Skinnerian and psychoanalytic—differ in practice. For the moment, though, it is important to note that both Lovaas and Bettelheim have had outstanding success with these severely disturbed children. Although Lovaas's success is more objectively documented, it is safe to say that both have helped a third or more of the children they have treated to make reasonably good social adjustments—an outcome that seemed impossible prior to their work.

Programmed instruction.   Skinner also made a significant contribution to the education of normal children through his invention of teaching machines and programmed instruction (Skinner, 1968). The teaching machine was a simple apparatus that permitted one to read a brief passage, answer questions, and then, by turning a knob, see if one were correct. Actually, the machine itself was far less important than the programmed material it contained, and today the material is presented in simple booklet form or installed in a computer. To get an idea of how programmed instruction works, read the material below[2] and pretend to fill in the blanks. As you do so, cover the answers on the left side with a piece of paper, sliding it down just far enough to check your answers.

---

[2]From Munn, N. L., Fernald, L. D., and Fernald, P. S., *Introduction to Psychology*, 3rd ed., Boston: Houghton Mifflin Co., 1974, pp. 249–50. By permission of the publisher.

small

small steps

active

active participation

small steps
active participation

knowledge

immediate
of results

immediate
knowledge of results

small steps
active participation
immediate knowledge
of results

1. Programmed instruction involves several basic principles of learning. One of these, called the principle of *small steps*, is based on the premise that new information must be presented in ＿＿ steps.

2. The learner gradually acquires more and more information, but always in ＿＿ ＿＿ .

3. Because active readers generally acquire more knowledge than passive readers, programmed instruction also is based on the principle of *active participation*. Writing key words as one is reading involves the principle of ＿＿ participation.

4. While reading a book, an uninterested learner may slip into a passive state and discover that he cannot recall what he has just "read." In using programmed instruction the learner is prompted to remain alert by writing the key words, thus utilizing the principle of ＿＿ ＿＿＿＿＿ .

5. In these two techniques of programmed instruction, information is presented in ＿＿＿＿＿ ＿＿ , and occasionally key words are missing, thus requiring the learner's ＿＿ ＿＿＿＿ to complete the statements.

6. A third principle, *immediate knowledge of results*, is illustrated when a professor returns quiz papers to his students at the end of the class in which they were written. These students receive almost immediate ＿＿＿＿＿ of results.

7. If a student makes an incorrect response at any point in programmed instruction, he discovers his mistake because the correct answer may be seen immediately after the frame, before the next one is considered. Thus, in programmed instruction, the learner receives ＿＿＿＿ knowledge ＿＿ ＿＿＿ .

8. Notice that in programmed instruction, unlike the evaluation of term papers, "immediate" does not mean a week or even a day but rather a few seconds. The reader of the program is continuously informed concerning his progress; he receives ＿＿＿＿＿ ＿＿＿＿＿ ＿＿ ＿＿＿ .

9. Let us review the three techniques of programmed instruction already considered. By means of ＿＿ ＿＿＿＿ , the reader learns new material, which he acquires through ＿＿＿ ＿＿ followed by ＿＿＿＿ ＿＿＿ ＿＿ ＿＿＿ .

Programmed instruction embodies several Skinnerian principles. First, it proceeds in small steps, because Skinner has found that the best way to establish new behavior is to shape it bit by bit. Second, the learner is active, because this is the natural condition of organisms. (Recall how Pavlov's dogs, in contrast, were harnessed in and simply reacted to stimuli.)   Third, feedback is immediate because Skinner found that learning is most rapid when promptly reinforced.   (Reinforcement here is the knowledge that one's answer is correct.)

A sample of programmed reading for children is found in Figure 8.4.

In programmed instruction, students work independently and at their own pace.   The instruction units are constructed so that each student may begin at a level that he or she can easily master.   One does not want the student making many errors at first, for then the student will lack positive reinforcement for learning.   As with shaping, one begins by reinforcing responses that are within the student's behavioral repertoire and gradually building up from there.

Surprisingly, programmed instruction bears some resemblance to Montessori methods.   Instruction in both is individualized, begins at the student's own level, and builds up skills gradually.   Instruction is designed so that students can readily master each task.   In both, the goal is not to tear down, through criticism or punishment, but to make learning a consistently positive experience.

However, programmed instruction also differs from Montessori methods.   In the first place, programmed instruction involves material that children read (see Figure 8.4), whereas Montessori materials are largely physical.   Even when learning to read, Montessori children begin with sandpaper letters, metal insets, and so on.   Montessori thought that young children find such physical activities more natural.

More fundamentally, there is a difference in the extent to which the child's work is free from adult direction.   Montessori children choose their own tasks and work on them while the teacher steps into the background. It is hoped that they will discover for themselves how something is out of place, how cylinders fit, how water is poured, and whatever else is important to them.   In programmed instruction, in contrast, adult direction is pervasive.   Although it might seem that children work independently on the booklets, in fact an adult (the program developer) has structured each small response.   The child follows the adult's lead, repeatedly checking with this

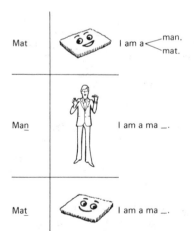

FIGURE 8.4
Programmed instruction for children.   (Adapted from Sullivan, M. W., Programmed learning in reading.   In A. D. Calvin (Ed.), *Programmed Instruction: Bold New Venture*.   Bloomington, Ind.: Indiana University Press, 1969, p. 111.   By permission of the publisher.)

social authority to see if he or she is right.   Children probably derive less sense that they are making their own discoveries about the world.

Nevertheless, it is important not to overlook the similarities between the two methods—especially the way both try to make learning a positive experience.   One can even imagine Skinner approving Montessori's physical tasks, albeit in his own terms.   He would say that they work not because they allow for spontaneous discoveries, but because they allow children to make responses that readily result in positive feedback from the physical environment.

Evaluation

Skinner considerably widened the scope of learning theory.   After noting the limitations of classical conditioning, he explored the nature of operant behavior, where the organism acts freely and is controlled by the consequences of its actions.   In a brilliant series of studies, Skinner showed how such control is exerted—by schedules of reinforcement, shaping, the influence of discriminative stimuli, and other factors.   Furthermore, Skinner amply demonstrated the practical importance of his ideas.

In the process, Skinner stirred up controversies on many fronts.   To some, his work lends itself to authoritarian practices—for he suggests ways to control, manipulate, and program others' behavior.   Skinner's (e.g., 1974, p. 244) reply was that environments do, in fact, control behavior, and how we use our knowledge of this fact is up to us.   We can create environments that suit humane purposes, or we can create ones that do not.

Developmentalists, too, often enter into heated, value-laden debates with Skinnerians.   Developmentalists cringe at talk of controlling and changing children's behavior, when one should, instead, try to understand children and give them opportunities to grow on their own.   To many Skinnerians, such sentiments are romantic and naive, for children chiefly develop through the molding influence of the external environment.

In a more objective vein, there are essentially three ways in which Skinner and writers in the developmental tradition disagree.   First, developmental theorists often discuss *internal* events.   Piaget describes complex mental structures, even though he might not be able to find direct evidence for all of them in any individual case.   Freudians discuss internal events, such as unconscious fantasies, that we cannot directly observe at all.   Skinner believed that such concepts divert us from scientific progress, which is made when we confine ourselves to the measurement of overt responses and environmental stimuli.   But on this point, Skinner is now generally considered too extreme.   Since the 1960s, there has been a dramatic new interest in cognition, and even growing numbers of learning theorists have been considering internal, cognitive events, even if the events cannot be directly measured.   In the next chapter we will discuss a major example of cognitive learning theory.

Second, developmental theorists and Skinnerians disagree on the meaning and importance of developmental *stages*—periods when children organize experience in very different ways.   In Piaget's theory, for example, a child's stage is a crucial variable; it is a predictor of the kind of experience the child can learn from. A child at the sensori-motor level will not learn tasks that involve language, nor will a child beginning to master concrete operations learn much from lectures covering abstract theory.

Skinnerians doubt the validity of stages as general, distinct ways of thinking or behaving; for the environment shapes behavior in a gradual, continuous manner (Skinner, 1953, p. 91; Bijou, 1976, p. 2). Skinner did acknowledge that one must note the child's age in any experiment, just as one must note an animal's species and characteristic behavior (1969, p. 89). Age contributes to the "topography" of behavior; it helps describe the behavior that the experimenter sets about to shape or maintain. However, such information is still merely descriptive; it is secondary to environmental variables that control behavior. The question is whether the child's developmental status deserves this secondary role.[3]

A third issue dividing Skinner and developmental theorists is the most important of all. This issue concerns the *source* of behavioral change. Developmentalists contend that in crucial instances a child's thoughts, feelings, and actions develop spontaneously, from within. Behavior is not exclusively patterned by the external environment. Gesell, for example, believed that children stand, walk, talk, and so on from inner maturational promptings. Piaget was not a maturationist, but he also looked primarily to inner forces underlying developmental change. In his view, children's behavior is not structured by the environment but by children themselves. Children, out of a spontaneous interest in moderately novel events, construct increasingly complex and differentiated structures for dealing with the world.

Consider, for example, a baby girl who drops a block, hears the sound, and drops it again and again, making this new and interesting sound last. In Skinner's theory, the sound is a reinforcer that controls her behavior. However, this reinforcer will soon lose its effectiveness, for she will soon become interested in more complex outcomes (Kohlberg, 1969a). She may, for instance, begin listening for different sounds as she drops objects from different heights. For Piaget, one cannot look to external reinforcements as the determinants of behavior, for these often vary with the child's developing interests. For him, the main variable is the child's spontaneous curiosity about increasingly complex events.

Developmental theorists, then, try to conceptualize ways in which children grow and learn on their own, somewhat independent of others' teachings or external reinforcements. At the same time, no one can deny that environments also reinforce and control behavior to a considerable extent, and often in ways Skinner described. Skinner's theory and research, moreover, have a clarity and elegant simplicity that others would do well to emulate. It is clear that Skinner's enormous contribution to scientific method and theory will be a lasting one.

---

[3]For further discussions on the topic of stage and principles of conditioning, see S. White, 1965, and Sameroff and Cavanaugh, 1979.

9

Bandura's Social Learning Theory

BIOGRAPHICAL INTRODUCTION

The pioneering learning theorists usually developed their concepts by experimenting with animals in physical settings. They watched how animals ran through mazes, solved puzzle boxes, or learned to press levers in Skinner boxes. These situations were not social; there were no other animals present. Skinnerians and others then showed that the same principles apply to learning in social contexts. Just as rats learn to press levers to get food, people learn to interact with others to obtain social rewards. However, some have questioned whether the analogy is really perfect. Bandura, in particular, argues that in social situations we learn a great deal through *imitation*, and that a full understanding of imitative learning requires several new concepts.[1]

Albert Bandura was born in 1925 in the province of Alberta, Canada. Like Skinner, he grew up in a very small town; his high school had only 20 students (Schultz, 1976, p. 302). Bandura attended the University of British Columbia as an undergraduate and the University of Iowa as a graduate student in psychology. At Iowa he studied with Robert Sears, one of the pioneers in social learning theory. In 1953 Bandura joined the

[1]There are social learning theories other than Bandura's, but Bandura is currently generating the most research. The reader interested in other social learning approaches might begin with Baldwin (1980).

faculty at Stanford, where he has been ever since. Bandura has established a high reputation in psychology, and in 1974 he served as president of the American Psychological Association. His students consider him a modern generalist, a man whose knowledge spans across many fields in the social sciences (Gelfand, 1969, p. 186).

BASIC CONCEPTS

Observational Learning

In Skinner's theory, learning often appears to be a gradual process in which organisms must act to learn. Organisms emit responses, which are gradually shaped by their consequences. Bandura (1962), however, argues that in social situations people often learn much more rapidly simply by observing the behavior of others. When, for example, children learn new songs or play house just like their parents, they often reproduce long sequences of new behavior immediately. They appear to acquire large segments of new behavior all at once, through observation alone.

The power of observational learning is well documented in the anthropological literature (Bandura and Walters, 1963, Ch. 2; Honigmann, 1967, p. 180). In one Guatemalan subculture, girls learn to weave almost exclusively by watching models. The teacher demonstrates the operations of the textile machine, while the girl simply observes. Then, when the girl feels ready, she takes over, and she usually operates it skillfully on her very first try. She demonstrates, in Bandura's (1965a) term, *no-trial learning*; she acquires new behavior all at once, entirely through observation. She does not need to fumble through any tedious process of trial-and-error learning with differential reinforcement for each small response.

When new behavior is acquired through observation alone, the learning appears to be *cognitive*. When the Guatemalan girl watches her teacher and then imitates her perfectly without any practice, she must rely on some inner representation of the behavior that guides her own performance. Thus Bandura, unlike Skinner, believes that learning theory must include internal cognitive variables.

Observation also teaches us the probable consequences of new behavior; we notice what happens when others try it. Bandura calls this process *vicarious reinforcement*. Vicarious reinforcement is also a cognitive process; we formulate expectations about the outcomes of our own behavior without any direct action on our part.

We learn from models of many kinds—not only from live models but from *symbolic* models, such as those we see on television or read about in books. Another form of symbolic modeling is verbal instruction, as when an instructor describes for us the actions for driving a car. In this case the teacher's verbal descriptions, together with a demonstration, usually teach us most of what we need to know. This is fortunate, for if we had to learn to drive exclusively from the consequences of our own actions, few of us would survive the process (Bandura, 1962, pp. 214, 241).

Let us now look more closely at the observational learning process, which Bandura divides into four subprocesses.

The Four Components of Observational Learning

1. Attentional processes.   First of all, we cannot imitate a model unless we pay attention to the model.   Models often attract our attention because they are distinctive, or because they possess the trappings of success, prestige, power, and other winsome qualities (Bandura, 1971, p. 17).   Television is particularly successful at presenting models with engaging characteristics and exerts a powerful influence on our lives (Bandura, 1977, p. 25).

Attention is also governed by the psychological characteristics of observers, such as their needs and interests, but less is known about such variables (1977, p. 25).

2. Retention processes.   Because we frequently imitate models some time after we have observed them, we must have some way of remembering their actions in symbolic form.   Bandura (1965a; 1971, p. 17) thinks of symbolic processes in terms of *stimulus contiguity*, associations among stimuli that occur together.   Suppose, for example, we watch a man use a new tool, a drill.   He shows us how to fasten the bit, plug it in, and so on.   Later, the sight of the drill alone arouses many associated images, and these guide our actions.

In the above example, the stimuli are all visual.   However, we usually remember events, Bandura (1971, p. 18) says, by associating them with verbal codes.   When we watch a motorist take a new route, we connect the route with words (e.g., "Route 1, then Exit 12 . . ."). Later, when we try to drive the route ourselves, the verbal codes help us follow it.

Young children, under the age of five years or so, are not yet accustomed to thinking in words and probably must rely quite heavily on visual images.   This limits their ability to imitate.   One therefore can improve on their imitations by directing them to use verbal codes—that is, by asking them to give verbal descriptions of a model's behavior while they are watching it (Coates and Hartup, 1969; Bandura, 1971, p. 19).

On many memory tasks, young children display a striking disregard for their own capacities and limitations.   For example, Vygotsky (1931b, p. 71) found that young children approach tasks, no matter how simple or difficult, with the same unbridled enthusiasm.   They act as if they can remember anything.   In contemporary terms, they lack *metacognitive* awareness; they do not yet observe and assess their own cognitive skills.   Between the ages of about five and 10 years, children gradually learn to evaluate their memory capacities and learn when to use memory aids such as verbal rehearsals (repeating something to themselves over and over to better remember it).   Bandura (1986, p. 89) summarizes experimental evidence that suggests that models can help children learn to use verbal rehearsal and other techniques.

3. Motor reproduction processes.   To reproduce behavior accurately, the person must have the necessary motor skills. For example, a boy might watch his father use a saw but find that he cannot imitate very well because he lacks the physical strength and agility. From observation alone, he picks up a new *pattern* of responses (e.g., how to set up the wood and where to place the saw) but no new physical abilities (e.g., cutting with power). The latter come only with physical growth and practice (Bandura, 1977, p. 27).

4. Reinforcement and motivational processes.   Bandura, like cognitive learning theorists before him (Tolman, 1948), distinguishes between the *acquisition* and the *performance* of new responses. One can observe a model, and thereby acquire new knowledge, but one may or may not perform the responses. A boy might hear his neighbor use some profane language, and thereby learn some new words, but the boy might not reproduce them himself.

Performances are governed by reinforcement and motivational variables; we will actually imitate another if we are likely to gain a reward. In part, it is our past history of *direct reinforcements* that matters. If, in the above example, the boy has himself received respect and admiration for swearing, he is likely to imitate his neighbor. If, on the other hand, he has been punished for swearing, he probably will hestiate to imitate him.

Performances also are influenced by *vicarious reinforcements*, the consequences one sees accrue to the model. If the boy sees his neighbor admired for swearing, the boy is likely to imitate him. If he sees the neighbor punished, he is less likely to do so (Bandura, 1971, p. 46; 1977, pp. 117–24).

Performances, finally, are partly governed by *self-reinforcements*, the evaluations we make of our own behavior. We will discuss this process in a later section.

Conclusion.   To successfully imitate a model, then, we must (1) attend to the model, (2) have some way of retaining what we have seen in symbolic form, and (3) have the necessary motor skills to reproduce the behavior. If these conditions are met, we probably know how to imitate the model. Still, we might not do so. Our actual performances are governed by (4) reinforcement contingencies, many of which are of a vicarious sort.

In reality, these four components are not totally separate. Reinforcement processes, in particular, influence what we attend to. For example, we often attend to powerful, competent, prestigious models because we have found that imitating them, rather than inferior models, leads to more positive consequences.

SOCIALIZATION STUDIES

Bandura's four-part model gives a fine-grained analysis of imitative learning. On a broader level, one of Bandura's primary, if sometimes implicit, concerns has been the socialization process—the process by which societies induce their members to behave in socially acceptable ways.

Socialization is an inclusive process that influences almost every kind of behavior, even technical skills.   Many American teenage boys, for example, feel that they will not fit into their social group unless they learn to drive a car.   Automobile driving, however, is not something that is required by all cultures, and there are classes of social behavior that have broader relevance.   All cultures seem to try to teach their members when it is acceptable to express aggression.   It also is likely that all cultures try to teach people certain modes of cooperation, sharing, and helping.   Aggression and cooperative behavior, then, are "targets" of socialization in all cultures (Hetherington and Parke, 1977, p. 231).   In the next few sections we will sample social learning analyses of some of the target behaviors in the socialization process.

Aggression

Bandura (1967; Bandura and Walters, 1963) believes that the socialization of aggression, as well as other behavior, is partly a matter of operant conditioning.   Parents and other socializing agents reward children when they express aggression in socially appropriate ways (e.g., in games or in hunting) and punish children when they express aggression in socially unacceptable ways (e.g., hitting younger children).   But socializing agents also teach children a great deal by the kinds of models they present.   Children observe aggressive models, notice when they are reinforced, and imitate accordingly.   Bandura has examined this process in several experiments, one of which is now considered a classic.

In this study (Bandura, 1965b), four-year-olds individually watched a film in which an adult male model engaged in some moderately novel aggressive behavior.   The model laid a Bobo doll[2] on its side, sat on it, and punched it, shouting such things as, "Pow, right in the nose," and "Sockeroo . . . stay down" (pp. 590–91).   Each child was assigned to one of three conditions, which meant that each child saw the same film but with different endings.

In the *aggression-rewarded* condition, the model was praised and given treats at the end of the film.   A second adult called him a "strong champion" and gave him chocolate bars, soft drinks, and the like (p. 591).

In the *aggression-punished* condition, the model was called a "big bully," swatted, and forced to cower away at the end of the film (p. 591).

In the third, *no-consequences* condition, the model received neither rewards nor punishments for his aggressive behavior.

Immediately after the film, each child was escorted into a room with a Bobo doll and other toys.   The experimenters observed the child through a one-way mirror to see how often he or she would imitate the aggressive model.

The results indicated that those who had seen the model punished exhibited significantly fewer imitations than did those in the other two groups.   Thus, vicarious punishment reduced the imitation of aggressive responses.   There was no difference between the aggression-rewarded and

[2]A large, inflated rubber doll.

no-consequences groups. This is often the finding with respect to behavior, such as aggression, that is typically prohibited. The observation that "nothing bad happens this time" prompts imitation just as readily as does vicarious reward (Bandura, 1969, p. 239).

The experiment also had a second, equally important phase. An experimenter came back into the room and told each child that he or she would get juice and a pretty sticker-picture for each additional response he or she could reproduce. This incentive completely eliminated the differences among the three groups. Now all the children—including those who had seen the model punished—imitated him to the same extent. Thus, vicarious punishment had only blocked the *performance* of new responses, not their *acquisition*. The children in the aggression-punished condition had learned new responses, but had not felt that it was wise to actually reproduce them until a new incentive was introduced.

One of Bandura's followers, Robert Liebert (Liebert et al., 1977, p. 145), suggests that this experiment has implications for aggression in television and movies. Children are frequently exposed to actors who demonstrate clever ways of committing homicides and other crimes. The widespread showing of such films is justified by the fact that the criminals are usually caught in the end. However, Bandura's work suggests that children probably learn about criminal behavior nonetheless, and only inhibit such behavior until a time when environmental contingencies clearly favor its occurrence.

In the above experiment, children performed *newly* acquired responses. Models also can influence the performance of *previously learned* behavior of the same general class. For example, a boy might watch a violent movie and then act roughly toward his sister. He does not actually imitate the behavior he saw in the film, but he feels freer to engage in previously learned behavior of the same kind. In such cases, we say that the behavior has been *disinhibited*. Models may also *inhibit* previously learned behavior, as when a girl sees a boy punished in class and therefore decides to check her impulse to do something else of a mischievous nature (Bandura and Walters, 1963, p. 72; Liebert et al., 1977, pp. 146–47).

Sex Roles

During socialization, children are taught to behave in sex-appropriate ways. Societies encourage boys to develop "masculine" traits and girls to develop "feminine" traits.

It is possible, of course, that sex traits are also, in part, genetically linked. Social learning theorists do not deny this possibility. However, they believe that more is to be gained from the study of socialization processes and the role of imitation in particular (Bandura and Walters, 1963, pp. 26–29; Mischel, 1970).

In the learning of sex roles, the acquisition/performance distinction is especially important (Mischel, 1970). Children frequently learn, through observation, the behavior of both sexes; however, they usually perform only the behavior appropriate to their own sex because this is what they

FIGURE 9.1
This young girl is imitating her father. After a while she probably will find that she receives more reinforcement for imitating females. However, she still may learn a good deal about "masculine" skills from observation alone.

have been reinforced to do. Margaret Mead (1964) told how Eskimo boys are encouraged to practice hunting and building snow houses, whereas girls are not. So ordinarily only the boys engage in these activities. Nevertheless, the girls watch the boys, and in emergencies they can execute the same skills, although not as well. They pick up the skills through observation alone, but they are not as adept as the boys because they have not practiced them.

Social reinforcements, then, only restrict the range of skills that boys and girls practice—not what they observe. After a while, however, children may even stop making quite as careful observations of opposite-sex models. Perhaps it is as if a boy, for instance, were to say: "I seem to make people happy only when I try things boys do; so I'm going to pay the closest attention to the things boys do." Thus, social reinforcements may even influence the observational process itself (Maccoby and Wilson, 1957; Grusec and Brinker, 1972).

Prosocial Behavior

Since the 1970s there has been considerable interest in the nature and roots of prosocial behavior—acts of sharing, helping, cooperation, and altrusim. Social learning theorists have taken the lead in this area, showing that prosocial behavior can be readily influenced by exposure to the appropriate models. In a typical study (Rushton, 1975), seven- to 11-year-old children watched an adult model play a bowling game and donate some of his winnings to a "needy children's fund." Immediately afterward, these children played the game alone, and they themselves made many donations—far more than did a control group who had not seen the altruistic model. Furthermore, the children who had observed the model still donated more two months later, even when placed in a different room with a different experimenter. Evidently, even a relatively brief exposure to a generous model exerts a fairly permanent effect on children's sharing.

Numerous other experiments have shown that models influence not only children's sharing but also their helpfulness toward others in distress, their cooperativeness, and their concern for the feelings of others (Bryan, 1975; Mussen and Eisenberg-Berg, 1977, pp. 79–90). The experimental findings in this area also seem supported by more naturalistic studies, in which parental behavior is linked to their children's altruism (Mussen and Eisenberg-Berg, 1977, pp. 86–90; Sroufe and Cooper, 1988, pp. 379–80).

Practicing and preaching. Socializing agents teach children not only by behavioral example, but by preaching virtue and telling children how to behave. Such verbal techniques have been most fully explored in research on prosocial behavior, so a brief review might be in order.

First of all, preaching seems ineffective unless it is forceful. If an adult simply says, "It is nice to share," the child will be far more influenced by what the adult actually does. If the adult shares, so will the child— regardless of whether the adult preaches altruism or greed (Bryan and Walbeck, 1970). When, however, the preaching becomes stronger, taking the form of long emotional sermons and commands, it can be effective (Mussen and Eisenberg-Berg, 1977, pp. 151–52).

Commands, however, are coercive and may backfire, as found in a study by G. M. White (1972). In this experiment some children took turns bowling with an adult who *told* them to share some of their winnings with needy children. Other children were simply given the opportunity to follow an altruistic example. The immediate result was that the children who were ordered to share did so to a greater extent, even when playing alone. In a posttest, however, these children's sharing decreased sharply, and they displayed a greater incidence of stealing, perhaps reflecting their resentment against the coercive technique.

Self-Regulation

As people become socialized, they depend less on external rewards and punishments and increasingly regulate their own behavior. That is, they establish their own internal standards and reward and punish themselves in accordance with them. For example, a woman might criticize herself for a moral transgression that no one else is even aware of. She punishes herself because her behavior violated her own standards.

Bandura has been very interested in how people evaluate their own performances as they strive for success and achievement. Some people set exceedingly high achievement goals and reward themselves only when they meet them.   An artist, for example, might approve of his own work only after he has corrected flaws that others would never detect.   Others are satisfied with less perfect work.

How are self-evaluative standards acquired?   In part, Bandura believes, they are the product of direct rewards and punishments.   For example, parents might give their daughter approval only when she earns very high grades, and after a while she adopts this high standard as her own.

However, Bandura's focus, once again, is on the influence of models, which he first demonstrated in a key experiment (Bandura and Kupers, 1964).   Basically, the design was as follows.   Seven- to nine-year-old children watched a model play a bowling game.   In one condition, the model rewarded himself with candy only when he obtained a high score, saying things such as, "I deserve some M&Ms for that high score" (1964, p. 3).   Otherwise, he made self-critical remarks, such as, "That does not deserve an M&M treat" (1964, p. 4).   In a second condition, the model followed a lower criterion for self-reward.   There was also a control group of children who saw no model.   The main finding was that afterward, when the children played the game alone, they adopted the patterns of self-reward of the model to whom they had been exposed.   The children in the control group, who had seen no model, adopted no consistent standards; they took treats whenever they felt like it.   The models, then, exerted clear-cut effects on the children's self-evaluative behavior.

In ordinary life, the situation is more complicated because children are exposed to a variety of models (e.g., parents, TV characters, and peers), some of whom exemplify high self-evaluative standards and some of whom do not.   Which models will children follow?

Bandura (1986, pp. 342–43) says that children tend to adopt the self-evaluative standards of peers rather than adults because children can more easily achieve the lower standards that peers set.   But Bandura also points out that we can do things to get children to adopt higher standards.   For example, we can encourage children to associate with high-achieving peers (peers who set high self-evaluative standards).   We can also expose children to models who are rewarded for adhering to high standards.   For example, we can read children stories about scientists and athletes who settled for nothing short of excellence and who eventually achieved great success and public acclaim.

People who set high self-evaluative standards are generally hard workers, and hard work produces real accomplishments.   At the same time, high goals are difficult to achieve, and people who set high goals are prone to disappointment and depression.   Such people, Bandura says, can avoid depression by focusing on subgoals.   That is, instead of measuring their progress in terms of distant aims, they should set realistically attainable goals for each day and reward themselves when they achieve them (1986, pp. 354, 359–60).

Self-Efficacy

When we regulate our own behavior, we engage in self-observation. We evaluate our ongoing performances in terms of our standards and goals.   On other occasions, we reflect on our general abilities, reaching conclusions such as, "I'm good at algebra" and "I'm a poor swimmer." Bandura calls such general judgments *self-efficacy appraisals* (1986, Ch. 9).

Bandura believes that our self-efficacy appraisals exert powerful effects on our levels of motivation.   When we believe we are good at tasks, we work on them vigorously and persist with them despite temporary setbacks.   When we doubt our abilities, we work less energetically and are more likely to give up when we encounter difficulties (1986, p. 394).

The importance of perceived self-efficacy was demonstrated in an experiment by Collins (1982, cited in Bandura, 1986, p. 391).   Collins divided children into two groups according to their level of ability in mathematics, and he also asked the children about their own opinions of their abilities.   Collins then gave all the children some difficult problems.   As one would expect, the children in the high-ability group outperformed those in the low-ability group.   But perceived self-efficacy also had an effect.   Within each ability group, the children who believed they were good at math solved more problems, chose to work on more of the problems they failed, and displayed a more positive attitude toward mathematics.

It is possible, of course, for a person to have *too* high an estimate of his or her abilities.   A girl who overestimates her ability as a skier might start too fast down a treacherous slope and risk injury.   A boy who has an exaggerated sense of himself as a dancer might enter a dance contest before he is ready and experience unnecessary failure.

In general, Bandura says, it is best to *slightly* overestimate one's abilities.   Then one will attempt tasks that are "realistically challenging" and solve many tasks that one couldn't solve before (1986, p. 394).

Sources of self-efficacy appraisals.   Bandura (1986, pp. 399–408) suggests that self-efficacy appraisals are based on four sources of information.

1.   The most influential source of knowledge is *actual performance*.   If we repeatedly succeed at tasks, our sense of efficacy increases.   If we repeatedly fail, our sense of efficacy drops.   Once we have developed a robust sense of self-efficacy in an area, we are not too troubled by temporary setbacks.   We are likely to attribute failures to our lack of effort or to poor tactics and to try again.   And if we succeed, our sense of efficacy goes up even higher.
2.   Self-efficacy appraisals are also influenced by *vicarious experiences*.   If we see others succeed at a task, we infer that we can do it too.   This is especially true if we believe that others have roughly the same abilities as we do.
3.   Another variable is *verbal persuasion*—pep talks.   When someone convinces us we can perform a task, we usually do better on it.   Pep talks cannot, of course, enable us to accomplish tasks that are far too difficult.   But outside encouragement can help, largely because success usually depends more upon the effort we put into a task than upon any inherent ability.
4.   Finally, we judge our abilities partly on the basis of *physiological cues*.   For example, we might interpret fatigue or tension as signs that a task is becoming too difficult for us.   At the same time, people often react differently to the same bodily cues.   One girl, warming up for the 400-meter race, may interpret her anxiety as a sign that she is too tense to do well.   Another girl may interpret

the same bodily cues as an indication that she is getting "fired up," that her "adrenaline is flowing," and that she is ready to do her best.

ABSTRACT MODELING AND PIAGET'S STAGES

In many instances, imitation produces exact copies of a model's behavior. For example, a child might imitate a friend's new way of writing the letter "L." Psychologists sometimes assume that all imitation is of this variety— exact copies of specific behaviors. But Bandura suggests that people also engage in a more general process he calls *abstract modeling*. People induce the general rules or principles underlying particular behaviors, and they then use these rules to generate entirely new behavior of their own. For example, English-speaking children induce, from all the language they hear, that the rule for forming the plural is to add the "s" sound, and they then use this rule to generate countless new sentences.

Bandura claims that abstract modeling accounts for a great deal of conceptual learning, including the concepts investigated by Piaget. By observing a model, a child might, for example, induce a new moral rule or the principle underlying conservation of liquid. But Bandura's view of this process differs from Piaget's. Like Piaget, Bandura sees the child as an active cognitive agent; the child induces rules and grasps concepts. But Bandura's emphasis is much more on the way the external environment— especially models—influence the kinds of concepts that children learn. Later we will review some of the research of Bandura and his colleagues on how models might influence children's conceptual development. But first let us compare the theories of Piaget and Bandura a bit more thoroughly.

Bandura and Piaget. Piaget, you will recall, thought that children learn much on their own, from an intrinsic interest in the world. Children are especially curious about stimuli that are moderately novel, that do not quite fit into their existing cognitive structures. When, for example, our son Tom was 11 months old, he could grasp many things with his hands, so he was surprised to discover one day that he couldn't grasp water. He kept trying and failing, intently studying the way the water responded to his actions. Tom was not motivated by adult approval or any other external reinforcement. He was engrossed in the problem itself. And because he was so interested in the problem, he continued to work on it, and over the next several months he invented some ways of holding water.

In Piaget's view, then, children construct their own cognitive structures as they work on intrinsically interesting problems. In the process, their thinking undergoes a series of broad transformations called *stages*. These stages, in turn, indicate the kinds of new problems children will find most interesting; for they continue to be most curious about events and activities that are just beyond their current level. This principle of moderate discrepancy holds for imitation too; children are spontaneously interested in models whose behavior is slightly more complex than their own (Kohlberg, 1966b; 1969a, p. 434; Kuhn, 1974). This is why we often see children tagging along after somewhat older ones, trying to do the same things. Thus, Piagetians do not spend much time examining the modeling influences in a child's life; they study, instead, the child's cognitive behavior at each stage, for the child's stage determines the kinds of models the child will seek out.

Bandura, in contrast, is much more of an environmentalist. It is appealing, he says, to imagine children making their own discoveries and creating their own ideas. In reality, however, children's minds are structured by the environment, by the models and the social training practices the environment provides (Bandura, 1977, p. 183; Bandura and Walters, 1963, p. 44).

In some major works (1977, 1986, 1989), Bandura has softened his environmentalism somewhat. He talks about "reciprocal influences" among individuals, their behavior, and the environment. But Bandura is still much more an environmentalist than Piaget, and Bandura continues to raise strong objections to Piagetian theory. Specifically, he disagrees with two basic Piagetian tenets.

First, Bandura doubts that children learn much on their own, out of an intrinsic interest in moderately novel events. If children were motivated to figure out everything that is slightly beyond their grasp, they would be learning all the time. But this is not the case. If we want children to learn, we must motivate them and assist them. We must teach them things, administer rewards and punishments, and provide them with appropriate models. After a while, to be sure, children do become self-motivated learners. But this does not mean that they now learn for learning's sake, because of their natural curiosity about the world. Rather, they learn to meet their internal achievement standards (e.g., to master 90 percent of the material for a test). These internal standards, moreover, are themselves the products of social teaching and modeling influences (Bandura, 1986, pp. 340, 480–88; 1989, pp. 8–9, 34–35).

Second, Bandura questions the validity of Piagetian stages. At first the stages seem plausible because children do often master material in sequences. But this is only because people usually solve easier problems before they solve more difficult ones. There is nothing special about Piaget's stage sequences, and they are not as absolute as he claims.

Moreover, the stage concept implies that thinking becomes organized and reorganized into broad, unitary structures that underlie children's thinking across a wide range of tasks. For example, the child at the stage of concrete operations should apply the same logical operations to a wide variety of problems. But stages in this sense, Bandura argues, do not exist. Thinking actually consists of numerous discrete skills that vary from one cognitive domain to the next. For example, reading, writing, and arithmetic all involve many of their own particular skills and subskills. Piagetian stages, which lump children's thinking into broad categories, tell us little about the particular thinking skills in each area.

Bandura argues, then, that Piaget's view of development is false. Children do not primarily learn on their own, nor does their thinking undergo broad stage transformations. To understand development, we must adopt a social-learning perspective. We must examine the ways in which societies, through direct teaching and the provision of models, transmit particular knowledge and skills.

To demonstrate the superiority of their approach, Bandura and his colleagues have tried to show that Piaget's stages can be readily modified through social-learning procedures. In one classic study, Bandura and McDonald (1963) examined the effects of models on Piaget's stages of moral reasoning.

Moral reasoning. Piaget, you will recall, proposed a two-stage theory of moral judgment, one aspect of which concerns consequences versus intentions. That is, younger children tend to judge wrongdoing in terms of its consequences, whereas older children base their judgments on the intentions behind the act. For example, a young child is likely to say that a boy who broke 15 cups by accident is naughtier than one who was trying to steal but broke only one cup. The young child focuses on the consequences—the amount of damage. The older child, in contrast, usually puts more weight on the underlying motive.

Bandura gave five- to 11-year-old children 12 such items and found the age shift that Piaget and others (Kohlberg, 1969a) have documented. However, Bandura emphasized, children of all ages evidenced at least some reasoning of both kinds, suggesting that the stages are not rigidly demarcated.

Following this pretest, Bandura tried to show that the children's thinking could be altered by modeling influences. In a key part of the experiment, children individually observed an adult model who was praised for giving responses *contrary* to their own dominant mode. If, for example, a child had typically judged wrongdoing in terms of intentions, the model always based her judgment on the consequences. An experimenter presented the model with a moral dilemma, praised her when she gave her answer, and gave the child a turn on a new item. Taking turns in this way, the model and child each responded to 12 new items (different from the pretest items).

This training procedure did have a strong effect. Prior to the training, children gave one type of moral response only about 20 percent of the time; during the treatment, this number increased to an average of about 50 percent.

The experiment also included an immediate posttest in which the children responded once again to the pretest items. The results indicated that the children persisted with their new mode of responding (about 38 to 53 percent of the time).

The study, Bandura says, shows that "the so-called developmental stages were readily altered by the provision of adult models . . . " (Bandura and Walters, 1963, p. 209). There seems to be nothing fixed or invariant about them.

A group of cognitive-developmentalists (Cowan et al., 1969) replicated Bandura's modeling treatment and obtained similar results. Nevertheless, cognitive-developmentalists have viewed the study suspiciously. They acknowledge that modeling can influence cognitive stages, but the influence should be small. This is because stages represent broad, deeply rooted cognitive structures. We cannot, in theory, effortlessly get a child to reason in any way we wish. And when we do produce change, it should be primarily in the direction of the stage sequence—one stage forward. Several experiments have, in fact, found that these are the kinds of changes that do occur when Kohlberg's, rather than Piaget's, stages are used (Gardner, 1982, p. 219). This, Kohlberg (1969a) argued, is because his stages represent broader cognitive structures than Piaget's moral stages do, so his are harder to change. However, as Bandura (1986, pp. 494–96) notes, the modeling influences in these studies were brief and weak.

We can see, then, that Bandura's experiment has stirred up a good deal of controversy. He has presented a serious challenge to cognitive stage theory.

Conservation. Social learning theorists have also tried to show that conservation can be altered through modeling. Some of the key experiments have been performed by Rosenthal and Zimmerman (Rosenthal and Zimmerman, 1972; Zimmerman and Rosenthal, 1974). In a typical study (1972, Experiment I), five- and six-year-olds were first given a battery of conservation tasks (e.g., conservation of number, liquid, and weight). Those who showed little knowledge of conservation were assigned to one of two groups. Some children were assigned to a modeling group in which they observed an adult model perform the tasks correctly. Others were placed in a control condition; they saw no model. All the children were then readministered the same test battery and were also given a new series of items to test for generalization. Actually, the generalization tasks were of the same kind (e.g., conservation of number, liquid, and weight); they differed only in colors and shapes and in other superficial ways.

The results indicated that the modeling group outperformed the control group; they gave significantly more correct conservation responses. This was true for both the repeated tasks and the generalization tasks.

In this study the amount of change produced by the modeling treatment was impressive, but such is not always the case. In another experiment (Rosenthal and Zimmerman, 1972, Experiment IV), for example, four-year-olds acquired new conservation skills only to a very modest degree.

On the basis of their several experiments, Rosenthal and Zimmerman enthusiastically concluded that modeling can produce rapid and substantial changes in conservation behavior (1972, p. 399; 1974, p. 268). Conservation skills, they believe, are probably the product of socialization—of the teachings of adults in the child's culture. Developmentalists would be more skeptical and would point to the weaker results with children who were not ready to benefit from the modeling experience.

PRACTICAL IMPLICATIONS

Bandura's work should do a good deal to increase our awareness of the importance of models in child-rearing and education. Although most parents and teachers are already somewhat aware of the fact that they teach by example, they probably have also overlooked just how influential modeling can be. A case in point is physical punishment. Many parents try to prevent their children from fighting by spanking them when they fight — only to find, it seems, that their children fight all the more (Bandura and Walters, 1963, p. 129). The likely explanation is that the parents, by spanking, are inadvertently providing a good demonstration of how to hurt others (Bandura, 1967). Similarly, whenever we find that we are unable to rid a child of some distressing bit of behavior, we might ask whether we have been inadvertently modeling the behavior ourselves.

Modeling, according to Bandura, takes many forms. The familiar kind is behavioral modeling; we exemplify an activity by performing it. Modeling may also be done verbally, as when we give instructions or issue commands. Social learning researchers have evaluated the effectiveness of the varous kinds of modeling, and their findings should be of importance to parents and educators. Of particular interest are studies such as G. M. White's (1972), which examined the effects of commanding children to share. At first, the commands seemed to work, but their impact diminished over time, and the commands also produced resentment and rebelliousness. In the long run, we may do better simply to model generosity and helpfulness through our own behavior. Then children can follow our example without feeling forced to do so.

Social learning theorists have also shown that behavior is influenced not only by personal or live models, but also by those presented in the mass media. Filmed models, in particular, seem to exert a powerful impact, and one major implication is that television, which many children watch for hours on end, is shaping young lives. Social learning theorists have been especially concerned with the effects of televised violence on children and have found that, in fact, it can increase children's aggressiveness in their daily lives. The findings are complex—the effects seem strongest, for example, on young children—but the findings are substantial enough to warrant our concern (Gardner, 1982, pp. 334–36; Huston et al., 1989).

The kinds of models presented in the mass media have been of concern to those seeking social change, such as African-Americans and women's groups. These activists have pointed out that films, books, and magazines have typically depicted women and people of color in stereotyped roles and, by doing so, have restricted people's sense of what they might become in life. Accordingly, these groups have tried to get the media to present new kinds of models, such as women and African-Americans as doctors and scientists, rather than housewives and delinquents. The social learning research suggests that the activists have, in this case, adopted a good strategy for social change.

Because modeling can have a strong impact on behavior, it has significant promise as a therapeutic device. You might recall that in Mary Cover Jones's (1924) famous experiment, modeling was part of the method used to eliminate Peter's fear of furry objects. Bandura and others have conducted a number of studies that have more systematically shown how modeling can help reduce fears. In one experiment (Bandura et al., 1967), for example, four-year-olds who were afraid of dogs observed a child calmly play with one, and then the children themselves became less fearful. Modeling can also help in other ways, such as making overly submissive clients more assertive (Rosenthal, 1976).

Bandura (1986) has begun to urge therapists to pay special attention to self-efficacy appraisals when they diagnose and treat their clients. For example, Bandura believes that whatever technique a therapist uses to treat a phobia—whether it is modeling or some other technique—the treatment will work best if it gives the client the sense that he or she can now exert some control over the feared stimulus. Similarly, techniques for dealing with pain, such as relaxation or guided imagery, work best when they give clients the feeling that they can now exert some influence on the amount of pain they feel (1986, pp. 425–445).

EVALUATION

The concept of imitation is an ancient one, but Bandura has greatly increased our awareness of its importance. He has shown how models can rapidly influence a wide range of behavior and has thus given us a better appreciation of how the social environment alters behavior. Furthermore, Bandura and his colleagues have made their points through a number of well-designed experiments, employing elegant and rigorous methodologies, which are often lacking in developmental research.

At the same time, because social learning theorists have concentrated so heavily on laboratory research, we cannot yet be certain of how well their principles and findings hold up in ordinary life situations. Although Bandura showed that models can change children's moral thinking in the laboratory, we cannot be sure that modeling influences account for the growth of moral thinking in real life.

In some cases the experimental situations may contain artificial conformity pressures that make the modeling effects look greater than they really are. In a typical experiment, the child is taken from the classroom and led into a room where he or she meets unfamiliar adults. Naturally the child feels a bit overwhelmed and searches for clues as to the "right" way to behave. So, for example, if the child sees a model praised for discussing morals in terms of consequences, the child infers that he or she is supposed to do the same (see Cowan et al., 1969).

Social learning theorists are aware of this problem and often do what they can to eliminate any artificial conformity pressures. Furthermore, some social learning theorists have begun to explore how modeling works in everyday life (Grusec and Abramovitch, 1982).

For us, the most important issues are those that divide Bandura and the developmentalists. To developmentalists, Bandura is too environmentalistic. This is not to say that most developmentalists deny the effects of the environment. They do recognize that environments influence behavior, and often in the ways that Bandura specifies. But developmentalists place a high value on the kinds of growth that emerge from within the child—from the child's inner maturational promptings and spontaneous interest in the world. Bandura, developmentalists believe, minimizes the importance of such growth.

Among the developmentalists, it has been the Piagetians who have become most embroiled in debates with Bandura. Piagetians believe that children learn from a spontaneous interest in moderately novel events. Bandura (1986, pp. 480–82) dismisses this suggestion; children, he says, really learn in order to obtain reinforcements, such as praise, which they eventually come to administer to themselves. But Bandura's own research may contradict his argument. In several experiments, models perform what he calls "moderately novel" or "relatively unique" behaviors (Bandura, 1962, pp. 250, 252; 1965b, p. 116). Models sock Bobo dolls, march about, knock objects off shelves, and engage in other zany physical antics. As Kohlberg (1969a, p. 435) pointed out, these behaviors seem intuitively designed to capture the imagination of four-year-old subjects, and in several experiments the subjects readily imitated them, even though there were no reinforcements available (Bandura and Huston, 1961; Bandura et al., 1963; Bandura, 1965b). Quite possibly, the children reproduced such behaviors because they found them intrinsically interesting. Reinforcement variables, to be sure, can increase or alter imitation, but a spontaneous interest in moderate novelty might also be at work.

Bandura (1986, pp. 480–82) argues that the principle of moderate novelty does not fit with everyday observations. If people learned from their intrinsic interest in moderately novel events, they would be learning all the time; for they are constantly encountering slightly new information. In reality, however, people usually restrict their learning to one or two areas of life, such as their areas of occupational expertise.

Piagetians (e.g., Kamii, 1980) and other developmentalists (e.g., Montessori, 1936b) would agree that people often seem to be fairly apathetic when it comes to learning. But this observation does not prove that humans have no intrinsic interest in the world. Rather, the observation shows that the child's natural curiosity has been stifled.

Children, in the developmental view, begin life full of enthusiasm for learning, and during the first few years they learn a tremendous amount on their own, without adult instruction. Then adults get hold of them, sending them to schools and taking charge of their learning. Adults give them "socially guided instruction" and provide them with modeling influences, teaching them what and how to think. Children, feeling the pressure to please grownups, try to give the adults the answers the adults want— the "right answers." As a result, children stop trusting their own judgment, and lose the thrill that comes from making their own discoveries.

Bandura says that he, too, believes in self-motivated learning, but of a different kind. People, in Bandura's view, do not learn out of a spontaneous interest in the world, but to achieve their internal goals and standards. Children internalize external standards and make their own positive self-evaluations contingent upon the achievement of these standards. For example, a college student, studying for exams, might only be pleased with himself when he is certain that he has mastered enough material to earn straight "A"s.

Bandura makes learning sound like a very self-conscious process. Learners, in his view, seem to be at least as interested in their own personal progress as in the subject matter itself. This is certainly true of a good deal of learning. Yet the deepest and most creative thinkers seem to engage in their work much less self-consciously. They forget themselves and become totally absorbed in the matter at hand (Dewey, 1916, p. 173; Montessori, 1936a, pp. 50–53; Maslow, 1970, pp. 45, 65). Like young children, highly creative people are interested in learning for its own sake. Piagetians and other developmentalists would like all of us to retain this kind of learning.

Piagetians also believe that Bandura overlooks the importance of cognitive structures or stages. Bandura, as we have seen, does acknowledge that cognitive skills set limits on what children can learn and imitate. But he does not believe that cognitive skills are best described as broad stage structures. Instead, he thinks of cognition much more atomistically, as a large number of specific, isolated skills.

Bandura's position has received support in recent years (Flavell, 1985, pp. 290–95), but the concept of general stage is not as untenable as he makes it sound. As we discussed in Chapter 6 on Piaget, there is reason to believe that Piaget's stages, despite certain problems, are valid. And social learning research itself occasionally suggests that the child's general stage is at work. For example, Liebert et al. (1969) found that 14-year-olds, but not eight- or six-year-olds, could imitate a new grammatical rule. The oldest subjects were able to figure out the rule underlying the model's behavior because they had capacities for abstract thinking that the younger children lacked. They had, it seems, formal operations.

It might be, then, that Bandura underestimates the importance of developmental variables. He certainly seems to overlook the extent to which children learn on their own, from an intrinsic interest in the world. He might also overlook the extent to which modeling is influenced by cognitive stages. Nevertheless, Bandura has significantly broadened learning theory and contributed enormously to our understanding of how environmental factors shape behavior.

10

Vygotsky's Social-Historical Theory of Cognitive Development

BIOGRAPHICAL INTRODUCTION

This book focuses on theorists in the developmental tradition—scholars who have seen developmental change primarily in terms of inner forces. For example, Gesell emphasized inner maturational promptings, while Piaget saw children making their own discoveries. By way of contrast, we have also examined the ideas of learning theorists, who have emphasized the role of the external environment.

Some readers, however, may be dissatisfied with this theoretical division. Why, they might ask, must we view development in either/or terms? Can't a theory assign major roles to both inner and outer forces?

The construction of such an integrative theory is a worthy goal, but few people have made much progress in attaining it. Bandura, as we saw, pronounces behavior to be multidetermined—to be influenced by various internal and external variables—but he also continues to discredit the developmentalist perspective on how change comes from within. Later we will discuss the ways Freud and Erikson weave inner and outer forces into their psychoanalytic theories. In the realm of cognitive development, the major theorist who had a deep appreciation of both developmental and environmental forces was the Russian L. S. Vygotsky (1896–1934).

Vygotsky had read the early writings of Gesell, Werner, and Piaget, and he recognized the importance of the kinds of intrinsic development they were addressing.   At the same time Vygotsky was a Marxist who believed that one can only understand human beings in the context of the social-historical environment.   Thus Vygotsky tried to create a theory that allowed for the interplay between the two "lines of development"—the "natural line" that emerges from within and the "social-historical line" that influences the child from without (Vygotsky, 1931a, p. 17).

Vygotsky was only partly successful.   He had only sketched out an integrative theory of development when, at the age of 38, his life was cut short by tuberculosis.   Nevertheless, many psychologists believe that if we eventually do construct a solid integrative theory, it will build on the start Vygotsky gave us.

Lev Semenovich Vygotsky grew up in Gomel, a port city in western Russia.   His father was a banking executive, and his mother was a teacher, although she spent most of her life raising her eight children.   The family loved interesting conversation, a trait that rubbed off on the young Vygotsky.   As a teenager, he was known among his friends as the "little professor" because he was constantly leading them in discussions, mock trials, and debates.   Vygotsky also loved to read history, literature, and poetry (Wertsch, 1985, pp. 3–4).

When Vygotsky was 17, he wanted to attend the University of Moscow, but because he was Jewish he had to struggle with the state's quota system; the university's enrollment was only 3 percent Jewish.   Initially, Vygotsky seemed assured of a spot because he was so bright.   But before he completed his oral examinations, the educational ministry shifted to a lottery system for Jewish applicants.   Vygotsky felt he had lost all hope, but then he won a position by chance alone.

At the university, Vygotsky specialized in law, but he also took a wide variety of courses in other fields, as well as courses at Shanyavskii People's University, where a number of professors had gone after being expelled from the University of Moscow for anti-Czarist leanings.   Vygotsky graduated with a law degree from the University of Moscow in 1917 and returned to his home of Gomel (Wertsch, 1985, pp. 5–6).

Between 1917 (the year of the Communist Revolution) and 1924, Vygotsky taught literature in a secondary school and psychology at the local teacher's college, and he became interested in the education of the physically disabled.   He also worked on his doctoral dissertation on the psychology of art.   During this period he became ill with tuberculosis (1985, pp. 7–8).

On January 6, 1924, Vygotsky travelled to Leningrad to deliver a lecture on the psychology of consciousness.   The clarity and brilliance of his speech—by the unknown young man from the provinces—had an electrifying effect on the young psychologists in the audience.   One, A. R. Luria (1902—1977), recommended Vygotsky for a position at the Moscow Institute of Psychology, which Vygotsky received.   During his first year of work at the institute, he finished his dissertation and received his doctorate (1985, p. 8).

In Moscow, Vygotsky soon became a commanding presence.   When he lectured, students stood outside the packed auditorium and listened through open windows.   When he travelled, students wrote poems in honor of his journey. Vygotsky inspired such enthusiasm not only because his ideas were exciting, but because he led a group of young Marxists on a mission—to create a psychology that would help build a new socialist society (1985, p. 10).

Perhaps sensing that his life would be short, Vygotsky worked at a breakneck pace. He read, lectured, and conducted research as rapidly as he could, and he also travelled extensively to help clinics working with children and adults with neurological disorders. Vygotsky's daily schedule was often so busy that he did his writing after 2 A.M., when he had a few quiet hours to himself. During the last three years of his life, his coughing spells became so severe that he was sometimes left exhausted for days at a time. Nevertheless, he worked until he died (1985, pp. 12–14).

A few of Vygotsky's writings were published shortly after his death in 1934, but in 1936 the Soviet government banned his work—a ban that lasted until 1956. The primary reason for the ban was that Vygotsky conducted some research with intelligence tests, which the Communist Party condemned. Actually, Vygotsky criticized the conventional use of intelligence tests and employed them in new ways, but such subtleties were lost on the authorities. Fortunately, Vygotsky's colleagues and students kept his work alive, and in the past decade or so, there has been a great interest in Vygotsky's ideas in the West. This interest will doubtlessly grow as more of Vygotsky's writing is translated from the Russian (Cole and Scribner, 1978; Kozulin, 1986, pp. xxiv–xxv).

MARX'S VIEWS ON HUMAN NATURE

Since Vygotsky tried to create a psychology along Marxist lines, it will be helpful to briefly review some of the ideas of Karl Marx (1818–1883) on human nature before discussing Vygotsky in detail.

Marx's comments on human nature were relatively brief, and they primarily appeared in his early writings (Marx, 1844, 1845; Marx and Engels, 1846). Marx recognized that humans have biological needs, but he emphasized the human capacity for tool-use and production. It is by inventing and using tools that humans master their environments, satisfy their needs, and, ideally, fulfill their deepest creative potentials. Production, Marx also emphasized, is an inherently social process. People join together to plant and harvest crops, exchange goods, assemble machines, and so on.

Beyond these general comments, Marx had little to say about human nature. Indeed, he argued that it is a mistake to describe human nature in the abstract, apart from its social-historical context. Although humans are distinguished by their capacity for tool-use and technological production, the conditions under which they work and produce change throughout history. The working conditions of the medieval artisan, for example, were quite different from those of the nineteenth-century factory worker. To understand humans, then, we need to understand history and the dynamics of historical change (Marx, 1845, pp. 107–9; Marx and Engels, 1846, pp. 118–21, 129).

History, in Marx's view, is a *dialectical* process, a series of conflicts and resolutions. New forces of production (e.g., new ways of manufacturing) come into conflict with the existing social system, and a new social system is installed. For example, in eighteenth- and nineteenth-century Europe, the creation of new factories gave a rising class of capitalists the opportunity to make vast sums of money, but the ancient feudal system stood in their way. The result of this conflict was the overthrow of the feudal system and the establishment of a new system—the free enterprise system which allowed the capitalists to make as much money as they liked (Marx, 1859; Marx and Engels, 1872, pp. 336–40; Mills, 1962, pp. 82–83).

Marx believed that his own age—the second half of the nineteenth century—was experiencing a new phase in the dialectic of history. Technological progress was now being impeded by the free enterprise system. The resolution of this conflict would be a communist revolution in which the workers would take over the industries and organize them for the benefit of all.

We have encountered the concept of dialectic—of conflict and resolution—earlier (Chapter 6). Marx, like so many other scholars, adopted the concept from Hegel. However, Marx used the concept in a very different way.

For Hegel, the dialectic of history occurs in the realm of consciousness and ideas; one viewpoint comes into conflict with its opposite, leading to a new synthesis. Marx, in contrast, believed that conflicts in ideas are superficial. The conflicts that really matter are social and economic. In fact, most ideas and values merely justify particular social and economic interests. The medieval lords praised loyalty and honor; the rising capitalists heralded liberty and free competition; and both groups believed they were giving expression to the highest of all values. In reality, both groups were merely spouting opinions that justified their own social and economic interests.

Marx, then, was highly critical of those scholars who analyzed the nature of consciousness—people's ideas, values, and outlooks—as if these had an independent existence. What people think, Marx said, depends on their material life—the ways in which they work, produce, and exchange goods—at a certain point in historical development.

But it is not just the *content* of thinking that depends on historical development. Our species' cognitive *capacities*, too, have changed as a result of historical change, especially technological development. This, at least, was the position of Marx's collaborator Friedrich Engels (1820–1895), who forcefully argued that early technology—early tool use—gave rise to uniquely human traits such as advanced intelligence and speech.

Engels on tool-use and human evolution. According to Engels (1925, pp. 47–49, 238–46), our ancestors became capable of tool-use when they came down from the trees and began living on level ground. This new mode of life enabled them to develop an upright posture, which freed the hands for the production of stone implements. Once people began making tools, their minds expanded. They began discovering new properties of natural objects, such as the properties of stone and wood that facilitate cutting. They also became aware, however dimly at first, of the scientific principles underlying tool-use, principles such as leverage, mass, and force.

Tool-use also led to new modes of cooperation and communication. As technologies advanced, people discovered the advantages of working together. For example, they found that they could more effectively build a hut or a boat by joining forces. But they now needed some way of communicating beyond grunts and gestures. People needed to give one another instructions, such as, "Turn right," and "Pull harder." "Men in the making," Engels said, "arrived at the point where *they had something to say* to one another" (1925, p. 232). Thus, they developed speech.

More generally, technology promoted a new orientation toward the environment. With tools in hand, humans no longer had to accept the environment as they found it. They could change it. At a certain point, for example, they stopped picking fruit and vegetables wherever they found them; they began clearing land and planting their own crops. This new orientation promoted planning and foresight. Successful farming requires people to plan months and years ahead. Such foresight, Engels observed, has not always been a capacity that humans have exercised as well as they should. Nevertheless, once people saw the power of tools and technology, they began transforming the environment according to their own plans and designs.

VYGOTSKY'S THEORY OF PSYCHOLOGICAL TOOLS

In the Marxist view, then, we cannot study human nature in the abstract, as something that is fixed and eternal. Human capacities, as Engels said, have changed as a result of historical development—especially technological development. As our species developed new tools for dealing with the environment, it became more aware of the properties of objects, developed new ways of cooperating and communicating, and developed new capacities for planning and foresight. Further changes in human technology will undoubtedly produce further changes in human cognition.

Vygotsky was deeply impressed by Engels's writing on tool-use, and he attempted to extend Engels's insights. Just as people have developed tools to master the environment, Vygotsky proposed, they also have created "psychological tools" to master their own behavior. For example, early peoples used notched sticks and knotted ropes to help them remember events, much as a person might tie a string around his or her finger today. Later, as cultures developed, they created other mental tools. Voyagers began using maps to help them retrace prior routes and plan future expeditions. Vygotsky called the various psychological tools that people use to aid their thinking and behavior *signs*, and he argued that we cannot understand human thinking without examining the signs that cultures provide (Vygotsky, 1930, pp. 39–40; 1931).

Undoubtedly, the single most important sign system is *speech*. Speech serves many functions, but most fundamentally it frees our thought and attention from the immediate situation—from the stimuli impinging upon us at the moment. Because words can symbolize things and events that go beyond the present situation, speech enables us to reflect upon the past and plan for the future (Vygotsky, 1930, p. 26; Luria, 1976, p. 10).

For example, I know a farming family whose vegetables were being raided by deer. For a while the family members simply reacted to each immediate situation as it occurred. Whenever someone saw a deer eating the vegetables, he or she chased it away. After a while, however, the family sat down and discussed long-term solutions. They talked about building a new fence, how high it should be, and whether a ditch would be useful. One family member shared an idea she heard from a neighbor a few months earlier. By using words to symbolize things and events that were not immediately present—"a fence," "a ditch," "the neighbor's idea"—the family developed a plan. (They decided to build a higher fence.)

When humans use signs, Vygotsky said, they engage in *mediated* behavior. That is, they do not just respond to environmental stimuli; their behavior is also influenced or "mediated" by their own signs. In the present example, the family did not just respond directly to the environmental stimuli (the deer), but also acted on the basis of a verbally formulated plan ("O.K., we've decided to build a 10-foot fence") (Vygotsky, 1930, pp. 19–40).

The acquisition of speech is of major importance to the growing child; it enables the child to participate intelligently in the social life of his or her group. But speech does more than this. It also facilitates the child's own, individual thinking. By the age of three or four years, Vygotsky noted, children begin to carry out the kinds of dialogues they had had with others with themselves alone. At first they do this aloud, and we can hear children at play saying things such as, "I wonder where this wheel goes? Does it go here?" After a while, at the age of six or seven years, children begin to carry out such dialogues more inwardly and silently. Vygotsky believed that our ability to talk to ourselves—to think with the help of words—contributes enormously to our powers of thought.

Two other important sign systems are *writing* and *numbering systems*. The invention of writing was a great human achievement; it enabled people to keep permanent records of information. For most children, however, learning to write (and read) is a real struggle because writing forces children to detach themselves from physical, expressive speech, which comes so naturally to them, and to use abstract symbols for words. Learning to write usually requires a good deal of formal instruction (Vygotsky, 1934, p. 181; 1935, p. 105).

Numbering systems have also been of great importance in human evolution. Vygotsky suggested that early peoples created numbering systems because they found that they were unable to quantify objects (such as vegetables or cattle) by sight alone. They needed sets of symbols to help them count. For example, the Papaus of New Guinea invented a method of counting that used their fingers and many parts of their bodies to stand for objects. As societies evolved, they developed other numbering systems, such as the abacus and written notation. They also increasingly dealt with quantities in abstract and theoretical ways, apart from particular objects. Algebra, for example, deals with general quantitative categories without even specifying particular numbers. If $a + 10 = b$, then $a = b - 10$, regardless of the particular values of *a* and *b*.   The mastery of algebra and other theoretical uses of number, like the mastery of reading and writing, usually requires formal instruction (John-Steiner and Souberman, 1978).

Vygotsky argued that cultural sign systems have a major impact on cognitive development—an impact overlooked by developmentalists such as Gesell and Piaget.   Gesell and Piaget looked at development as if it comes from the child alone, from the child's inner maturational promptings or spontaneous discoveries.   Vygotsky acknowledged that such intrinsic development, the "natural line" of development, is important.   It even dominates cognitive development up to the age of two years or so.   But after this, the growth of the mind is strongly influenced by the "cultural line" of development, the sign systems the culture provides.   In fact, all our uniquely human powers of thought—those that distinguish us from other species—would be impossible without speech and other sign systems.

Vygotsky speculated, in addition, that the highest levels of thinking—the levels of purely abstract or theoretical reasoning—require instruction in writing, math, and other kinds of abstract concepts.   Children might, to be sure, develop some concepts on their own, in their everyday experience, but they will not develop purely abstract modes of thought without instruction in abstract sign systems.   And since this instruction is only widespread in technologically advanced societies, we will find purely abstract thinking prevalent only in these societies (Vygotsky, 1934, pp. 103, 206; 1935, p. 90; Luria, 1976, pp. 8, 161).

In 1931 Vygotsky saw a unique opportunity to test this latter hypothesis—that abstract thinking is a product of relatively advanced levels of social-historical development.   At this time, there were many remote areas of the Soviet Union, including Central Asia, where peasants still lived a feudal existence.   The peasants worked on small farms and were completely dependent on wealthy landowners and feudal lords.   Most were illiterate.   The new Soviet government, attempting to develop the entire nation into a modern socialist state, instituted collective farming practices, in which peasants met in groups to plan production, measure output, and so on.   The government also gave the peasants short courses in writing, reading, and the theoretical uses of number.   Because, in 1931, the government was still phasing in the new programs, Vygotsky saw the opportunity to compare the mental processes of those adults who had begun to participate in the modern forms of social life with those who were still living in the old ways.

Actually, Vygotsky himself was too ill to go to Central Asia to conduct field work, but he encouraged Luria and others to do so.   In one aspect of the study, the interviewers presented the subjects with syllogisms such as the following:

> In the Far North, where there is snow, all bears are white.   Novaya is in the Far North.   What color are the bears there?   (Luria, 1976, p. 108)

The nonliterate subjects refused to deal with the question in a purely theoretical way.   They said things such as, "I don't know what color the bears there are, I never saw them" (1976, p. 111).   When the interviewer pressed them, asking them to answer "on the basis of my words," the peasants still refused to speak beyond their personal experience. As one said, "Your words can be answered only by someone who was there, and if a person wasn't there he can't say anything on the basis of your words" (1976, p. 109). Those who had been participating in the new programs, in contrast, were willing to deal with the syllogisms on a theoretical plane and they answered them correctly (1976, p. 116).

This study wasn't perfect. In particular, it didn't pinpoint the particular aspects of historical change that had produced the greatest change in the peasants' thinking. Was the main factor the course work in reading and writing, or in math, or was it schooling in general? Or was the main factor collective farm planning? Such questions were left to other investigators (e.g., Scribner and Cole, 1981).

Nevertheless, the study did support the Marxist contention that the mind is a product of social-historical change. The study suggested that we cannot meaningfully discuss the "principles of thinking" or "cognitive development" in the abstract, as psychologists usually do. We need to examine the culture into which the child is growing, and the sign systems the culture provides. For, as Vygotsky said, "If one changes the tools of thinking available to the child, his mind will have a radically different structure (cited in John-Steiner and Souberman, 1978, p. 126).

Not all Marxist psychologists, we should note, have enthusiastically endorsed Vygotsky's ideas. Several Marxists have argued that Vygotsky stretched the metaphor of tools too far. Tools, they say, mean real tools—not speech, writing, math, and other "psychological tools" (see Kozulin, 1986, pp. xlviii–l).

But whatever his standing as a Marxist, Vygotsky pointed developmental psychology in a promising new direction. Vygotsky recognized the role of intrinsic forces, but he suggested that a complete understanding of cognitive development requires the study of the psychological tools the culture provides and expects the child to use.

These two forces—intrinsic and cultural—generally seem to be opposed. Perhaps it is for this reason that scholars have generally emphasized one force or the other, but not both. Vygotsky, in contrast, was schooled in dialectical theory and was therefore primed to consider the ways in which opposing forces interact and produce new transformations. The growing child, trying to make sense of the world in her own way, encounters a culture that expects her to use its particular sign systems. These interactions are complex and difficult to study. Vygotsky himself only began to investigate them, and he generally focused on only one side of the dialectic—the impact of culture on the child. In the following sections, we will review his work on the acquisition of memory aids, the internalization of speech, and the impact of schooling.

MEMORY AIDS

Vygotsky suggested that some of humankind's earliest psychological tools were memory aids, and these tools are still very important to us today.

Thus, Vygotsky and his colleagues conducted various experiments to try to gain insights into the ways in which children acquire them.

In one experiment, Vygotsky (1931a, pp. 70–71) instructed children and adults to respond in different ways when they saw different colors. He told them to lift a finger when they saw red, to press a button when they saw green, and so on for other colors. Sometimes he made the task simple, sometimes he made it difficult, and at certain points he offered memory aids.

In such experiments, the youngest children, between the ages of four and eight years, typically acted as if they could remember anything. Whether the task was simple or difficult, they rushed into it as soon as they heard the instructions. When the experimenter offered them pictures and cards "to help you remember," they usually ignored the aids, or used them inappropriately. Young children, Vygotsky concluded, "do not yet know their capacities and limitations" or how to use external stimuli to help them remember things (1931b, p. 71).

Older children, from about nine to 12 years, typically used the pictures Vygotsky offered, and these aids did improve their performance. Interestingly, the addition of such aids did not always improve the memory of the adults. But this was not because they had become like young children and no longer used memory devices. Rather, it was because they now rehearsed instructions and made mental notes to themselves inwardly, without the need for external cues (Vygotsky, 1930, pp. 41–45).

By today's standards, these experiments were very informal. Vygotsky and his colleagues did not systematically test predetermined hypotheses but used the experiments to explore the child's thinking. The investigators tried out varous procedures and watched how the child responded, and in this way they tried to gain insights into the steps through which the child acquires some of the cognitive tools of his or her culture.

But as informal as these experiments were, they were pioneering investigations into an area that has become a major topic in contemporary psychology. This is *metacognition*, the awareness people have of their own thought processes. (People's specific awareness of their own memory processes is sometimes called *metamemory*). Like Vygotsky, contemporary psychologists are trying to discover how children become aware of their thinking and how they learn to use psychological tools and strategies to improve it (Flavell, 1985, pp. 105–7, 230–38).

SPEECH

As mentioned earlier, the single most important psychological tool is speech (Vygotsky, 1930, p. 24; 1934, p. 256). Speech frees our thought and attention from the immediate perceptual field. This freedom sets us apart from other species.

To illustrate this difference, Vygotsky called attention to research by Kohler (1925) on the problem-solving of apes. Kohler found that if one places a banana within an ape's visual field—but behind some bars so the ape cannot grab it—the ape's attention will be so riveted on the banana that it will hardly consider anything else.   The ape won't even consider using a stick lying nearby, unless the stick also happens to lie directly in front of the bars.   The stick, that is, must also be part of the immediate visual field (Kohler, 1925, pp. 37–38; Vygotsky, 1930, pp. 35–37).

Human thinking, in contrast, can range much more freely beyond the immediate perceptual field, and it is speech that enables it to do so. Because words frequently refer to absent objects, we can, in a situation like that of the ape, ask ourselves, What object might reach that banana?   Is there a stick or a pole around here that will reach it?   Thus, we use words to contemplate and direct our search for objects not in our visual field.

Vygotsky suggested that the ability to engage in such internal dialogues develops in three steps.

1.   Initially, references to absent objects occur in the child's interactions with others.   For example, a two-year-old girl might ask her mother to help her find something.   Or the mother might say, "We're going to the park now, so get your pail and shovel," directing the girl's attention to objects she had not been looking at.

2.   Next, at the age of three years or so, the child begins to direct similar comments to herself.   While playing with her toys, she might say, "Where's my shovel?   I need my shovel," and begin looking for an object that had not been within her immediate surroundings.

    For a time, this self-guiding speech is said aloud; we frequently hear children talking as they play or work on problems.   Then, beginning at about six years of age, chidren's self-directed speech becomes increasingly quiet, abbreviated, and less comprehensible to us.

3.   Finally, by age eight or so, we cannot hear this talk at all.   But the child's self-directed speech has not disappeared; it has merely gone underground. It has turned into *inner speech*, the silent dialogue that one has with oneself (Vygotsky, 1934, pp. 29–40).

The general process, then, is one of *internalizing* social interactions. What begins as an interpersonal process, occurring between the parent and the child, becomes an intrapsychic process, occurring within the child. Vygotsky believed that this general progression characterizes the development of all the "higher mental processes," all the forms of thought and attention that depend on cultural signs.   In fact, he stated that the progression is a general law:

> Any function in the child's cultural development appears on the stage twice, on two planes, first on the social plane and then on the psychological.   (1931a, pp. 44–45).

This law, in the view of Vygotsky and his followers, was a cornerstone of a Marxist psychology.   A Marxist does not seek the origins of thinking within the individual child, spontaneously sprouting from the child's mind, but in external social existence (Vygotsky, 1930, p. 45).   "The child," Vygotsky said, "learns the social forms of behavior and applies them to himself" (1931a, p. 40).

Egocentric Speech

In the process of internalizing social speech, children go through a phase (step 2) in which they spend considerable time talking to themselves aloud. The first person to call attention to this kind of speech was Piaget (1923), who called it *egocentric speech*. Piaget observed, for example, that if two five-year-old girls are playing in a sandbox, each might talk enthusiastically about topics without considering the fact that the other couldn't possibly know what she was referring to. Piaget called this speech "egocentric" because he thought it reflects the child's general egocentrism; the child doesn't adjust her speech to the perspective of the listener because she egocentrically assumes that the listener's perspective is the same as her own. Piaget estimated that between the ages of four and seven years about 45 percent of all speech is egocentric (1923, p. 51).

Vygotsky agreed that egocentric speech is very prevalent in this age group, but he disagreed with Piaget about its theoretical meaning. In Piaget's view, egocentric speech is basically useless. It merely reflects a deficiency in the child's thinking. Vygotsky, in contrast, emphasized its positive function; it helps the child solve problems. In one of Piaget's studies (1923, p. 14), 6½-year-old Lev says to no one in particular, "I want to do that drawing, there . . . I want to draw something, I do. I shall need a big piece of paper to do that." In Vygotsky's view, Lev's self-directed talk helps Lev plan and direct his activities (Vygotsky, 1934, p. 29).

Vygotsky also disagreed with Piaget about egocentric speech's ultimate fate. Piaget implied that as children overcome their egocentrism, egocentric speech simply dies out. Vygotsky argued that it doesn't just fade away, but it goes underground and turns into inner speech, the kind of silent dialogue that we so often have with ourselves when we try to solve problems. Interpreting the decline of egocentric speech as an indication that it is dying, Vygotsky said, "is like saying that the child stops counting when he ceases to use his fingers and starts adding in his head" (1934, p. 230).

Vygotsky argued, then, that egocentric speech is highly useful and is an important way station on the road to inner speech. But even if one were to agree with Vygotsky on these points, one would still have to agree with Piaget that there is something puzzling about it. The child seems to be talking to someone, yet doesn't do so in any full way. For example, a child playing alone with a tinkertoy while an adult is silently seated across the room says,

> The wheels go here, the wheels go here. Oh, we need to start it all over again. We need to close it up. See, it closes up. We're starting it all over again. Do you know why we wanted to do that? Because I needed it to go in a different way. (Kohlberg et al., 1968, p. 695)

The child seems to be talking to the listener (e.g., asking him, "Do you know why . . . ?"), but the child doesn't wait for the listener to respond.

According to Vygotsky, the child's self-directed speech is puzzling because it is not yet differentiated from social speech. The child is trying to use speech to direct her own activities, but she still casts her speech in the form of social communication. It takes a while for self-directed speech to "differentiate out" and take on its own character. Only gradually does self-directed speech become quieter and more abbreviated and turn into inner speech (Vygotsky, 1934, pp. 229–32).[1]

Studies Bearing on the Vygotsky-Piaget Issue

Vygotsky and others have conducted a number of studies bearing on the Vygotsky-Piaget debate on egocentric speech.

Task difficulty.   Vygotsky reasoned that if egocentric speech serves a problem-solving function, it should increase when tasks become more difficult. Because Piaget saw no positive function to egocentric speech, his theory makes no such prediction.

So Vygotsky did various things to make children's tasks more difficult. "For instance, when a child was getting ready to draw, he would suddenly find that there was no paper, or no pencil of the color he needed. In other words, by obstructing his free activity, we made him face problems" (Vygotsky, 1934, pp. 29–30). In these situations, the proportion of egocentric speech (the amount of egocentric speech compared to all speech) nearly doubled among five- to seven-year-olds (Luria, 1961, p. 33). The children tried to solve problems by talking to themselves. For example, one boy said, "Where's the pencil? I need a blue pencil. Never mind, I'll draw with the red one and wet it with water; it will become dark and look like blue" (Vygotsky, 1934, pp. 29–30). This study suggested, then, that egocentric speech does serve a problem-solving function in young children, a finding that has been replicated by Kohlberg et al. (1968).

Age trends.   Vygotsky also suggested that his theory, in comparison to Piaget's, predicts different age trends. If, as Piaget implied, egocentric speech merely reflects the child's cognitive immaturity, it should decline as the child develops. It should simply drop off, as indicated by the solid line in Figure 10.1.

In Vygotsky's view, in contrast, egocentric speech is a new achievement, a new alternative to social speech. It provides the child with a new problem-solving tool—one that we might expect the child to increasingly use. Thus Vygotsky predicted that egocentric speech would actually rise before it declines as it turns into inner speech. This trend is indicated by the dotted line in Figure 10.1.

Basically, the empirical research on age trends has supported Vygotsky's position, as has nearly all other research that has pitted Vygotsky's views versus those of Piaget on this matter (Kohlberg et al., 1968). Nevertheless, it still seems possible that Piaget was partly correct. Even if some

---

[1]As evidence that the child's overt self-directed speech is still partly social, Vygotsky reported that the child stops talking aloud when it is clear that the listener cannot hear (1934, p. 233). Vygotsky believed that this evidence contradicted Piaget's view that the egocentric child isn't trying to communicate, but Piaget denied that this was ever his belief. The child, Piaget said, wants to communicate but cannot (Piaget, note in Vygotsky, 1934, p. 275).

egocentric speech serves the self-guiding function that Vygotsky emphasized, it also seems that *some* egocentric speech might reflect the child's inability to consider the audience's viewpoint. Thus it may be that both Piaget and Vygotsky were correct.

Verbal Self-Regulation and Personality Development

So far, we have focused on the way children use speech to help them solve problems of an intellectual sort. For example, we saw how a boy talked to himself to figure out how to draw a picture despite the absence of a blue pencil. But verbal self-regulation also helps us understand personality development more broadly. In particular, it helps account for those personality traits we ordinarily associate with character strength, such as conscience and will power.

Conscience. As we shall see in Chapter 11, Freudians suggest that at six or seven years of age, children begin to behave as if they are governed by internal moral standards. They no longer seem solely concerned with parental punishments; they begin to criticize themselves for thoughts and actions that no one else is even aware of. In Freudian terms, they are developing a *superego.*

Many of Freud's thoughts on the superego have to do with the Oedipus complex, and these thoughts go beyond Vygotsky's concerns. But when Freud discussed the process by which the superego develops, his explanation was completely in tune with Vygotsky's theory. Children develop a superego, Freud said, by internalizing parental prohibitions; they

FIGURE 10.1. Piaget's theory predicts a general decline in egocentric speech as children overcome their egocentrism. Vygotsky's theory predicts a curvilinear trend; since egocentric speech is a positive new achievement, it should increase for a time before declining as it turns into inner speech.

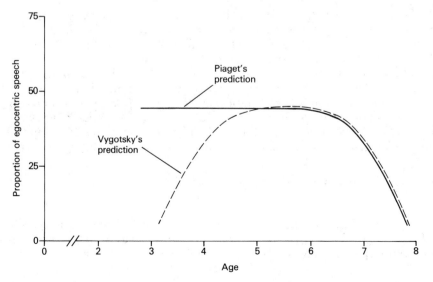

reproach themselves in the same way their parents had reproached them (Freud, 1933, p. 62). Vygotsky would have added that this internalization occurs largely through speech, and that there is a period when we can directly observe it because children speak to themselves aloud. Munn provides an example.

> A three-year-old, awakening full of pep at six A.M., starts tuning up for the day. His weary and irate father from the next bedroom tells him in no uncertain terms to get back into bed, and adds, "Don't you dare get me up until seven o'clock."
>
> The boy obeys, but within a few moments mutterings from his room again disturb the father.
>
> Getting out of bed, and going to the door of the boy's room, this is what the father hears:
>
> "Not till seven o'clock," to his arm as he jerks it back from the edge of the bed.
>
> And, as his body squirms half out of bed, he throws himself back vigorously, saying, "You heard what I told you." (1946, p. 255)

Thus, this little boy gives himself moral directions in the same way his father had given them to him a short time earlier.

Will-Power. Another dimension of personality is will or will-power. Most of us feel that will-power is an important matter in our daily lives, but psychologists largely ignore it. Skinnerians believe that will-power doesn't exist. We might believe we are exercising our wills, but we are really behaving according to external reinforcements. Other psychologists avoid the concept because they would rather leave issues of free will and determinism to the philosophers.

Vygotsky, however, thought that will-power is a real phenomenon and a legitimate topic for psychological study. Basically, the question of will-power is: How is it possible for us to take action in situations in which forces pull us strongly against it? How, for instance, do we stop watching TV and go study instead?

Vygotsky's (1932) answer was that we use words to create artificial stimuli to direct our behavior. If we are watching TV, we might say to ourselves, "O.K., I'm going to watch it until 8:00 o'clock; then I'll study." We create a new, verbal signal to control our behavior.

As always, Vygotsky argued that we initially acquire such signals through social interactions. When we were young, adults frequently used signals to direct our behavior. They might have told us, "I want you to jump in the water on the count of three," or, "You can watch TV until the big hand on the clock reaches the 12." Thus, when we find ourselves in situations when we need to motivate ourselves, we apply the same signals to ourselves.

Luria's Research on the Verbal Regulation of Behavior

Vygotsky described the stages through which children internalize speech and regulate their own behavior, but his description was fairly general. A more fine-grained analysis was provided by his student Luria.

Luria focused on the internalization of adult commands. He wanted to see how the child comes to obey adult commands and then applies them to herself, regulating her own behavior. Vygotsky, we should note, did not imply that all self-regulation is limited to the internalization of commands. Children internalize all kinds of dialogue. But Luria focused on commands.

Luria found that the child's ability to follow adult commands develops rather slowly. Suppose a toy fish is lying on a table. If we tell a 14-month-old child, "Bring me the fish," the child will do so. But if we place a shiny toy cat closer to the child and again say, "Bring me the fish," the child will bring us the shiny cat. Our verbal instructions cannot overcome the power of an attractive stimulus (Luria, 1960, p. 360).

There are other difficulties as well. In one experiment, Luria gave a two-year-old a rubber balloon and told him to press it, which the child did. But Luria noted, "He does not stop his reaction, for he presses a second, a third, and a fourth time" (1960, p. 360). Luria gave the boy only one instruction, but the boy's action *perseverated*—it kept going.

What's more, our commands, which can so easily set a child's behavior in motion, do not have nearly the same power to *inhibit* it. If an experimenter tells a two-year-old who is pressing a balloon, "That's enough," the command usually has little effect. In fact, in many cases the command only intensifies the child's reaction; the child presses even more energetically (Luria, 1961, p. 53).

To get an idea of the difficulty, Luria said, "Try . . . giving a child of twenty months or two years verbal instructions to take its stockings *off* while it is pulling them *on* . . . and you will see that your verbal instructions are unable to alter the action already begun; on the contrary, they will merely intensify it" (1961, p. 53).

By the ages of three or three-and-a-half, children can follow specific adult commands fairly well (Luria, 1961, p. 70; Slobin, 1966, p. 131). But can they follow their *own* verbal instructions?

In one experiment, Luria told children to say "Press" and press a balloon when they saw one light and to say "Don't press" and to refrain from pressing when they saw another light. But three- and three-and-a-half-year-olds pressed at every light. They said "Press" and pressed, and they said "Don't press" and pressed. Once again, words excite action, but they have a weak inhibiting effect (Luria, 1960, pp. 374–75; 1961, pp. 90–91).

Luria believed that a good part of the difficulty is that young children respond to the *excitatory* function of speech rather than to its *semantic* content or *meaning*. Thus, the phrase "Don't press" excites action simply because it is a signal, regardless of its meaning. Luria found that the only way to prevent three- and three-and-a-half-year-olds from responding to a light is to tell them to remain silent when they see it. Then they won't press. But if they give themselves any verbal signal at all, they will press, regardless of the meaning of their words (1960, pp. 374–75; 1961, pp. 90–91).

A number of Luria's experiments suggest that children can verbally regulate much of their own behavior by the age of five or six years. They can easily handle the kinds of experiments previously described. In fact, an experimenter need only give them instructions at the outset, and they will perform correctly without saying anything to themselves aloud. But Luria believed that they are still giving themselves verbal instructions— only now they are doing so silently, through inner speech. To support his interpretation, Luria reported that when he made tasks more compli- cated or speeded them up, the five- and six-year-olds spontaneously began giving themselves instructions aloud once again (1961, p. 93).

   Self-regulation and neurological functioning. Luria emphasized the social origins of self-regulation. First children submit to the commands of others; then they command themselves. At the same time, Luria rec- ognized that the child's ability to regulate his or her behavior depends on the maturation of the nervous system. In fact Luria devoted a great por- tion of his life studying the neurological mechanisms underlying self- regulation and other mental functioning, and he is considered one of his- tory's great neurologists.

   Many of Luria's insights came during his work with patients who suffered brain injuries during the Second World War. Luria, like others, found that the kinds of difficulties the patients experienced depended greatly on the specific location of their injuries. The ability to regulate one's own behavior, Luria found, is tied to the frontal lobes, particularly in the left hemisphere. Patients who suffered frontal lobe injuries could still speak and perform simple habitual tasks, such as greeting others and dressing themselves. But in new situations, they were unable to regulate their own behavior and, as a result, they were slaves to environmental stimulation.

   For example, one patient was supposed to take a train to Moscow, but when he arrived at the station he stepped onto the first train he saw boarding and travelled in the opposite direction. Apparently the call "All aboard" and the sight of the others getting onto the train was more than he could resist. He couldn't tell himself, "This isn't my train," and use these words to regulate his own behavior.

   Patients with severe frontal lobe damage also have problems with perseveration; once they begin an activity, they cannot easily stop it. Luria told about a patient "who began occupational therapy after the war. He was instructed to plane a piece of wood. He planed a board down com- pletely and continued to plane the work bench, being unable to stop" (1982, p. 111).

   In such cases, we must guess that the patients were unable to use speech to control their behavior. We suppose that they could not effec- tively tell themselves, "Stop," or "Hold it." Some of Luria's other research added more direct support for this speculation.

   In one study, Luria asked patients to imitate him and raise a finger or a fist whenever he did so. This they could do. But when Luria reversed the instructions, they had difficulty. They could repeat his instructions, but they couldn't apply them to their behavior. A patient would say, "Yours is a fist, so now I must raise my finger," but he still imitated Luria and raised his fist. Such studies more directly suggest that frontal lobe damage impairs the self-regulatory function of speech (1982, p. 112).

Inner Speech

Under ordinary circumstances, adults have developed the capacity to give themselves verbal instructions inwardly and silently, through inner speech. Inner speech, however, is very difficult to investigate. Vygotsky obtained some clues from writers and poets, but he relied primarily on the study of egocentric speech in children. That is, he assumed that the changes we see in egocentric speech just before it goes underground forecast what inner speech is like (Vygotsky, 1934, pp. 226–27).

Inner speech, in comparison to social speech, seems more abbreviated. In particular, it omits the "psychological subject" of a sentence while preserving the "psychological predicate"; it omits that which we already know and focuses upon that which is new. Sometimes we can observe the same phenomenon in social situations. Vygotsky asked us to imagine several people waiting for a bus. "No one will say, on seeing the bus approach, 'The bus for which we are waiting is coming.' The sentence is likely to be abbreviated to 'Coming,' or some such expression because the subject is plain from the situation" (1934, p. 236). Similarly, when we talk silently to ourselves, we already know the subject that is on our minds, so for the sake of brevity, we restrict our words to what is new (1934, pp. 220, 236).

Another characteristic of inner speech is the dominance of "sense" over "meaning." The sense of a word is the feeling it arouses in us, and this feeling is heavily dependent on the context in which the word occurs. For example, the word *lion* may evoke feelings ranging from fear to tender sympathy depending on the story in which the word appears. The "meaning" of a word, when contrasted with its sense, refers to its precise meaning, as in its dictionary definition. A word's meaning is stable across contexts and is very important when we wish to communicate clearly. But in our inner experience, when we are using words to think about something just to ourselves, we are strongly affected by the sense of words (1934, pp. 244–45).

To understand inner speech more fully, Vygotsky (1934, pp. 245–49) said, we need to examine its role within a microgenetic process. Microgenesis, you will recall from Chapter 5, is the relatively brief developmental process that occurs every time we form a thought or a perception. The formation of a verbal statement, too, unfolds microgenetically, and inner speech enters this process at a critical point.

The act of making a verbal statement begins with a motive—an interest, a need or a problem. This is followed by some dim stirring of a thought, and it is at this point that inner speech comes into play. We engage in inner speech to try to formulate and articulate our thoughts. This process is fluid and dynamic, and both our thoughts and our words undergo several transformations as we struggle to make a clear statement without losing the inner sense of our original thought.

Recently I wanted to tell my nine-year-old daughter about a vivid personal experience. I had found that every time I jogged past a certain part of a park, I was attacked by a red-winged blackbird. Inwardly, two words strongly evoked my *sense* of the experience, my emotional image of the bird in the context. These words were *red* and *black*. Before speaking, however, I realized that these words wouldn't mean much to anyone who hadn't shared my experience.   So I changed my words so that my daughter would have a clearer image of what had occurred, while still preserving my own sense of the experience as best I could.

Sometimes we cannot find words to express our thoughts at all.   By way of illustration, Vygotsky referred to a novel by Gelb Uspensky, in which "a poor peasant, who must address an official with some life-important issue, cannot put his thoughts into words" (1934, p. 249).   The poor man asks the Lord for help, but to no avail.

Some writers have felt that the process of translating thoughts into words so routinely distorts the original thought that, as the poet F. Tiutcheve put it, "A thought once uttered is a lie" (Vygotsky, 1934, p. 254). Vygotsky recognized this danger.   Nevertheless, he argued that we need words to develop our thoughts.   A thought that fails to realize itself in words remains unfulfilled.   A "voiceless thought," as the poet O. Mandelstam said, "returns to shadow's chambers" (Vygotsky, 1934, pp. 210).

SCHOOLING

Children master most speech spontaneously, with hardly any direct teaching (Vygotsky, 1935, p. 105).   Indeed, they learn speech so readily that they seem biologically programmed to do so.   In this sense, speech seems to be as much a part of the natural line of development as the cultural line.   The acquisition of other sign systems, however, usually requires more formal instruction.   Most children learn writing and mathematics in school, and Vygotsky was one of the first psychologists to give careful consideration to the impact of school instruction on the mind of the developing child. As was his custom, he developed his ideas by comparing them to those of others, particularly to the ideas of Piaget.

Vygotsky vs. Piaget

Piaget drew a sharp distinction between development and teaching. Development, he said, is a spontaneous process that comes from the child. It comes from inner maturational growth and, more importantly, from the child's own efforts to make sense of the world.   The child, in Piaget's view, is a little intellectual explorer, making her own discoveries and formulating her own positions.

Piaget did not mean that the child develops in isolation, apart from the social world.   Other people do have an impact on the child's thinking. But they do not help the child by trying to directly teach her things.   Rather, they promote development by stimulating and challenging the child's own thinking.   This often occurs, for example, when children get into discussions and debates with friends.   If a girl finds that a friend has pointed out a flaw in her argument, she is stimulated to come up with a better argument, and her mind grows.   But the girl's intellectual development is an independent process.   For it is the girl herself—not an outside person— who must construct the new argument.

As a proponent of independent thinking, Piaget was highly critical of the teacher-directed instruction that occurs in most schools. Teachers try to take charge of the child's learning, acting as if they could somehow pour material into the child's head. They force the child into a passive position. Moreover, teachers often present abstract concepts in math, science, and other areas that are well beyond the child's own grasp. Sometimes, to be sure, children appear to have learned something, but they usually have acquired mere "verbalisms"; they repeat back the teacher's words without any genuine understanding of the concepts behind them. If adults want children to genuinely grasp concepts, they must give children opportunities to discover them on their own (Piaget, 1969).

In Vygotsky's view, spontaneous development is important, but it is not all-important, as Piaget believed. If children's minds were simply the products of their own discoveries and inventions, their minds wouldn't advance very far. In reality, children also benefit enormously from the knowledge and conceptual tools handed down to them by their cultures. In modern societies, this usually occurs in schools. Teachers do, as Piaget said, present material that is too difficult for children to learn by themselves, but this is what good instruction should do. It should march ahead of development, pulling it along, helping children master material that they cannot immediately grasp on their own. Their initial understanding might be superficial, but the instruction is still valuable, for it moves the children's minds forward.

Scientific Concepts

Vygotsky saw particular value in the kinds of abstract concepts that are taught in schools. He called them *scientific concepts*, and he included in this category concepts in math and science (e.g., Archimedes' Law) as well as concepts in the social sciences (e.g., class conflict). He contrasted these concepts with the *spontaneous concepts* that children learn on their own. Because children develop most of their spontaneous concepts outside of school, in their everyday lives, Vygotsky also referred to spontaneous concepts as *everyday concepts* (although there is no reason why schools cannot also give children opportunities to make their own discoveries, as Montessori, Dewey, and Piagetians such as Kamii have shown).

In any case, Vygotsky argued that instruction in scientific concepts is very helpful because it provides children with broader frameworks in which to place their spontaneous concepts. For example, a seven-year-old boy might have developed the spontaneous concept of *grandmother*, but his concept is primarily based on his image of his own grandmother. If we ask him to define the term, he might reply, "She has a soft lap." Formal instruction, in which the teacher diagrams family trees (including concepts such as *grandparents*, *parents*, and *children*) can give the child a broader framework in which to place his spontaneous concept and help him understand what a grandmother really is (Vygotsky, 1930, p. 50).

Vygotsky argued that this kind of formal instruction brings two specific benefits. First, it brings consciousness to the child's thinking. As long as the child thinks of the concept *grandmother* as a particular person, he is not really conscious of the concept. His awareness is directed to the person, not the concept. Only when he sees that *grandmother* is a category within a more general system of categories does he become aware of the concept as such (Vygotsky, 1934, p. 171).

Second, as children gain awareness of their concepts, they can put them to deliberate use. A 10-year-old girl who has some understanding of the concept of *grandmother* can use the concept to compare the size and composition of her family to that of a new friend. She can ask, "How many grandmothers do you have?" Later on, she might use this formal category to study genetics or kinship systems in anthropology. She can use the concept in various ways.

By learning concepts on a more general or "scientific" level, then, children become more aware of the concepts and can put them to deliberate use.

A similar process occurs when children learn to write. Before they are introduced to writing, they have mastered a great deal of spoken language, but their mastery is not at a very conscious level. Speaking is a bit like singing; it is physically expressive and flows rather naturally. Writing, in contrast, uses more formal and abstract systems of symbols and forces one to behave much more consciously and deliberately. When one writes, one is constantly making conscious decisions with respect to the proper verb form, the point at which a sentence should end, and so forth. Learning to write takes great effort, but it helps children see how language is structured. Writing, Vygotsky said, "brings awareness to speech" (1934, p. 183).

Support for Vygotsky's speculation has come from the research of Sylvia Scribner and Michael Cole (1981, pp. 151–56) on the effects of literacy among the Vai people in Liberia. The investigators presented both literate and nonliterate Vai adults with several sentences, some of which were ungrammatical. Both groups were perfectly able to say which sentences were ungrammatical. But the literate Vai were better able to explain why (for example, to explain that the subject and the verb of a sentence didn't agree). Apparently, literacy training had given them a greater conceptual awareness of their speech. In contemporary terms, they had gained *metacognitive* knowledge of their own speech.

To get a better sense of what it feels like to learn on a newly conceptual level, we might recall the experience of studying a foreign language in school. The process probably felt awkward, scholastic, and self-conscious. But we might also have felt that we were becoming aware of our native language for the first time because we were seeing it within a broader, abstract framework, as employing one set of rules where other options are possible (Vygotsky, 1934, p. 196). As Goethe said, "He who knows no foreign language does not really know his own" (Vygotsky, 1934, p. 160).

Vygotsky, then, saw much more value in scientific concepts than Piaget did. In Vygotsky's view, both scientific and spontaneous concepts have their own specific virtues. Spontaneous concepts, such as the child's own concepts of *grandmother* and *brother*, are "saturated with experience" (1934, p. 193); they are full of rich personal sensations and imagery. Scientific concepts, such as *Archimedes' Law* and *class conflict* are comparatively dry and abstract. But scientific concepts give children broader frameworks in which to view their own concepts, thus enabling children to gain awareness of and control over them.

Interactions between scientific and spontaneous concepts.

In school, the two kinds of concepts typically influence and benefit each other in the following way. Scientific concepts, which the teacher hands down "from above," lead the way. They give cognitive development a new goal, pressing children to think more abstractly than they ordinarily would.

For a while, however, children usually have difficulty understanding the new concepts. That the children understand them at all must be credited to their spontaneous concepts. When, for example, a typical Soviet class of third graders listens to the teacher discuss the concept of *class conflict*, it is only because the children have already developed spontaneous concepts of rich and poor people that they have an inkling of what the teacher is talking about. In this sense, spontaneous concepts pave the way for scientific concepts (1934, p. 194).

In any event, the teacher presses on and gives more instruction, prompting the children to think about the concepts further. After a while the pupils come to a fuller understanding of them.

Instruction, then, propels the mind forward. Instruction, Vygotsky emphasized, does not just add something new to the child's development, like adding clothes to the child's body. Rather, it interacts with development, awakening it, charting new paths for it. Vygotsky said that psychologists should do all they can to learn about this interaction (1935, pp. 80, 91).

Vygotsky himself, however, found that this interaction is difficult to study; the developmental processes stimulated by instruction are largely hidden from view. The one thing that is certain, Vygotsky found, is that development does not follow instruction in any straightforward way. When he plotted the two curves—one for the course of instruction, the other for the child's subsequent mental development—he found that the curves do not coincide. For example, it often happens that three or four steps in instruction produce no change in the child's understanding of arithmetic, and then

> ... with a fifth step, something clicks; the child has grasped a general principle, and his developmental curve rises markedly. For this child, the fifth operation was decisive, but this cannot be a general rule. The turning points at which a general principle becomes clear to the child cannot be set in advance by the curriculum. (1934, p. 185)

Thus, the teacher cannot prescribe the manner in which the child learns. The teacher might create a curriculum that progresses in a step-by-step manner, but this doesn't mean that the child will develop according to the teacher's plan. Development has its own rhythms. Still, adult teaching is necessary. Without it, the child's mind wouldn't advance very far (Vygotsky, 1934, p. 185).

The Zone of Proximal Development

Most teachers would probably agree with Vygotsky's general view-point. They would agree that it is their job to move the child's mind forward, and to do this they must directly teach children new concepts, not wait for them to make their own discoveries. At the same time, how-ever, teachers know that they cannot teach any concept to any child. They cannot, for example, effectively begin teaching algebra to most first graders. Teachers need ways of determining the kinds of lessons that children are ready for.

Most schools have made such decisions with the help of standardized achievement and intelligence tests. A school might give a third grade child an achievement test, find that he or she is doing math at the third grade level, and assign the child to a middle level math group. Vygotsky argued, however, that the conventional tests are inadequate. They only measure the child's actual level of development, telling us how far the child has developed so far. They do not tell us about the child's ability to learn new material beyond his or her present level.

The reason for this shortcoming, Vygotsky said, is that conventional tests only evaluate what the child can accomplish when working indepen-dently. But before children can perform tasks alone, they can perform them in collaboration with others, receiving some guidance or support. To determine a child's potential for new learning, then, we need to see how well the child can do when offered some assistance.

Vygotsky asked us to consider two boys who scored at the eight-year-old level on a conventional intelligence test (1934, p. 187). They scored at this level, that is, when working independently, as the test requires. Then, however, the examiner presented some new problems, too difficult for the boys to solve on their own, and offered each some slight assistance, such as a leading question or the first step in a solution. With this help, one boy scored at the nine-year-old level while the other boy scored at the 12-year-old level. Clearly, the boys' potential for new learning was not the same. Vygotsky called the distance that children can perform beyond their current level the *zone of proximal development*. More precisely, he defined the zone as

> the distance between the actual developmental level as determined by inde-pendent problem solving and the level of potential development as deter-mined through problem solving under adult guidance or in collaboration with more capable peers. (1935, p. 86)

The zone of proximal development, Vygotsky hoped, would give educators a much better indication of each child's true potential.

Actually, Vygotsky wrote just as enthusiastically about the concept's usefulness to developmental psychology. He discussed the concept as if it provides a new, improved searchlight that illuminates not only those functions that have already matured, but those that are in the process of maturing. By focusing on the activities that children can accomplish with assistance, the zone reveals those abilities that are just beginning to develop—like the ability to walk in an infant who can do so only if she has a hand to hold.   The zone of proximal development casts light not so much on "the ripe as the ripening functions"—those that the child can only carry out with assistance today but will be able to perform alone tomorrow (Vygotsky, 1934, p. 188).

But how do we know that Vygotsky was correct, that the zone of proximal development does illuminate the stirrings of inner development? When a *slight* amount of assistance quickly enables a child to succeed, we can be fairly certain we are observing a spontaneously developing capacity. The rapid success suggests that the adult aided a capacity that had already been emerging from within.

But Vygotsky also suggested that adults occasionally provide a *great deal* of assistance.   He approvingly noted, for example, that a child could use an abstract concept "because the teacher, working with the child, [had] explained, supplied information, questioned, corrected, and made the pupil explain" (1934, p. 191).   In this case, the teacher appears to have treated the child like a puppet, and it isn't clear that the teacher has stimulated anything spontaneous within the child.

Perhaps the only way to know if the child's spontaneous development is activated is to watch the child.   Is the child enthusiastic, curious, and actively involved?   Or does the child look off into space?   In fact, some research (e.g., Rogoff et al., 1984) suggests that adults who teach effectively within the zone of proximal development do continually look for signs of spontaneous interest on the child's part.

PRACTICAL APPLICATIONS

Education

Vygotsky wanted to help build a new society, and he deliberately set out to construct a theory that addressed practical matters.   As we have just seen, he tried to show how school instruction can promote child development, and he offered a new concept, the zone of proximal development, to assess each child's potential for new learning.   If we want to know what a child is ready to learn, Vygotsky said, we cannot look at what the child can do when working alone; we must see how far ahead he can go when offered some assistance.

The idea of the zone of proximal development has captured the interest of a growing number of researchers.   For example, Ann Brown and her colleagues (e.g., Brown and Ferrara, 1985) have evaluated the extent to which the concept does in fact help test a child's potential for new learning, and Brown's findings have been encouraging.   The concept has also stimulated new interest in the teaching process itself—in what happens when adults help children solve problems that they cannot solve by themselves (e.g., Rogoff et al., 1984; Griffin and Cole, 1984; Valsiner, 1984).   These studies are providing new insights into the ways in which adults gradually shift the responsibility for solving a problem from themselves to the child, how adults monitor the child's interest and enthusiasm, and other details of the teaching process.

Vygotsky also made another major educational contribution—one for which he has only recently begun to receive credit. He was perhaps the first theorist to call attention to the importance of metacognition, the person's awareness of his or her own thinking. Vygotsky did not use this particular term, but his work on memory aids and on scientific concepts indicated ways in which children become conscious of their thinking and ideas and begin to exercise some control over them. Vygotsky tried to show that consciousness and deliberate control are "the principal contributions of the school years" (1934, p. 186). In the past two decades, there has been an enormous amount of research into these processes, and educators are increasingly inclined to agree with Donaldson (1978, p. 129) that Vygotsky put his finger on the essential value of formal education.

Clinical Applications

Although Vygotsky's theory has had its widest impact in educational circles, it has also influenced other areas of practical activity. As we saw in our discussion of Luria's work, Vygotsky's insights into the self-regulative function of speech have informed the thinking of those who diagnose people suffering from neurological disorders. In addition, Vygotsky's ideas on verbal self-regulation have inspired several new psychological treatment approaches for many kinds of problems. A good example is provided by Meichenbaum and Goodman (1971), who showed how one can train hyperactive second graders to use self-directed speech to gain self-control.

First an adult experimenter modelled self-guiding speech. The following is an excerpt of what the experimenter said aloud while the child observed:

> Okay, what is it I have to do? . . . I have to go slow and be careful. Okay, draw the line down, down, good; then to the right, that's it; now down some more and to the left. Good, I'm doing fine so far. Remember to go slow. . . . No, I was supposed to go down. That's okay, just erase the line carefully. . . . Good. (Meichenbaum and Goodman, 1971, p. 117)

After this modeling, the experimenter gave the child similar instructions while the child performed the task.

Up to this point, the child's behavior was controlled by the adult's verbal commands. The next step was to shift the control to the child; the child was asked to perform the task while instructing herself aloud. Finally, the experimenter helped the child fade out her vocalized instructions; the child performed the task while whispering to herself, and then without making any sounds or lip movements at all.

Step-by-step, then, Meichenbaum and Goodman trained the impulsive children to acquire verbal control over their behavior and to exercise this control on an increasingly covert level. Meichenbaum and Goodman reported that the children who received this training subsequently outperformed the other impulsive children in their class on cognitive tasks and measures of self-control.

Other psychotherapists have also focused on self-directed speech, even if they have not traced the historical origins of their work to Vygotsky.

This is the case, for example, with Albert Ellis and his rational-emotive therapy (Ellis, 1962). Ellis zeroes in on the irrational content of his clients' silent sentences. For example, one man reported that he felt miserable because his golfing partners didn't like him. The man assumed that the event, the golfing partners' reactions to him, caused his unhappiness. In reality, Ellis contends, it was the man's internal dialogue, his telling himself that it was terrible that they didn't like him, that caused his misery (1962, pp. 126–27). And invariably it is some irrational belief, such as the belief that one must have everyone's love and approval, that causes neurotic suffering. Ellis therefore tries to get his clients to think and talk to themselves in more realistic ways. In general, psychotherapies that focus on internal dialogues come under the heading of cognitive-behavioral therapies, and they are becoming more popular every day (see Bandura, 1986, pp. 515–22 for a review).

EVALUATION

Much as psychologists rediscovered Piaget in the 1960s, they are rediscovering Vygotsky today. Vygotsky's impact is unlikely to reach the monumental proportions of Piaget's, but Vygotsky's ideas are generating a great deal of excitement because they suggest important ways to expand and balance traditional developmental theory.

Vygotsky recognized that intrinsic development, as studied by Gesell, Piaget, and others, is important; children do grow and learn from their inner maturational promptings and their active curiosity. But these forces alone, Vygotsky said, will not take children very far. To fully develop their minds, children also need the intellectual tools provided by their cultures—tools such as language, memory aids, numerical systems, writing, and scientific concepts. Thus a major task of developmental theory is to understand how these tools are acquired.

Vygotsky's proposal was that children first learn these tools in their social interactions with others; then they apply them to their own, individual thinking. For example, children first learn to speak in order to communicate with others; then they internalize their speech, talking to themselves to plan and direct their thought and behavior. Similarly, children learn many conceptual tools in social interactions in schools before they use these tools on their own. Vygotsky's accounts of the internalization of cultural tools are now recognized as classic contributions to the psychological literature.

But Vygotsky did more. He suggested that we should study how intrinsic developmental and cultural forces interact and produce new transformations. It is the interaction between these conflicting forces that psychology must eventually understand.

Vygotsky's suggestion is more impressive than it might initially sound. Many psychologists have called for eclectic approaches, saying we need to consider a variety of intrinsic and environmental variables when we study development. Such statements sound reasonable, but they overlook the legitimate conflicts between theorists who emphasize one force or the other.

Piagetians believe the child grasps a concept on his own; environmentalists believe that he learns it from others; how can both be right?   There is a logical contradiction.

Vygotsky, as a dialectical theorist, offered a new perspective.   According to dialectical theory, life is full of contradictions, and what we need to study is what happens when opposing forces meet.   We need to see what happens when the growing child, trying to figure things out for herself, encounters adults who try to teach her things.   These interactions, Vygotsky observed, are complex and largely hidden from view.   Indeed, Vygotsky frequently used the metaphors of magnifying glasses, x-rays, and telescopes to convey the need to get a better view of them (1933, p. 102; 1935, p. 91; Cole and Scribner, 1978, p. 12).   Nevertheless, by calling attention to the interactions between opposing forces, Vygotsky pointed developmental theory in an exciting new direction.

At the same time, Vygotsky has been criticized for one-sidedness.   For example, Wertsch (1985, pp. 43–48, 57, 72–73) argues that although Vygotsky said we should study the interactions between developmental and cultural forces, his own research focused largely on cultural forces.   He studied the ways in which speech, memory aids, writing, and scientific concepts transform the child's mind, but he didn't examine the ways in which the child's inner, spontaneous development might affect cultural forces (1985, p. 43).   He gave us a good picture of how children internalize their culture, but he told us little about how they might challenge or criticize their culture, as a stubborn two-year-old or an idealistic adolescent might do.

In a sense, it is easy to forgive any one-sidedness in Vygotsky's own research.   A person can only do so much in his or her research career, and Vygotsky's career was cut tragically short.   Others can study the interactions between development and culture in fuller and more balanced ways.

The problem is that Vygotsky did not restrict himself to academic matters.   He also tried to shape educational practices, and his educational ideas are rapidly gaining popularity.   In this realm, then, any one-sidedness becomes a more urgent matter, and we need to take a close look at it.   In the following comments, I will evaluate Vygotsky's educational theory from a strongly developmentalist perspective—the perspective of writers such as Rousseau, Montessori, and Piaget.

Vygotsky, compared to developmentalists, was enthusiastic about school instruction.   Instruction, he said, gives development a forward thrust.   It "does not preclude development, but charts new paths for it" (1934, p. 152).

On a day-to-day basis, the teacher moves the child forward by working within the zone of proximal development.   That is, the teacher does not just give children tasks that they can solve by themselves, but more difficult tasks, tasks that they can only solve with some assistance.   In this way, instruction stimulates capacities that are still in an embryonic state and pushes development forward.

At first glance, this kind of forward-looking instruction would seem desirable.   But developmentalists have always been wary of attempts to accelerate development. One danger is that we can push children forward before we give them the chance to fully develop their capacities at their present stage.

Imagine an ordinary five-year-old, let's say a boy. If Piaget is right, he is more strongly influenced by his perceptions than by logic. He is impressed by what he sees, hears, and feels—not rational discourse. His imagination is lively, and he likes to be physically active. In outlook and temperament, he is a natural artist; he loves to draw, sing, dance, and engage in dramatic play. As mentioned in our discussions of Werner and Piaget (pp. 92–93, 132), it is quite possible that children this age are naturally disposed to develop the artistic side of their personalities.

The danger is that the child's parents and teachers, armed with Vygotsky's ideas about instruction, will focus too exclusively on the child's future development. They will want to get him started on the 3 R's and conceptual and analytic reasoning. And the adults will probably find that they can, by providing assistance, get the boy to work on academic tasks. But in the process they may ignore the boy's need to develop his current capacities—his senses and perceptions and his artistic orientation.

In the Rousseauian view, every stage of life has its own particular virtues, and children need the time to perfect their capacities at each stage. If we constantly try to move children forward, we will deprive them of the opportunities they need to do so.[2]

But Vygotsky's educational philosophy contains a second, equally serious danger. Instruction, Vygotsky said, propels the child forward because teachers and more capable peers give the child assistance. With the help of others, children can solve problems that are beyond them as individuals. Vygotsky was undoubtedly correct about this, but he overlooked the extent to which outside assistance undermines the child's independence. Developmentalists have repeatedly warned that when we give children assistance and direction, we encourage them to depend on others to know what and how to think, undermining their ability to think for themselves.

Vygotsky, to be sure, usually recommended that we only provide children with slight amounts of assistance (such as a leading question or the first step in a solution). In such cases, the threat to the child's independence does not seem too great. But on occasion, Vygotsky implied that we might give the child a great deal of assistance. He implied this, for example, when discussing his research on the concept of *because*.

Vygotsky found that eight-year-olds frequently use *because* correctly when speaking on theoretical topics learned in school before they do so with respect to their everyday concerns. For example, a girl might correctly say, "Planned economy in the USSR is possible because there is no private property" (1934, p. 191). The reason for the girl's success, Vygotsky said,

[2]In a small number of writings, Vygotsky showed a definite appreciation of childhood's special qualities. He wrote, for example, on the child's natural inclination to draw and to play (1935, pp. 105–119; 1933, pp. 92–104). But even in these writings, he valued art and play because they move development forward. Art can lead to writing; play frees the child from the concrete situation and leads to abstract thought. Vygotsky focused on the child's future, not on the child's need for time to fully develop his or her current orientation toward life.

is that "the teacher, working with the child, has explained, supplied information, questioned, corrected, and made the pupil explain" (1934, p. 191). So, when the girl responds alone, she speaks correctly because the teacher's help is "invisibly present" (1934, p. 191).

To a developmentalist, however, the girl's correct response is no cause for celebration. When the teacher's assistance is this pervasive, it is difficult to imagine that the girl is in any way thinking for herself. She is merely saying what the teacher has trained her to say.

Vygotsky (1935) had little patience with the developmentalists' concerns. Developmentalists, he said, are so worried about the harmful effects of instruction that they constantly keep it at bay. They only introduce instruction when the child is "ready" for it, which usually means waiting for a capacity to fully mature before adding any relevant instruction. Instruction then becomes superfluous, doing nothing to move the child forward.

Actually, developmental educators—educators in the tradition of Montessori, Dewey, and Piaget—are also concerned about the child's forward movement. But they believe that children themselves will tell us the experiences they need to move forward. When a task enables a child to develop an emerging capacity, the child will show a keen interest in it and work on it with tremendous energy and concentration. For example, Montessori found that children of four years or so become deeply engrossed in cutting vegetables and other practical activities, probably because these activities help them develop their perceptual-motor skills. Thus, the teacher's job is to observe the child's interests and inclinations and to provide activities that engage the child in a full way.

Teachers will, of course, be tempted to introduce materials that they know the child will need in the future. But education is most effective when it is geared to the child's own interests and inclinations, not the teacher's goals for the future. And in no case should the teacher present tasks that are so far ahead of the child that the child can only solve them with the teacher's assistance. The teacher should introduce activities that stimulate, challenge, and engage the child, and then let the child solve them on his or her own.

In recent years, several of Vygotsky's followers have narrowed the gap between Vygotsky and the strong developmentalists. Rogoff et al. (1984), Griffin and Cole (1984), and others believe that we should pay close attention to the child's interest and enthusiasm as we lead children through tasks. These investigators do not want to squash the child's imagination, creativity, or participation in the learning process. In fact, in one essay, Vygotsky (1935, pp. 116–19) himself argued that writing instruction should arouse the child's vital interests and correspond to the child's natural way of learning.

Yet neither Vygotsky nor his followers have completely endorsed a thoroughgoing developmental position. They resist the idea that the child should take the sole initiative with respect to his or her own development. As Bruner (1984, p. 96) has said, Vygotskians oppose the "image of human development as a lone venture for the child," in which the child must figure everything out on his or her own. Instead, society has a responsibility to provide the child with the intellectual tools it has developed, and this means providing the child with instruction and assistance. If this assistance forces the child to lean on others for intellectual support, so be it. Children simply cannot discover everything on their own. To develop their minds they need the help of adults and more capable peers.

In the last analysis, then, Vygotsky and the developmentalists disagree over the extent to which development can be entrusted to the child, to the child's own interests and efforts. And this disagreement, at least on the practical level, is likely to continue for a long time. But this may be a good thing. For disagreement can be part of an ongoing dialectic, a series of challenges and responses that keep both sides thinking and coming up with new ideas.

11

Freud's Psychoanalytic Theory

BIOGRAPHICAL INTRODUCTION

In most of the chapters so far, the primary focus has been on motor or cognitive development. In this chapter we will begin discussing a group of theorists—the psychoanalysts—whose special province has been the inner world of feelings, impulses, and fantasies. The principal founder of psychoanalytic theory was Sigmund Freud (1856–1939).

Basically, Freud was a developmentalist; he believed that psychological change is governed by inner forces, especially biological maturation. But Freud also thought that maturation brings with it unruly sexual and aggressive energies, which societies must harness. Thus, social forces also play a powerful role in Freud's theory.

Freud was born in Freiberg, Moravia (now a part of Czechoslovakia). He was the first child of a 20-year-old mother and a 40-year-old father, although his father also had two grown sons from a previous marriage. The father was a wool merchant who never became very successful in business, and financial troubles forced the family to move twice when Freud was young—first to Leipzig, and then, when Freud was four, to Vienna, where Freud lived until the last year of his life (Jones, 1961, Ch. 1).

As a boy, Freud was a brilliant student, and the family encouraged his studies. His parents made sure that he had an oil lamp to study by, while the other family members had only candles (Schultz, 1975, p. 302).

Freud's intellectual interests covered a wide variety of topics, and when he was old enough to enter the university he had difficulty deciding on an area of study. With some reluctance, he chose medicine, primarily because it gave him an opportunity to do research. In medical school Freud conducted important investigations of the spinal cord of the *Petromyzon*, a type of fish (Jones, 1961, Chs. 3 and 4).

Between the ages of 26 and 35, Freud restlessly searched for a field in which he might make some important discovery. He continued to do research in established areas of neurology, but he was more excited by other possibilities. For a while, he thought he might find revolutionary uses for cocaine, a drug to which he seemed temporarily addicted. Freud also visited Charcot's laboratory in Paris, where Charcot was investigating the mysteries of hysteria. The study of this disorder became the starting point of Freud's great contributions (Jones, 1961, Chs. 5, 6, 10, and 11).

The term *hysteria* is applied to physical ailments as well as to losses of memory for which there is no physiological explanation. A woman might complain of a "glove anesthesia," a loss of feeling in the hand up to the wrist, even though physiologically there is no way she could lose sensation in precisely this part of the body.

Freud's first work on hysteria followed the example of Josef Breuer, who had treated a woman ("Anna O.") by helping her uncover buried thoughts and feelings through hypnosis. It seemed to Breuer and Freud (1895) that hysteric patients had somehow blocked off, or *repressed*, wishes and emotions from awareness. The blocked-off energy had then become converted into physical symptoms. Therapy, then, consisted of uncovering and releasing emotions that had been relegated to a separate part of the mind—the *unconscious*.

Freud's early work (1895) with hysterics can be illustrated by the case of a woman he called Elizabeth von R. Elizabeth suffered from hysterical pains in her thighs, pains that became worse after walks with her brother-in-law, toward whom she "grew to feel a peculiar sympathy . . . which easily passed with her for family tenderness" (Freud, 1910, p. 23). The sister (his wife) then died, and Elizabeth was summoned to the funeral. As Elizabeth "stood by the bedside of her dead sister, for one short moment there surged up in her mind an idea, which might be framed in these words: 'Now he is free and can marry me' " (1910, p. 23). This wish was totally unacceptable to her sense of morality, so she immediately repressed it. She then fell ill with severe hysterical pains, and when Freud came to treat her, she had completely forgotten the scene at her sister's bedside. Many hours of psychoanalytic work were necessary to uncover this and other memories, for Elizabeth had strong reasons for barring them from consciousness. Eventually, she was able to gain awareness of her feelings, and, to the extent she could accept them, they no longer needed to be redirected into bodily symptoms.

In Freud's work with Elizabeth and many other patients, he did not use hypnosis, the technique Breuer had employed. Freud found that hypnosis, among its other drawbacks, could only be used with some patients, and even with those it often produced only temporary cures. In its place he developed the method of *free association*, in which the patient is instructed to let his or her mind go and to report everything just as it occurs, making no effort to order or censor the thoughts in any way.

Freud found, however, that although free association eventually leads to buried thoughts and feelings, it is by no means completely free. Patients strongly resist the process. They block on certain topics, change the topic, insist that their thoughts are too trivial or embarrassing to mention, and so on (Freud, 1920, pp. 249–50). Freud named these interruptions *resistance* and considered resistance new evidence for the power of repression in the mind (Breuer and Freud, 1895, p. 314). That is, Freud saw new evidence for his theory that the patient's mind is at war with itself, that certain wishes are unacceptable to the patient's "ethical, aesthetic, or personal pretensions," and that the wishes therefore need to be repressed (Freud, 1910, p. 22).

As Freud built his theory, he speculated that not only hysterics and other neurotic patients suffer from this kind of internal conflict. We all have thoughts and desires that we cannot admit to ourselves. In neurosis, repression and conflict become particularly intense and unmanageable, and symptoms result. Nevertheless, conflict characterizes the human condition (Freud, 1900, p. 294; 1933, p. 121).

Breuer and Freud published a book together—*Studies on Hysteria* (1895)—which became the first classic work in psychoanalytic theory. Afterward, however, Breuer discontinued his work in the area. Breuer's decision was largely influenced by the direction the work was taking. Freud was increasingly finding that the central emotions that hysterics blocked from awareness were sexual ones—a finding that Breuer sensed was true but which he also found personally distasteful and troubling. Moreover, the sexual theory brought ridicule from the scientific community, and this hurt Breuer deeply. Consequently, Breuer left it to Freud to investigate this new area by himself.

As Freud pressed on with the work, he found that his patients' buried memories led farther back into their pasts—into their childhoods. Freud had great trouble understanding what he was finding. His patients repeatedly told stories about how their parents had committed the most immoral sexual acts against them as children—stories that Freud finally concluded must mainly be fantasies. For a while, it seemed that his research had gone up in smoke. It was not built on truth, but on fiction. But he then concluded that fantasies, too, govern our lives. Our thoughts and feelings can be as important as actual events (Freud, 1914a, p. 300; Gay, 1988, p. 95).

In 1897, the year in which Freud was puzzling over the truth of his patients' memories, he began a second line of investigation—a self-analysis. Motivated by the disturbance he felt when his father died, he began examining his own dreams, memories, and childhood experiences. Through this analysis, he gained independent confirmation of his theory of childhood sexuality and discovered what he considered his greatest insight: the Oedipus complex in the child. That is, he discovered that he (and presumably all children as well) develop an intense rivalry with the parent of the same sex for the affection of the parent of the opposite sex. Freud first published this theory in the *Interpretation of Dreams* (1900). He called the intepretation of dreams "the royal road to the unconscious" (1900, p. 647).

Freud's self-analysis was not an easy process. He had begun delving into an area—the unconscious—out of which "God knows what kind of beast will creep" (Jones, 1961, p. 213). At times, Freud was unable to think or write; he experienced "an intellectual paralysis such as I have never imagined" (1961, p. 213). And, on the top of this, what he was finding—evidence for childhood sexuality—was unacceptable to most of the scientific community. Most of his colleagues believed, with everyone else, that sexuality begins at puberty, not before. Freud's suggestion that innocent children experience sexual desires indicated that he was little more than a perverted sex maniac. In the face of this reaction, Freud felt "completely isolated" and said that he often dreaded losing his way and his confidence (Freud, 1914a, p. 302).

About 1901 (when Freud was 45 years old), he finally begin to emerge from his intellectual isolation. His work attracted various younger scientists and writers, some of whom began meeting with him for weekly discussions. These discussion groups gradually evolved into a formal psychoanalytic association. Among Freud's early disciples were Alfred Adler and Carl Jung, who, like several others, eventually broke with Freud and established their own psychoanalytic theories.

Freud continued to develop and revise his theory until the end of his life, the last 16 years of which he spent in pain from cancer of the jaw. In 1933 the Nazis burned his books in Berlin, and in 1938 he had to leave Vienna for London, where he lived his last year and died at the age of 83.

THE STAGES OF PSYCHOSEXUAL DEVELOPMENT

We have seen how Freud's work led him to believe that sexual feelings must be active in childhood. Freud's concept of sex, however, was very broad. In his view (1905), "sex" includes not just sexual intercourse but practically anything that produces bodily pleasure. In childhood, in particular, sexual feelings are very general and diffuse. Sexual feelings may be included in activities such as sucking for pleasure, masturbation, the wish to show off one's body or to look at the bodies of others, anal excretion or retention, body movements such as rocking, and even acts of cruelty, such as pinching or biting (1905, pp. 585–94).

Freud had two major reasons for considering such diverse activities as sexual. First, children seem to derive pleasure from them. Babies enjoy sucking even when they are not hungry; they suck their hands, fingers, and other objects because it produces pleasurable sensations on the mucous membranes of the mouth (1905, p. 588). Second, Freud regarded many childhood activities as sexual because they later reemerge in adult sexual activity. Most adults engage in sucking (i.e., kissing), looking, exhibitionism, or cuddling immediately prior to and during sexual intercourse. Sometimes, in the cases of so-called perversions, adults reach orgasm through childhood sexual activities alone (without sexual intercourse). A "Peeping

Tom" may reach orgasm simply by looking at the bodies of others. Neurotic adults, too, retain childhood sexual wishes, but they feel so much guilt and shame that they repress them (Freud, 1920, Chs. 20 and 21; 1905, pp. 577–79).

In Freud's theory, the term for one's general sexual energy is *libido*, and any part of the body on which this energy becomes focused is called an *erogenous zone* (Freud, 1905, pp. 585–94, 611). Almost any part of the body can become an erogenous zone, but in childhood the three most important zones are the mouth, the anus, and the genital area. These zones become the center of the child's sexual interests in a specific *stage sequence*. The child's first interests center on the mouth (the oral stage), followed by the anus (the anal stage), and finally the genital region (the phallic stage). Freud thought that this sequence is governed by a *maturational* process—by innate, biological factors (1905, pp. 587, 621). At the same time, the child's *social experiences* also play a decisive developmental role. For example, a child who experiences a great deal of frustration at the oral stage may develop a lasting preoccupation with things having to do with the mouth. Let us now look at Freud's stages in more detail.

The Oral Stage

The first months. Freud said that "if the infant could express itself, it would undoubtedly acknowledge that the act of sucking at its mother's breast is far and away the most important thing in life" (1920, p. 323). Sucking is vital, of course, because it provides nourishment; the baby must suck to stay alive. But, as mentioned, Freud thought that sucking also provides pleasure in its own right. This is why babies suck on their thumbs and other objects even when they are not hungry. Freud called such pleasure-sucking *autoerotic*; when babies suck their thumbs, they do not direct their impulses toward others but find gratification through their own bodies (Freud, 1905, p. 586).

Autoerotic activities are not confined to the oral stage. Later on, for example, children masturbate, and this too is autoerotic. However, Freud emphasized the autoerotic nature of the oral stage because he wanted to stress the extent to which babies are wrapped up in their own bodies. Like Piaget, Freud thought that during the first six months or so of life the baby's world is "objectless." That is, the baby has no conception of people or things existing in their own right. When nursing, for example, young infants experience the comfort of the mother's hold, but they do not recognize the existence of the mother as a separate person. Similarly, when cold, wet, or hungry, babies feel mounting tension and even panic, but they are unaware of any separate person who might relieve the pain. They simply long for a return of pleasurable feelings. Thus, although babies are completely dependent on others, they are unaware of this fact because they do not yet recognize other people's separate existence.

Sometimes Freud described this initial objectless state as one of *primary narcissism* (e.g., 1915a, p. 79). The term *narcissism* means self-love and is taken from the Greek myth about a boy called Narcissus, who fell in love with his reflection in a pond. As some scholars have observed (e.g., Jacobson, 1954), this term is somewhat confusing because it implies that babies have a clear conception of themselves to love, when they still cannot distinguish themselves from the rest of the world. Still, the term *narcissism* does convey the idea that at first babies focus primarily inward, on their own bodies. The basic narcissistic state, Freud (1916) said, is sleep, when infants feel warm and content and have absolutely no interest in the outside world.

The second part of the oral stage.

Beginning at about six months, babies begin to develop a conception of another being, especially the mother, as a separate, necessary person. They become anxious when she leaves or when they encounter a stranger in her place (Freud, 1936a, p. 99).

At the same time, another important development is taking place: the growth of teeth and the urge to bite. At this point, Karl Abraham (1924a) pointed out, babies dimly form the idea that it is they, with their urge to bite and devour, who can drive their mothers away. Life at this stage, then, becomes increasingly complex and troubling. It is little wonder that we may often unconsciously wish to return to the earlier oral stage, when things seemed so much simpler and more gratifying.

An illustration: Hansel and Gretel.

Freud was aware of the difficulty in reaching conclusions about the infant's mental life. Babies cannot talk and tell us about their feelings and fantasies. To some extent, we are forced to reconstruct the infant's psychic life from the analyses of adults who seem to revert to early ways of thinking, namely psychotics. But Freudians also suggest that many myths and fairy tales reveal the child's early fantasies and concerns.

Bettelheim (1976, pp. 159–66) wrote about the oral themes contained in the story of Hansel and Gretel. Briefly, Hansel and Gretel are two children who are sent into the forest by their parents, especially the mother, because they are careless with food (milk) and there is no longer enough to feed them. In the forest, they come upon a gingerbread house, which they proceed to devour. They sense that it may be dangerous to eat so much of the house and hear a voice that asks, "Who is nibbling at my house?" But they ignore it, telling themselves, "It is only the wind" (The Brothers Grimm, 1972, p. 90). The woman who owns the house then appears, and she is at first completely gratifying. She gives them all kinds of good things to eat and nice beds in which to sleep. But the next day she turns out to be worse than their mother. She is a witch who intends to eat them.

In Bettelheim's analysis, the themes are largely those of the second oral stage. The story begins with the children experiencing the dreaded separation from their caretakers. There is some hint that the children's own inner urges are at the root of their troubles; they have been reckless with their mother's milk and they greedily devour the gingerbread house. The children's wish is to return to the first oral stage, which seemed so blissful. So they meet the witch, who is temporarily "the original, all-giving mother, whom every child hopes to find again later somewhere out in the world" (Bettelheim, 1976, p. 161). However, this proves impossible. Because they are dimly aware of their own oral destructiveness, they imagine that others will take an oral revenge, which is what the witch attempts to do.

Bettelheim says that fairy tales facilitate growth by addressing children's deepest fears while, at the same time, showing them that their problems have solutions. In this story, Hansel and Gretel finally quit acting solely on the basis of their oral impulses and use more rational parts of the personality. They employ reason to outwit the witch and kill her, and they return home as more mature children.

Fixation and regression.
According to Freud, we all go through the oral stage as well as every other stage of psychosexual development. However, we also can develop a *fixation* at any stage, which means that no matter how far we have advanced beyond it, we maintain a lasting preoccupation with the pleasures and issues of the earlier stage. For example, if we are fixated at the oral stage, we might find ourselves continually preoccupied with food; or we find that we work most comfortably when we are sucking or biting on objects, such as pencils; or we gain the most pleasure from oral sexual activities; or we find ourselves addicted to smoking or drinking partly because of the oral pleasure involved (Freud, 1905; Abraham, 1924b).

Freud said that he was not certain about the causes of fixation (1920, p. 357), but psychoanalysts generally believe that fixations are produced by either excessive gratification or excessive frustration at the stage in question (Abraham, 1924b, p. 357; Fenichel, 1945, p. 65). The baby who receives prolonged and very satisfying nursing may continue to seek oral pleasures. Alternatively, the baby who experiences sharp frustrations and deprivations at the oral stage may act as if he or she is unwilling to give up oral satisfactions or as if there is a persistent danger that oral needs will not be met. Such a person might, for instance, become anxious when meals are not served on time and devour the food as if it might disappear at any moment. In general, it seems that severe frustrations, rather than excessive gratifications, produce the strongest fixations (Whiting and Child, 1953; R. W. White and Watt, 1973, pp. 136, 148, 189).

Sometimes people show few oral traits in their daily lives until they experience some frustration, and then they *regress* to the oral fixation point. A little boy who suddenly finds himself deprived of parental affections when his baby sister is born might regress to oral behavior and once again take up thumb-sucking—something he had previously given up. Or a teenage girl may not be particularly concerned about oral matters until she loses a boyfriend, and then she becomes depressed and finds comfort in eating.

The tendency to regress is determined by both the strength of the fixation in childhood and the magnitude of the current frustration (Freud, 1920, Ch. 22). If we have a strong oral fixation, a relatively small frustration in our current life may be sufficient to cause an oral regression. Alternatively, a major frustration might cause a regression to an earlier developmental stage even if the fixation was not particularly strong.

The kinds of regressions we have been discussing might occur in any of us—in relatively "normal" people. We all find life frustrating at times, and now and then we regress to earlier, more infantile, ways of behaving. Such regressions are not pathological, because they are only partial and temporary. For example, the boy who resumes thumb-sucking when his baby sister is born usually does so only for a while; in any case, he does not become like an infant in other respects.

Freud also believed, however, that the concepts of fixation and regression can help clarify more serious emotional disorders. In certain forms of schizophrenia, there is a very complete regression to the first developmental stage. The schizophrenic often withdraws from interaction with others and entertains grandiose ideas concerning his or her importance. The patient may think that he or she is God and that his or her ideas affect the whole world. In such a case, the person has undergone a fairly complete regression to a state of primary narcissism, in which the libido is invested solely in the self, and the boundaries between self and the rest of the world have once again become unstable (1920, pp. 422–24).

According to Abraham (1924a), regression to the oral stage is also evident in severe cases of depression. Such depressions frequently follow the loss of a loved one, and a common symptom is the patient's refusal to eat. Perhaps patients are punishing themselves because they unconsciously feel that it was their own oral anger that destroyed the love object.

The Anal Stage

During the second and third years of the child's life, the anal zone becomes the focus of the child's sexual interests. Children become increasingly aware of the pleasurable sensations that bowel movements produce on the mucous membranes of the anal region. As they gain maturational control over their sphincter muscles, they sometimes learn to hold back their bowel movements until the last moment, thereby increasing the pressure on the rectum and heightening the pleasure of the final release (Freud, 1905, p. 589). Children also frequently take an interest in the products of their labors and enjoy handling and smearing their feces (Freud, 1913, pp. 88–91; Jones, 1918, p. 424).

It is at this stage that children are first asked to renounce their instinctual pleasures in a fairly dramatic way. Few parents are willing to permit their children to smear and play with feces for very long. Most parents, as well-socialized individuals, feel a certain repugnance over anal matters and soon get children to feel the same way. As soon as their children are ready, if not sooner, parents toilet-train them.

Some children initially fight back by deliberately soiling themselves (Freud, 1905, p. 591). They also sometimes rebel by becoming wasteful, disorderly, and messy—traits which sometimes persist into adulthood as aspects of the "anal expulsive" character (Brown, 1940; Hall, 1954, p. 108).

Freud, however, was most interested in the opposite reaction to parental demands. He observed that some people develop an excessive stake in cleanliness, orderliness, and reliability (1908a). It seems as if they felt, as children, that it was too risky to rebel against parental demands, and so they anxiously conformed to parental rules. Instead of messing and smearing, they became models of self-control, acquiring a disgust for anything dirty or smelly, and developing a compulsive need to be clean and orderly. Such people, who are sometimes labeled "anal compulsive" characters, also harbor resentment over submitting to authority, but they do not dare to express their anger openly. Instead, they frequently develop a passive obstinacy; they insist on doing things according to their own schedule— often while others are forced to wait. They may also be frugal and stingy. It is as if they feel that although they were forced to give up their feces when others demanded it, they will hold onto other things, such as money, and nobody will take them away.

Toilet-training probably arouses sufficient anger and fear to produce some measure of fixation in most children, especially in the United States, where we tend to be strict about this matter (Munroe, 1955, p. 287). Consequently, most people probably develop at least some tendency toward "anal expulsiveness," "anal compulsiveness," or some combination of both. Sometimes these traits have little serious impact on one's life but then emerge in a more pronounced way when one is under stress. For example, writers may be prone to compulsive behavior when they become anxious about their work. A writer may be unable to finish a manuscript because of a compulsive need to check and recheck it for mistakes. To a Freudian, such behavior probably represents a regression to the anal stage, where the individual learned that his or her natural actions met with unexpected disapproval. That is, the writer might have learned that his or her first "productions" were considered dirty and revolting when done spontaneously but prized if done properly. Thus, the writer, anxious about the impact of the manuscript, tries to protect himself or herself by seeing that everything is done precisely as it is supposed to be.

The Phallic or Oedipal Stage

Between the ages of about three and six years, the child enters the phallic or oedipal stage. Freud understood this stage better in the case of the boy than in the case of the girl, so we will begin our discussion with the boy.

The boy's oedipal crisis. The oedipal crisis begins when the boy starts to take an interest in his penis. This organ, which is "so easily excitable and changeable, and so rich in sensations," fires his curiosity (Freud, 1923, p. 246). He wants to compare his penis to those of other males and of animals, and he tries to see the sexual organs of girls and women. He may also enjoy exhibiting his penis and, more generally, imagines the role he might play as an adult, sexual person. He initiates experiments and spins fantasies in which he is an aggressive, heroic male, frequently directing his intentions toward his primary love-object, his mother. He may begin kissing Mommy aggressively, or want to sleep with her at night, or imagine marrying her. He probably does not yet conceive of sexual intercourse per se, but he does wonder what he might do with her.

The boy soon learns, however, that his most ambitious experiments and plans are considered excessive and improper. He learns that he cannot, after all, marry Mommy or engage in any sex play with her. He cannot even touch, hug, or cuddle with Mommy as much as he would like, since he is now a "big boy."   At the same time, he notices that Daddy seems to be able to do whatever *he* wants: Daddy seems to kiss and hug Mommy at will, and he sleeps with her all night long (doing with her whatever grown-ups do at night).   Thus, the lines of Oedipus complex are drawn: The boy sees the father as a rival for the affections of the mother.

The little boy's oedipal wishes are illustrated by Freud's case of Little Hans (1909).   When Hans was about five years, he asked his mother to touch his penis, and he wanted to cuddle with her at night.   His father, however, objected.   Soon after, Hans had the following dream:

> In the night there was a big giraffe in the room and a crumpled one; and the big one called out because I took the crumpled one away from it.   Then it stopped calling out; and then I sat down on top of the crumpled one (p. 179).

According to Freud, Han's dream probably represented his wish to take his mother (the crumpled giraffe) from the father (the big giraffe).

The little boy, of course, cannot realistically hope to carry out his rivalrous wishes; the father is too big.   Of course, he could still entertain rivalrous fantasies, but these too become dangerous.   For one thing, he not only feels jealous of his father, but also loves and needs his father, so he is frightened by his destructive wishes toward him.   But more important, the boy begins to consider the possibility of *castration*.   In Freud's day, parents often made outright threats of castration when a boy masturbated. Today, parents may discourage maturbation more delicately, but the boy does probably begin to worry about castration when he realizes that his sister or other females are missing a penis.   He then concludes that they once had one, but it was cut off, and the same thing could happen to him. Thus, the oedipal rivalry takes on a new, dangerous dimension, and the boy must escape the whole situation (Freud, 1924, p. 271).

Typically, the boy resolves the oedipal predicament through a series of defensive maneuvers (Freud, 1923; 1924).   He fends off his incestuous desires for his mother through *repression*; that is, he buries any sexual feelings toward her deep into his unconscious.   He still loves his mother, of course, but he now admits only to a socially acceptable, "sublimated" love—a pure, higher love.   The boy overcomes his rivalry with his father by repressing his hostile feelings and by increasing his *identification* with him.   Instead of trying to fight the father, he now becomes more like him, and in this way vicariously enjoys the feeling of being a big man.   It is as if the boy were to say, "If you can't beat him, join him."

To overcome the oedipal crisis, finally, the boy internalizes a *superego*. That is, he adopts his parents' moral prohibitions as his own, and in this way establishes a kind of internal policeman who guards against dangerous impulses and desires.   The superego is similar to what we ordinarily call the *conscience*; it is an inner voice that reprimands us and makes us feel guilty for bad thoughts and actions.   Before the child internalizes a superego, he suffers only from external criticism and punishment.   Now, however, he can criticize himself, and thus he possesses an inner fortification against forbidden impulses.

FIGURE 11.1   Drawings by a five-year-old boy and a six-year-old girl suggest sexual interests of the phallic stage.

The foregoing review suggests the complexity of the Oedipus complex, but it actually is far more complex than we have indicated.   The boy's rivalry and love work both ways—he also rivals the mother for the affection of the father (Freud, 1923, pp. 21–24).   The situation is also complicated by the presence of siblings, who also become the objects of love and jealousy (Freud, 1920, p. 343), and by other factors, such as the loss of a parent. We cannot begin to go into the limitless variations here, but the interested reader can refer to Fenichel (1945, pp. 91–98).

Typical outcomes.   Typically, when the boy resolves the Oedipus complex at the age of six years or so, his rivalrous and incestuous wishes are temporarily driven underground.   As we shall see, he enters the latency period, during which he is relatively free of these worries.   Nevertheless, oedipal feelings continue to exist in the unconscious.   They threaten to break into consciousness once again at puberty and exert a strong influence on the life of the adult. This influence has many variations, but it typically is felt in two central areas: competition and love.

As the adult male enters into competition with other men, he carries with him the dim knowledge of his first forays into this area. The first time he dared to rival a man his masculinity suffered a sharp setback. Consequently, he may be apprehensive about rivaling men again. In the back of his mind, he is still a little boy, wondering if he can really be a big man (Freud, 1914b; Fenichel, 1945, p. 391).

The adult may also feel a sense of guilt over competitive urges. The first time he rivaled a man, he wished to do away with his competitor. He repressed these hostile wishes and established a superego to help fend them off, but he still may dimly feel that the wish to become more successful than others is somehow wrong (Freud, 1936b, p. 311).

Oedipal feelings also influence a man's experiences in love. Freud said that the man "seeks above all the memory-image of the mother" (1905, p. 618). However, this desire has its problems. In the early years, it became associated with castration anxiety and guilt. Consequently, men are sometimes impotent with women who evoke too much of the mother's presence. They become sexually inhibited with women who arouse the deep and tender feelings associated with her, and they are most potent with women whom they regard as mere outlets for their physical needs (Freud, 1912).

Freud thought that everyone undergoes an oedipal crisis, so all men have some of these feelings to a certain degree. Severe problems usually stem from excessive fears experienced as a child. Still, oedipal problems are not as serious as those that develop at earlier periods, when the personality is in a more formative stage.

The girl's Oedipus complex.
Freud thought that there was an Oedipus complex for the little girl too, but he admitted that "here our material—for some reason we do not understand—becomes far more shadowy and incomplete" (1924, p. 274). Freud's views on this topic, in broad outline, were as follows. He noted (1933, pp. 122–27) that the girl, by the age of five years or so, becomes disappointed in her mother. She feels deprived because her mother no longer gives her the constant love and care that she required as a baby, and, if new babies are born, she resents the attention they receive. Furthermore, she is increasingly irritated by the mother's prohibitions, such as that on masturbation. Finally, and most upsetting, the girl discovers that she does not have a penis—a fact for which she blames the mother, "who sent her into the world so insufficiently equipped" (1925a, p. 193).

The little girl's genital disappointment is illustrated by an anecdote from Ruth Munroe (1955, pp. 217–18), a psychologist who said that she was skeptical about Freud's theory until one day when she observed her four-year-old daughter in a bathtub with her brother. The daughter suddenly exclaimed, "My weewee (penis) is all gone,"—apparently comparing herself with her brother for the first time. Munroe tried to reassure her, but nothing worked, and for some weeks she objected violently even to being called a girl. Thus, this little girl felt what Freud called *penis envy*, the wish to have a penis and to be like a boy (Freud, 1933, p. 126).

The little girl does, however, recover her feminine pride. This happens when she begins to appreciate the attentions of her father. The father may have not paid any special attention to his daughter when she was in diapers, but now he may begin to admire her cuteness and growing femininity, calling her his little princess and flirting with her in other ways. Thus inspired, she begins to spin romantic fantasies involving herself and her father. At first her thoughts include a vague wish for his penis, but this soon changes into a wish to have a baby and give it to him as a present.

As with the little boy, the little girl discovers that she lacks sole rights to her new love-object. She realizes that she cannot, after all, marry Daddy, nor can she cuddle, hug, or sleep with him as much as she would like. However, the mother seems to be able to do these things, so she becomes the rival for his affections. Freud said that this oedipal situation might be called the *Electra complex* (1940, p. 99).

What most puzzled Freud about the girl's Oedipus complex was the motivation for its resolution. In the case of the little boy, the primary motivation seemed clear: The boy is frightened by the threat of castration. But the little girl cannot fear castration, for she has no penis to lose. Why, then, does she renounce her oedipal wishes at all? In one essay, Freud said that he simply did not know the answer (1925a, p. 196), but his best guess was that the girl resolves the oedipal crisis because she fears the loss of parental love (1933, p. 87). Thus, she does after all repress her incestuous desires, identify with her mother, and institute a superego to check herself against forbidden impulses and wishes.[1] Still, lacking castration anxiety, her motivation to erect strong defenses against oedipal feelings must be weaker, and, as a result, she must develop a weaker superego. Freud knew that this last conclusion would anger the feminists, but this was where his reasoning led and he argued that women in fact are less rigid about moral issues (1933, p. 129).

Like a boy, then, the little girl entertains and then abandons rivalrous and incestuous fantasies. In some ways, the later consequences of the oedipal experience would seem similar to those for the boy. For example, the girl too may carry within her the dim knowledge that her first attempt at rivaling a woman for a man's love failed, and she may therefore doubt her future prospects. At the same time, though, the girl's oedipal experiences differed from the boy's, so the effects may differ as well. She had less need to resolve the Oedipus crisis, so her oedipal desires may be more open and transparent later in life (Freud, 1933, p. 129). Furthermore, just before she entered into the oedipal rivalry, she experienced a deep disappointment over being female. This feeling, Freud felt, may lead to a "masculinity complex," in which the woman may avoid intimate relationships with men, since these only remind her of her inferior state, and, instead, try to outdo men by becoming very aggressive and assertive (Freud, 1933, p. 126).

---

[1]As with the boy, the girl's Oedipus complex is exceedingly complex. Rivalries develop with both parents and with siblings as well.

The Latency Stage

With the establishment of strong defenses against oedipal feelings, the child enters the latency period, which lasts from about age six to 11 years. As the name suggests, sexual and aggressive fantasies are now largely latent; they are kept firmly down, in the unconscious. Freud thought that the repression of sexuality at this time is quite sweeping; it includes not only oedipal feelings and memories, but oral and anal ones as well (Freud, 1905, pp. 580–85). Because dangerous impulses and fantasies are now kept underground, the child is not excessively bothered by them, and the latency period is one of relative calm. The child is now free to redirect his or her energies into concrete, socially acceptable pursuits, such as sports and games and intellectual activities.

Some of Freud's followers have argued that sexual and aggressive fantasies do not disappear at this time as completely as Freud implied (Blos, 1962, pp. 53–54). For example, an eight-year-old boy is still interested in girls' bodies, and he typically discovers the real facts of life at about this age. Nevertheless, most Freudians agree that sexual concerns lose their frightening and overwhelming character. In general, the latency-age child possesses a new composure and self-control.

Puberty (The Genital Stage)

The stability of the latency period, however, does not last. As Erikson says, "It is only a lull before the storm of puberty" (1959, p. 88). At puberty, which begins at about age 11 for girls and age 13 for boys, sexual energy wells up in full adult force and threatens to wreak havoc with the established defenses. Once again, oedipal feelings threaten to break into consciousness, and now the young person is big enough to carry them out in reality (Freud, 1920, p. 345).

Freud said that from puberty onward the individual's great task is "freeing himself from the parents" (1920, p. 345). For the son, this means releasing his tie to the mother and finding a woman of his own. The boy must also resolve his rivalry with his father and free himself of his father's domination of him. For the daughter, the tasks are the same; she too must separate from the parents and establish a life of her own. Freud noted, however, that independence never comes easily (1905, p. 346). Over the years we have built up strong dependencies upon our parents, and it is painful to separate ourselves emotionally from them. For most of us, the goal of genuine independence is never completely attained.

Anna Freud on Adolescence

Although Freud sketched the general tasks of adolescence, he wrote little about the distinctive stresses and behavior patterns of this stage of life. It was his daughter, Anna Freud, who made many of the first contributions to the psychoanalytic study of adolescence.

Anna Freud's starting point was the same as Freud's: The teenager experiences the dangerous resurgence of oedipal feelings. Typically, the young person is most aware of a growing resentment against the parent of the same sex. Incestuous feelings toward the other parent remain more unconscious.

Anna Freud said that when adolescents first experience the welling up of oedipal feelings, their first impulse is to *take flight*. The teenager feels tense and anxious in the presence of the parents and feels safe only when apart from them. Some adolescents actually run away from home at this time, while many others remain in the house "in the attitude of a boarder" (A. Freud, 1958, p. 269). They shut themselves up in their rooms and feel comfortable only when with their peers.

Sometimes adolescents try to escape their parents by developing a blanket *contempt* for them. Instead of admitting any dependence and love, they take an attitude that is exactly the opposite. It is as if they think that they can become free of parental involvement by thinking absolutely nothing of them. Here, again, teenagers may fancy themselves suddenly independent, but their parents still dominate their lives, for they spend all their energy attacking and deriding their parents (1958, p. 270).

Adolescents sometimes attempt to defend themselves against feelings and impulses altogether, regardless of the objects to whom their feelings are attached. One strategy is *asceticism*. That is, the adolescent tries to fend off all physical pleasure. Boys or girls might adhere to strict diets; deny themselves the pleasures of attractive clothes, dancing, or music, or anything else fun or frivolous; or try to master their bodies through exhausting physical exercise.

Another defense against impulses is *intellectualization*. The adolescent attempts to transfer the problems of sex and aggression onto an abstract, intellectual plane. He or she might construct elaborate theories on the nature of love and the family, and on freedom and authority. While such theories may be brilliant and original, they are also thinly disguised efforts to grapple with oedipal issues on a purely intellectual level (A. Freud, 1936).

Anna Freud observed that adolescent turmoil and the desperate defenses and strategies of this period are actually normal and to be expected. She did not usually recommend psychotherapy; she thought that the adolescent should be given time and scope to work out his or her own solution. However, parents may need guidance, for there "are few situations in life which are more difficult to cope with than an adolescent son or daughter during the attempt to liberate themselves" (A. Freud, 1958, p. 276).

THE AGENCIES OF THE MIND

We have now reviewed the stages of development. Freud's theory contains many other concepts, and we cannot review them all. However, an introduction to Freud does require a look at one other cluster of concepts, those pertaining to the agencies of the mind. Freud was continually revising his ideas on this topic, but his best-known concepts are those of the id, ego, and superego.

The Id

The *id* is the part of the personality that Freud initially called "the unconscious" (e.g., 1915b). It is the most primitive part of the personality, containing the basic biological reflexes and drives. Freud likened the id to a pit "full of seething excitations," all pressing for discharge (1933, p. 73). In terms of motivation, the id is dominated by the *pleasure principle*; its goal is to maximize pleasure and minimize pain. Pleasure, in Freud's view, is primarily a matter of reducing tension (1920, p. 365). During sexual intercourse, tension mounts and its final release is pleasurable. Similarly, we find that the release of hunger or bladder tensions brings pleasurable relief. In general, the id tries to remove all excitation and to return to a quiet state—namely, that of deep, peaceful sleep.

At first, the baby is almost all id. Babies worry about little besides bodily comfort, and they try to discharge all tensions as quickly as possible. However, even babies must experience frustration. For example, they sometimes must wait to be fed. What the id does then is to *hallucinate* an image of the desired object, and in this way it temporarily satisfies itself. We see such *wish-fulfilling* fantasies at work when a starving person hallucinates an image of food, or when a thirsty dreamer dreams that a glass of water is at hand and therefore does not have to wake up and get one (Freud, 1900, pp. 158, 165). Such fantasies are prime examples of what Freud called *primary process thinking* (1900, p. 535).

In the course of life, many impressions and impulses are repressed into the id, where they exist side by side with the basic drives. In this "dark and inaccessible" region of the mind, there is nothing that corresponds to logic or a sense of time (Freud, 1933, pp. 73–74). Impressions and strivings "are virtually immortal; after the passage of decades they behave as though they had just occurred" (1933, p. 74). Images in the id, furthermore, are very fluid and easily merge into one another. The id is oceanic, chaotic, and illogical. It is completely cut off from the external world. Our best knowledge of this mysterious region comes from the study of dreams.

The id, then, contains basic drives and reflexes, along with images and sensations that have been repressed. So far we have focused on the id's sexual drives and those associated with the preservation of life, such as hunger and thirst. The id also contains aggressive and destructive forces. Freud's views on aggression are complex and underwent drastic revisions, but in a sense we can see how aggression follows the id's basic principle of reducing tension. In the id, any image that is associated with pain or tension should be instantly destroyed. It does not matter to the id that one may be wishing for the destruction of someone one needs and loves; contradictions such as these have no importance in this illogical region of the mind. The id simply wants a reduction in disturbing tensions immediately.

The Ego

If we were ruled by the id, we would not live for long. To survive, one cannot act solely on the basis of hallucinations or simply follow one's impulses. We must learn to deal with reality. For example, a little boy soon learns that he cannot just impulsively grab food from wherever he sees it. If he takes it from a bigger boy, he is likely to get hit. He must learn to consider reality before acting. The agency that delays the immediate impulse and considers reality is called the *ego*.

Freud said that whereas "the id stands for the untamed passions," the ego "stands for reason and good sense" (1933, p. 76). Because the ego considers reality, it is said to follow the *reality principle* (1911). The ego tries to forestall action until it has had a chance to perceive reality accurately, to consider what has happened in similar situations in the past, and to make realistic plans for the future (1940, p. 15). Such reasonable ways of thinking are called *secondary process thinking* and include what we generally think of as perceptual or cognitive processes. When we work on a math problem, plan a trip, or write an essay, we are making good use of ego functions. At first, though, the ego's functioning is largely bodily or motoric. For example, when a child first learns to walk, he or she inhibits impulses toward random movement, considers where he or she is headed to avoid collisions, and otherwise exercises ego controls (1940, p. 15).

The term *ego* is one that we hear a great deal in everyday language. Quite often, we hear that someone has a "big ego," meaning that this person has an inflated self-image. Although Freud himself occasionally wrote about the ego in just this way (e.g., 1917), many Freudians (e.g., Hartmann, 1956; Beres, 1971) contend that we should distinguish between the ego and the self-image. Strictly speaking, they say, the ego refers only to a set of functions—judging reality accurately, regulating impulses, and so on. The self-image, the picture we have of ourselves, is different from the ego itself.

Freud emphasized that although the ego functions somewhat independently from the id, it also borrows all its energy from the id. He likened the ego's relation to the id to that of a rider on a horse. "The horse supplies the locomotive energy, while the rider has the privilege of deciding on the goal and guiding the powerful animal's movement. But only too often there arises between the ego and the id the not precisely ideal situation of the rider being obliged to guide the horse along the path by which it itself wants to go" (1933, p. 77).

The Superego

The ego is sometimes called one of the "control systems" of the personality (Redl and Wineman, 1951). The ego controls the blind passions of the id to protect the organism from injury. We mentioned how a little boy must learn to inhibit the impulse to grab food until he can determine whether it is realistically safe to do so. But we also control our actions for other reasons. We might also refrain from taking things from others because we believe such actions are morally wrong. Our standards of right and wrong constitute the second control system of the personality, the *superego*.

We referred earlier to Freud's view on the origin of the superego: It is a product of the oedipal crisis. Children introject parental standards to check themselves against the dangerous impulses and fantasies of this period. Freud did note, though, that the superego continues to develop after this period as well. Children continue to identify with other people, such as teachers and religious leaders, and to adopt their moral standards as their own (1923, p. 27).

Freud wrote about the superego as if it contained two parts (1923, pp. 24–25). One part is sometimes called the *conscience* (Hall, 1954). It is the punitive, negative, and critical part of the superego that tells us what *not* to do and punishes us with feelings of guilt when we violate its demands. The other part is called the *ego ideal*, and this part consists of *positive* aspirations. For example, when a little boy wants to be just like a famous basketball player, the athlete is his ego ideal. The ego ideal may also be more abstract. It may include our positive ideals, such as the wish to become more generous, courageous, or dedicated to principles of justice and freedom.

Levels of Awareness of the Three Agencies

The id, ego, and superego function at differing levels of awareness, as Freud tried to show by means of a diagram (1933, p. 78), reproduced here as Figure 11.2.

The id, at the bottom of the drawing, is completely removed from the region labeled *pcpt.-cs*, from consciousness and the perception of reality. The id is entirely unconscious, which means that its workings can be made conscious only with a great deal of effort.

The ego extends into consciousness and reality; it is the part of the id that develops in order to deal with the external world. The ego, you will note, largely inhabits a region labeled *preconscious*. This term refers to functioning that is below awareness but can be made conscious with

FIGURE 11.2 Freud's sketch of the personality structure. (Reprinted from *New Introductory Lectures on Psychoanalysis* by Sigmund Freud. Translated and edited by James Strachey. Copyright © 1933 by Sigmund Freud. Copyright renewed 1961 by W.J.H. Sprott. Copyright © 1965, 1964 by James Strachey. By permission of W. W. Norton & Co., Inc., Sigmund Freud Copyrights, the Institute of Psycho-Analysis, and the Hogarth Press.

relatively little effort. The ego is also partly unconscious; for example, it represses forbidden thoughts in a completely unconscious way.

The superego is drawn on top of the ego, illustrating its role of criticizing the ego from above. The superego, too, is partly unconscious; although we are sometimes aware of our moral standards, they also frequently affect us unconsciously. For example, we might suddenly become depressed without any idea why, because our superego is punishing us for forbidden thoughts.

The Central Role of the Ego

In the last analysis, our ability to deal with life—our mental balance—rests with our ego's ability to meet the various pressures put upon it. More specifically, the ego is the executive agency that must somehow serve three "tyrannical masters"—the id, reality, and the superego (1933, p. 78). The ego must eventually meet the biological demands of the id, but in a way that also respects external reality and does not violate the precepts of the superego. The task is difficult because the ego is basically weak; as mentioned, it has no energy of its own, but borrows it from the id. Consequently, the ego is quite prone to anxiety—to the fear that it might not satisfy any one of its three dictators. First, the ego experiences "neurotic anxiety" when it feels it cannot master the impulses of the id, as when a dangerous, repressed wish threatens to break out, or when we feel helpless to meet a basic biological need. Second, the ego feels "moral anxiety" when it anticipates punishment from the superego. And third, the ego is always subject to "realistic anxiety" when we face the dangers in the external world.

"Thus the ego, driven by the id, confined by the superego, repulsed by reality, struggles to master its economic task of bringing harmony among the forces and influences working in and upon it; and we can understand how it is that so often we cannot suppress a cry: 'Life is not easy!'" (Freud, 1933, p. 78)

In much of Freud's writing, the ego seems to regard the id and the superego as adversaries, as powerful combatants it must somehow appease and control. However, Freud also recognized the vital necessity of the id and superego, and some of Freud's closest followers have elaborated on the positive ways the ego utilizes these agencies. In an important contribution, Kris (1952) described how the ego can utilize the fluid, sensuous, dreamlike imagery of the id as a source of creative thinking. Artists, for example, may temporarily abandon their tight ego controls and realistic thinking in order to delve into the unconscious for its rich imagery and inspirational power. Kris called this process "regression in the service of the ego," and Kris's concept has become very important in Freudian theory. You might recall that Werner (Chapter 5) also emphasized a similar process in his discussions of microgenesis. For both Werner and the Freudians, then, primordial thinking is not just something to be overcome but may continually serve as a rich resource for creative work.

Dreams

Freud was very interested in dreams, which can tell us much about the mysterious workings of the unconscious. Actually, however, all three agencies are at work.

Dreams begin as wishes from the id. For example, a child who is hungry dreams that he or she is eating a delicious meal. Such dreams are innocent enough and directly express the id's wishes. However, many wishes violate the standards of the superego, so the ego requires some distortion or disguise of the original wish before permitting the dream to surface into consciousness (Freud, 1940, p. 51). In one of Freud's examples, a little boy was told that it was wrong for him to eat very much because of his illness; so one night, when he was especially hungry, he dreamt that someone else was enjoying a sumptuous meal (1900, pp. 301–2). Similarly, many sexual and aggressive wishes must be disguised and distorted before surfacing. Because the dream we remember upon waking has undergone disguise, we cannot interpret it in any simple, straightforward way. In psychoanalysis, the patient is asked to free-associate to the dream. That is, he or she is asked to say whatever comes to mind in connection with each aspect of it. Patients do not find it easy to associate freely—without censoring "immoral" thoughts and fantasies—but eventually the process can reveal the dream's underlying meanings (Freud, 1920, pp. 249–50; 1940, p. 53).

The Ego's Development

Many of the most important elaborations on Freud's theory have concerned the ego. In 1936 Anna Freud pointed out that although the ego may be weak, it is the ego that employs various mechanisms of defense, such as repression and intellectualization. The healthiest defense mechanism is sublimation, by which the ego desexualizes energy and channels it into socially acceptable pursuits (S. Freud, 1920, p. 354).

Freudians have also been concerned with the process by which the ego develops. Freud wrote little on this subject. His main suggestion (1911) was that the ego develops because the drives are frustrated. As long as babies are gratified, they have no reason for dealing with reality. But they do experience frustration. At first they try to reduce tensions through hallucinations, but these do not work for long. So they must seek need-gratifying objects in reality.

The difficulty with Freud's proposal is that it implies that the ego only acts when the id activates it. Construed in this way, the ego is weak. It only serves the id.

Hartmann's revision. One of Freud's most influential followers, Heinz Hartmann, suggested that Freud's theory might permit a different picture of the ego—one that gives it more autonomy. Hartmann (1939, 1950) noted that Freud wondered whether the ego might not have genetic roots of its own. If so, ego functions such as motility (body movement), language, perception, and cognition might develop according to their own *matura-tional timetable*. Children, then, might begin to walk, talk, grasp objects, and so on from inner promptings that are biologically governed, but which are also independent of the instinctual drives. Children have a matura-tional need to develop ego functions when the id is at rest, when life is "conflict-free." Thus, the ego might develop independently from the id. Hartmann's proposal is widely considered a major breakthrough in the study of ego development.

Ego development and object relations. Freudians have also studied the kind of environment most conducive to ego growth. When Freudians talk about the environment, they usually are speaking not about the physical world but the world of other people. They call interactions with others *object relations*.

According to Hartmann (Hartmann et al., 1946), Benedek (1938), and others, the optimal interpersonal environment at first is a consistently gratifying one. When caretakers are consistently loving, babies become interested in them and learn about the external world of people. Con-sistent care seems especially important for the development of one essential ego function—the ability to postpone gratification. As Benedek says, when the mother is consistent and loving, the baby gains *confidence* in her. The baby does not grow unduly impatient the minute his or her needs are not met but learns to wait. The baby knows that care is forthcoming.

When, in contrast, babies suffer painful deprivations and inconsistent care, they often have great difficulty postponing gratification. They may become overly aggressive and impulsive, feeling that if they do not take something immediately, it may be missing when they need it (Redl and Wineman, 1951).

Many of Freud's followers, then, have modified and expanded upon Freud's ideas about the ego and its development. They have been partic-ularly concerned with how the ego gets the strength and energy to somehow deal with the internal and external demands it encounters. In the next chapter, we will discuss Erikson's insights into the ways children develop ego strength and vitality through their interactions with the widening social world.

PRACTICAL IMPLICATIONS

It is impossible to make any sharp distinctions between Freudian theory and practice. Freud's theory emerged from the clinical treatment of pa-tients, and his followers continue to use therapy as a main source of data. In this chapter we have focused on Freud's theory of normal growth and development, rather than pathology and treatment, but we still have found it necessary to mention topics in the latter areas (e.g., hysteria).

A description of Freud's therapeutic work is well beyond our scope. What we can say here is that a major goal of psychoanalysis is to recover repressed or blocked-off experience. We mentioned how this was nec-essary in the case of Elizabeth von R. Elizabeth had repressed sexual feelings toward her brother-in-law, and these feelings, far from disappearing, became diverted into painful bodily symptoms. The only solution, Freud thought, is for us to become more conscious of our thoughts and feelings so that, instead of their controlling us, we can gain a measure of control over them. As he put it, "Where id was, there ego shall be" (1933, p. 80).

Therapy with children usually proceeds somewhat differently from that with adults, for children are not given to verbal discussions and recollections. Instead, they learn to express, accept, and master feelings and fantasies through play. In the Bettelheim chapter, we will discuss a therapeutic approach with extremely disturbed children.

It is important to note that Freud never believed that psychoanalysis can completely cure our problems. Because we all live in society, which demands some repression of our instinctual urges, we all suffer to some extent. Further, Freud saw the therapist's role as limited. A psychiatrist was once asked by Freud if he was really able to cure. The psychiatrist replied: "In no way, but one can, as a gardener does, remove some impediments to personal growth." "Then," Freud answered, "we will understand each other" (Ellenberger, 1970, p. 461).

The practical implications of Freud's ideas extend far beyond the treatment of patients. His ideas have influenced practically every area of life, including the practice of law, art, literature, religion, and education. The area of most interest to us here is education. Freud's thoughts on education were not as radical as it is sometimes supposed. He believed that societies will always exact some instinctual renunciation, and he said it would be unfair to send children into the world expecting that they can do just as they please (1933, p. 149). On the other hand, Freud thought that discipline is usually excessive; it makes children feel unnecessarily ashamed and guilty about their bodies and their natural functions. Freud was particularly emphatic on the need for sex education (1907). He recommended that sex education be handled by the schools, where children could learn about reproduction in their lessons on nature and animals. They themselves would then draw the necessary conclusions with respect to humans.

Freudian ideas have motivated some more adventurous experiments in education. For example, at Summerhill, A. S. Neill (1960) gave children a great deal of liberty of all kinds, including sexual freedom. However, such radical innovations are rare, and Freud's influence is more typically found in the general attitude a teacher takes toward children. This attitude is particularly evident when a teacher refrains from automatically disciplining some unwanted behavior and instead tries to understand the emotional reasons behind it (Russell, 1971). When a teacher takes a closer look at a child's life, the teacher may discover that the angry or sullen child is not really mad at the teacher but is finding something at home, such as the neglect of a parent, deeply frustrating. Or the teacher may find that the shy child has for many years been made to feel inferior in the presence of adults. Or the teacher may discover that the seemingly lazy teenager is actually brooding endlessly over sex or social failure (White and Watt, 1973, p. 34). The teacher may not always be able to correct such problems, or even feel that it is prudent to discuss them with the student, for the student may need his or her privacy in certain matters. Nevertheless, a measure of understanding can help the teacher. For the teacher is then not so quick to criticize or punish but has a reason for being patient and encouraging—attitudes that have helped many a child.

EVALUATION

Freud was one of the great thinkers of this century. Before Freud, some poets, artists, and philosophers may have known about the unconscious and early sexual fantasies, but it was Freud's remarkable work that made us take these matters seriously. At the same time, Freud was more bitterly attacked than any other psychological theorist before or since. Even today many consider his ideas scandalous.

It is not surprising, then, that Freud and his followers have sometimes reacted dogmatically and defensively. At times they have behaved like members of a religious sect, isolating themselves from other scientists and gathering in their own groups to reaffirm the truth of their own beliefs. At other times, Freudians have resorted to *ad hominem* arguments— arguments directed not against others' ideas, but against their personalities. In one essay (1925b) Freud argued that his critics objected to his ideas because of their own resistances and repressions.

In the midst of such emotionally charged debates, several criticisms of psychoanalysis have been offered that have merit, and some Freudians have tried to face them openly and to correct the weaknesses in the theory.

Some of the most important criticisms of Freud have come from anthropologists, who have argued that Freud's theory is culture-bound. In the 1920s Malinowski and others zeroed in on Freud's theory of the Oedipus complex, pointing out that it is not nearly as universal as Freud imagined. Malinowski noted that the family constellation on which this complex is based—the nuclear triangle of mother, father, and child—is not found in all cultures. Among the Trobriand Islanders, Malinowski found, the child's chief disciplinarian was not the father but the maternal uncle. Further, the strongest incest taboo was not between children and parents but between brothers and sisters. In this situation, Malinowski pointed out, repressed fears and longings were very different. "We might say that in the Oedipus complex there is a repressed desire to kill the father and marry the mother, while in the . . . Trobriands the wish is to marry the sister and to kill the maternal uncle" (Malinowski, 1927, pp. 80–81). Thus, the oedipal situation is by no means just as Freud described.

Malinowski, however, did not wish to dispense with Freud altogether. On the contrary, he was indebted to Freud for the insight that repressed wishes emerge in projections such as dreams, magic, and folklore. This insight provided him with an important theoretical tool. Malinowski's argument was that such projections vary with the cultural setting. Among the Trobriand Islanders, he found no oedipal myths or dreams, but many that centered on their own strongest temptations and taboos—especially brother-sister relations. For example, although they themselves never admitted to incestuous wishes toward siblings, they told stories about how magic originated long ago when a brother and sister did commit incest.

At the time of Malinowski's writings, Freud and his followers resisted anthropological modifications of psychoanalytic theory. However, later Freudians (e.g., Kardiner, 1945; Erikson, 1963; Parsons, 1964) have tried to combine psychoanalytic and anthropological insights.

Freud has also been sharply criticized for cultural bias on the topic of women. Psychoanalytically oriented writers such as Clara Thompson (1950) and modern feminists have charged that Freud's views on women reflect his own unexamined Victorian attitudes. Freud's limitations, Thompson said, are most evident in his concept of penis envy. She agreed that girls envy boys, but not for the reasons Freud thought. Freud assumed that penis envy is based on a real biological inferiority—a view that fit well with his society's prejudice. Actually, she said, penis envy is much more of a cultural problem; girls feel inferior to boys because girls lack the same privileges in a male-dominated society. That is, they lack the opportunities for adventure, independence, and success. Freud ignored women's legitimate desire for social equality.

Writers have also accused Freud of cultural bias in his discussions of women's sense of morality. Freud thought that girls, not fearing castration, have less need to internalize a strong superego. As evidence he pointed to women's greater emotionality and flexibility in moral matters. Such observations, his critics contend, simply reflect his own cultural stereotypes.

Empirical evidence does suggest that Freud would have done well to question his theory on superego formation. Most evidence suggests that children do not acquire an initial sense of morality because they fear harm, whether castration or some other physical punishment. The child who only fears physical punishment simply tries to avoid getting caught (and perhaps learns to hate the punisher). A sense of morality, instead, appears to develop when the child experiences love and wishes to keep it. The child who receives love tries to behave properly to gain parental approval (Brown, 1965, pp. 381–94; White and Watt, 1981, pp. 359–60.) Thus, if a girl is loved as much as a boy, she should develop an equally strong conscience.

Freud's theory of the girl's Oedipus complex, then, has met with justifiable criticisms. Still, thoughtful critics such as Clara Thompson have not wished to overturn Freud altogether. The task is to sort out what is valid in the theory. Girls still may develop sexual longings, fears, and rivalries during the oedipal period, and it is important not to overlook these developments.

Freud has also been criticized on scientific grounds. Although his theory hinges on universal childhood developments, his evidence came primarily from adults—from the memories and fantasies of adults in treatment. Freud did not investigate his hypotheses in an unbiased way with representative samples of normal children.

Some psychologists think that Freud's theory is of little scientific value because it is so hopelessly opaque and complex. Sometimes, in fact, the theory predicts equally probable but contradictory outcomes. For example, children who experience frustration at the anal stage might develop habits of orderliness, cleanliness, and obedience, or they might develop the opposite characteristics, rebelliousness and messiness. How does one predict which set of traits any given child will develop?

Finally, there is the unnerving experience of never seeming able to disconfirm Freud's hypotheses. If one does a study and finds no relationship between weaning and later oral behavior, some Freudians will argue that one failed to understand Freud's thoughts in sufficient depth.

Nevertheless, despite all the problems that people have encountered, an enormous amount of research on Freud's ideas has been done and will continue, and investigators will eventually sort out the valid and invalid propositions. Researchers will continue to struggle with Freud's theory and to test it the best they can because they sense that Freud was basically on the right track. As Hall and Lindzey say (1975), his theory has a fundamental appeal because it is both broad and deep.

> Over and above all the other virtues of his theory stands this one—it tries to envisage a full-bodied individual living partly in a world of reality and partly in a world of make-believe, beset by conflicts and inner contradictions, yet capable of rational thought and action, moved by forces of which he has little knowledge and by aspirations which are beyond his reach, by turn confused and clear-headed, frustrated and satisfied, hopeful and despairing, selfish and altruistic; in short, a complex human being. For many people, this picture of man has an essential validity. (p. 72)

12

Erikson
and the Eight
Stages of Life

BIOGRAPHICAL INTRODUCTION

Among the advances in the psychoanalytic theory of development, none has been more substantial than that made by Erik H. Erikson. Erikson has given us a new, enlarged picture of the child's tasks at each of Freud's stages. Beyond this, he has added three new stages—those of the adult years—so the theory now encompasses the entire life cycle.

Erikson was born in 1902 in Frankfurt, Germany. His parents were Danish, but they separated a few months before he was born, so his mother went to Frankfurt to have her baby among friends. There she raised Erikson by herself until he was three years old, when she married a local pediatrician, Dr. Homburger. Erikson's mother and stepfather were Jewish, but Erikson looked different—more like a tall, blond, blue-eyed Dane. He was even nicknamed "the goy" (non-Jew) by the Jewish boys (Coles, 1970, p. 180).

Young Erikson was not a particularly good student. Although he excelled in certain subjects—especially ancient history and art—he disliked the formal school atmosphere. When he graduated from high school, he felt lost and uncertain about his future place in life. Instead of going to college, he wandered throughout Europe for a year, returned home to study art for a while, and then set out on his travels once again. He was going through what he would later call a *moratorium*, a period during which young people take time out to try to find themselves. Such behavior was acceptable for many German youth at the time. As Erikson's biographer, Robert Coles (1970), says, Erikson "was not seen by his family or friends as odd or 'sick,' but as a wandering artist who was trying to come to grips with himself" (p. 15).

Erikson finally began to find his calling when, at the age of 25, he accepted an invitation to teach children in a new Viennese school founded by Anna Freud and Dorothy Burlingham. When Erikson wasn't teaching, he studied child psychoanalysis with Anna Freud and others, and he was himself analyzed by her.

At the age of 27 Erikson married Joan Serson and started a family. Their life was disrupted in 1933 when the rise of Hitler forced them to leave Europe. They settled in Boston, where Erikson became the city's first child analyst.

Nevertheless, the urge to travel seemed firmly implanted in Erikson's nature. After three years in Boston, he took a position at Yale, and two years later he made another trip—to the Pine Ridge Reservation in South Dakota, where he lived with and learned about the Sioux. Erikson then moved on to San Francisco, where he resumed his clinical practice with children and participated in a major longitudinal study of normal children at the University of California. He also found time to travel up the California coast to study another Indian tribe, the Yurok fishermen. We can see that Erikson was exploring areas that Freud had left uncharted—the lives of normal children and of children growing up in different cultural contexts.

In 1949, during the McCarthy era, Erikson came into conflict with his employer, the University of California. The university demanded a loyalty oath of all its employees, which Erikson refused to sign. When some of his colleagues were dismissed, he resigned. Erikson took a new job at the Austin Riggs Center in Stockbridge, Massachusetts, where he worked until 1960. He was then given a professorship at Harvard, even though he had never earned a formal college degree. He has been at Harvard ever since.

Erikson's most important work is *Childhood and Society* (1950; 2nd ed. 1963). In this book he maps out his eight stages of life and illustrates how these stages are played out in different ways in different cultures. Two other highly influential books are *Young Man Luther* (1958) and *Gandhi's Truth* (1969), which bridge psychoanalytic insights with historical material.

ERIKSON'S STAGE THEORY

General Purpose

Freud, you will recall, postulated a sequence of psychosexual stages that center on body zones. As children mature, their sexual interest shifts from the oral to the anal to the phallic zone; then, after a latency period, the focus is once again on the genital region. Thus, Freud presented a completely new way of looking at development.

At the same time, however, Freud's stage theory is limited. In particular, its focus on body zones is too specific. As you will recall from Chapter 6, a rigorous stage theory describes *general* achievements or issues at different periods of life. For example, we do not call shoe-tying a stage because it is too specific. Similarly, the focus on zones also tends to be specific, describing only parts of the body. Even though it is interesting to note that some people become fixated on these zones—and, for example, find the mouth or the anus the main source of pleasure in life—there is more to personality development than this.

Freud's writings, of course, were not limited to descriptions of body zones. He also discussed crucial interactions between children and significant others. Erikson has tried to do this more thoroughly. At each Freudian stage, he has introduced concepts that gradually lead to an understanding of the most decisive, general encounter between the child and the social world.

1. The Oral Stage

Zones and modes. Erikson first tries to give the Freudian stages greater generality by pointing out that for each libidinal zone we can also speak of an ego mode. At the first stage, the primary zone is the mouth, but this zone also possesses a mode of activity, *incorporation*, a passive yet eager taking in (Erikson, 1963, p. 72). Further, incorporation extends beyond the mouth and characterizes other senses as well. Babies not only take in through the mouth, but through the eyes; when they see something interesting, they open their eyes eagerly and widely and try to take the object in with all their might. Also, they seem to take in good feelings through their tactile senses. And even a basic reflex, the grasp reflex, seems to follow the incorporative mode; when an object touches the baby's palm, the fist automatically closes around it. Thus, incorporation describes a general mode through which the baby's ego first deals with the external world.

Freud's second oral stage is marked by the eruption of teeth and aggressive biting. According to Erikson, the mode of *biting* or *grasping*, like incorporation, is a general one that extends beyond the mouth. With maturation, babies can actively reach out and grasp things with their hands. Similarly, "the eyes, first part of a relatively passive system of accepting impressions as they come along, have now learned to focus, to isolate, to 'grasp' objects from a vaguer background, and to follow them" (1963, p. 77). Finally, the organs of hearing conform to the more active mode of grasping. Babies can now discern and localize significant sounds and can move their heads and bodies so as to actively take them in. Thus, the mode of biting or grasping—of active taking—is a general one that describes the central way in which the ego now deals with the world.

The most general stage: Basic Trust vs. Mistrust. The most general stage at each period consists of a general encounter between the child's maturing ego and the social world. At the first stage, as babies try to take in the things they need, they interact with caretakers, who follow their own culture's ways of giving to them. What is most important in these interactions is that babies come to find some consistency, predictability, and reliability in their caretakers' actions. When they sense that a parent is consistent and dependable, they develop a sense of basic trust in the parent. They come to sense that when they are cold, wet, or hungry, they can count on others to relieve their pain.   Some parents come promptly, while others minister on schedules, but in either case babies learn that the parent is dependable and therefore trustworthy.   The alternative is a sense of mistrust, the feeling that the parent is unpredictable and unreliable, and may not be there when needed (1963, p. 247).

Babies must also learn to trust themselves. This problem becomes particularly acute when babies experience the rages of teething and hurt the nursing mother with their sharp bites and grasps.   When babies learn to regulate their urges—to suck without biting and to hold without hurting—they begin to consider themselves "trustworthy enough so that the providers will not need to be on guard lest they be nipped" (1963, p. 248). For her part, the mother needs to be careful not to withdraw too completely or to wean too suddenly.   If she does, the baby will feel that her care is not dependable after all, for it may be suddenly taken away.

When babies have developed a sense of trust in their caretakers, they show it in their behavior.   Erikson says the first sign of trust in a mother comes when the baby is willing "to let her out of sight without undue anxiety or rage" (1963, p. 47).   The word "undue" is probably important here, for we saw in the discussion of Bowlby that most babies experience some separation anxiety.   Nevertheless, if parents are dependable, babies can learn to tolerate their absences.   If caretakers are undependable, babies cannot afford to let them go and panic when they begin to do so.

Trust is similar to what Benedek calls confidence (see p. 242 in the preceding chapter).   It is a basic faith in one's providers.   Erikson says that he prefers the term *trust* because "there is more naivete and more mutuality in it" (1963, p. 248).   But trust results in the same attitude that Benedek was concerned about—the calm patience that comes from the certainty that one's providers will be there when needed.

Trust, then, is the sense that others are reliable and predictable.   At the same time, however, Erikson implies that trust ultimately depends on something more.   Ultimately, he says, trust depends on the *parents' own confidence*, on their sense that they are doing things right.   Parents "must be able to represent to the child a deep, an almost somatic conviction that there is a meaning to what they are doing" (1963, p. 249).   This sense of meaning, in turn, requires cultural backing—the belief that the "way we do things is good for our children."

At first glance, Erikson's emphasis on the caretaker's own confidence is puzzling.   What does the parent's confidence have to do with the baby? Erikson might have in mind thoughts similar to those of the psychiatrist H. S. Sullivan.   Sullivan (1953, pp. 49–109) believed that in the first months of life the infant has a special kind of physical empathy with the mother-figure such that the baby automatically feels the mother's state of tension. If the mother feels anxious, the baby feels anxious; if the mother feels calm, the baby feels calm.   These early interactions, in turn, influence later attitudes.   Thus, it is important that parents feel reasonably confident and self-assured, so babies will not become too wary of interpersonal contact. Babies need to feel that it is basically good and reassuring to be close to others.

Erikson (1959, p. 64) observes that it is not always easy for American parents to have an inner confidence in their child-rearing practices. Whereas parents in simpler, more stable cultures follow practices that have been handed down over the generations, the modern American parent has fewer traditions to fall back on. Modern parents receive all kinds of advice on newer, "better" child-rearing techniques, and the advice is by no means uniform.

In this situation, Erikson thinks that books such as Spock's (1945) are helpful. Throughout his book, Spock encourages parents to trust themselves. He tells parents that they know more than they think and that they should follow their impulses to respond to their babies' needs. It is almost as if Spock had read Erikson and understood the importance of the parent's possessing an inner assurance.

Beyond reading Spock, parents can gain an inner security from religion. Their own faith and inner assurance will be transmitted to the child, helping the child feel that the world is a trustworthy place. If parents are without religion, they must find faith in some other area, perhaps in fellowship, or the goals of their work, or in their social ideals (Erikson, 1959, pp. 64–65).

Erikson has sometimes given readers the impression that babies should develop trust but not mistrust. But he does not mean this. He sees each stage as a vital conflict or tension in which the "negative" pole is also necessary for growth. In the present case, infants must experience both trust and mistrust. If they only developed trust, they would become too gullible. "It is clear," Erikson says, "that the human infant must experience a goodly measure of mistrust in order to learn to trust discerningly" (1976, p. 23).

At the same time, it is critical that infants emerge from this stage with a favorable balance of trust over mistrust. If they do, they will have developed the core ego strength of this period: *hope*. Hope is the expectation that despite frustrations, rages, and disappointments, good things will happen in the future. Hope enables the child to move forward into the world and take up new challenges (Erikson, 1982, p. 60).

Conclusion. We see, then, that Erikson has considerably broadened Freud's description of the oral stage. Erikson has shown that it is not just the oral zone that is important, but the corresponding ego modes of dealing with the world. The infant incorporates and later grasps things in the world through the various senses. The infant's maturing ego, in turn, meets the social world—in this case, the caretakers—in a general, decisive encounter. The critical issue is that of trust vs. mistrust. The baby needs to know that the caretakers are predictable and to sense their inner assurance. If the baby can develop a favorable balance of trust over mistrust, the baby develops the core ego strength of this period: hope. Hope enables the child to move forward and enthusiastically confront the world despite current and past frustrations.

Issues of trust, mistrust, and hope are, of course, with us throughout our lives. Erikson recognizes this. But he also claims that the struggle between trust and mistrust reaches its own particular crisis and is the dominating event in the first year of life. And the way in which infants resolve this first crisis, with or without a firm sense of hopefulness, determines the energy and vitality they bring to subsequent stages.

2. The Anal Stage

Zones and modes.   In Freud's second stage, which occurs during the second and third years, the anal zone comes into prominence.   With the maturation of the nervous system, children gain voluntary control over their sphincter muscles; they can now retain and eliminate as they wish. They often hold on to their bowel movements to maximize the sensations of the final release.

Erikson agrees with Freud that the basic modes of this stage are retention and elimination, of holding on and letting go.   However, Erikson also points out that these modes encompass more than the anal zone.   For example, children begin to use their hands to hold stubbornly onto objects and, just as defiantly, to throw them away.   Once they can sit up easily, they carefully pile things up one moment, only to discard them the next. With people, too, they sometimes hold on, snuggling up, and at other times insist on pushing the adult away (1959, pp. 82, 86).

The general stage: Autonomy vs. Shame and Doubt.   Amidst these contradictory impulses—holding on one moment and expelling the next—the child is primarily trying to exercise a choice.   Two-year-olds want to hold on when they want and to push aside when they do not.   They are exercising their will, their sense of autonomy.

In other ways, too, maturation ushers in a sense of autonomy during the second and third years.   Children can now stand up on their own two feet, and they begin to explore the world on their own.   They also insist on feeding themselves, even if this means exercising their right to make a mess.   Their language, too, reveals a new-found autonomy and sense of selfhood; they repeatedly use the words "me" and "mine."   Most of all, they express their autonomy in a single word—"no."   Two-year-olds seem unable to say "yes," as if any agreement means a complete forfeiture of their independence.   Through the strong and insistent "no," children defy all external control.

TABLE 12.1   The Stages of Freud and Erikson

AGE	FREUD'S STAGE	ERIKSON'S GENERAL STAGE
Birth to one	Oral	Trust vs. Mistrust: *Hope*
One to three	Anal	Autonomy vs. Shame, Doubt: *Will*
Three to six	Phallic (Oedipal)	Initiative vs. Guilt: *Purpose*
Six to 11	Latency	Industry vs. Inferiority: *Competence*
Adolescence	Genital	Identity vs. Role Confusion: *Fidelity*
Young Adulthood		Intimacy vs. Isolation: *Love*
Adulthood		Generativity vs. Self-Absorption, Stagnation: *Care*
Old Age		Ego Integrity vs. Despair: *Wisdom*

As children seem so much more in control of themselves and reach peaks of willfulness, societies, through parents, decide it is time to teach them the right ways to behave. As Freud observed, parents do not permit their children to enjoy their anality in any way they please; instead, they train them to behave in the socially proper way. Parents quite often toilet-train children by making them feel ashamed of messy and improper anal behavior. Children may resist training for some time, but they eventually submit to it.

Erikson agrees that the "battles of the toilet-bowl" are important. But he also is suggesting that the battles of this time—between the child's autonomy and the society's regulations—take place in a number of arenas. For example, when children insist on feeding themselves and making a mess, parents try to regulate their behavior. Similarly, parents sooner or later decide that their two-year-olds cannot say "no" to every single request. Two-year-olds, like everyone else, must live in society and respect others' wishes. Thus, the conflict at this stage is a very general one.

Erikson defines the conflict as that of autonomy versus shame and doubt. Autonomy comes from within; biological maturation fosters the ability to do things on one's own—to control one's own sphincter muscles, to stand on one's own feet, to use one's hands, and so on. Shame and doubt, on the other hand, come from an awareness of social expectations and pressures. Shame is the feeling that one does not look good in others' eyes. For example, a little girl who wets her pants becomes self-conscious, worried that others will see her in this state. Doubt stems from the real-ization that one is not so powerful after all, that others can control one and perform actions much better.

It is hoped that children can learn to adjust to social regulations without losing too much of their initial sense of autonomy. Parents in some cultures try to help the child with this. They gently try to help the child learn social behavior without crushing the child's independence. Other parents, unfortunately, are not so sensitive. They may shame children excessively when they have a bowel accident; they may try to break their children of any oppositional behavior; or they may ridicule their children's efforts to do things on their own. In such instances, children can develop lasting feelings of shame and doubt that override their impulses toward self-determination.

To the extent that children resolve this second crisis in a positive way, with a favorable ratio of autonomy over shame and doubt, they develop the ego strength of rudimentary *will*. "Will," Erikson says, is "the unbroken determination to exercise free choice as well as self-restraint" (1964, p. 119). Erikson includes self-restraint in his definition because he believes it is important for children to learn to control their impulses and to renounce what is not worth doing (or cannot be done). Still, it is the child—not external powers—who is in charge.

3. The Phallic (Oedipal) Stage

Zone and modes. During Freud's third stage (between about three and six years), the child's concern with the anal zone gives way to the primacy of the genital zone. Children now focus their interest on their genitals and become curious about the sex organs of others. They also begin to imagine themselves in adult roles and even dare to rival one parent for the love of the other. They enter the oedipal crisis.

Erikson calls the primary mode at this stage *intrusion*. By this term, he hopes to capture Freud's sense of the child as now exceedingly daring, curious, and competitive. The term intrusion describes the activity of the boy's penis, but as a general mode it refers to much more. For both sexes, the maturation of physical and mental abilities impels the child forward into a variety of intrusive activities. "These include the intrusion into other bodies by physical attack; the intrusion into other people's ears and minds by aggressive talking; the intrusion into space by vigorous locomotion; the intrusion into the unknown by consuming curiosity" (Erikson, 1963, p. 87).

The general stage: Initiative vs. Guilt.

Initiative, like intrusion, connotes forward movement. The child with a sense of initiative makes plans, sets goals, and perseveres in attaining them. I noted, for example, some of the activities of one of our sons when he was five years. In a single day, he decided to see how high he could build his blocks, invented a game that consisted of seeing who could jump the highest on his parents' bed, and led the family to a new movie containing a great deal of action and violence. His behavior had taken on a goal-directed, competitive, and imaginative quality.

The crisis comes when children realize that their biggest plans and fondest hopes are doomed for failure. These ambitions, of course, are the oedipal ones—the wish to possess one parent and rival the other. The child finds out that these wishes violate deep social taboos and that they are far more dangerous than imagined. Consequently, the child internalizes social prohibitions—a guilt-producing superego—to keep such dangerous impulses and fantasies in check. The result is a new form of self-restriction. Forever after, the individual's naive exuberance and daring will be offset by self-observation, self-control, and self-punishment.

In Erikson's view, the creation of a superego constitutes one of the great tragedies in life. Although the superego is necessary for socialized behavior, it stifles the bold initiative with which the child met life at the phallic stage. Still, Erikson is not completely pessimistic. He observes that three- to six-year-old children are, more than at any other time, ready to learn quickly and avidly, and they are willing to find ways of channeling their ambition into socially useful pursuits (1963, p. 258). Parents can help this process by easing their authority somewhat and by permitting children to participate with them as equals on interesting projects. In this way, parents can help children emerge from the crisis of this stage with a strong sense of *purpose*, "the courage to envisage and pursue valued goals," unimpaired by guilt and inhibition (Erikson, 1964, p. 122).

4. The Latency Stage

In Freud's theory, the resolution of the Oedipus complex brings about a latency period, lasting from about age six to 11. During this period the sexual and aggressive drives, which produced crises at earlier periods, are temporarily dormant. There is no libidinal (sexual) zone for this stage.

Of course the child's life at this time may not be entirely conflict-free. For example, the birth of a sibling may arouse intense jealousy. But as a rule, this is a period of calm and stability. In terms of the instincts and drives, nothing much is going on.

Erikson, however, shows that this is a most decisive stage for ego growth. Children master important cognitive and social skills. The crisis is *industry versus inferiority*. Children forget their past hopes and wishes, which were often played out within the family, and eagerly apply themselves to learning the useful skills and tools of the wider culture. In preliterate societies, children learn to hunt, farm, and make utensils. In these cultures, learning is often informal, and much of it comes from older children. In modern technological societies such as ours, children go to school, where they are asked to master more cerebral skills—reading, writing, and arithmetic. In either case, they are learning to do meaningful work and are developing the ego strengths of "steady attention and persevering diligence" (1963, p. 259). They also are learning to work and play with their peers.

The danger of this stage is an excessive feeling of inadequacy and inferiority (1963, p. 260). Most of us can probably remember the hurts of failure in the classroom or on the playground. A particularly deep sense of inferiority may have various roots. Sometimes children have difficulty at this stage because they have not successfully resolved the con-

FIGURE 12.1   A boy's drawing expresses daring initiative and disaster. There is a resemblance to the myth of Icarus, about a boy who went too far—too near the sun. This drawing, by a nine-year-old, may also suggest the industry theme of the next stage: the climbers on the left are engaged in skillful cooperation.

flicts at earlier stages.   For example, a girl may have developed more doubt than autonomy at the second stage, so she is unsure of herself as she tries to master new tasks.   At other times, school and community attitudes may hinder the development of a sense of industry.   An African-American boy, for example, may learn that the color of his skin counts for more than his wish and will to learn.   And all too often schools fail to discover and encourage the individual's special talents (1963, p. 260).

On the other hand, good teachers (who often are those who feel trusted and respected by the community) can help children at this time. Erikson (1959, p. 87) says that he has repeatedly observed that in the lives of inspired and gifted people just one teacher made a difference by encouraging the individual's talent.

In any case, the successful resolution of this stage leads to the ego strength Erikson calls *competence*, the free exercise of intelligence and skill in the completion of tasks, unimpaired by excessive feelings of inferiority (1964, p. 124).

5. Puberty (The Genital Stage)

According to Sigmund and Anna Freud, adolescence is a turbulent stage because of the dramatic physiological changes occurring at this time. Sexual and aggressive drives, which were dormant during the latency stage, now threaten to overwhelm the ego and its defenses.   The genital zone, in particular, is infused with tremendous sexual energy, and the adolescent is once again troubled by oedipal fantasies.   The teenager may find it difficult simply to be around his or her parents.

Erikson agrees that the great increase in drive energy is disruptive at adolescence, but he sees this as only part of the problem.   Adolescents also become disturbed and confused by new *social* conflicts and demands.   The adolescent's primary task, Erikson thinks, is establishing a new sense of *ego identity*—a feeling for who one is and one's place in the larger social order. The crisis is one of *identity versus role confusion.*

The upsurge of instinctual drives certainly contributes to the adolescent's identity problems.   Adolescents suddenly feel as if their impulses have a will of their own, that they are no longer one with themselves.   Also, the rapid physical growth at puberty creates a sense of identity confusion. Young people begin to grow so quickly and to change in so many ways that they barely recognize themselves.   It is probably for this reason that teenagers spend so much time looking in mirrors and pay so much attention to their appearance.

But identity problems are as much, if not more, a social matter.   It is not physical growth or sexual impulses per se that trouble young people, but it is the thought that one might not look good to others or meet others' expectations.   And, even more than this, young people begin to worry about their future place in the larger social world.   Adolescents, with their rapidly expanding mental powers, feel overwhelmed by the countless options and alternatives before them.

Because adolescents are so uncertain about who they are, they anxiously tend to identify with "in groups."   They can "become remarkably clannish, intolerant, and cruel in their exclusion of others who are 'different' . . . " (1959, p. 92). In their hurry to find some identity, they stereotype "themselves, their ideals, and their enemies" (1959, p. 92). They often put themselves and others to a "loyalty test." Some young people align themselves to political or religious ideologies. In all this, we can detect young people's search for values to which they can be true.

To understand identity-formation, it is important to recognize that it is a lifelong process. In part, we form our identities through identifications. Although we are not necessarily aware of it, we identify with those who appeal to us and therefore become like them. Each person's identity, then, is partly a synthesis of various partial identifications (1959, pp. 112–13).

We also develop a sense of identity through our accomplishments. The ability to stand up, walk, run, play ball, draw, read, and write all contribute to a sense of ego identity. We come to see ourselves as "one who can do these things." Such accomplishments become part of a positive and lasting sense of identity when they have importance for the culture (1959, pp. 89–90).

Still, even though identity-formation is a lifelong process, the problem of identity reaches its crisis at adolescence. It is at this time that so many inner changes are taking place, and so much in terms of future commitment is at stake. At this time, one's earlier identity seems inadequate for all the choices and decisions one must make.

Erikson (1959, p. 123) asks us to consider, for example, a young college girl from a conservative background. When she goes to college she meets people of very different backgrounds, among whom she must choose her friends. She also must decide what her attitude toward sex will be and what occupational goals she is willing to compete for. At this point, her previous identity and identifications offer little help. Each decision seems to affirm some aspect of her past while repudiating others. If, for example, she decides to become sexually active, she may violate her family's spoken values, while identifying with some of their hidden wishes. Similarly, if she chooses to compete in a male-dominated profession, such as medicine or law, she ventures beyond certain family values but aligns herself with others. Thus, as she makes decisions and commitments, she reworks prior identifications and forms a new identity. Her task is to forge for herself some "central perspective and direction, some working unity, out of the effective remnants of [her] childhood and the hopes of [her] anticipated adulthood" (Erikson, 1958, p. 14).

Identity-formation is a largely unconscious process. Still, young people are often painfully aware of their inability to make lasting commitments. They feel that there is too much to decide too soon, and that every decision reduces their future alternatives (Erikson, 1959, pp. 124–26). Because commitment is so difficult, they sometimes enter a *psychosocial moratorium*, a kind of "time out" period for finding oneself. Some young people, for example, drop out of college to travel or experiment with various jobs before making any final decisions. However, many young people have trouble achieving a free moratorium state. Until they know who they are and what they will do in life, they often experience a sense of isolation, a feeling that time is passing them by, an inability to find meaning in any kind of activity, and a feeling that life is simply happening to them. As Biff puts it in Arthur Miller's *Death of a Salesman*, "I just can't take hold, Mom, I can't take hold of some kind of life" (Erikson, 1959, p. 91).

Nevertheless, the adolescent frequently postpones commitments anyway, because of an inner need to avoid *identity foreclosure*, a premature acceptance of compartmentalized social roles. And although a protracted identity search can be painful, it can also eventually lead to a higher form of personal integration and to genuine social innovations. As we have seen, many of the theorists in this book resisted the temptation to settle into conventional occupational identities. Piaget, Freud, and Erikson, among others, spent some time searching for their true callings. And their search, while not always pleasant for them, eventually led to new ways of understanding and meaningful changes in their professions.

The adolescent's central task, then, is to find some way of life to which he or she can make a permanent commitment. The struggles of this stage lead to the new ego strength of *fidelity*, the ability to sustain one's freely pledged loyalties (1964, p. 125).

6. Young Adulthood

Erikson is the first Freudian and one of the few developmental writers of any persuasion to propose separate stages for the adult years. If, then, his thoughts seem sketchy, we should remember that he is writing about an uncharted area.

Erikson's stages of adult development describe steps by which people widen and deepen their capacities to love and care for others. The *adolescent* is preeminently self-centered. Adolescents are concerned with who they are, how they appear in the eyes of others, and what they will become. They do become sexually attracted to others and even fall in love, but such attachments most often are really efforts at self-definition. In their interactions, young people try to find out who they are by endlessly talking about their true feelings, their views of each other, and their plans, hopes, and expectations (1959, p. 95).

The adolescent, then, is too preoccupied with who he or she is to take up the task of young adulthood—the attainment of *intimacy*. Real intimacy is only possible once a reasonable sense of identity has been established (1959, p. 95). Only one who is secure with one's identity is able to lose oneself in true mutuality with another. The young man, for example, who is worried about his masculinity will not make the best lover. He will be too self-conscious, too worried about how he is performing, to abandon himself freely and tenderly with his sexual partner. To the extent that people fail to attain genuine mutuality, they experience the opposite pole of this stage—*isolation*.

Erikson observes that some young people marry before they have established a good sense of identity. They hope that they will be able to find themselves in their marriage. Such marriages, however, rarely work out. The partners sooner or later begin to feel hemmed in by their obligations as mates and parents. They soon complain that others are not giving them the opportunity to develop themselves. Erikson notes that a change in mate is rarely the answer. What the individual needs is some "wisely guided insight" into the fact that one cannot expect to live intimately with another until one has become oneself (1959, p. 95).

In his discussions of intimacy, Erikson, as a respectable Freudian, speaks glowingly of the experience of orgasm. It is a supreme experience of mutual regulation that takes the edge off the inevitable bitterness and differences between two people (1963, p. 265). He adds, though, that the "Utopia of genitality" is by no means a purely sexual matter. True intimacy means that two people are willing to share and mutually regulate all important aspects of their lives (1963, p. 266).

As with the other stages, no one develops only the positive pole of this stage. No couple experiences total intimacy. Because people are different (sexually and otherwise), there is inevitably a degree of antagonism between partners that leads to periodic isolation. Ideally, however, intimacy is stronger. If so, young adults develop the ego strength of mature *love*, the "mutuality of devotion forever subduing the antagonisms" between them (Erikson, 1964, p. 129).

7. Adulthood

Once two people have established some measure of intimacy, their interests begin to expand beyond just the two of them. They become concerned with raising the next generation. In Erikson's terms, they enter the stage of *generativity versus self-absorption and stagnation* (Erikson, 1982, p. 67). *Generativity* is a broad term, which refers not only to the creation of children, but also to the production of things and ideas through work. But Erikson has focused primarily on the former—the generation of children.

The mere fact of having children, of course, does not guarantee generativity. Parents must do more than produce offspring; they must protect and guide them. This means that parents must often sacrifice their own needs. They must overcome temptations to self-indulgence, which lead to an unproductive stagnation. To the extent they can positively cope with this conflict, they develop their ability to *care* for the next generation.

Some people, Erikson notes, develop generativity and care without having children of their own. Nuns and priests, for example, forego the right to raise their own children, as do others who apply their special gifts to other areas. Such persons can still teach and guide the next generation "by working with other people's children or helping to create a better world for them" (Erikson in Evans, 1969, p. 51). Such adults must, to be sure, withstand a certain amount of frustration. This is especially true of women, whose bodies are built for nurturing and nourishing offspring. But a sense of care and generativity is still possible.

On the other hand, there are many people who marry but lack generativity. In such cases, the couples often regress to a kind of "pseudo-intimacy" or "begin to indulge themselves as if they were their one and only child" (Erikson, 1959, p. 97).   Erikson might be thinking of couples who endlessly analyze their relationship in terms of how much each person is getting from the other.   The individuals seem more concerned with their own needs than those of their children.

There are several possible reasons for an inability to develop at this stage.   Sometimes the parent's own childhood was so empty or frustrating that the parent cannot see how it is possible to do more for his or her children.   In other cases, the difficulty seems more cultural.   In the United States in particular, our values emphasize independent achievement to such an extent that people can become too exclusively involved in themselves and their successes and neglect the responsibility of caring for others (1959, p. 97).

8. Old Age

The psychological literature on old age, which is still sparse, typically views this period as one of decline.   The elderly, it is repeatedly pointed out, must cope with a series of physical and social losses.   They lose their physical strength and health; they lose their jobs and much of their income through retirement; and, as time goes by, they lose their spouses, relatives, and friends.   Equally damaging, they suffer the inevitable loss of status that accompanies being old, inactive, and "useless" in America.   Occasionally, authors acknowledge that the aged are supposed to gain an inner wisdom, but this is probably only the case in some far-off culture or in some time long past.   By and large, successful aging consists in somehow adjusting to physical and social setbacks (see Havighurst, 1952 and 1968; Gitelson, 1975; Sze, 1975, pp. 569–74).

Erikson is aware of the many adjustments, physical and social, that the elderly must make.   He is aware of the fact that the aged cannot be as active as they once were.   But his emphasis is not on external adjustments but on the inner struggle of this period—a struggle that holds potential for growth and even wisdom.   He calls this struggle *ego integrity versus despair.*

As older people face death, they engage, Erikson implies, in what has been called a life review (Butler, 1963).   They look back on their lives and wonder whether they were worthwhile.   In this process, they confront the ultimate despair—the feeling that life was not what it should have been, but now time has run out and there is no chance to try alternative life styles.   Frequently, disgust hides despair.   Many older people are disgusted by every little thing; they have no patience for the struggles and failings of others.   Such disgust, Erikson says, really signifies their contempt for themselves (1959, p. 98).

As the older person faces despair, he or she is trying to find a sense of ego integrity.   Ego integrity, Erikson says, is difficult to define but includes the sense that there is an order to one's life and "the acceptance of one's one and only life cycle as something that had to be and that, by necessity, permitted of no substitutions . . ." (1963, p. 268).   Integrity, it would seem, expresses the feeling that, "Yes, I made mistakes, but given who I was at the time and the circumstances, the mistakes were inevitable.

I accept them, along with the good things in my life." Integrity is a feeling that also extends beyond the self and even transcends national and ideological boundaries. The older person, on some level, has a feeling of companionship "with the ordering ways of distant times and different pursuits, so expressed in the simple products and sayings of such times and pursuits" (1963, p. 268).

Erikson (1976) tells us that the crisis of old age is most admirably illustrated by Ingmar Bergman's film, *Wild Strawberries*. The film, in Erikson's words,

> records an old Swedish doctor's journey by car from his place of retirement to the city of Lund. There, in the ancient cathedral, Dr. Isak Borg is to receive the highest honor of his profession, a Jubilee Doctorate marking fifty years of meritorious service. But this journey by car on marked roads through familiar territory also becomes a symbolic pilgrimage back into childhood and deep into his unknown self. (1976, p. 1)

The film begins with Borg writing in his diary in which he expresses a self-satisfied view of what life has to offer. The film then plunges into a terrifying dream symbolizing his fear of death. Upon awakening, Borg decides to travel to Lund by car instead of by airplane and to take along his daughter-in-law, Marianne, who is in the midst of a marital crisis with which Borg has so far refused to help. As soon as they are in the car, they begin to quarrel, and Marianne tells him that "even though everyone depicts you as a great humanitarian . . . you are an old egotist, Father" (Bergman, 1957, p. 32). Along the journey, Borg engages in other encounters with Marianne and others, and he is visited by vivid dreams and memories about the past. These dreams and memories are extremely humiliating to him. He comes to realize that throughout his life he has been an isolated onlooker, moralistically aloof, and in many ways incapable of love. We see, then, that Borg's initial sense of integrity was superficial; as he imagines death and reviews his life, he confronts its many failures.

In the end, however, Borg's insights do not lead to a final despair but to a new acceptance of the past. While he is receiving his Jubilee Doctorate, which by now has become a rather trivial event, he begins to see "a remarkable causality" in the events of his life—an insight that sounds remarkably similar to Erikson's statement that ego integrity includes a sense of the inevitable order of the past. Equally impressive, though, is a change in character. At the end of the film, Borg expresses his love for Marianne and offers to help her and his son.

Through this film, we see why Erikson emphasizes the importance of both the positive and negative poles of his crises. Borg's initial sense of integrity was superficial and unconvincing. He acquired a more meaningful sense of integrity only after confronting his life thoroughly and answering to some existential despair (Erikson, 1976, p. 23).

Erikson and Bergman, then, are pointing to an inner struggle that we are apt to miss when we look at older people. We are aware of their many physical and social difficulties, and we may deplore the fact that older people seem so "useless." But such judgments are only partly valid. They are opinions formed by looking only at external behavior. We see that older people lack the zest and youthfulness that we so greatly prize, but we fail to consider the *inner* struggle. We fail to see that the quiet older person may be grappling in some way with the most important of all questions: Was my life, as I face death, a meaningful one? What makes a life meaningful?

This inner struggle tends to make the older person something of a philosopher, and out of the struggle grows the ego strength of *wisdom*. Wisdom may be expressed in many ways, but it always reflects a thoughtful, hopeful effort to find the value and meaning of life in the face of death (Erikson, 1976, p. 23; 1982, pp. 61–62).

THEORETICAL ISSUES

Why Erikson's Theory Is a Stage Theory

In Chapters 6 and 7 we saw that Piaget and Kohlberg believed that cognitive stages should meet several criteria. Erikson's stages deal more with emotional development, but they basically meet the same criteria. That is, the stages (1) describe qualitatively different behaviors, (2) refer to general issues, (3) unfold in an invariant sequence, and (4) are culturally universal. Let us examine these points in turn.

1. The stages refer to qualitatively different behavior patterns. If development were just a matter of gradual quantitative change, any division into stages would be arbitrary. Erikson's stages, however, give us a good sense of how behavior is qualitatively different at different points. Children at the autonomy stage sound very different from those at the trust stage; they are much more independent. Children at the initiative stage are different again. Whereas children who are establishing a sense of autonomy defy authority and keep others out, children with a sense of initiative are more daring and imaginative, running vigorously about, making big plans, and initiating new activities. Behavior has a distinctive flavor at each stage.

2. The stages describe general issues. As we have emphasized, stages refer to general characteristics or issues. Erikson has gone beyond Freud's relatively specific focus on body zones and has attempted to delineate the general issues at each period. At the oral stage, for example, he shows that it is not just the stimulation of this zone that is important but the general mode of taking in and, more generally still, the development of a sense of trust in one's providers. Similarly, at each stage Erikson tries to isolate the most general issue faced by the individual in the social world.

3. The stages unfold in an invariant sequence. All stage theories imply an invariant sequence, and Erikson's is no exception. He says that each stage is present in some form throughout life, but each reaches its own crisis at a specific time and in a specific order.

Erikson's claim is based on the assumption that his sequence is partly the product of *biological maturation*. As he puts it, the child obeys "inner laws of development, namely those laws which in his prenatal period had formed one organ after another and which now create a succession of potentialities for significant interaction with those around him" (1963, p. 67). At the second stage, for example, biological maturation ushers in a sense of autonomy. Because of maturation, children can stand on their own two feet, control their sphincter muscles, walk, use words such as "me," "mine," and "no," and so on. At the third stage, maturation prompts a new sexual interest, along with capacities for imaginative play, curiosity, and vigorous locomotion.

At the same time, *societies* have evolved such that they invite and meet this inner, maturational succession of potentialities. When, for example, the child at the autonomy stage demonstrates a new degree of self-control, socializing agents consider the child ready for training. For example, they begin toilet-training. The result is the battle of wills, between child and society, which creates the crisis of this period. Similarly, when children become recklessly ambitious with respect to sexual matters, societies decide it is now time to introduce their particular sexual prohibitions, creating the core conflict at the third stage. Thus, the succession of crises is produced by inner maturation on the one hand and social forces on the other.

4. The stages are cultural universals.

Erikson believes that his stages can be applied to all cultures. Readers might see how the stages would be universal to the extent that they are maturationally governed, but they may still be skeptical, for they know how widely cultures differ.

Erikson, too, is aware of the vast differences among cultures. In fact, one of his goals is to show how cultures handle the stages differently according to their different value systems. For example, the Sioux provide their children with a long and indulgent period of nursing; one of their goals is to get children to trust others and to become generous themselves (1963, pp. 134–40). Our society, in contrast, discourages dependency. Compared to other cultures, we wean our infants very early. We do not seem to want our children to learn to depend on or trust others too much, but to become independent. Independence and free mobility seem part of our cultural ethos, from the pioneer days to the present time (1963, Ch. 8).

What Erikson does claim is that all cultures address themselves to the *same issues*. All cultures try to provide their children with consistent care, regulate their extreme wish to do everything their own way, and instill incest taboos. And, as children grow, all cultures ask them to learn the tools and skills of their technology, to find a workable adult identity, to establish bonds of intimacy, to care for the next generation, and to face death with integrity. All cultures attempt to achieve these tasks because culture itself is a part of the evolutionary process; in the course of evolution, those groups that failed in these tasks had less chance of surviving. Unless cultures could get their members to sacrifice some of their independence for the needs of others (at the autonomy stage), to begin to learn the skills and tools of the society (at the industry stage), and to care for the next generation (at the generativity stage), they probably did not endure.[1]

The question of hierarchic integration.   Piagetians, you may recall, define their stages in terms of a fifth point; they view them as hierarchic integrations.   This concept has been used somewhat differently by different writers, but in a stage theory it basically means that earlier structures are reintegrated into new, dominant structures.   In Erikson's theory, such a process does occur at certain stages, such as adolescence.   As young people achieve a new sense of identity, they reorganize a good deal of their personality in the pursuit of dominant goals or life-plans.   However, the concept of hierarchic integration does not apply to all the stages.   For example, the issues at the stage of autonomy vs. shame and doubt are not reorganized or reintegrated into the next stage, initiative vs. guilt.   The new stage simply raises new concerns, leaving the earlier stage in the background, in much the same form as before.   Thus the concept of hierarchic integration does not seem to characterize development at all of Erikson's stages (see Kohlberg, 1969a, p. 353).

Must One Go through All the Stages?

We sometimes hear that if one doesn't achieve a good measure of success at one of Erikson's stages, one may be unable to go on to the next stage.   This is wrong.   In Erikson's theory, one must, if one lives long enough, go through all the stages.   The reason has to do with the forces that move one from stage to stage: biological maturation and social expectations.   These forces push one along according to a certain timetable, whether one has been successful at earlier stages or not.

Consider, for example, a boy who has been unable to attain much of a sense of industry.   When he reaches puberty, he must grapple with the issues of identity even though he is not really ready to do so.   Because of biological changes, he finds himself troubled by an upsurge of sexual feelings and by a rapidly changing body.   At the same time, social pressures force him to cope with problems of dating and to start thinking about his future occupation.   It matters little to the larger society that he is still unsure about his own skills.   His society has its own timetable, and by the time he is 20 years or so, he will feel pressure to decide on a career.   In the same way, he will find himself confronting each new stage in the sequence.

Each person, then, must go through all the stages, whether he or she has traversed the earlier stages well or not.   What is true is that success at earlier stages affects the chances of success at later ones.   Children who developed a firm sense of trust in their caretakers can afford to leave them and independently explore the environment.   In contrast, children who lack trust—who are afraid to let caretakers out of sight—are less able to develop a sense of autonomy.   (Conceptualized slightly differently, it is the

[1]Darwin had a similar view, as discussed in Chapter 3.

child who has developed a favorable balance of trust over mistrust who ventures into the world full of *hope* and anticipation, energetically testing new powers of independent action.)   In a similar way, a favorable outcome at each stage affects the chances of a positive outcome at the subsequent stage.   But whatever the outcomes, maturational and social forces require the child to face the issues at each new stage.

Comparison with Piaget

We have now reviewed the two most influential stage theories in the developmental literature: Piaget's cognitive-developmental theory and Erikson's psychoanalytic theory.   In many respects, the theories are different, as briefly noted before.   Broadly speaking, the most basic differences are these.

Erikson describes a variety of feelings we bring to tasks; Piaget focuses on intellectual development.   This development, for Piaget, is not motivated by biological maturation and social forces, but by the child's efforts to solve cognitive problems.   As children encounter problems they cannot handle with their existing cognitive structures, they become challenged and curious and construct more elaborate structures.   Since the driving force is the child's curiosity, there is no reason why the child must go through all the stages; if a child is not curious about an area (e.g., mathematics), he or she may never reach the highest stages in that area.   Thus, where maturation and social pressures drive us through all of Erikson's stages, ready or not, we only go through Piaget's stages to the extent we are intellectually motivated to build new structures.

Such differences seem large.   Nevertheless, both Erikson and Piaget are presenting stage theories, attempting to describe the most general qualitative shifts in behavior.   Moreover, they often seem to be presenting different perspectives on the same basic developments.   Let us look at how this is so.

1. Trust.   As Erikson (1964, pp. 116–17) observes, both Piaget and he are concerned with the infant's development of a secure image of external objects.   Erikson points to the child's growing reliance on the predictability and dependability of people, whereas Piaget documents the developing sense of permanent things.   Thus, both are concerned with the child's growing faith in the stability of the world.[2]

2. Autonomy.   As children develop a sense of trust in their caretakers, they become increasingly independent.   Secure in their knowledge that others will be there when needed, they are free to explore the world on their own.

Piaget points to a similar process.   As children gain the conviction that objects are permanent, they can act increasingly independently of them.   For example, when his daughter Jacqueline's ball rolled under the

---

[2]For research exploring these parallels, see Gouin-Décarie, 1965, Bell, 1970, and Flavell, 1977, p. 54.

sofa, she was no longer bound to the spot where she last saw it. She now knew that the object was permanent, even if hidden, and could therefore try out alternative routes for finding it.[3]

3. Initiative. At this stage, between about three and six years, Erikson and the Freudians emphasize the child's consuming curiosity, wealth of fantasy, and daring imagination. As Erikson says, "Both language and locomotion permit him to expand his imagination over so many things that he cannot avoid frightening himself with what he has dreamed and thought up" (1959, p. 75).

Piaget's view of the thinking at this period is remarkably similar. As Flavell says:

> The preoperational child is the child of wonder; his cognition appears to us naive, impression-bound, and poorly organized. There is an essential law-lessness about his world without, of course, this fact in any way entering his awareness to inhibit the zest and flights of fancy with which he approches new situations. Anything is possible because nothing is subject to lawful constraints. (1963, p. 211)

For Piaget, then, the fantasy and imagination of the phallic-age child owes much to the fact that the child is in the preoperational period—a time in which thoughts run free because they are not yet tied to the systematic logic that the child will develop at the next stage.

4. Industry. For Erikson and the Freudians, the fantasies and fears of the oedipal child are temporarily buried during the latency stage, which lasts from about six to 11 years. Frightening wishes and fantasies are repressed, and the child's interests expand outward; the child intently tries to master the realistic skills and tools of the culture. In general, this is a relatively calm period; children seem more self-composed.

Piaget, too, would lead us to believe that the six- to 11-year-old is more stable, realistic, and organized than the younger child. For Piaget, this change is not the result of the repression of emotions and dangerous wishes; rather, it comes about because, intellectually, the child has entered the stage of concrete operations. The child can now separate fact from fancy, can see different perspectives on a problem, and can work logically and systematically on concrete tasks. Intellectually, then, the child is in a stage of equilibrium with the world, and this contributes to his or her overall stability and composure. Erikson himself seems to have concrete operations in mind when he describes this period: He says that at this time the child's "exuberant imagination is tamed and harnessed by the laws of impersonal things . . ." (1963, p. 258).

5. Identity. In Erikson's view, the calm of the preceding period gives way to the turbulence and uncertainty of adolescence. Adolescents are confused by physical changes and pressures to make social commitments. They wonder who they are and what their place in society will be.

[3]For further thoughts on the parallels at this stage, see Kohlberg and Gilligan, 1971, p. 1076.

Piaget has little to say about physical changes in adolescence, but his insights into cognitive development help us understand why this can be an identity-searching time. During the stage of concrete operations, the child's thought was pretty much tied to the here-and-now. But with the growth of formal operations, the adolescent's thought soars into the distant future and into the realm of the purely hypothetical. Consequently, adolescents can now entertain limitless possibilities about who they are and what they will become. Formal operational capacities, then, may contribute to the self-questioning of this period (see Inhelder and Piaget, 1955, Ch. 18).

PRACTICAL IMPLICATIONS

Clinical Work: A Case Illustration

Clinical psychologists and other mental health workers have found Erikson's concepts very useful. We can get a sense of this from Erikson's own work with one of his cases, a four-year-old boy he calls Peter.

Peter suffered from a psychogenic megacolon, an enlarged colon that resulted from Peter's emotionally based habit of retaining his fecal matter for up to a week at a time. Through conversations with Peter and his family, Erikson learned that Peter developed this symptom shortly after his nurse, an Asian girl, had been dismissed. Peter, it seems, had begun "attacking the nurse in a rough-housing way, and the girl had seemed to accept and quietly enjoy his decidedly 'male' approach" (Erikson, 1963, p. 56). In her culture, such behavior was considered normal. However, Peter's mother, living in our culture, felt there was something wrong about Peter's sudden maleness and the way the nurse indulged it. So she got rid of the nurse. By way of explanation, the nurse told Peter that she was going to have a baby of her own, and that she preferred to care for babies, not big boys like Peter. Soon afterward, Peter developed the megacolon.

Erikson learned that Peter imagined that he himself was pregnant, a fantasy through which he tried to keep the nurse by identifying with her. But, more generally, we can see how Peter's behavior regressed in terms of stages. Initially, he had begun displaying the attacking, sexual behavior of the initiative stage, but he found that it led to a tragic loss. So he regressed to an anal mode. He was expressing, through his body, his central need: *to hold on*. When Erikson found the right moment, he interpreted Peter's wishes to him, and Peter's symptom was greatly alleviated.

Sometimes students, upon hearing of Peter's behavior, suggest that his symptom was a means of "getting attention." This interpretation is used frequently by the behaviorists. We note, however, that Erikson's approach was different. He was concerned with the meaning of the symptom for Peter, with what Peter was trying to express through it. Through his body, Peter was unconsciously trying to say, "I need to hold on to what I've lost." Erikson and other psychoanalysts believe that instead of changing a child's behavior through external reinforcements such as attention, it is best to speak to the child's fears and to what the child may be unconsciously trying to say.

Thoughts on Child-Rearing

Over the years, Erikson has applied clinical insights to many problems, including those in education, ethics, and politics. He has also had a special interest in child-rearing.

As we briefly mentioned in our discussion of trust, Erikson is concerned with the problem facing parents in our changing society. American parents are often unable or unwilling simply to follow traditional child-rearing precepts; they would like to bring up their children in more personal, tolerant ways, based on new information and education (Erikson, 1959, p. 99). Unfortunately, modern child-rearing advice is often contradictory and frightens the new parent with its accounts of how things can go wrong. Consequently, the new parent is anxious and uncertain. This is a serious problem, Erikson thinks, for, as we have seen, it is important that the parent convey to the child a basic security, a feeling that the world is a calm and secure place.

Erikson suggests that parents can derive some inner security from religious faith. Beyond this, he suggests that parents heed their fundamental "belief in the species" (1963, p. 267). By this, Erikson means something similar to Gesell. Parents should recognize that it is not all up to them to form the child; children largely grow according to an inner, maturational timetable. As Erikson says, "It is important to realize that . . . the healthy child, if halfway properly guided, merely obeys and on the whole can be trusted to obey inner laws of development . . ." (1963, p. 67). Thus, it is all right for parents to follow their inclination to smile when their baby smiles, make room for their child to walk when he or she tries to, and so on. They can feel secure that it is all right to follow the baby's own biological ground plan.

Erikson also hopes that parents can recognize the basic inequality between child and adult. The human child, in contrast to the young of other species, undergoes a much longer period of dependency and helplessness. Parents, therefore, must be careful to resist the temptation to take out their own frustrations on the weaker child. They must resist, for example, the impulse to dominate the child because they themselves feel helpless with others. Parents should also be careful to avoid trying to shape the child into the person they wanted to become, thereby ignoring the child's own capacities and inclinations. Erikson says, in conclusion, "if we will only learn to let live, the plan for growth is all there" (1959, p. 100).

EVALUATION

Erikson has certainly broadened psychoanalytic theory. He has delineated the most general issues at each of Freud's stages and has enlarged the stage sequence so that it now covers the entire life cycle. Erikson has also given us a new appreciation of how social factors enter into the various stages. For example, he shows that adolescents are struggling not just to master their impulses but to find an identity in the larger social world.

Erikson, finally, has given Freudian theory new insights into the possibilities for healthy development. He has done this primarily by making wider use of the concept of maturation than Freud did. In Freud's view, maturation directs the course of the instinctual drives, which must undergo a good measure of repression. For Erikson, maturation also promotes the growth of the ego modes and the general ego qualities such as autonomy and initiative.[4] Erikson, to be sure, discusses the difficulties in attaining these qualities, but he does give us a better picture of how ego growth is possible. By suggesting that healthy development is tied to a maturational ground plan, Erikson has moved Freudian theory in the developmental direction of Rousseau, Gesell, and others.

Erikson's theory has also met with various criticisms. Robert White (1960) argues that Erikson has tried too hard to link the various aspects of ego development to Freud's libidinal zones. Erikson says that for each zone, there is a characteristic ego mode of interaction with the world. However, White argues, these modes fail to capture many of the child's activities. For example, many of the young child's efforts to achieve autonomy—such as the child's loud "no's" and vigorous walking—seem unrelated to the anal modes of retention and elimination. White himself proposes that we think of ego growth as a general tendency toward competence—a tendency that includes locomotion, exploration, and autonomous action without any necessary connection to Freud's zones.

A more general criticism is that Erikson is frequently vague with respect to theoretical issues. He writes in a beautiful flowing prose, but he leaves many conceptual matters unclear. For example, he provides new insights into the potential for growth in old age, when people examine their lives and search for wisdom, but he does not clearly indicate how this is part of the maturational process. It may be that there is a biologically based tendency to review one's life (Butler, 1963), but Erikson is not explicit on this matter. Similarly, he fails to spell out how maturation contributes to the other stages of adulthood, and he treats many other issues in a very implicit way.

Erikson is aware of his general vagueness. As he once said, "I came to psychology from art, which may explain, if not justify, the fact that the reader will find me painting contexts and backgrounds where he would rather have me point to facts and concepts" (1963, p. 17).

This conceptual vagueness may partly explain why interesting empirical research on his theory has been slow to develop. Nevertheless, some good research has occasionally emerged. Marcia (1966), for example, has thoughtfully constructed measures of different identity states, and these measures seem related to other variables. For example, young people with a foreclosed identity—who have simply accepted handed-down occupational goals and values without themselves struggling with alternatives— seem to be most often found at the level of conventional moral thought on Kohlberg's scale. Those, in contrast, who have achieved a sense of

---

[4]Erikson's suggestion that ego growth has maturational roots follows the lead of Hartmann, discussed in the preceding chapter (pp. 241–42).

identity after a personal struggle are more often represented by postconventional moral thinking (Podd, 1972).

Thus, it does appear that Erikson's theory can generate good empirical research. Erikson's thought, like Freud's, is so rich and profound that it rewards efforts to master it—both for personal insights into human nature and for scientific progress.

13

A Case Study in Psychoanalytic Treatment:
Bettelheim on Autism

BIOGRAPHICAL INTRODUCTION

In this chapter we will try to get a better understanding of psychoanalytic treatment. `Such treatments vary, of course, and we will not attempt to review the variations here. Instead, we will examine a "case study": Bettelheim's work with autistic children. Bettelheim's work is especially important to us because, as we shall see, it is squarely within the developmental tradition.

Bruno Bettelheim (1903–1990) grew up and became interested in psychoanalysis in Vienna. In 1932 Bettelheim and his wife took into their home and began caring for a girl who later would have been diagnosed as suffering from *autism* (Kanner, 1943)—a mysterious condition in which children are totally unresponsive to people. But in 1938 Hitler's invasion of Austria disrupted this home treatment, along with everything else (Goleman, 1990). From 1938 to 1939 Bettelheim was a prisoner in the concentration camps of Dachau and Buchenwald. Bettelheim wrote detailed accounts of this experience (e.g., 1960) and drew upon it in all of his work. After his release, he came to the United States and, in 1944, took over the direction of the Orthogenic School in Chicago with the hope that if it was possible to build prison camps powerful enough to destroy human personalities, perhaps it was also possible to create environments that can foster their rebirth (Bettelheim, 1967, p. 8). In this special school and home for children, Bettelheim and his staff treated a wide variety of emotional disorders, but Bettelheim always had a special interest in autistic children, and he wrote movingly about his school's treatment of them in *The Empty Fortress* (1967). Bettelheim retired as director of the school in 1973, but he continued to write on many topics, including fairy tales (1976), reading instruction (Bettelheim and Zelan, 1981), and parenting (1987). Bettelheim died at the age of 86, taking his own life.

Bettelheim was a complex man. In his writings, he emphasized the need for a warm, accepting environment in which even the most disturbed children will feel free to develop according to their inner promptings. This is the philosophy that the staff at the Orthogenic School has followed. Yet Bettelheim himself was an autocratic man who sometimes insulted his students and staff. And soon after he died, former patients from the school wrote that he sometimes lost his temper and hit them and humiliated them (e.g., Jatich, 1990). The extent to which he did this is still a matter of debate (Bernstein, 1990), but there definitely was a contradiction between Bettelheim's philosophy and his personal behavior.

Still, we do not study Bettelheim because of his personal attributes. We study him because of his ideas and insights and the hope his school has provided for the treatment of troubled children.

THE AUTISTIC SYNDROME

Autism is relatively rare; it is much rarer, for example, than mental deficiency. However, it is important because it is the earliest of the severe personality disturbances, usually showing up by the second year of life (Bettelheim, 1967, p. 392; Treffert, 1970). Autistic children appear to be physically healthy, but they differ dramatically from normal children in other ways. As mentioned, these chidren are completely aloof; they do not interact with others. If you try to relate to them, they either avoid eye contact or "look right through you" (Lovaas, 1973).

Much of the time, these children engage in repetitive behavior called self-stimulation. That is, they endlessly spin objects, such as ashtrays, or stare at their hands as they rapidly shake them, or they rock themselves like babies. In a minority of cases, the children are self-destructive—they hit their heads or tear at their skin, especially when placed in a new situation or when physically restrained (Lovaas et al., 1973).

Autistic children, in addition, frequently display severe disturbances in language. About half of them are mute. Those who do talk often engage in echolalia, the meaningless repetition of sounds. For example, if you ask a child, "What's your name?" the child answers, "What's your name?" (Lovaas, 1973, p. 2).

Another characteristic is an obsessive need for sameness. Once a behavior pattern is established, the child insists on its ritualistic execution. For example, a bedtime ritual must always consist of precisely the same actions. If one interferes with the pattern, the child flies into a rage or into an acute panic (Eisenberg and Kanner, 1956).

Some of these symptoms appear in children with other psychiatric diagnoses, so one would not, for example, label a child "autistic" simply because he or she engaged in self-rocking. The most distinctive feature of autism is the extreme isolation.

THE CAUSE OF AUTISM

The cause of autism is still unknown. Because the onset is so early, many workers believe that it is a product of some inborn impairment, perhaps some brain dysfunction (e.g., Rimland, 1964). Others, including Bettelheim, speculate that autism is primarily the outcome of early interactions with the social environment, with parents or caretakers. More specifically, Bettelheim proposed that early in life these children fail to develop a sense of *autonomy*, which he defined as the feeling that one can have an effect on the environment.

According to Bettelheim, the issue of autonomy occurs much earlier in life than most writers have supposed. In the psychoanalytic tradition, infancy is frequently portrayed as a period of passive dependency, as a "golden age when all [the infant's] wants are taken care of by others and he neither wishes nor needs to do anything on his own" (Bettelheim, 1967, p. 15). Bettelheim countered that there are many ways in which babies ordinarily develop a sense of autonomy, a conviction that their own actions make a difference in the world. For example, babies are active in nursing, searching for the nipple on their own and expending great energy in sucking, and they probably feel that it is their own actions that produce the satisfactions of feeding. Similarly, babies' cries may give them a sense of autonomy and power. Although we adults may consider the babies' cries as a sign of their dependency, this probably is not the way babies see it. If their cries repeatedly bring comfort, they may get the sense that "When I cry, things happen." Also, babies may get a sense that their emotions and actions count for something when their smiles bring about smiles in return. Or, when babies are held too tightly, and their gestures of discomfort produce a more comfortable grip, they acquire further confirmation that their own actions make a difference. In Bettelheim's view, when we see children who act autonomously in the second year—for example, vigorously walking, exploring, and trying to do things on their own—they are only continuing to express a sense of autonomy that they began to develop in the first year of life (1967, pp. 14–32).

Bettelheim thought that the baby's growing sense of autonomy is not only important in its own right but is also central to the development of a personality and a self (1967, pp. 24–25, 33–35). For Bettelheim, the sense of self—the sense of "I"—is bound up with the feeling that "I did it" and "It was my own actions that made the difference."

Autism, Bettelheim said, is the failure to develop autonomy. Early on, autistic children seem to get the notion that their attempts to influence the key figures in their lives will meet only with indifference, anxiety, or retaliation. They might conclude that their efforts to find the mother's nipple and to feed themselves produce mainly irritation or anxiety. Or, when they show discomfort at being held too tightly, they might experience the caretaker's reaction as one of indifference (or a further tightening of the hold). If such reactions dominate the infant's experience, they will begin to give up their own active efforts to better their lot (1967, pp. 72–74).

But the basic reason children give up autonomous action, Bettelheim said, is that they somehow get the feeling, correctly or incorrectly, that their existence is not desired. They feel that any actions or willfullness— even any fussing—might be the last straw that brings about their destruction. In this respect, Bettelheim speculated, autistic children feel something like the prisoners in concentration camps for whom any action risked death. Thus, autistic children conclude that it is too dangerous to be independently assertive. Through a monumental act of will, they decide to do nothing and to be nothing, or to limit their actions to the small world that they can control (for example, endlessly spinning an ashtray, apparently oblivious to the happenings in the rest of the room). Moreover, since the sense of self depends on active interchange with the world, they forfeit the opportunity to build a self. Walling themselves off from the world, with no self inside, they live in an empty fortress (1967, pp. 73–83, 223).

It is sometimes thought that Bettelheim blamed autism on the parents. Bettelheim said that this was not his intention. Although he attributed the disorder to parent-child interactions, he believed that inborn temperamental differences between parent and child may play a large role. For example, a fast, hyperactive baby boy may be out of tune with a slow-moving mother, and the boy will have difficulty finding appropriate feedback from his mother (1967, p. 29). In any case, Bettelheim said that the important thing is not what the parent does, but what the baby experiences—whether the baby can find the desired responses to his or her own actions (1967, p. 70).

THERAPY

For a long time, autism was considered essentially untreatable. Then Bettelheim (1967) and a few others (especially Lovaas, 1969) reported some success. In the Orthogenic School, the treatment for all children is on a residential basis; the children live in the school full-time. When Bettelheim was its director, the school generally housed 45 to 50 children, but it never attempted to treat more than six or eight autistic children at a time (Bettelheim, 1967, p. 90; 1974, p. 5). The treatment for these children usually lasted at least five years. Bettelheim's therapeutic principles emerge from his detailed descriptions of three case studies (1967).

Love and Care

A crucial part of the school's environment, in Bettelheim's day and today, is the provision of a tremendous amount of love, care, and protection—a nurturance that probably counteracts any feelings by the autistic children that others wish their destruction. The school's counselors are extremely devoted to the children, and after a while this loving care seems to register with them. For example, Joey, a nine-year-old boy who had given up on people and had made himself into a machine, seemed to like being bathed,

> though for a long time this too was a mechanical procedure. In the tub he rocked hard, back and forth, with the regularity of an engine and without emotion, flooding the bathroom. If he stopped rocking, he did that too, like a machine. . . . Only once, after months of being carried to bed from his bath, did we catch a slight puzzled pleasure on his face and he said, in a very low voice, "They even carry you to your bed here." This was the first time we heard him use a personal pronoun. (1967, p. 255)

Autonomy

Apart from this care, though, there is a sense in which Bettelheim believed that the staff cannot do things for the autistic children; for the most important thing that the children must develop is autonomy; and if autonomy is to be genuine, the children must gain it on their own. All the staff can do is create the right conditions of love and respect for the children and then hope that the children will begin to trust them sufficiently to take the first steps on their own.

The way in which love and care set the stage for autonomous action is illustrated by an incident with Laurie, a girl who came to the school at the age of seven years. Although Laurie was pretty and well dressed, she was completely inert and withdrawn. She had not uttered a word in more than four years. She also ate and drank very little and for months had kept her mouth slightly open, which parched her lips. Laurie's counselor tried to

> wet her lips and also to oil them, to make her more comfortable. Her counselor rubbed her lips softly, and then gently put a finger in her mouth and on her tongue. . . . At first Laurie barely reacted, but later she seemed to like it, and for an instant she touched the finger with her tongue, may even have licked it for a moment. (1967, p. 100)

Thus, the counselor's loving care seemed to inspire Laurie to take a small, but spontaneous initial action on her own.

Usually the children's first efforts at self-assertion occurred around the issue of elimination, which is what happened, for example, in the case of Marcia. When Marcia came to the school at the age of 10½ years, she was completely unresponsive to people or objects, and she spoke only in single words that had some personal meaning to her alone. A central problem in her life was her constipation; she had stopped moving her bowels on her own after her mother had begun training her at two years. Since then, her parents had given her repeated enemas, an experience which, her doll-play later revealed, represented for her the feeling of being completely overpowered by huge adults. The staff's attitude toward her constipation illustrates the importance they put on the concept of autonomy. Bettelheim wrote:

> From the moment Marcia came we were convinced that if we were to force her to do anything, to give anything up, we could never help her out of her isolation. Nothing seemed more important than her acquiring the feeling that she was at least in charge of her own body. So from the beginning we assured her that we would not force her to move her bowels, that at the school she would never be given enemas, or any laxatives, and that in regard to elimination she could do as she wished. (1967, p. 170)

She did not have to defecate in the toilet, "but could do it wherever and whenever it was easiest for her" (1967, p. 172). Soon Marcia began to soil, and the first place she defecated with any regularity was in the bathtub, the place where she seemed to feel the most relaxed and comfortable. After defecating in the tub, she frequently played with her stools. "After about a year and again in her own good time—though we occasionally made tentative suggestions—she began to eliminate in the toilet" (1967, p. 172).

The children's progress continued when they made initial attempts to relate to others. After a year at the school, Marcia invited her counselor Inge to play a chasing game, exclaiming, "Chase!" However, Inge always had to maintain a certain distance, and Marcia never chased Inge in turn. Bettelheim speculated that through this game, in which Marcia was never caught, she was trying to master her feelings of being overpowered by adults. That is, she may have been trying to establish "through thousands of repetitions of the game that never again would anyone get hold of her and overpower the now barely emerging 'me'" (1967, p. 179). Thus, Bettelheim interpreted Marcia's initial attempts to relate to others in terms of her need to establish autonomy. The counselors respected her wishes and always played the game on her own terms. Their attitude, in turn, seemed to win Marcia's trust to the point where she then tried new ways of relating to them.

The three cases suggest, finally, that progress in relating gave the children the courage to begin a new phase: Through symbolic play, they attempted to reexperience and master conflicts at the earliest developmental stage, the oral stage. For Marcia, it took some time before she could engage in purely oral play. For days, she repeatedly forced water in and out of a baby doll's mouth and rectum in exactly the same manner. Apparently, she first had to free herself of the death grip that enemas had on her total experience before she could work on feeding as a separate function (1967, p. 208). Finally, she separated the two activities by performing them in different rooms. When, however, her play did take on distinctively oral themes, she revealed that orality was fraught with its own grave dangers, as when, for example, she viciously beat a toy dog for daring to drink some milk (1967, p. 224). Marcia seemed to believe that oral intake was bad and could bring about the severest retaliation. Gradually, though, she was able to experiment with pleasurable ways of drinking in doll play and even to enjoy drinking itself.

The course of therapy, it should be noted, was not something that Bettelheim determined beforehand. The children took the lead in acting and exploring their problems, and the staff supported them the best it could. This was often difficult. Marcia's water play, for example, flooded the floors and required enormous work mopping up. But the staff members usually tolerated such behavior, for the children were trying to master their experience (1967, pp. 204, 217).

Marcia eventually made a partial recovery. After five years in the school, she was talking to others and seemed capable of the full range of emotional expression. Her intellectual abilities, however, lagged behind; she was only reading at the fourth grade level. Perhaps she had entered the school at too late an age ($10\frac{1}{2}$ years) to permit a full recovery. Still, when she returned home, after seven years in the school, she was able to take care of herself and perform useful tasks. More importantly, she was no longer the frozen child she once had been.

Attitude toward Symptoms

One of the most radical aspects of Bettelheim's philosophy was his attitude toward symptoms. For most mental health workers, symptoms (e.g., self-stimulation and peculiar gestures) are to be directly eliminated, or, at best, tolerated. Bettelheim, however, pointed out that the symptoms are what the children have spontaneously developed to gain some relief from, and even some mastery over, their tensions. They represent the child's greatest spontaneous achievement to date. Accordingly, they deserve our respect. If, instead, we disparage the symptoms—if, for example, we encourage the child to drop them—we cannot convey our respect for the child either (1967, p. 169).

The staff's attitude toward symptoms is illustrated by its approach to Marcia's behavior in the dining room. When Marcia first came to the school, she ate only candy, and in the dining room she plugged her ears with her forefingers and her nose with her little fingers, apparently to protect herself from something dangerous in the situation. This habit made it impossible for her to eat with her hands. The staff thought about telling her that it was O.K. to unplug her ears and nose, but they realized that this communication would fall woefully short. For if it were O.K. for her to unplug them she would do it herself. Similarly, they did not feel that an offer to feed her themselves would convince her that they understood her plight; if she could trust anyone to feed her, she would not need to plug herself up.

> Our solution was to offer to plug the ears for her; then she could have some fingers free to eat with. Hearing our offer, Marcia promptly plugged her nose with her forefingers and with her other fingers brought food to her mouth by bending as close to the plate as she could—a performance that astonished both the other children and all adults present. (1967, pp. 169–70)

Many professionals would consider the staff's approach completely wrong; what they did was reinforce the psychotic behavior. However, they were trying to show a respect for the child's own devices for handling frightening feelings.

Sometimes the autistic symptoms included self-destructive behavior; the children tried to hurt and damage themselves. In these cases, the staff did step in; they had to protect the children (e.g., 1967, p. 268). However, other symptoms were respected as far as possible, for they were the children's autonomous constructions.

Phenomenology

Bettelheim's work has a phenomenological orientation. As a philosophy, phenomenology is exceedingly complex, but in psychology it generally means suspending our preconception that others think in some customary way and trying to enter into the other's unique world from the inside. It means putting onself in the other's shoes (Ellenberger, 1958).

The school's phenomenological approach is illustrated by the attitude toward Marcia's plugging of her ears and nose. Although the *staff members* knew it was O.K. for Marcia to unplug herself, they guessed that this was not *Marcia's* experience. Thus, they tried to see the world in terms of Marcia's unique inner experience and to act accordingly.

Bettelheim believed that autistic children will never leave their defensive positions as long as others are simply interested in getting them to see the world as they (adults) see it.

> This is exactly what the psychotic child cannot do. Instead, our task . . . is to create for him a world that is totally different from the one he abandoned in despair, and moreover a world he can enter right now, as he is. This means, above all, that he must feel we are with him in his private world and not that he is once more repeating the experience that "everyone wants me to come out of my world and enter his." (1967, p. 10)

The phenomenological task is especially difficult in the case of autistic children for two reasons. First, because we have become fairly well adjusted to the external world, we have difficulty understanding the horror with which the autistic child regards it. Second, autistic children in many ways have never transcended the experiential modalities of the infant— modalities that are largely preverbal and foreign to us as adults.

Summary

In Bettelheim's view, then, therapy should include (1) a great deal of love and care for the autistic children, which (2) enables them to trust others to the point where they will dare to take steps toward autonomous action. Bettelheim also believed (3) that the children will make progress only if they are given full respect as human beings, including respect for their symptoms as their greatest efforts to date to relieve their suffering. Finally (4), they will move out of the autistic position only if the staff somehow communicates to them that it does not simply want them to enter its own world, but that it is trying to understand the children's own unique experience.

EVALUATION

Bettelheim tried to evaluate the school's success with the 46 autistic children it treated up to 1967 (1967, pp. 414–16). He believed the school had good success with four-fifths of these children. That is, about this number were able to make a decent adjustment to society, including meaningful relationships with others. Of these, about half, for all intents and purposes, were cured; although they sometimes showed some personality quirks, they were doing well in their studies or were earning a living on their own. It is difficult to evaluate such statistics, however, because there are no reports on the reliability of these judgments. We do not know, that is, if neutral observers would have agreed with Bettelheim's assessments. Nevertheless, Bettelheim's case reports and films indicate that the children did make substantial progress, so we can have some confidence in his impressions.

Bettelheim's success is, for our purposes, very important because his school took a decidedly developmental approach and showed it can work. Unlike most mental health institutions, the school did not actively try to change the children's behavior. The staff was, in a sense, more passive. It assumed that if it established the right conditions of love and care, the children would begin to take the steps toward health on their own. The staff allowed the children to take the lead. Bettelheim's school, working in the developmental tradition, had faith that even in these very disturbed children there were inner forces toward growth and autonomy that would emerge in the right environment.

Rousseau, Gesell, and other developmentalists distinguish between autonomous growth and socialization. If we actively try to change children's behavior, we usually become socializers. We adopt socially appropriate behavior as our goal and try to teach children accordingly. The behaviorist Lovaas (1973), for example, tries to reinforce socially appropriate behavior, such as language, while eliminating socially inappropriate behavior, such as peculiar psychotic gestures. Bettelheim, in contrast, put such a high premium on autonomous development that he frequently tolerated socially "deviant" acts. We saw how he respected many psychotic symptoms, for they are the child's autonomous creations. We also saw how the staff permitted Marcia to move her bowels in the bathtub and to flood the floors. It did so because she was taking steps on her own and exploring her problems. Bettelheim said that "too often children's progress is viewed not in terms of a move toward autonomy but of the convenience of a society that cares less about autonomy than conformity, and of parents who prefer not to clean their children's underclothes, no matter what" (1967, p. 294). The real question, he says, is "when, and for what gains, we ought to strip away social adjustment for the sake of personal development" (1967, p. 293).

Bettelheim, then, provided valuable support for the developmentalist position, which tries to let the children take the lead and do their own growing. His treatment is not the only one that has been effective; Lovaas, in particular, has had fairly equal success with behavioral techniques. But Bettelheim gave us a reason to consider the developmentalist alternative.

I have implied that Bettelheim's approach differs not only from the behaviorists' but from that of most mental health workers. At the same time, a number of child psychoanalysts would substantially agree with his approach. Most child analysts of course, work with less disturbed children and therefore do not need to become active caretakers. Nevertheless, they often share Bettelheim's developmentalist orientation. That is, they do not try to get children to behave in the "correct" ways, but they try to create a climate of acceptance and understanding that will enable children to take the initiative in exploring their problems.

The major weakness of Bettelheim's work is a lack of respect for standard scientific methodology. As mentioned, we would like more reliable outcome data. We also would like information on the relative effectiveness of Bettelheim's specific procedures, as indicated by objective measures. Bettelheim did not even attempt these. Nevertheless, Bettelheim's work and moving case reports are a significant contribution to the psychoanalytic and developmental literature.

14

Schachtel
on Childhood
Experiences

BIOGRAPHICAL INTRODUCTION

Freud, Erikson, and Bettelheim share the developmentalist concern for
how growth might occur from inner forces, from the organism itself. Although I have made somewhat less a point of it, they also share the developmentalist view that thought and behavior are qualitatively different
at different stages. A writer who provided special insights into the unique
qualities of early experiences was Ernest Schachtel.

Ernest Schachtel (1903–1975) was born and grew up in Berlin. His
father wanted him to become a lawyer, which he did, even though he was
more interested in philosophy, sociology, and literature. Schachtel practiced law for eight years until 1933, when the Nazis had him jailed and
then sent to a concentration camp. After his release he worked on family
research in England and Switzerland and then in 1935 came to New York,
where he received psychoanalytic training. Schachtel worked as a psychoanalyst the rest of his life, with a special interest in Rorschach (inkblot)
testing. However, Schachtel was always something of a maverick among
psychoanalysts, a man with his own ideas on development (Wilner, 1975).

BASIC CONCEPTS

Schachtel was most specifically interested in the problem of *infantile amnesia*, our inability to remember most of the events of our first five or six years of life (Schachtel, 1959, p. 286). This curious gap in our memories was first noted by Freud, who pointed out that as infants we had many intense experiences—loves, fears, angers, jealousies—and yet our recall for them is very fragmentary. Freud's explanation was that this amnesia is the product of repression. Early sexual and aggressive feelings became linked to shame, disgust, and loathing, and therefore were repressed into the unconscious (Freud, 1905, pp. 581–83).

Schachtel believed that Freud was partly right, but he pointed out two problems with the repression hypothesis. First, childhood amnesia is quite pervasive; we forget not only the sexual and hostile feelings that we might have had cause to repress but almost every other aspect of our early childhoods as well. Second, even psychoanalytic patients, who sometimes can get beneath the repression barrier, are still unable to remember much of their first few years. Thus, childhood amnesia must have an additional source (Schachtel, 1959, p. 285).

Schachtel suggested that childhood amnesia primarily has to do with *perceptual modes of experience*. Most adult experience and memory is based on verbal categories. We look at a painting and say to ourselves, "That is a picture by Picasso," and this is how we remember what we have seen (see Slobin, 1979, pp. 155–56). Childhood experience, in contrast, is largely preverbal. It is, as Rousseau said, more directly based on the senses. As a result, it cannot be tagged, labeled—and later recalled—through verbal codes, and it is therefore lost to us as we grow up.

Schachtel divided childhood experience into two stages: infancy and early childhood. Let us look at the modes of perception during these two stages and compare them with the orientations of the adult.

Infancy (Birth to One Year)

In infancy we rely on certain senses in particular. One vital sense is *taste*. Babies, who take many things into their mouths, have more taste buds than adults do and probably can make rather fine discriminations through this modality (Schachtel, 1959, pp. 138, 300). Babies also experience objects and people by their *smells*. Since babies are often held on the lap, and since young children, when standing, reach up only to the adult's waist, they are probably quite sensitive to the smell of legs, lap, and the sexual and excretory organs of the adult (1959, p. 138). Infants, Schachtel said, know what the mother tastes and smells like long before they know what she looks like. They probably can tell when she is tense or calm through these senses (1959, p. 299). Babies are also very sensitive to *touch* and react, for example, to the state of the mother as revealed by her relaxed or tense hold. Babies, finally, react sensitively to temperature through the *thermal sense* (1959, p. 92).

Schachtel called these senses *autocentric*—the sensations are felt in the body. When we taste or smell food, our sensations are felt in the mouth or in the nostrils. Similarly, the experiences of hot and cold, and of being held and touched, are felt in or on the body. The autocentric senses are distinguished from the predominantly *allocentric* senses—*hearing* and, especially, *sight*. When we use these sensory modalities, our attention is directed to the outside. When we look at a tree, we usually focus outward, on the object itself (1959, pp. 81–84, 96–115).

The autocentric senses are intimately bound up with feelings of pleasure and unpleasure, of comfort and discomfort. Good food, for example, produces a feeling of pleasure; rancid food produces disgust. The allocentric senses, in contrast, are usually more neutral. We experience no keen pleasure or disgust, for instance, in looking at a tree. The baby's predominantly autocentric experience, then, is tied to the pleasure principle, as Freud said.

Adult memory categories—which are predominantly verbal—are poorly suited for the recall of autocentric experience. We have a fair number of words for describing what we see but very few for describing what we smell, taste, or feel. "A wine," for example, "is said to be dry, sweet, robust, fine, full, and so on, but none of these words enables one to imagine the flavor and bouquet of the wine" (1959, pp. 298–99). Poets can sometimes create vivid images of visual scenes, but they are unable to do so with respect to smells and tastes. The world of the infant, then, which is so much a world of smells, tastes, and bodily sensations, is not subject to verbal codes and recall.

Schachtel called special attention to the sense of smell. Western cultures practically outlaw discriminations based on this sense. If, upon being introduced to a man, I were to go up and sniff him, I would be considered extremely uncouth (although it is perfectly acceptable to inspect him visually at a distance). In English to say, "He smells," is synonymous with saying, "He smells badly." We do, of course, use perfumes and are aware of some fragrances, but on the whole our discriminations based on this sense are very limited.

The taboo on smell is probably related to the fact that odor is the primary quality of fecal matter. Babies, as Freud noted, seem to enjoy the smell of their feces, but socializing agents teach them otherwise. The result is that children repress specific anal experiences, as Freud said. But it is more than this. Children quit making fine discriminations based on this sense altogether. Consequently, their early experiences are lost, for they do not fit into the accepted categories of experience.

Early Childhood (One to Five Years)

During infancy we do not generally welcome changes in internal or external stimulation. Sudden changes—such as sharp hunger pains, shivering cold, or the loss of bodily support—can be quite threatening. The infant would, as Freud said, like to remain embedded in a warm, peaceful, protective environment, much like the womb (Schachtel, 1959, pp. 26, 44–68).

At about one year of age, however, the child's basic orientation undergoes a change. Children become relatively less concerned about their security; under maturational urging, they take a much more active and persistent interest in new things.   To some extent they still rely on the autocentric senses, as when they put objects into their mouths.   But they now increasingly utilize the pure allocentric senses—hearing and especially sight.   They examine and explore new objects by looking at them.

The young child's attitude is one of openness to the world.   The child has the capacity to take everything in, no matter how small or insignificant to us, in a fresh, naive, and spellbound manner.   A little girl, coming across an insect, will stop and examine it intently.   To her, the insect is full of new and fascinating possibilities.   She perceives each new object with a sense of wonder and awe.

This openness contrasts markedly with the predominant attitude of adults.   Most adults simply label objects—for example, "That is an ant"—and then go on to something else.   Adults use the same allocentric senses—sight and hearing—but not in a fully allocentric way, not with an openness to things themselves.   As adults, our greatest need is not to explore the world in all its richness but to reassure ourselves that everything is familiar, as accustomed and expected.

It is not easy to understand why adults are in such a hurry to name, label, and classify things, but the answer probably has to do with the process of socialization.   As children grow up, they find that grown-ups and peers have standard, conventional ways of describing the world, and the pressure is great to adopt them.   The older child and the adult become afraid of looking at things in any way that might be different from others.   There is always the threat of feeling odd, ignorant, or alone.   Just as infants need the security of caretakers, adults need the security of belonging and conforming to their cultural group.   Consequently, they come to see what others see, to feel what everyone feels, and to refer to all experiences with the same clichés (1959, pp. 204–6, 176–77).   They then think that they know all the answers, but they really only know their way around the conventional pattern, in which everything is familiar and nothing a cause for wonder (1959, p. 292).

What the adult becomes capable of remembering, then, is that which fits into conventional categories.   For example, when we take a trip, we see all the sights we are supposed to see, so we can be sure to remember exactly what everybody else remembers, too.   We can tell our friends that we saw the Grand Canyon, that we stopped at six Howard Johnson restaurants, that the desert looked beautiful at sunset (just like in the postcards).   We cannot, however, give any real idea of what the country was like.   The trip has become a mere collection of clichés (1959, p. 288).

Similarly, our journey through life is remembered in terms of conventional signposts.   A man can tell us about his birthdays, his wedding day, his jobs, the number of children he had and their positions in life, and the recognitions he received.   But he will be unable to tell us about the truly special qualities of his wife, of his job, or of his children, for to do so would mean opening himself to experiences that transcend the conventional categories of perception (1959, p. 299).

Among adults, Schachtel said, it is primarily the sensitive artist who has retained the young child's capacity to view the world freshly, vividly, and openly. Only the exceptional artist can experience things with the young child's sense of wonder at watching an insect walk; at the way a ball squeezes, bounces, and responds to the hand; or at the way water feels and looks as it is poured. For most of us, unfortunately, "the age of discovery, early childhood, is buried deep under the age of routine familiarity, adulthood" (1959, p. 294).

In summary, then, neither the autocentric experiences of the infant nor the allocentric experiences of the young child fit into the adult's way of categorizing and remembering events. The infant's world of tastes, smells, and touch, as well as the young child's fresh and open experience of things in all their fullness, are foreign to the adult and are not subject to recall.

IMPLICATIONS FOR EDUCATION

Most of Schachtel's thoughts on child-rearing and education concerned the child as he or she begins actively to explore the world. Schachtel wanted us to preserve and encourage the young child's bold curiosity. Unfortunately, we usually stifle it.

For example, when babies begin to handle and examine everything they see, parents often become overly anxious. Parents, as Montessori observed, are afraid that their children are acting too rough, that they might break things, or that they might hurt themselves. Actually, it is usually simple enough to "child-proof" a house—to remove all breakable and dangerous objects—and then permit the child to explore. Nevertheless, parents often become anxious at this point, and the result is that children learn that it is dangerous to become too curious about the world (1959, p. 154).

Adults may also discourage children's curiosity by the way they name, label, and explain things to children. For example, when a child becomes curious about something, the adult often simply tells the child the object's name, implying that there is nothing more to know about it (1959, p. 187). If a little girl shouts, "Da!" and points excitedly at a dog, the father says, "Yes, that's a dog," and then urges her to continue on with their walk. He teaches her that the conventional category, the word, "explains" the object. Instead, he might say, "Yes, that's a dog!" and stop and observe it with her. In this way, he respects and encourages her active interest in the world.

Schachtel, on the whole, told us more about how parents, teachers, and peers stifle the child's curiosity than how we might protect and encourage it. Like Rousseau, he implied that the most important thing is to avoid negative influences. If we can lessen our tendency to close off their world, children themselves will take an open, active interest in it, from their own spontaneous tendencies.

EVALUATION

Freud thought that the great tragedy of life was that in order for us to live in society, we repress so much of ourselves. Freud had in mind the repression of instinctual drives. Erikson elaborates on this theme, suggesting that positive potentials for autonomy, initiative, and other strengths usually become somewhat curtailed in the course of socialization. Schachtel's contribution is an enlarged conception of just how much we do lose. It is not just that we repress our drives, or even that ego strengths such as autonomy are restricted, but that we lose touch with entire modes of experience. The baby who is in direct contact with objects through the senses of smell, taste, and touch and the child who is openly curious about the world grow into well-socialized adults who view the world through very narrow, verbal, conventional schemes. Perhaps Schachtel, by helping us appreciate the extent of the problem, also puts us in a position to begin to correct it.

Schachtel also demonstrated, in the course of his writings, the value of a phenomenological approach to childhood. He provided glimpses of how the infant's world might appear from the inside—how differently they may experience the world because different senses are dominant. The phenomenological approach deserves wider application in developmental psychology.

At the same time, Schachtel's work suffered from certain oversimplifications. For one thing, he probably underestimated the importance of vision in infancy. For example, we saw in our chapter on ethology how the baby's attention to visual patterns, such as the face, is very important. Schachtel also gave a one-sided picture of language. He felt that the acquisition of language stifles creativity, for the child learns to substitute the conventional label or word for the experience itself. Although this may be true, language can also be creative, as we shall see in our chapter on Chomsky.

Still, Schachtel did much to keep psychologists and psychoanalysts mindful of the value of the radical Rousseau-like way of thinking. He pointed out how very different the child's world is from ours and how much human potential for fresh creative experience may be lost in the process of becoming a well-adjusted member of the conventional social order.

15

Jung's Theory of Adulthood

BIOGRAPHICAL INTRODUCTION

We have noted that few theorists have concerned themselves with development during the adult years. Erikson is one notable exception. Another was C. G. Jung (1875–1961), whose psychoanalytic theory dealt primarily with the issues of adulthood and aging.

Jung was born in Kesswil, a village in northeastern Switzerland. His childhood was mostly unhappy. He experienced the tensions of his parents' marital difficulties and was usually quite lonely. School bored him and even precipitated fainting spells when he was 12 years old (Jung, 1961, p. 30). Because his father was a pastor, Jung went to church, but he disliked it and got into bitter religious arguments with his father. Jung's primary enjoyments during childhood and adolescence were exploring nature and reading books of his own choosing—drama, poetry, history, and philosophy.

Despite his problems, Jung did well in high school and went on to earn a medical degree. He then began practicing psychiatry in Zurich, where he quickly developed a lasting interest in psychotic disorders. Jung's work—including his invention of the word-association test—suggested the importance of Freud's ideas. His colleagues warned him that any alignment with Freud would jeopardize his career, but he went ahead and indicated the importance of Freud anyway (1961, p. 148). Freud, of course, appreciated Jung's support, and when the two men met they found they had much in common. For some time, Freud treated Jung like a son and chosen disciple. Jung, however, disagreed with aspects of Freud's theory, particularly with the attempt to reduce all unconscious events to sexual drives. Jung believed the unconscious contains many kinds of strivings, including religious and spiritual ones. In 1912 Jung decided to develop his own ideas, and in 1913 the two men severed ties.

After parting with Freud, Jung lost his footing. He began having uncanny, deeply symbolic dreams and experienced frightening visions during his waking hours. In one vision he saw the Alps grow and then saw mighty yellow waves drown thousands of people and turn into a sea of blood. Since World War I broke out the next year, he believed that his vision carried a message that related to events far beyond himself (1961, pp. 175–76).

Jung realized that he was on the brink of psychosis, but he nevertheless decided to submit to the unconscious—to whatever was welling up and calling him from within. It was his only chance of understanding what was happening to him. Thus he embarked on a terrifying inner journey in which he frequently felt himself descending into lower and lower depths. At each region, he saw archaic symbols and images, and he communicated with demons, ghosts, and strange figures from the distant historical past. During this period, his family and professional practice served as bases of support in the outer world. Otherwise, he was certain, the images welling up from within would have driven him completely out of his mind (1961, p. 189).

Gradually, after about four years, he began to find the goal of his inner quest. This happened when he increasingly found himself drawing geometrical figures, symbols composed of circles and squares that he would later call *mandalas* (see Figure 15.1). The drawings represented some basic unity or wholeness, a path to the center of his being. Jung said that during his psychotic state

> I had to let myself be carried along by the current, without knowing where it would lead me. When I began drawing mandalas, however, I saw that everything, all the paths I had been following, all the steps I had taken, were leading back to a single point—namely to the midpoint. It became increasingly clear to me that the mandala is the center (1961, p. 196)

Jung thus began to understand his break as a necessary inner journey that led to a new personal integration. Support for this, however, came some eight years later, when he dreamed of a curiously Chinese-looking mandala, and the next year he received a book in Chinese philosophy that discussed the mandala as the expression of the unity of life. Jung then believed that his own experience partook of an unconscious universal quest for psychic wholeness.

FIGURE 15.1   A Tibetan mandala.   (Reprinted from *The Collected Works of C. G. Jung,* trans.
R. F. C. Hull, Bollingen Series XX. Vol. 9, I, *The Archetypes and the Collective
Unconscious,* copyright © 1959, 1969 by Princeton University Press.   Figure 1,
''Concerning Mandala Symbolism.''

Jung made the exploration of the unconscious and its symbols the center of his research for the rest of his life. He continually explored his own dreams and fantasies and those of his patients. He also extensively studied the myths and art of numerous cultures, finding in these productions the expression of universal, unconscious yearnings and tensions.

PERSONALITY STRUCTURE

Although Jung was most concerned with the nature of the unconscious, he developed a theory of personality that encompasses various systems of personality functioning. We will first describe Jung's ideas on personality structure, and then discuss his views on how the personality develops.

The ego. The ego is roughly equivalent to consciousness. It includes our awareness of the external world as well as our consciousness of ourselves (Jung, 1933, p. 98; Whitmont and Kaufmann, 1973, p. 93).

The persona. The persona is the ego's mask, the image one presents to the outer world. Our personas vary with our roles. A man presents one image to his business associates, another to his children. Some people develop their personas to the exclusion of deeper parts of the personality. At some point they, or others, sense that there is little of substance beneath the superficial front (Jung, 1961, p. 385). It also is true, however, that we need this part of the personality to deal effectively with others. It is often necessary, for example, to convey an image of confidence and decisiveness if we want others to listen to us (Jacobi, 1965, p. 37). To the extent that the personality is balanced, the persona will be developed, but not to the exclusion of other parts.

The shadow. The shadow consists of those traits and feelings that we cannot admit to ourselves. It is the opposite of our ego or self-image; it is the Mr. Hyde of Dr. Jekyll. In dreams, the shadow is projected onto people of the same sex, as when we dream about evil and sadistic people who are the same sex as ourselves. In our daily lives, our shadow often shows when we are in awkward situations and, for example, suddenly blurt out a hostile remark that "doesn't sound like me at all." We also see the projections of our shadows when we complain about "the one thing I cannot stand in people"; for such vehemence suggests that we are really defending against an awareness of this quality in ourselves (von Franz, 1964, p. 174).

In most cases the shadow is largely negative, for it is the opposite of our positive self-image. However, to the extent that our conscious self-image contains negative elements, the unconscious shadow will be positive (Jung, 1961, p. 387). A young woman who considers herself unattractive may dream about a beautiful lady. She considers this lady somebody else, but it may really represent her own beauty wishing to emerge. Whether the shadow is positive or negative, it is important to get in touch with it.

Insight into the nature of one's shadow is the first step toward self-awareness and the integration of the personality (Jung, 1933, p. 33).

The anima and animus. Chinese Taoists speak of the Yin and the Yang, the feminine and the masculine sides of our personalities. According to Jung, the feminine principle includes capacities for nurturance, feeling, and art, and a oneness with nature. The masculine principle includes logical thinking, heroic assertion, and the conquest of nature (Jung, 1961, pp. 379–80; Whitmont and Kaufmann, 1973, p. 94). We are all biologically bisexual, and we all identify with people of both sexes, so we all possess both masculine and feminine traits. However, there are also genetic sex differences, which socialization pressures exaggerate, forcing women to overdevelop their feminine side and men to overemphasize their masculine nature. The result is that the "other side" is repressed and weak. Men tend to become one-sidedly independent, aggressive, and intellectual; they neglect capacities for nurturance and relatedness to others. Women develop their nurturant and feeling sides but neglect their capacities for self-assertion and logical thought. Nevertheless, the neglected aspects do not disappear but remain active and call out to us from the unconscious. In men, the feminine side emerges in dreams and fantasies as "the woman within," the *anima*. In women, the "man within" is called the *animus* (Jung, 1961, p. 380).

The personal unconscious. Jung thought that the unconscious consists of two layers. The first is the personal unconscious, which contains all the tendencies and feelings that we have repressed during our lifetime (1961, p. 389). Much of the shadow is in the personal unconscious. It might include, for example, a man's tender feelings toward his father which, as a child, he needed to repress. The anima and animus are also partly, but not completely, found in this unconscious region. A woman may have repressed her experiences of her father as seductive—experiences that then contribute to her animus and reside in her personal unconscious.

The collective unconscious. Each individual's personal unconscious is unique, for each person has repressed different thoughts and feelings during his or her lifetime. However, Jung also believed that there exists, at the deepest layer of the psyche, a collective unconscious that is inherited and shared by all humankind. The collective unconscious is made up of innate energy forces and organizing tendencies called *archetypes* (see Fig. 15.2). We can never know the archetypes directly, but we can learn about them through archetypal images found in the myths, art, dreams, and fantasies of peoples throughout the world. Through these images, people try to express their deepest inner yearnings and unconscious tendencies. They include the image of the Earth Mother, the Wise Old Man, rebirth, death, the trickster, the witch, and God.

The archetypes also influence the nature and growth of the other parts of the personality. For example, a woman's animus results not only from her experiences with her father and other men but from an unconscious, universal tendency to find some Wise Man or Good Father.

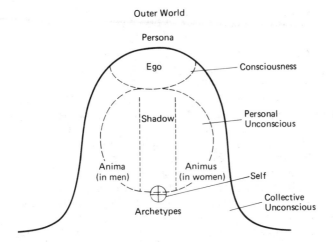

FIGURE 15.2   The psyche in Jung's theory.

Different cultures express archetypal themes in somewhat different ways, but humans everywhere have always been fascinated and impressed by them. Jung said:

> The concept of the archetype . . . is derived from the repeated observation that, for instance, the myths and fairytales of world literature contain definite motifs which crop up everywhere. We meet these same motifs in the fantasies, dreams, deliria, and delusions of individuals living today . . . They have their origin in the archetype, which in itself is an irrepresentable unconscious, pre-existent form that seems to be part of the inherited structure of the psyche and can therefore manifest itself spontaneously anywhere, at any time. (1961, p. 380)

Although Jung said archetypes are essentially unknowable, he also likened them to instincts in animals—for example, a bird's innate schema of the parent (Jung, 1964, p. 58). Perhaps archetypes can also be likened to the innate perceptual tendencies Gestalt psychologists talk about (Arnheim, 1954; R. Watson, 1968, Ch. 19). For example, we may have an inner sense of what constitutes a harmonious form. Mandalas probably strike us as beautiful because they correspond to our senses of proportion, balance, and good organization.

The Self.   The most important archetype is that of the Self, our unconscious striving for centeredness, wholeness, and meaning (Jung, 1961, p. 386). The Self is an inner urge to balance and reconcile the opposing aspects of our personalities. It is represented throughout the world in drawings of mandalas, figures in which all sides are perfectly balanced around a center point. The Self is also expressed by our search for God, the symbol of wholeness and ultimate meaning (1961, p. 382).

Introversion and extraversion.   Although the Self is the ultimate goal in life, no one ever fully attains it. We all develop in one-sided ways. Most of us, for example, develop our consciousness and neglect our unconscious lives. Women neglect their masculine side, men their feminine side. Jung developed other concepts to describe opposite tendencies, of which we develop one to the exclusion of the other. One such polarity is introversion-extraversion. The extravert confidently engages in direct action; the introvert hesitates and reflects upon what may happen. At a party an extraverted young woman immediately walks over to others and strikes up a conversation with them. The introverted woman hesitates; she is caught up in her inner state, her fears, hopes, and feelings. The extravert moves outward, toward the world; the introvert is more secure in his or her inner world and takes more pleasure in activities such as reading and art. We all have both tendencies but are predisposed toward one, leaving the other underdeveloped and unconscious (Jung, 1945).

THEORY OF DEVELOPMENT

The First Half of Life

The personality develops along different lines during the first and second halves of the life cycle. The first period, until the age of 35 or 40, is a time of outward expansion. Maturational forces direct the growth of the ego and the unfolding of capacities for dealing with the external world. Young people learn to get along with others and try to win as many of society's rewards as possible. They establish careers and families, and they do what they can to advance up the social ladder of success. To do so, women usually experience social pressure to develop their feminine traits, and men their masculine traits.

During this phase, Jung thought, a certain degree of one-sidedness is necessary; the young person needs to dedicate himself or herself to the task of mastering the outer world. It is not especially advantageous for young people to be too preoccupied with their self-doubts, fantasies, and inner natures (Jung, 1933, p. 109). For the task is to meet the demands of the external environment confidently and assertively. As one can imagine, extraverts, rather than introverts, have an easier time of it during this period (Jacobi, 1965, p. 42).

The Mid-Life Crisis

About age 40 the psyche begins to undergo a transformation. The individual feels that the goals and ambitions that once seemed so eternal have lost their meaning. Quite often the person feels depressed, stagnant, and incomplete, as if something crucial is missing. Jung observed that this happens even among people who have achieved a good measure of social success, for " . . . the achievements which society rewards are won at the cost of a diminution of personality. Many—far too many—aspects of life which should have been experienced lie in the lumber-room among dusty memories" (1933, p. 104).

The psyche itself provides the way out of this crisis. It urges the person to turn inward and examine the meaning of his or her life. This turning inward is prompted by the unconscious, the region in which all the repressed and unlived aspects of the self have grown and now clamor to be heard. The unconscious calls out for recognition in order to bring about psychic balance and harmony (1933, pp. 17–18, 62–63).

The unconscious speaks to us primarily through dreams. For example, early in his analysis, a man who was depressed and felt that his life was meaningless had the following dream:

> I am standing totally perplexed, in the midst of a Casbah-like city with serpentine and winding small streets, not knowing where to turn. Suddenly I see a young, mysterious woman whom I had never seen before, pointing with her hand the direction out. It had a very awesome quality to it. (Whitmont and Kaufmann, 1973, p. 95)

The dream's message is that the man must pay attention to his anima (the mysterious young woman) for the direction out of his impasse. For it is this side of himself that he has so far failed to appreciate and develop.

As adults examine their lives and listen to unconscious messages, they sooner or later encounter images of the Self, the symbols of wholeness and centeredness. For example, a middle-aged man, a highly successful executive who had been increasingly experiencing tension and a suicidal depression, had a dream in which a water devil attacked him and maneuvered him to the edge of an abyss. The creature then rescued him and gave him a drill, which the dreamer was supposed to use to dig to the center of the earth. In Jungian terms, the dream's key figure, the water devil, is initially evil, for it represents elements in the unconscious that the conscious ego has considered inadmissible—destructive urges. Yet the devil turns into a helper, indicating that the man must confront the negative aspects of himself if he is ever to become whole and find his true center (Whitmont, 1969, pp. 224–25).

As the dream continued, the man found himself in a secret chamber where a meeting was in progress around a square table. Presiding were a splendid knight and a Lord Mayor. However, the dreamer was led to the table by a delinquent boy and a dirty, tramplike man who looked like a friar. They sat at the table and gave him some repulsive food which he ate anyway. He then pushed his drill into the ground, and flowers grew around the drill, and the drill was transformed into a blossoming tree.

According to a Jungian analysis, the splendid knight and the Mayor represent the heroic and authoritative aspects of the personality that the man had consciously realized as a business administrator. The delinquent and the ragged friar stand for the neglected, devalued aspects of the self, elements he has so far repressed. In particular, this man had regarded his religious inclinations as soft and escapist, as tendencies that would undermine his manhood. But it is the monk and the delinquent—repressed shadow figures—who lead him to the square table, the symbol of psychic unity. There he eats repulsive food—for no one likes looking into the repressed parts of the personality—but in so doing he sees that new growth (the blossoming tree) will emerge (1969, pp. 224–27).

You will notice that the Jungian approach to dreams differs from that of the Freudians. Freud considered dreams to be the end-products of distortion and disguise. Jung, in contrast, believed that dreams express unconscious meanings fairly directly (Jung, 1933, p. 13). In the dream cited above, the delinquent and the monk are interpreted quite literally, as symbols for the delinquent and religious aspects of the personality. Further, the unconscious, the source of dreams, is not just a seething pit of base impulses and desires, as it was for Freud. Rather, the unconscious, as a part of nature, can be a creative force, directing us out of our current stalemates, as the above dreams illustrate. Dreams tell us which aspects of the self we have neglected and must get in touch with (1933, pp. 62–63). This does not mean that we should actually live out our evil tendencies. However, it does mean that we should learn about them, so we can control them, rather than the other way around (Whitmont, 1969, pp. 227–30).

The road toward health and growth—toward the unattainable goal of the Self—is called *individuation* (Jung, 1933, p. 26). Individuation involves not only achieving a measure of psychic balance, but also separating ourselves from our ordinary conformity to the goals and values of the mass culture. It means finding one's individual way. Each person's true nature partakes of universal archetypes, but it is also based on unique experiences and potentials that must be discovered (Jung, 1961, p. 383; Jacobi, 1965, pp. 83–87).

The middle of life, then, is marked by a transformation in the psyche. We are prompted to begin turning our energy away from the mastery of the external world and to begin focusing on our inner selves. We feel inner urgings to listen to the unconscious to learn about the potentials we have so far left unrealized. We begin to raise questions about the meaning of our lives, which, after all, are now half over.

Although the focus from middle age onward becomes increasingly inward, the middle-aged adult still has the energy and resources for making changes in his or her external situation. In middle age, adults quite often take up long-neglected projects and interests and even make seemingly incomprehensible career changes. Men and women, Jung observed (1933, p. 108), begin giving expression to their opposite sexual sides. Men become less aggressively ambitious and become more concerned with interpersonal relationships. As an older colleague once told me, "As you get older you find that achievement counts for less and friendship counts for far more." Women, on the other hand, become more aggressive and independent. If, for example, a man loses interest in the family business, the wife may willingly take it over. The woman, like the man, is becoming increasingly inner-directed as she ages, but her enthusiasm for aggressive pursuits may temporarily counterbalance or stall this general inner orientation.

The changes of life in middle age can create marital problems. The wife may tire of her husband's intellectual condescension, for she is now trying to develop her own thinking side. The husband, on the other hand, may feel oppressed by his wife's tendency to treat him emotionally like a child. He no longer simply wants to be calmed and pampered for his moodiness, but he wants to explore the realm of feelings and relationships in a more mature manner.   Changes such as these can disturb the marital equilibrium (Jung, 1931).

Although growth during the second half of life creates tensions and difficulties, the greatest failures come when adults cling to the goals and values of the first half of life (Jung, 1933, p. 109).   A middle-aged woman may desperately try to maintain the physical attractiveness of her youth. Or the middle-aged man may talk incessantly about his past athletic glories. In such cases, adults miss out on further development, which can emerge only when they risk a confrontation with the neglected parts of themselves.

Old Age

Jung said that "with increasing age, contemplation, and reflection, the inner images naturally play an ever greater part in man's life. . . .   In old age one begins to let memories unroll before the mind's eye . . . " (1961, p. 320).   The old person tries to understand the nature of life in the face of death (1961, p. 309).

Jung believed that we cannot face death in a healthy way unless we have some image of the hereafter.   If "I live in a house which I know will fall about my head within the next two weeks, all my vital functions will be impaired by this thought; but if on the contrary I feel myself to be safe, I can dwell there in a normal and comfortable way" (1933, p. 112).   When Jung recommended that the aged entertain thoughts of an afterlife, he did not feel that he was simply prescribing some artificial tranquilizer.   For the unconscious itself has an archetype of eternity that wells up from within as death nears.

Jung could not say, of course, whether our archetypal image of the hereafter is valid, but he believed that it is a vital part of psychic functioning and therefore tried to get some picture of it.   He based his picture on his own last dreams and those of others near death.   The archetypal image of eternity, in Jung's view, is not of some hedonistic paradise.   Instead, he pictured the souls of the dead to be like a spell-bound audience listening to a lecture, seeking information from the newly deceased on the meaning of life.   Apparently they know only what they knew at the moment of death.   "Hence their endeavor to penetrate into life in order to share in the knowledge of men.   I frequently have the feeling that they are standing directly behind us, waiting to hear what answer we will give them, and what answer to destiny" (1961, p. 308).   They continue to strive to attain in death that share of awareness that they failed to win in life.

In Jung's view, then, life after death is a continuation of life itself. The dead, like the aged, continue to struggle with the questions of existence; they wonder what it is that makes a life whole and gives it meaning— they search, in Erikson's term, for integrity.   Jung's view of the continuation of this questioning fits well with his theory of the unconscious as something that extends beyond any finite life and participates in the tensions of the universe.

PRACTICAL IMPLICATIONS

As with the Freudians, Jung's theory is inseparable from its practical applications. Much of Jung's theory came out of his work with patients who helped him understand the nature of the unconscious and the kinds of experiences that were necessary to integrate their lives. Jungian psychoanalysis is most applicable to adults and older people. In fact, over two-thirds of Jung's own clients were in the second half of their lives (Whitmont and Kaufmann, 1973, p. 110).

Jung's ideas would also seem of value even to those who never find their way to the analyst's office. Most adults, at one time or another, probably experience the special problems that come with growing older. Some knowledge of the kinds of changes that typically occur may help them get their bearings. For this reason, adults seem to derive benefits from a book such as *Passages* (Sheehy, 1976), which discusses the expectable crises of adulthood. Since this book popularizes ideas of Levinson (1977, 1978), and Levinson, in turn, owes much to Jung, one ultimately may find the deepest rewards from Jung himself.

Jung's relevance for psychology and psychiatry extends beyond his special insights into adult development. Because he considered religious questions vital and meaningful in their own right, ministers, priests, and others, who themselves must often work with emotionally distressed people, have found that Jung provides a valuable bridge between the religious and psychiatric professions.

Jung's writings, furthermore, anticipated some bold thinking on the nature of psychotic disorders, especially the thinking of Laing (1967). Laing argued that it is wrong to view psychotic experiences as simply abnormal and bizarre. This attitude characterizes technological cultures that refuse to admit the validity of the inner world and, instead, make outer adjustment the sole objective. Laing contended that the psychotic experience, for all its pain, can be a meaningful inner voyage and a healing process. In this voyage, the therapist can serve as a guide, helping the patient understand his or her inner symbols. Jung's view was somewhat similar, and a knowledge of Jung would seem essential for anyone who wishes to understand psychosis.

EVALUATION

Jung occupies an unusual place in contemporary psychology. On the one hand, many of his ideas are too mystical for most psychologists. He not only posited a collective unconscious, but he also believed in ESP and related phenomena (e.g., Jung, 1961, p. 190). Sometimes, in addition, he seemed unnecessarily determined to keep his concepts shrouded in mystery. For example, he said that the archetypes are unknowable, yet he compared them to instincts in animals—a topic certainly open to scientific investigation.

On the other hand, psychologists in general, and developmentalists in particular, are increasingly recognizing the importance of Jung's ideas. Developmentalists, as we have seen, have long been concerned with how we seem to lose so much of ourselves and our potentials as we become socialized, as we become adjusted to the external world. Jung agreed that this happens, but he saw new opportunities for individual growth in the adult years.

Moreover, some very significant empirical research lends support to Jung's ideas. In a major study of adult men, Levinson (1977, 1978) interprets his findings in a Jungian context. Levinson found that the vast majority of his subjects underwent a crisis at about age 40 or 45, during which they began to experience "internal voices that have been silent or muted for years and now clamor to be heard" (1977, p. 108). Levinson concludes that the life structure of the 30s necessarily gives high priority to certain aspects of the self, those oriented toward social adjustment and achievement. But in the 40s, "the neglected parts of the self urgently seek expression and stimulate a man to reappraise his life" (1977, p. 108).

The impressive studies of Neugarten and her colleagues at the University of Chicago have also lent support to Jung's insights. Neugarten reports that for both sexes the 40s and 50s mark a "movement of energy away from an outer-world to an inner-world orientation" (1964, p. 201). Introspection, contemplation, and self-evaluation increasingly become characteristic forms of mental life (Neugarten, 1968, p. 140). Furthermore, men "become more receptive to their own affiliative, nurturant, and sensual promptings; while women seem to become more responsive toward, and less guilty about, their own aggressive, egocentric impulses" (Neugarten, 1964, p. 199). Thus, Neugarten's research, like Levinson's, documents some of the personality shifts Jung outlined.

These shifts, it is important to note, seem to occur consistently before external situations demand them (Havighurst et al., 1968, p. 167). Adults seem to turn inward before they might be forced to do so by external losses, such as retirement, reduced income, or the loss of a spouse. Thus, there seems to be an intrinsic developmental process at work. Adults may have an inherent need to take stock, to resist the pressures of conventional roles, and to concern themselves with the neglected and unrealized aspects of the personality.

16

Chomsky's Theory of Language Development

BIOGRAPHICAL INTRODUCTION[1]

In 1949 Montessori tried to get us to see that the child's mastery of language is an amazing achievement. It was not the learning of words that impressed her, but the acquisition of grammar or syntax—a system of rules for creating and understanding correct sentences. Grammatical rules are so complex and so deeply buried within spoken language that adults are hardly aware of them, yet children somehow unconsciously master most of them by the age of six years. Developmental psychology must understand how this happens.

Psychologists might have agreed with Montessori, but for a long time they were handicapped by their own ignorance of grammatical rules and structures. They were largely limited to counting children's nouns and verbs. Then, in 1957, Chomsky published *Syntactic Structures*, in which he described some of the operations we use to form and transform sentences. Researchers then had an idea of the kinds of operations to look for in children's speech, and the whole new field of developmental psycholinguistics emerged.

Noam Chomsky was born in 1928 in Philadelphia. He learned something about linguistics from his father, who was a respected Hebrew scholar, and studied linguistics, mathematics, and philosophy at the University of Pennsylvania. Actually, he was bored by college after two years and was ready to drop out when he met the linguist Zellig Harris. He became

---

[1]This chapter was written in collaboration with Stephen Crain.

299

absorbed in Harris's work and then began making his own innovations. In the meantime, Chomsky earned both a B.A. and a Ph.D. degree from Pennsylvania, although he spent several graduate school years in a special program at Harvard which permitted him to work on whatever he wanted. Chomsky's new theory, a combination of mathematics and linguistics, was so different from anything that had been done before that the universities had no place for him within their traditional departments. His only job offer came from the Massachusetts Institute of Technology (MIT), where he has been since 1955 (Chomsky, 1977, p. 80).

Chomsky is known not only for his innovations in linguistics, but also for his political activities and writings. He grew up in what he has called a "radical Jewish community" (Lyons, 1970, p. xi) and became one of the first intellectuals to speak out against the Vietnam War. He has also written extensively on American foreign policy and has opposed other U.S. military interventions, including the war with Iraq. Many of his colleagues disagree with his radical politics, but they almost unanimously recognize his accomplishments as a linguist. He has already been awarded eight honorary doctorate degrees and has received many other forms of recognition.

BASIC CONCEPTS

The Importance of Rules

Prior to Chomsky, most people probably believed in what Brown has called the "storage bin" theory of language learning. Children imitate others and acquire a large number of sentences that they store in their heads. They then reach in for the appropriate sentence when the occasion arises (Brown and Herrnstein, 1975, p. 444).

Chomsky has shown that this view is incorrect. We do not simply learn a set number of sentences, for we routinely create new ones. As I write this book, I use the same words over and over, but I create a novel sentence practically every time. We all do the same thing when we speak or write. We can do this because we have internal *rules* that enable us to decide which sentences are grammatical and convey our intended meanings. If we could use only sentences that we had already heard and memorized, our language would be severely limited. Because we have a system of rules—a grammar—we can invent and understand sentences that we have never heard before (Chomsky, 1959, p. 56).

The Child's Remarkable Grasp of Rules

Chomsky has focused on the rules for making transformations, as when we transform a statement into a question. For example, we might turn the sentence, "The dog bit the lady," into the question, "Did the dog bite the lady?" Chomsky has shown that the rules for making transformations can be quite complex, and he therefore considers it remarkable that they are routinely mastered by children.

Chomsky himself has observed children only informally. However, we can illustrate the child's linguistic capacities with some findings by Roger Brown (1973), whom Chomsky inspired. Brown unobtrusively tape-recorded a few children's spontaneous speech over a number of years and found, among other things, how they begin making a transformation called *tag questions*. Here are some tag questions produced by a boy called Adam one day when he was four-and-a-half years old.

Ursula's my sister, isn't she?
I made a mistake, didn't I?
Diandros and me are working, aren't we?
He can't beat me, can he?
He doesn't know what to do, does he?

The "tags" are the little questions on the end (Brown and Herrnstein, 1975, p. 471).

The first thing we might notice is the creative nature of Adam's speech. These do not seem to be sentences he has heard, but sentences he is making up. He can create new sentences that are grammatical because he is following rules.

Yet the rules are complex. First of all, to create the tags, Adam must reverse the negative or affirmative statement in the first part of the sentence. When Adam says, "I made a mistake," an affirmative statement, the tag must be negative, "Didn't I?" When he begins with a negative statement, such as "He can't beat me," the tag must be positive, "Can he?" Adam does this correctly every time.

Also, Adam must locate the subject of the sentence and then convert it into the correct pronoun in the tag question. In the sentence, "Diandros and me are working, aren't we?," Adam correctly sees that the subject is the noun-phrase "Diandros and me," and he converts it into "we."

Also, Adam implicitly recognizes that there are specific times when one must move the auxiliary verb to the front in the question. Note, however, that in the sentence, "I made a mistake, didn't I?," the auxiliary "did" is not even present in the statement. So Adam creates it, following an abstract rule that we weren't even aware of until Chomsky (1957) discovered it.

Thus Adam is simultaneously employing several operations, and these are only some of them. It is truly remarkable that he can produce correct tag questions at age four-and-a-half, yet he is not unusual in this respect (Brown and Herrnstein, 1975, p. 471).

An interesting aspect of Adam's verbal record is the frequency distribution of these sentences over time. Adam produced no tag questions at all until he was four-and-a-half, and then he suddenly burst out with them. In one hour he created 32 such questions, whereas the average adult frequency is three to six. His behavior is reminiscent of Piaget's circular reactions and Montessori's repetitions. Children seem to have an inner need to solidify new capacities through repeated exercise.

In any case, the development of tag questions illustrates Chomsky's point: Children master complex linguistic rules and procedures in a very short time. They seem to master most of the intricacies of grammars by the age of six or so, and the rest by puberty. This is not to say that they become consciously aware of grammatical rules; even Chomsky is still trying to make them explicit. But they gain a working knowledge of them on an intuitive level. They rapidly learn the rules of their own language—and, if need be, those of a second language as well. It is a common observation, Chomsky says, that a young child of immigrant parents may learn a second language in the streets, from other children, with amazing rapidity, and the child will speak the new language as fluently as the other children (1959, p. 42).

Chomsky acknowledges that everyone's speech, including that of adults, contains errors, slips, false starts, and interrupted fragments. These mistakes are caused by such factors as carelessness, fatigue, and memory lapses. These deficits in *performance*, however, are far outweighed by an underlying *competence*, which is best revealed by an ability to distinguish between poorly formed and well-formed sentences (Chomsky, 1962, p. 531).

The Innateness Hypothesis

Chomsky says that the linguistic accomplishments of the ordinary child are too great to be explained in terms of any kind of input from the environment. Children hear only a limited body of speech, much of which is poorly formed, yet they rapidly and uniformly develop an intricate system of rules for creating an unlimited number of sentences. Their knowledge extends far beyond their experience. One can only conclude, Chomsky says, that children do not build grammars primarily from the evidence they hear, but according to an inner design—a genetic program (1972, p. 171; 1980, pp. 232–34).

Chomsky likes to compare the development of grammar to the growth of physical organs, such as the embryonic heart or the visual apparatus. Here it is obvious that the structures that emerge are too intricate to explain in terms of environmental inputs (e.g., oxygen, nutrients). The environment is vital, but it primarily supports or activates intrinsically determined patterns. In a roughly similar way, the linguistic environment primarily triggers the construction of grammatical systems whose pattern is determined by the genetic blueprint (1980, p. 33).

But there is a problem. Languages, unlike physical organs, vary considerably from culture to culture, and the language a child learns depends on the culture in which he or she is raised. How, then, can an innate language-learning process be at work?

Chomsky's most recent proposal (1986, pp. 145–50) is this. When children master a grammar, they are guided by an innate knowledge of *universal grammar*; they automatically know the general form that any language must take. But universal grammar (UG) has holes in it; it leaves certain parameters open. For example, one principle of UG is that all sentences must contain a subject, but some languages allow speakers to routinely leave the subject implicit; the speakers do not have to voice it. In Italian one can simply say "Went" where in English one must say "She went" (Hyams, 1986). Thus children need information from the environment to set this parameter, to determine which rule their particular language follows.

Usually, Chomsky (1986, p. 146) speculates, setting parameters is a simple matter, like setting a switch + or −. Furthermore, the number of switches that a child must set may be fairly small. Thus, grammar acquisition may require only a small amount of environmental input.[2]

It is not yet clear that this parameter-setting model actually describes the way children learn their particular grammars. Few linguists would be surprised if Chomsky were to propose a new model before long. But Chomsky is committed to the general theory of universal grammar. Regardless of how children pick up the details of their particular grammars, they must have an innate knowledge of the general form that all languages must take. As they put words together, they must intuitively know that certain combinations are possible and others are not. If children lacked this knowledge, if they had to learn grammar primarily from experience, they could never master such a complex system in so short a time.

The child's capacity to learn languages, Chomsky also postulates, is species-specific (found only in humans) and is a highly specialized faculty within the human mind. That is, it is quite unlike the faculty for learning science, music, and so on. It has its own genetic design (1980, Ch. 6; 1983, p. 37).

Innate Constraints

What, precisely, are the genetically determined aspects of language? We are a long way from knowing for sure. We cannot have an innate knowledge of many of the rules for creating tag questions, for these are not universal.

On a universal level, Chomsky believes that we are probably disposed to construct languages out of certain building-blocks, such as nouns and verbs. Primarily, however, Chomsky argues that our minds possess built-in *constraints* that limit the rules we will even consider. As children learn languages, these constraints tell them, in effect, "Don't waste your time considering such-and-such rules; these are wrong." Such constraints free the child of the predicament of the scientific linguist, who must entertain and rule out all conceivable grammatical systems and rules. Children already know that grammars must be of a certain type (Chomsky, 1972, p. 113).

A major innate constraint is that all transformational rules must be *structure-dependent*. To get an idea of what this means, let us consider transforming the following sentences into yes/no questions.

(1) The man is tall. — Is the man tall?
    The book is on the table. — Is the book on the table?
    I can go. — Can I go?

---

[2]The idea of UG with gaps filled in by experience reminds one of the imprintinglike process by which some species of birds learn songs (see Chapter 3). However, Chomsky has not suggested this analogy.

What is the rule for forming these questions? Chomsky says that a neutral scientist, looking at these questions for the first time, would doubtlessly infer that the rule is to read from left to right until we come across the first verbal element ("is," "can," etc.) and then to move it to the front of the sentence. We can call this Hypothesis 1, and it works almost every time with sentences of this type. It is a simple, straightforward rule, one we would use if we were programming a computer. But look what happens when we apply it to the following sentence:

(2)   The man who is tall is in the room.   — Is the man who tall is in the room?

The sentence is ungrammatical. Hypothesis 1 is therefore wrong, and our scientist would be surprised.

When we correctly transform sentences, we first analyze them into abstract phrases (e.g., the noun phrase and the verb phrase). The phrases are called abstract because nothing marks off their boundaries; our sense of them is intuitive. Then we locate the first verbal element ("is," "can," etc.) *after the first noun phrase*, and it is this that we move to the front of the sentence. Thus (to use a diagram suggested by Aitchison, 1976),

(1)	The man	is	tall
	The book	is	on the table
	I	can	go
(2)	The man who is tall	is	in the room

In this way, then, Sentence 2 is correctly transformed. In Chomsky's terms, we follow a structure-dependent rule; we do not operate on strings of single words, but we analyze the structure of the phrases before making transformations, and we always keep the noun phrase intact (Chomsky, 1975, pp. 30–32).

Chomsky claims that the ordinary child, unlike our imaginary scientist, will never even consider Hypothesis 1. This is because structure-dependence is an innate mode of organizing experience, not something derived from evidence. In fact, Chomsky says, people may go through a considerable part of their lives without hearing any evidence that would enable them to choose between Hypothesis 1 and structure-dependence, and yet the very first time they must transform a sentence like Sentence 2 they will unhesitatingly use the structure-dependent rule (1975, p. 32).

It would be difficult to test Chomsky's assertion directly; for we would need a complete record of a speaker's experience. However, there is some evidence that supports Chomsky's position. When three- to five-year-old children were asked to transform sentences like Sentence 2, they sometimes had difficulty, but they seemed to do whatever was necessary, such as cutting up the sentences, to avoid violating the principle of structure-dependence (S. Crain and Nakayama, 1987). When, moreover, we consider the fact that all languages, as far as we know, employ only structure-dependent rules, it begins to appear that structure-dependence may very well be an innate property of the human mind.

Structure-dependence, then, is submitted as an innate constraint that restricts the kinds of transformational rules that children must learn. Children growing up in different cultures will learn somewhat different transformational rules, but they will automatically know that all rules must be structure-dependent. Children learning English, for example, will learn some tag-question rules that are not universal, but they will always respect structure-dependence. When Adam created the tag question, "Diandros and me are working, aren't we?," he automatically knew that it is the entire noun phrase (Diandros and me) that is converted into a pronoun in the question. The great task of linguistics, Chomsky believes, is to discover what principles, such as structure-dependence, set limits on the kinds of rules we will automatically follow. Such principles will tell us much about the nature of the human mind.

Surface and Deep Structure

When we create, comprehend, and transform sentences, we intuitively work on two levels. We attend both to the surface structure and to the deep structure of sentences. Chomsky's use of these concepts gets very abstract and technical but we can get a flavor of his ideas through some examples. Consider the following two sentences:

(3) John is eager to please.
(4) John is easy to please.

On the surface, the two sentences have the same structure: subject (John), verb (is), modifier (eager/easy), and infinitive (to please). Yet we intuitively know that their underlying meanings, revealed by their deeper structures, are different. In Sentence 3, John is the subject; he is the one who pleases. In Sentence 4, John is the object; others please him. Thus, the two sentences have different underlying structures.

The surface/deep structure distinction is important with respect to transformations. Consider these sentences:

(5) Susan ate the apple.
(6) The apple was eaten by Susan.
(7) Susan did not eat the apple.
(8) What did Susan eat?
(9) Susan ate the apple, didn't she?

Of these sentences, Sentence 5 is the most straightforward. It is a simple, active, declarative sentence and follows the subject-verb-object word order. In English, this form is closest to (but not identical with) the abstract deep structure; Sentence 5 is the basic kernel upon which one can perform certain operations to generate all the other sentences. One could not take any other sentence—say Sentence 6—and derive a clear set of operations for creating the others (Chomsky, 1957, pp. 45, 91; 1965, pp. 138–41).

Some writers, such as McNeill (1971), have been struck by the possibility that deep structures have more universal features than surface structures. Consequently, McNeill has hypothesized that children will initially speak in deep structures. This hypothesis may have some merit, but Chomsky has not endorsed it. He has implied (1968; 1972, p. 71) that all languages may utilize distinctions between deep and surface structures, but he has placed greater emphasis on innate constraints, such as structure-dependence.

NOTES ON THE GROWTH OF GRAMMAR

As indicated, Chomsky has not himself studied children, and his views on development are rather vague and inconsistent. In general, he suggests that we begin with the assumption that development is "instantaneous," that children instantly develop the grammatical structures of the adult. But this is just an initial working assumption, a way to get research started. For Chomsky also realizes that grammatical capacities, like any biological system, do mature and may even undergo qualitatively different stages (1972, pp. 88–90; 1975, pp. 119–23).

In any case, Chomsky's work has inspired many researchers—psycholinguists—to study children's language development in great detail. The following notes summarize only some of the main findings.[3]

Early Language

Right at birth, babies seem tuned into language. Careful film analyses suggest that infants make very slight body movements in response to speech, and their movements vary with the boundaries of sounds and words. Such movements are not made in response to other sounds, such as tapping (Condon and Sander, 1974).

At about one month of age babies begin gurgling and cooing, and by six months or so they are usually making babbling sounds such as "ba ba" and "da da." Babies' early vocalizations appear to be highly similar throughout the world (Sachs, 1976, p. 148).

One-Word Utterances

At about one year, babies begin producing single words. Some researchers believe that they are trying to use single words to express entire sentences. For example, "cookie" might mean, "I want a cookie" or "There is a cookie," depending on the context. There is a danger, however, of reading too much into the baby's speech (Sachs, 1976).

Two-Word Utterances

Beginning at about one-and-a-half years, children put two words together, and their language takes on a definite structure. Researchers have disagreed widely, however, about how best to characterize this structure.

[3]This summary basically follows that outlined by Cairns and Cairns, 1976, pp. 193–97.

Table 16.1 lists some typical two-word utterances, as characterized by some psycholinguists.

Notice how, in utterances 6 through 8, children are separating out agents, actions, and objects. Some people (e.g., McNeill, 1966) have proposed that children possess an underlying knowledge of subject-verb-object relationships. This, however, is not certain. When children employ agents, they are not necessarily using subjects. An agent is a limited semantic (word-meaning) category; it refers to something that takes action. A subject is a broader syntactic category that refers to parts of sentences that may or may not be taking action (e.g., there is no action in "He is tall"). Thus researchers who infer adult syntax in children's speech may once again be reading too much into it (Gardner, 1982, pp. 168–70).

Developing Grammar

Between two and three, children typically begin putting three and more words together, saying things like "I making coffee." Occasionally they say things like "Eve is girl" (Brown, 1973, p. 314), now apparently using subjects and verbs that go beyond agents and actions (Eve isn't *doing* anything). English-speaking children usually follow the subject-verb-object word order, which is integral to deep structure in our language (Brown et al., 1969, p. 42).

As soon as children begin putting three or more words together, they indicate a sense of structure-dependence—that *noun-phrases* are whole units. They reveal this, for example, by their pauses, as when a child says, "Put ... the red hat ... on," rather than "Put the ... red hat ... on." The child knows that the phrase "the red hat" functions as a unit that is not to be broken up (Brown and Bellugi, 1964, p. 150). Later, when children begin making transformations, they will respect the integrity of these units.

During this phase children also begin making use of *word endings*, and when they do, they *overregularize*, saying things like "I runned," "It doed," and "She doed it." A similar process occurs with respect to plurals; children routinely say things like "foots," "mans," and "mouses" (Ervin, 1964; Slobin, 1972).

Interestingly, children do not begin with overregularizations, but first use correct irregular forms. For example, a child might say "went" before

TABLE 16.1   Some Typical Two-Word Utterances

TYPE	EXAMPLE
1. Naming	that doggie
2. Repetition	more jump
3. Negation	allgone ball, no wet
4. Possession	my truck
5. Attribution	big boy
6. Agent-action	Johnny hit
7. Action-object	hit ball
8. Agent-object	Mommy bread (meaning, "Mommy is cutting the bread")

Adapted from Brown and Herrnstein (1975, p. 478) and Slobin (1979, pp. 86–87).

saying "goed." But after a month or so children begin to overregularize word endings and continue to do well into the elementary school years.

What children seem to be doing, most psycholinguists believe, is formulating rules. They discover that the rule for forming the past tense is to add the "-ed" sound, which they then apply to all cases, assuming that the language is more consistent than it actually is. Similarly, they induce that the rule for creating plurals is to add the "-s" sound, which they then apply across the board.

As mentioned earlier, psycholinguists sometimes seem to be looking for adult syntax in children's speech. Developmentalists in the Rousseauist tradition, in contrast, would be interested in the ways children's speech might be qualitatively different from that of adults. Overregularizations do give children's speech a unique flavor. However, children are actually overregularizing adult rules. Consequently, we would like to know if children sometimes also formulate their own rules.

This possibility struck Klima and Bellugi (1966) when examining children's *negatives*. Initially children act as if their rule is: Put the negative in front of the whole sentence (or after it). For example, they say, "No play that," "No want stand head," and "Car go no."

A bit later children seem to form a new rule: Put the negative after the first noun phrase and before everything else. They say things like, "He no bite you" and "I no want envelope."

At different stages, then, children structure negatives in their own ways. Some researchers (e.g., Dale, 1972, p. 169; Pierce, 1989) suggest that children's early sentences are close to deep structure—even though deep structure is a purely theoretical structure that children never directly hear. In any case, children's negatives do have a quality of their own. As Klima and Bellugi (1966) say, "It has seemed to us that the language of children has its own systematicity, and that the sentences of children are not just an imperfect copy of those of an adult" (p. 191).

Transformations

Between about three and six years, children's grammar rapidly becomes quite complex; most notably, children begin making transformations. Bellugi-Klima (1968) has studied how children form Where, What, and Why questions, which are transformations of their deep-structure representations. For example, "Where can I put it?" is essentially a transformation of "I can put it where."

Children do not master the transformational operations all at once, and they seem to go through stages somewhat like those with respect to negatives. For example, they go through a period where they say things like, "Where I can put it?" and "What he wants?" They move the "Where" or "What" to the front of the sentence, but leave the rest of the sentence alone (retaining the subject-verb-object word order). Even when they are asked to imitate, they commonly stick to their own way of speaking. For example,

Adult: "Adam, say what I say: Where can I put them?"
Adam: "Where I can put them?" (Slobin, 1979, p. 96).

Near Adult Grammar

Although children master most aspects of grammar by the age of five or six years, some of the most complex transformations are still beyond their grasp. For example, they seem to have difficulty with the passive voice until age seven or so (Turner and Rommetveit, 1967). The years five to 10 may be important for the acquisition of the subtlest and most complex grammatical skills (C. Chomsky, 1969).

Universals

As indicated, many psycholinguists believe there may be universals in the developmental process. So far the evidence is strongest for the earliest phases. Children everywhere probably proceed from babbling to one-word to two-word utterances. Babbling and two-word structures, in particular, appear to be highly similar throughout the world (Brown and Herrnstein, 1975, pp. 477–79; Sachs, 1976).

The search for syntactic universals after the two-word phase becomes very difficult, and the search has really just begun. Some evidence suggests that children everywhere may initially handle negatives in the same manner, and they may overregularize some parts of speech (Slobin, 1972, 1973; Cairns and Cairns, 1976, p. 205). By the time children are mastering transformations, they are clearly using rules that differ somewhat from language to language. Still, there may be universal constraints, such as structure-dependence, which limit the rules they will form.

CHOMSKY AND LEARNING THEORY

Chomsky suggests that language is something structured by children themselves. Hearing only a fragmentary body of speech, they nevertheless discover its rules, guided by an innate sense of what the rules must be like. Learning theorists, in contrast, believe that we must look to the social environment for the source of linguistic patterning. Language, in their view, is shaped primarily by others through operant conditioning or through modeling influences.

Operant Conditioning

The Skinnerian view of early language learning, which we have already discussed to some extent (Chapter 8), is sometimes called the "babble-luck" theory. Babies babble away until, by luck, they hit on a sound that resembles a word, and it is reinforced. For example, they say "da da" in the presence of Daddy, and the parents show their approval. Gradually, parents make their approval contingent upon increasingly accurate and complex utterances.

Skinner (1957) and his followers (e.g., Lovaas, 1977) have recognized that such meticulous shaping of each utterance would be too slow a process to account for the rapid development of language. Accordingly, they have pointed out that when children are taught specific linguistic behaviors, they may rapidly generalize their learning to new situations. For example, a child who has been taught to pluralize a word may automatically pluralize new words without any further training. Because children generalize, they readily produce entirely new expressions—behavior that Chomsky considers so important.

The principle of generalization would seem to explain overregularizations (e.g., "mans"). However, the picture is complicated because, as you may recall, children initially emit correct irregular forms (e.g., "men") which are presumably reinforced. Clearer demonstrations of operant principles have come from laboratory research, most of which has been done with retarded children or disturbed children who are behind in their speech. Such children have been taught plurals, prepositions, and other relatively simple grammatical elements, which they have rapidly generalized to new situations (Lovaas, 1977, pp. 110–16). However, it has not yet been shown that operant techniques can produce anything like complex grammatical transformations.

Furthermore, research by Brown and Hanlon (1970) suggests that normal children would have great difficulty learning language on the basis of parental conditioning, because parents are such poor language teachers. These investigators found that parents correct surprisingly few ungrammatical utterances. Instead, they concentrate on the truthfulness of their children's remarks. For example, when one girl, Sarah, said, "Her curl my hair," her mother said, "That's right," because that was what she was doing. The mother ignored Sarah's grammatical error. When, on the other hand, Sarah said, "There's the animal farmhouse," a grammatically impeccable sentence, her mother corrected her, because it was a lighthouse (1970, p. 202). Thus, it is unlikely that Sarah learned grammar as a consequence of her parents' effective use of approval and disapproval.

Perhaps it is not parental approval, but some other form of feedback that constitutes effective reinforcement. Perhaps children learn to use increasingly correct grammar because parents can comprehend and respond accurately to it. However, Brown and Hanlon also failed to find that well-formed utterances met with any better understanding than poorly formed utterances. Brown and Hanlon's data were based on only three children, but these three seemed to learn correct grammar despite the poorest kind of direct reinforcement from their parents.

Some of the most energetic learning-theory research has been devoted to teaching sign language to apes. By doing so, learning theorists hope to demonstrate the effectiveness of their procedures and to refute Chomsky's assertion that language learning is an innate propensity specific to humans. Some researchers have relied on operant techniques alone, whereas others have mixed their methods. The results, in many cases, have been quite remarkable, but it is not yet apparent that one can teach apes to handle language with anything like the flexibility and creativity of the ordinary human child at the two-word phase (Gleitman and Gleitman, 1986a, pp. 331–32). To Chomsky, these results are hardly surprising. The discovery that apes can learn language, he says, "would be similar to the discovery, on some unexplored island, of a species of bird that had never thought to fly until instructed to do so through human intervention" (1980, p. 239).

Operant theory, then, has yet to mount a case that seriously weakens Chomsky's position. In fact, operant theorists have increasingly come to recognize innate constraints which influence what different species can and cannot readily learn. Still, operant theory and research is still developing and may yet challenge Chomsky's proposals in some interesting ways.

Bandura and Modeling

Bandura emphasizes the influence of models. He recognizes that modeling does not always work through a process of exact imitation, for children produce novel utterances that they have never heard. For example, children's overregularizations (e.g., "mans") cannot be exact imitations, for adults do not talk this way.[4] However, Bandura contends that modeling is still at work; the process is one of "abstract modeling." Children imitate the rules they hear (e.g., add the "s" sound to form the plural), which they imitate too well (Bandura, 1977, p. 175).

Some laboratory research supports Bandura's position. Whitehurst et al. (1974), for example, showed that the careful modeling of passive sentences produced passives in children's speech. The children did not just copy the model's exact words, but they picked up the general structure of passive sentences and created new sentences of this type.

Chomsky has not commented directly on Bandura's proposal, but we can imagine what his response would be. In the real world, models may exemplify some rules with sufficient clarity for children to infer them on this basis. By and large, however, models present children with a limited body of speech that is frequently ambiguous. For example, they produce countless sentences that are consistent with either a structure-dependent or a structure-independent rule, but very few sentences that would enable the child to choose between these rules. Furthermore, much adult speech is degenerate; it is full of errors, slips, false starts, and so on. Thus, although children do pick up rules from the speech they hear, they can do so only because they are guided by an innate sense of what the rules are. Instead of focusing on the behavior of models, then, we should study the processing mechanisms of the child.

A good deal of research has challenged Chomsky's view of the quality of speech children hear (Snow, 1979; Sroufe and Cooper, 1988, pp. 278–79). Although speech between adults may be full of errors, adults commonly talk to children in a very simple, clear, and grammatical fashion. Such speech has been called "motherese" and is illustrated by the following early record of it (Brown and Bellugi, 1964, p. 135):

Adam: See truck, Mommy. See truck.
Mother: Did you see the truck?
Adam: No I see truck.
Mother: No, you didn't see it? There goes one.
Adam: There go one.

[4]It is conceivable that overregularizations are exact imitations of the speech of other children, but it is unlikely. Overregularizations occur in all children, including two-year-old first-borns whose primary linguistic models are their parents (Slobin, 1979, p. 94).

> *Mother:*   Yes, there goes one.
> *Adam:*   See a truck. See truck, Mommy. See truck. Truck. Put truck, Mommy.
> *Mother:*   Put the truck where?
> *Adam:*   Put truck window.
> *Mother:*   I think that one's too large to go in the window.

Except for the last sentence, the mother's speech is short, and it is perfectly grammatical. It is simple enough for Adam to imitate, which he does at one point, saying, "There go one." The mother follows with an *expanded imitation*—"Yes, there goes one." That is, she imitates Adam's sentence and expands a bit upon it. Perhaps expanded imitations gradually lead the child toward new grammatical forms.

The discovery of motherese, then, suggests that models may be far more effective than Chomsky implies. If adults model speech in simple, clear, and correct forms, children can learn it from them.

However, we cannot yet draw any firm conclusions about the impact of modeling influences. For one thing, we do not yet know how important motherese is. Current evidence suggests that motherese can speed up some language acquisition a bit, but children can certainly learn language without it. The adults in some cultures, such as the Kulali in New Guinea, do not believe in using simplified speech, yet their children learn language at roughly the same rate as U.S. children (Sroufe and Cooper, 1988, pp. 279–82).

Furthermore, even if simplified speech can accelerate language learning slightly, it still may be uninformative on key points. It probably doesn't provide children with the information they would need to know that all rules must be structure-dependent by the age they know this. This knowledge, as Chomsky says, may be innate, a part of the mind's natural way of organizing linguistic experience.

There is, finally, another kind of evidence that must caution us against placing too much emphasis on the role of modeling influences. Children sometimes create grammatical structures that are quite unlike those of adults. For example, we noted earlier how children initially put the "no" at the beginning or the end of the rest of the sentence—something that adults never exemplify. Adam does this in the above excerpt, saying, "No I see truck." Thus, children do not seem to be merely imitating adult rules but forming rules of their own. Ironically, Chomsky and his co-workers (e.g., Lightfoot, 1982, p. 184) have minimized the significance of these structures, emphasizing instead the early development of adult grammar. Yet these unique structures suggest that children do not just imitate adult rules but also organize speech in their own ways.

In summary, then, the discovery of simplified speech suggests that models may be more helpful to children than Chomsky implies. However, we should not jump to the conclusion that speech is primarily a product of modeling influences. It still seems possible that children possess an innate sense of general grammatical forms and that they sometimes structure language differently from that of models.

CHOMSKY AND PIAGET

Early in his career Chomsky wrote strong attacks on learning theory—namely, Skinner's theory (e.g., 1959). Later he became more concerned with the differences between his theory and that of Piaget, and he even met with Piaget for a series of debates in 1975 (Piatelli-Palmarini, 1979).

Piaget and Chomsky, to be sure, have much in common. Both argue that children are not molded by the external environment, but spontaneously create mental structures. However, Chomsky is much more nativistic than Piaget. Chomsky believes that language is largely wired into the genes. Children will, upon receiving appropriate stimulation, automatically create grammatical forms according to the genetic blueprint. Piaget, in contrast, placed much less emphasis on genetically controlled development. In his view, cognitive structures emerge simply from the child's own efforts to deal with and make sense out of the world.

Another difference concerns the specificity or the autonomy of language development. For Chomsky, language is a highly specialized "mental organ" which develops fairly independently from other forms of cognition (much as the heart develops apart from the liver or lungs). Piaget and his followers, in contrast, have viewed language as more closely related to general cognitive development.

For example, Sinclair (1971) proposed that the basic grammatical relations—subject-verb-object sequences—actually rest on prior sensori-motor achievements. At first babies fail to distinguish between themselves, their actions, and objects. If a girl drops a ball, she thinks it is gone because it is no longer part of her own actions. At the end of the sensori-motor period, children's searches for missing objects imply a differentiation between themselves, their actions, and the objects themselves. Thus, they develop the cognitive requirements for separating the self (subject), action (verb), and object.

Piaget also suggested that language is related to cognition at other periods. He noted (1983), for instance, that children begin using linguistic symbols (words) at about the same time that they begin using nonlinguistic symbols, such as play-actions to represent absent objects. It therefore seems that language emerges as part of a more general symbolizing process.

Piagetians have proposed, in addition, that the ability to perform linguistic transformations requires the development of concrete operations. Until this time, children may not be able to fully understand passive transformations because they require reversible operations. Similarly, they cannot understand a sentence such as "The wolf is easy to bite" because they would need to reverse it into something like "Someone can easily bite the wolf" (Cromer, 1970; Ingram, 1975). In the Piagetian view, then, concrete operations are necessary before basic linguistic transformations are possible.

Piagetians, then, contend that language is related to general cognitive development—and even depends on prior cognitive achievements. This view hardly sits well with Chomsky and his followers. Chomsky acknowledges that language is partially related to other forms of cognition, but he cannot believe that the intricate, complex grammars that children develop, with specific properties such as structure-dependence, are best understood in terms of more general cognitive principles.

As they assess the Chomsky-Piaget debate, researchers will probably turn a good deal of attention to the years between two and six. During this time, Piaget believed, the child's thought is basically illogical and unsystematic. If, during this time, the child's linguistic accomplishments emerge as rapidly and as impressively as Chomsky and his followers suggest, it will be difficult to maintain that language rests entirely on logic or other forms of cognition. Language development will look like a more specialized activity with its own period of rapid growth. At the same time, it seems unlikely that research will ultimately show language to be as divorced from other cognitive activities as Chomsky implies.

IMPLICATIONS FOR EDUCATION

Chomsky says that children learn an extensive, intricate grammatical system almost entirely on their own. All they need is to hear a language spoken, and they will master it, without any special training program. This is as true of the child in the ghetto as it is of the child in the middle-class suburb. The child picks up language off the streets, without anyone paying much attention to his or her progress. In fact, it is often the immigrant child in a poor neighborhood who masters not just one language but two (Chomsky, 1977, p. 88).

Since Chomsky believes that children learn language spontaneously, he proposes no new instructional methods. This does not mean, however, that his work has no practical value. It can help change our attitudes and deepen our appreciation of the child's mind. The teacher who considers the child's linguistic accomplishments will realize how ridiculous it is to focus on the child's shortcomings. Whatever the child may lack, it is trivial in comparison to the complex grammatical system he or she has mastered. The teacher, upon meeting each new elementary school child, will think: "This child has developed a remarkable grasp of linguistic structures. This mind deserves my greatest respect." One can only wonder about the effect such an attitude would have.

Despite the work of Chomsky and others, many psychologists cannot accept the possibility that children really learn language on their own. Instead, they believe that it is up to us to teach children a proper grammar. For example, Bandura (1977, p. 175) implies that we should correct children's overregularizations (e.g., "We digged the hole"). Chomsky's work suggests otherwise. What children are doing is searching for underlying rules, a search that will eventually lead to the mastery of an intricate grammar. It is wrong to interfere with this process. By correcting children's mistakes, we only confuse them and undermine their confidence. Their mistakes will correct themselves in time. Instead of correcting children, it would be more appropriate simply to admire their progress. Our quiet admiration and joy can be as helpful as any corrections we might make.

Nevertheless, many psychologists and educators continue to explore ways of facilitating and accelerating children's speech—even among pre-schoolers (Wells, 1985; Whitehurst et al., 1988). Some of these efforts include the use of expanded imitations—something many parents naturally do. For example, we noted how one of Brown's subjects, Adam, said, "There go one," and his mother responded, "Yes, there goes one" (Brown and Bellugi, 1964, p. 140). Children then sometimes imitate their parents' expansions. Many parents seem naturally to talk to children in this way, and children may enjoy such conversations. But it is not at all clear that expanded imitations can help language acquisition in any major way (Dale, 1972, pp. 116–20; Wells, 1985; Cole and Cole, 1989, p. 303).

Some educators have felt that it is important to teach children with African–American dialects the standard English form. These educators have commonly assumed that African–American dialects are inferior to standard English, which they are not (Labov, 1970; Bartlett, 1972). The likely outcome of such teaching is that the African–American child is made to feel deficient and inadequate.

In most schools, teachers describe the parts of speech, writing the familiar tree diagrams on the blackboard. Prior to Chomsky, we might have thought that these lessons were necessary. But the work of Chomsky and others suggests that children already have an implicit grasp of almost everything the teacher is explaining by the age of six years. Tree diagrams, to be sure, can make children more *conscious* of their language, a point Vygotsky emphasized. Since tree diagrams are abstract, they probably benefit children primarily after the age of 11 or so, when the capacity for abstract thinking begins. Before this age, tree diagrams probably just baffle the child.

In general, the lesson to be gained from Chomsky's work is this: Since children independently master an intricate system of grammatical rules, we should respect their independent efforts. It is presumptuous of us to try to structure the child's learning, and our attempts to do so are likely to lead only to the child's loss of faith in his or her own intuitions. While it is good to talk to children in ways they find enjoyable, it is not necessary to do anything that undermines their confidence or depreciates their immense accomplishments.

EVALUATION

It is remarkable that Chomsky, who is more of a linguist or even a philosopher than a psychologist, has inspired so much psychological research. This research is a testament to the importance of his ideas.

We have focused on the descriptive studies of children's emerging grammar. At the same time, Chomsky has stimulated other lines of investigation. Some researchers have been exploring the possibility that there is a neurologically based critical period for language learning. Once the brain has completed a certain degree of maturation—perhaps at the onset of puberty—it may be very difficult for children to acquire language with anything like the ease with which they do so before this time. This may be why, for example, deaf children can readily learn sign language only if they receive instruction before this time. Similarly, children seem able to learn aspects of a second language more readily before puberty. Also, if a child suffers damage to a language center of the brain, the brain may be able to compensate if the damage occurs before the circuits are set— before the critical period has ended. Much needs to be learned about such matters, including the age at which any critical period might end (it might end before puberty). But we can see how Chomsky's strongly biological theory has inspired new research (Krashen, 1975; Gleitman and Gleitman, 1986b; Pinker, 1989).

The criticisms we might make of Chomsky are primarily from a developmental perspective. First, Chomsky has promoted a kind of revival of preformationism. His comments on the "instantaneous" emergence of mature grammar make it sound as if children are miniature adults as far as their language is concerned. Also, Chomsky has inspired research that frequently tends to read adult linguistic structures into children's speech. It has, in Rousseau's words, been "looking for the man in the child without considering what he is before he becomes a man." From a developmental perspective, more attention needs to be given to the possibility that children's speech, like their thought, sometimes has a quality all its own.

The second developmental criticism is one Werner might make. Chomsky contends that grammar can be studied separately from other psychological processes. He even suggests that this is the scientific way to proceed, since biologists study organs such as the heart and the lungs apart from one another (1983, p. 35). However, biologists recognize that organs and systems differentiate out of more primitive and global configurations, and this may be true of language as well. Early speech, for example, may be difficult to classify either in terms of syntactic or action categories because these two systems are still undifferentiated (see Hass, 1975). Thus, while one may disagree with Piaget's claim that language rests upon prior sensori-motor and cognitive achievements, one still may consider the ways in which language is initially bound up with actions, feelings, and perceptions.

These criticisms notwithstanding, one can only marvel at the excitement and energy Chomsky has generated. Earlier, a few writers, such as Montessori, indicated that language development merits special study because children are mastering so many complex rules so soon, but it was not until Chomsky began to specify the nature of these rules that the research really got underway.

__17__

Conclusion:
Humanistic Psychology and Developmental Theory

In this, the concluding chapter, we will discuss the emergence of humanistic psychology and indicate the extent to which developmental theorists have shared the humanists' concerns.

HUMANISTIC PSYCHOLOGY

Background

Humanistic psychology is only a single recent expression of an old intellectual tradition, a tradition with roots in ancient philosophies throughout the world. There really is no one set of humanistic beliefs; humanism has taken different forms in different historical eras. It has emerged whenever people have felt that some system or authority—political, moral, or intellectual—was undermining human dignity or human unity (Hawton, 1961; Fromm, 1967).

Much early humanistic writing was directed against religious dogma. For example, sixteenth-century writers such as Desiderius Erasmus and Sir Thomas More protested that the Church often asked people to blindly adhere to religious doctrines, thus undermining their dignity by robbing them of the freedom to think for themselves. Furthermore, the Church often pitted Christians against non-Christians, when it should have been promoting tolerance and brotherhood (de Santiallana, 1956, pp. 27–30, 92–95).

Humanistic philosophy flourished most widely during the eighteenth-century Enlightenment, when the writings of Locke struck such a responsive chord. Before Locke, political and religious authorities often argued that people were innately wicked and therefore required repression. But if Locke were right—if people were solely the products of their environments—then one had only to change the environments to perfect them and make repression unnecessary. Furthermore, if inequalities were not innate but the products of circumstances, one could erase these too.

The Enlightenment spirit, then, was quite optimistic; unlimited human progress seemed possible. To achieve the greatest progress, Locke, Voltaire, and others turned to science. They believed that the scientific method—the open-minded, cautious verification of hypotheses through empirical evidence—would produce the knowledge that would better the condition of all (Berlin, 1956, pp. 11–29).

The Enlightenment beliefs in science and environmentalism have continued to play a role in some humanistic thinking. However, no single set of beliefs has ever claimed the complete loyalty of all humanists. In fact, in modern psychology, the combination of science and environmentalism took on a form that began to strike some as too rigid and narrow, leading to a new humanistic revolt.

Modern Scientific Psychology

Modern scientific psychology grew out of a deep admiration for the achievements of physics, chemistry, and the other natural sciences. Many psychologists felt that if psychology could only follow the example of these sciences, it too could accomplish great things. They proposed that psychology, like physics, strive for the objective, quantitative measurement of isolated variables and the formulation of abstract laws. At first, in the latter part of the nineteenth century, scientific psychology was led by Wundt and his colleagues, who tried to analyze consciousness into basic elements, as physicists and chemists had done for matter. This effort, however, seemed to lead to a dead end, and by the second decade of the twentieth century, the scientific banner had been taken over by another group, the behaviorists. The behaviorists, as we have seen, argued that we should confine ourselves to the measurement of overt behavior and the way it is controlled by observable stimuli in the external environment. The inner world of thoughts, feelings, and fantasies, they argued, has little place in scientific psychology.

Many behaviorists have seen themselves within the humanistic tradition; they have been trying to develop scientific techniques that will better the human lot. As we have seen, experimenters have used behavior modification techniques to alleviate fears, temper tantrums, and other problems. They also have devised new instructional methods. Behaviorists, like their Enlightenment predecessors, have held that their environmental, scientific approach will produce the greatest human progress.

The Humanistic Revolt in Psychology

Early on, however, some psychologists had misgivings about the behavioristic brand of science. During the first half of this century, Gordon Allport, Carl Rogers, Abraham Maslow, and others argued that behaviorism, whatever its merits, was producing a very one-sided picture of human nature. Humans, they argued, do not consist of only overt responses, nor are they completely controlled by the external environment. People also grow, think, feel, dream, create, and do many other things that make up the human experience. The behaviorists and others, in their emulation of the physical sciences, were ignoring most aspects of life that make humans unique and give them dignity. These humanists were not at all opposed to scientific investigation, but they argued that psychology should address itself to the full range of human experience, not just the aspects that are most readily measurable and under environmental control. For some time, these writers were calling out in the wilderness; their views were far removed from the mainstream in American psychology. But in the 1950s their writings began to attract increasing attention, and a humanistic movement in psychology was born (Misiak and Sexton, 1973, pp. 108–9).

The humanistic psychologists' call for renewed attention to inner experience has aligned them with the existential and phenomenological movements. With the existentialists, the humanists have held that the living person must take priority over any abstract, scientific system. With the phenomenologists, the humanists have pointed to the need to suspend our ordinary ways of classifying people from the outside; instead we should try to understand how the world feels to people from the inside.

Modern humanistic psychology, then, developed primarily in reaction to behavioristically oriented approaches. Humanistic psychology's relationship to the second main branch of psychology, psychoanalysis, has been more ambivalent. Many humanists have appreciated the psychoanalytic attempt to explore the inner world at its deepest levels. However, humanists have also felt that the psychoanalysts have been too pessimistic about human capacities for growth and free choice. Whereas the behaviorists have seen people as exclusively controlled by the external environment, psychoanalysts have viewed people as dominated by irrational forces in the unconscious. Perhaps, humanists have suggested, psychoanalytic theory has been too colored by the study of patients with crippling emotional disorders. Humanists have proposed that people, to a much greater extent than has been realized, are free and creative beings, capable of growth and self-actualization (Maslow, 1962, pp. 189–97).

The modern humanistic movement in psychology, then, sees itself diverging from the two dominant forces in psychology, scientific behaviorism and psychoanalysis. For this reason, humanists sometimes call their movement the "third force." To get a more concrete picture of the kind of work humanistic psychologists have been doing, we will now review some of the ideas of the man who is considered the father of modern humanistic psychology, Abraham Maslow.

Maslow

Biographical introduction.   Maslow (1908–1970) was born in Brooklyn, New York, the son of poor, Russian immigrant parents.   He was a shy, unhappy boy.   Although he liked high school, he had trouble adjusting to college.   He attended the City College of New York, Cornell University, and finally the University of Wisconsin, where he earned his B.A. degree and stayed on for graduate work in psychology.   Maslow began his career squarely within the scientific mainstream.   He received rigorous experimental training under E. L. Thorndike and Harry Harlow and wrote a standard textbook on abnormal psychology (Wilson, 1972, pp. 115–34). In fact, Maslow said that early in his career he was sold on behaviorism (Misiak and Sexton, 1973, p. 113), and in a sense he never repudiated it; he always realized that people are subject to conditioning from the external environment.   What increasingly annoyed him was behaviorism's onesidedness; people also have an inner life and potentials for growth, creativity, and free choice.

Maslow's ideas.   Maslow's first step in the direction of a humanistic psychology was the formulation of a new theory of motivation (1943). According to this theory, there are six kinds of needs: physiological needs, safety needs, belongingness needs, love needs, self-esteem needs, and, at the highest level, self-actualization needs.   These needs are arranged in a hierarchical order such that the fulfillment of lower needs propels the organism on to the next highest level.   For example, a man who has a strong physiological need, such as hunger, will be motivated by little else, but when this need is fulfilled, he will move on to the next level, that of safety needs, and when these are satisfied, he will move on to the third level, and so on.

In his major works, Maslow was most interested in the highest need, the need for self-actualization.   Self-actualization, a concept borrowed from Goldstein (1939), refers to the actualization of one's potentials, capacities, and talents.   To study it, Maslow examined the lives and experiences of the most healthy, creative people he could find.   His sample included contemporaries and acquaintances, such as the anthropologist Ruth Benedict, as well as public and historical figures, such as Thomas Jefferson and Eleanor Roosevelt (1954, pp. 202–3).

Maslow's key finding was that the self-actualizers, compared to most people, have maintained a certain independence from their society.   Most people are so strongly motivated by needs such as belongingness, love, and respect that they are afraid to entertain any thought that others might disapprove of.   They try to fit into their society and do whatever brings prestige within it.   Self-actualizers, in contrast, are less conforming.   They seem less molded and flattened by the social environment and are more spontaneous, free, and natural.   Although they rarely behave in unconventional ways, they typically regard conventions with a good-natured shrug of the shoulders.   Instead, they are primarily motivated by their own inner growth, the development of their potentials, and their personal mission in life (1954, pp. 223–28).

Because self-actualizers have attained a certain independence from their culture, they are not confined to conventional, abstract, or stereotyped modes of perception. When, for example, most people go to a museum, they read the name of the artist below the painting and then judge the work according to the conventional estimate. Self-actualizers, in contrast, perceive things more freshly, naively, and as they really are. They can look at any painting—or any tree, bird, or baby—as if seeing it for the first time; they can find miraculous beauty where others see nothing but the common object (Maslow, 1966, p. 88). In fact, they seem to have retained the creative, open approach that is characteristic of the young child. Like the child, their attitude is frequently "absorbed, spellbound, popeyed, enchanted" (1966, p. 100).[1] Unfortunately, most children lose this approach to life as they become socialized.

In a sense, then, self-actualizers are good phenomenologists. They can suspend or go beyond conventional ways of ordering experience. Maslow also likened their approach to a "Taoistic letting be," to an appreciation of objects without interfering with them or attempting to control them (1962, p. 86). He suggested that psychologists can learn much from self-actualizers' phenomenological and Taoistic approaches. Instead of fitting people into theoretical categories and performing experiments on them, psychologists should first simply watch and listen to people with a naive openness. If they did this, they would be open to new discoveries.

Maslow reworked his ideas over the years and was not always systematic in the process. But by and large, his overall position was as follows:

1. Humans possess an essential, biological, inner nature, which includes all the basic needs and the impulses toward growth and self-actualization (1962, p. 190; 1971, p. 25).

2. This inner core is partly species-wide and partly idiosyncratic, for we all have special bents, temperaments, and abilities (1962, p. 191).

3. Our inner core is a positive force that presses toward the realization of full humanness, just as an acorn may be said to press toward becoming an oak tree. It is important to recognize that it is our inner nature, not the environment, that plays the guiding role. The environment is like sun, food, and water; it nourishes growth, but it is not the seed. Social and educational practices should be evaluated not in terms of how efficiently they control the child or get the child to adjust, but according to how well they support and nourish inner growth potentials (1962, pp. 160–61, 211–12).

4. Our inner nature is not strong, like instincts in animals. Rather, it is subtle, delicate, and in many ways weak. It is easily "drowned out by learning, by cultural expectations, by fear, by disapproval, etc." (1962, p. 191).

5. The suppression of our inner nature usually takes place during childhood. At the start, babies have an inner wisdom with respect to most matters, including food intake, amount of sleep, readiness for toilet-training, and the urges to stand up and to walk. Babies will also avidly explore the environ-

---

[1]When such perception is intense, it can be called a "peak experience." Peak experiences may emerge during almost any activity—not only when observing nature, but during work, artistic production, love, or athletics. During a peak experience, people lose themselves in the moment and things seem to flow and to come almost without striving or effort. People are at the peak of their powers (Maslow, 1962, Chs. 6 and 7).

ment, focusing on the particular things in which they take delight. Their own feelings and inner promptings guide them toward healthy growth. However, socializing agents frequently lack respect for children's choices. Instead, they try to direct children, to teach them things. They criticize them, correct their errors, and try to get them to give the "right" answers. Consequently, children quit trusting themselves and their senses and begin to rely on the opinions of others (1962, pp. 49–55, 150, 198–99).

6. Even though our inner core, with its urge toward self-actualization, is weak, it rarely disappears altogether—even in adulthood. It persists underground, in the unconscious, and speaks to us as an inner voice waiting to be heard. Inner signals can lead even the neurotic adult back to buried capacities and unfulfilled potentials. Our inner core is a pressure we call the "will to health," and it is this urge on which all successful psychotherapy is based (1962, pp. 192–93).

7. There are a few people—"self-actualizers"—who have remained deeply responsive to their inner natures and urges toward growth. These people are less molded and flattened by cultural pressures and have preserved the capacity to look at the world in a spontaneous, fresh, childlike manner (1962, pp. 207–8).

DEVELOPMENTALISTS AS HUMANISTS

If Maslow's ideas sound familiar, they are. Maslow and the modern humanistic psychologists have, without making much note of it, drawn heavily upon the developmental tradition. Since Rousseau, developmentalists have been preoccupied with the same basic problem as Maslow: Children, as they become socialized, quit relying on their own experience and judgments; they become too dependent on conventions and the opinions of others. Thus, the developmentalists, like the humanists, have been searching for an inner force that will guide the individual toward a healthier, more independent development.

Intrinsic Growth Forces

Where Maslow speaks of a biological core that directs healthy growth, developmentalists refer to maturation. Maturation is an internal mechanism that prompts children to seek out certain experiences at certain times. Under maturational urging, children regulate their cycles of sleep and eating; learn to sit up, walk, and run; develop an urgent need for autonomy; master language; explore the widening environment; and so on. According to Gesell and others, children, following their own inner schedule and timing, are eminently wise regarding what they need and can do. So, instead of trying to make children conform to our own set schedules and directions, we can let them guide us and make their own choices—as Maslow proposed.

Nevertheless, as Maslow observed, it is often difficult for us to trust children and the growth process. We seem to have particular difficulty believing that children can really learn on their own, without our direction and supervision. But developmentalists have tried to show that they can. Montessori, in particular, tried to show that if we will open-mindedly observe children's spontaneous interests, they will direct us to the tasks on which they will work independently and with the greatest concentration and sense of fulfillment. They will become absorbed in such tasks because the tasks meet inner needs to perfect certain capacities at certain points in development. Thus, we are not forced to take charge of children's learning, to choose tasks for them, to motivate them by our praise, or to criticize their mistakes—practices that force them to turn to external authorities for guidance and evaluation. Instead, we can trust their maturationally based urges to perfect their own capacities in their own ways. Maslow might have pointed to Montessori as an educator who was thoroughly humanistic in her faith in children's intrinsic creative powers.

Not all developmentalists, of course, are as nativistic as Gesell or Montessori. As we have seen, Piaget, Kohlberg, and the cognitive-developmentalists doubt that biological maturation directly governs the stages of cognitive development. Nevertheless, these theorists also look to children's independent activities, rather than to external teachings, as the source of development. Children, in their view, are intrinsically curious about the world and reach out for new experiences that lead them to reorganize their cognitive structures. Thus, the cognitive-developmentalists also share the humanists' faith in intrinsic capacities for self-directed learning.

Interestingly, Maslow's thoughts on adulthood were also foreshadowed by earlier developmental theorists—especially by Jung. Maslow pointed out how the well-socialized adult, whose inner potentials for self-actualization lie dormant, will still hear inner voices calling for attention. Jung used nearly identical language to describe the crisis of middle life. Prior to middle age, the individual typically concentrates on adjusting to the external, social world, trying to do things that bring social success and prestige and developing those parts of the personality that are suited for this goal. In middle life, however, social success loses its importance, and inner voices from the unconscious direct one to attend to the previously neglected and unrealized parts of the self. The individual increasingly turns inward and considers the discovery and rounding out of the personality more important than social conformity.

Thus, developmental theorists, like the modern humanistic psychologists, have tried to uncover intrinsic growth factors that stand apart from pressures toward social conformity. At the same time, however, some developmental theorists have been more pessimistic than the humanists about the chances for any substantial improvement based on intrinsic forces. In particular, the Freudians have felt that because maturation brings with it unruly sexual and aggressive impulses, a good measure of social repression will always be necessary. Erikson has viewed maturational growth somewhat more positively than Freud, calling attention to the maturation of autonomy, initiative, industry, and so on, but he too has felt that the other sides of these qualities—shame, doubt, guilt, inferiority, and so on—are inevitable. No child, for example, can become completely autonomous, for societies will always need to regulate the child to some extent. Still,

Erikson hopes that we can raise children so that they can gain as much autonomy, initiative, and as many other virtues as possible.

Furthermore, Freudian therapy relies heavily on inner growth forces. Recall how Freud once asked a psychiatrist if he could really cure. When the psychiatrist responded that he could not—that he could only remove some impediments to growth as a gardener removes some stones or weeds— Freud said that they would then understand each other. The psychoanalyst's reliance on intrinsic growth processes is quite evident in Bettelheim's school. Bettelheim did not try to make disturbed children behave in normal ways, but he tried to provide certain conditions—love, acceptance, empathy—that will enable children to feel it is safe to take steps toward growth on their own. The physician treats patients in essentially the same way. The doctor does not actually heal a cut but only cleans and stitches the wound. The rest is up to Nature. Any cure, in psychotherapy or in medicine, partly relies on forces toward health that are out of the doctor's control. The doctor puts his or her faith in innate forces toward health.

Thus, developmental theorists, like the humanists, have tried to discover the nature of intrinsic growth forces and to devise educational and therapeutic methods based upon them. And, to a considerable extent, developmental writers had been working on these tasks long before the modern humanistic movement in psychology even began.

Romanticism

Theories that extol the virtues of Nature and biological forces, as opposed to society, are often called Romantic. In this sense, Maslow, as well as Rousseau and the maturationists, are strongly Romantic. Rousseau, in fact, is often credited with the origin of Romantic thought.

Another aspect of Romanticism is a fondness for the past. This attraction is quite evident in Maslow; he looked upon infancy and childhood as times when we were more closely in touch with our natural urges and possessed a more spontaneous and creative outlook. As children, he said, we perceived the world more freshly, directly, and imaginatively than we typically do as well-socialized adults. Maslow recognized the value of mature, adult thought, but he also felt that we need to learn to regress temporarily to more childlike modes of experience.

Rousseau, too, "romanticized the past." He suggested that we were happier and more independent as savages, and he saw childhood as a potentially happy and innocent time in which we live in close harmony with Nature. In modern developmental theory, perhaps the most thoroughgoing Romantic was Schachtel, who contrasted the richly sensuous experiences of infancy and the open curiosity of childhood with the stereotyped, conventional thought of most adults.

Neither Rousseau nor Schachtel, however, clearly specified ways in which we, as adults, might recapture childlike modes of experience. For such a conceptualization, we are particularly indebted to Werner. Werner suggested that we continually engage in a process called microgenesis, beginning each new thought or perception at primitive levels before moving on to more advanced forms of cognition. Thus, the primitive modes of experience are continually available to us. Ordinarily, Werner observed, we do not engage in primitive imagery in a very full way, but we do so when we are most creative, when we truly begin anew. At these moments our impressions become particularly rich and sensuous; for primitive images are fused with emotion, sensation, and imaginative qualities. Creative thinking, of course, does not stop with such images; it goes on to articulate and structure them. Nevertheless, Werner emphasized, creativity begins with a responsiveness to early forms of experience—a view shared by the psychoanalysts who speak of "regressions in the service of the ego."

Not all developmentalists, we should note, have been very Romantic. The cognitive-developmentalists, in particular, have generally been unimpressed by the distinctive virtues of childlike thinking. Piaget observed that we continue to use early sensori-motor schemes and cognitive operations, but he saw nothing special in the imaginative, fanciful thinking of the preoperational child, and he never suggested that creative people regress to it. Similarly, Kohlberg never seemed impressed by the concept of regression. In his view, stages of moral reasoning simply reflected increasing levels of cognitive adequacy, so there was no point to regressing to earlier stages.

Not all developmentalists, then, have placed a special premium on childlike modes of thought. All developmentalists, to be sure, have argued that childhood thinking has unique qualities, but not all developmentalists have been so enamored with these qualities that they have urged us to recapture them. Still, a Romantic attraction to childhood is one theme that runs through a good deal of humanistic psychology and developmental theory.

Phenomenology

Another central component of modern humanistic psychology is a phenomenological orientation. This orientation or method includes what may be called a "phenomenological suspension." One tries to suspend one's theoretical preconceptions and customary categories and tries to see people and things as openly and freshly as possible—to see them as they really are. This approach, as we have seen, was the starting point of Rousseau's developmental philosophy. Rousseau argued that children have their own ways of seeing, thinking, and feeling, and that we know nothing about these; we therefore must refrain from investing children with our own thoughts and take the time to simply observe them, listen to them, and let them reveal their unique characteristics to us. Later, Piaget and Montessori emphasized the same point. The ethologists, too, may be said to employ a phenomenological suspension. Before an ethologist forms any hypothesis or builds any theory, he or she first simply tries to learn about and describe as much about a particular species as possible. To do this, ethologists believe, we must observe animals in their natural habitats, not in the laboratory.

In psychology, phenomenology usually implies a second step. Phenomenological psychologists usually suspend preconceptions in order to enter into the *inner* world of the other. They try to open themselves to the other's direct experience, to see things through the other's eyes.

Developmental theorists have been less consistent in taking this second step. Those who have worked the hardest to learn about children's inner worlds are Schachtel and the psychoanalysts. Schachtel tried to gain insight into the infant's unique modes of perception, and the psychoanalyst Bettelheim, for example, constantly asked himself, "How does the world look and feel to this child?" Other writers, however, have been less interested in perceiving the world through the child's eyes. Gesell wanted us to be open to children's own needs and interests, but he primarily observed their external motor behavior. Werner gave us insights into how the world might look to the child—how, for instance, it might appear full of life and feeling—but he mostly discussed the child's mental life from the *outside*, analyzing it in terms of concepts such as differentiation and integration. Similarly, Piaget provided valuable insights into the young child's unique experiences—how objects change with momentary perceptions, how dreams seem real, how morals seem imposed by authorities, and so forth—but Piaget, too, primarily examined the young child's thought from the outside, analyzing it in terms of logical structures. The ethologists also primarily look at behavior from an external point of view.

A knowledge of how the world looks to children (and adults) at different stages will not be easy to come by. Young children are not sufficiently verbal to tell us how the world appears to them, and infants cannot tell us anything at all. One approach may be the study of spontaneous interests. For example, Montessori showed how young children attend to minute details and are concerned about anything out of place. These observations give us two clues concerning the young child's perceptual world. Young children also seem to perceive life where we do not, and they may be particularly interested in objects, such as cars, balls, or balloons, which, with a little imagination, take on human qualities. It would seem important to record every aspect of the environment that children find uniquely interesting. To structure such studies, we might follow the lead of Martha Muchow (discussed in Chapter 5), who observed how children of different ages responded to typical settings in their everyday environments, including a landing dock and a department store. By noting the things that children find particularly interesting, as well as those that they ignore, we can begin to form a picture of how the world appears to the child at different phases of life.

Universals

Readers who have already learned something about developmental psychology will notice that this book neglects or skims over certain topics. We have barely mentioned, for example, differences among children or adults on I.Q. tests. Other topics that have received only minor coverage include cultural differences in personality development and sex differences. The various differences among people, which are partly the product of environmental factors, are tremendously important. If we are ever to redress artificial social inequalities, we need to know how they are formed.

However, the differences among people have not been the developmentalists' primary concern. Instead, they have searched for developmental forces and sequences common to all people. This search, as Chomsky suggests (1975, pp. 130–33), probably reflects, as much as anything, an ethical orientation. Developmentalists, like humanists, are trying to show how, at the deepest levels, we are all the same. Developmentalists shy away from topics concerning how one person is better than another and focus, instead, on what Maslow calls our "biological brotherhood" (1962, p. 185). They want to show that, at bottom, we all have the same yearnings, hopes, and fears, as well as the same creative urges toward health and personal integration. Hopefully, an appreciation of the positive strivings that we all share can help in the building of a universal human community.

SUMMARY

Humanistic thought has taken various forms through the decades. During the Enlightenment, humanism became linked to an environmental outlook and the scientific enterprise. The hope was that the creation of improved environments, aided by scientific knowledge, would lead to better living conditions for us all. In contemporary psychology, the behaviorists continue to pursue the goals of the Enlightenment.

In recent years, however, the behavioristic approach has struck many humanistic psychologists as too one-sided. Maslow and others have objected that behaviorism leaves out too much that gives human life its richness and dignity. By focusing on how external behavior comes under environmental control, it has ignored our inner world and our spontaneous urges toward health and independence. If we are to create better environments, they must not simply be those that control behavior but those that foster and support the intrinsic creative forces.

In formulating a new version of humanism, Maslow and others have, without making much note of it, drawn heavily upon the developmental tradition in psychology. First and foremost, they have joined the developmentalists in their search for intrinsic growth forces that can lead to healthy development. Second, the humanists have joined those Romantic developmentalists who have looked fondly upon earlier periods as times when we were more in tune with Nature and had a more spontaneous outlook. Third, the humanists' call for a more phenomenological science has been, to an extent, anticipated by developmentalists; for many developmentalists have suggested that we cannot appreciate the growing child's unique ways of thinking and learning unless we approach them with something of a naive openness. Finally, both humanists and developmentalists have been primarily concerned with the universal aspects of human development, with the urges toward growth and health that we all share.

POSTSCRIPT

It has been more than 20 years since Maslow's death in 1970, yet Maslow remains a central figure in humanistic psychology. At the same time, humanistic theory has moved forward to meet new challenges.

During Maslow's career, the dominant force in psychology was behaviorism. But during the 1970s and 1980s, behaviorism lost its grip on the field. In a broad shift, psychologists abandoned the belief that they must restrict their research to observable behavior and turned their attention to cognitive processes—to internal, mental events.

This cognitive revolution was largely the result of two events. One was Chomsky's work on linguistics. Chomsky convinced most psychologists that they would never be able to understand language solely in terms of overt behavior and environmental conditioning. They also need to uncover the internal rules and operations people use to comprehend and generate sentences (Miller, 1989, p. 275).

The dramatic new interest in cognition was even more powerfully influenced by advances in science and technology, particularly in computer technology. Psychologists, like people everywhere, were enormously impressed by the achievements of high-speed computers, and they quickly saw similarities between computers and human thinking. Both computers and humans, psychologists noted, encode, store, and retrieve information, and psychologists began using computer models to build new theories of the mind. And psychologists were not alone in this effort. They were joined by philosophers, mathematicians, linguists, and computer scientists, all working under the new banner of "cognitive science." Thus, the 1970s and 1980s experienced the emergence of a powerful intellectual movement, a movement that is still gaining momentum today (Miller, 1989, pp. 275–78).

During the 1940s and 1950s, humanists would have welcomed any new interest in cognition. During those years, when behaviorists were restricting research to overt behavior, the study of internal mental events promised a fuller picture of human experience. As it turned out, however, the new cognitive science is nearly as limited and one-sided as the old behaviorism. Cognitive scientists study thinking as if it consists of nothing but rational problem-solving mechanisms and procedures. They make little room for the emotional aspects of thinking—for wonder, imagination, empathy, and inspiration.

Compared to cognitive science, Piagetian theory seems downright warm-blooded. Piagetians, too, focus on cognitive processes, but they also see people as emotionally engaged in the world. Children, in their view, eagerly explore their surroundings, become engrossed in problems that arouse their curiosity, get into discussions and debates with their peers, and, in adolescence, become social critics and utopian thinkers.

Cognitive scientists, in contrast, write about human information-processing as if it were a purely cerebral, task-oriented affair. They provide step-by-step descriptions of problem-solving strategies and procedures, using numerous flow charts and diagrams, but they give us little sense that these operations take place in a living, feeling person. As Sigel

(1986) observes, one can read major collections of essays and literature reviews in cognitive science (e.g., Sternberg, 1984; Klahr, 1989) without ever coming across the terms *emotion* or *affect*.

It would be one thing if this new cognitive orientation were confined to academic circles. But a similar preoccupation with rational, technological thinking is sweeping through our entire culture, including our educational system.

Today's schools, our nation's policy-makers constantly warn us, must give children the intellectual tools they will need for the hi-tech world of the twenty-first century. Otherwise our nation will lose its competitive edge. Thus, our schools are doing all they can to make children computer literate, to increase their knowledge of math and science, and to teach them rational, analytic kinds of reasoning at the earliest possible ages.

The new educational focus is illustrated by the growing popularity of thinking-skills programs (Costa, 1985). These programs attempt to teach numerous specific "skills," such as observing, classifying, and predicting, in a systematic, step-by-step manner. The program developers do not give much attention to the philosophical assumptions underlying their work, but they use computer terminology every chance they get and they share the general technological assumption that the best thinking is goal-directed, systematic, and self-conscious. They encourage children to clearly define their goals, to develop systematic plans to achieve their goals, and to monitor their progress each step of the way.

Maslow (1966, 1971) had important things to say about the limitations of such an approach. The most creative scientists and thinkers, Maslow observed, do not rely exclusively on this kind of systematic, rational thinking. They also call upon more intuitive, empathic, and emotional ways of knowing, especially during the early phases of their work. Like young children, they look upon the world with innocence and wonder and are open to the wide range of feelings and impressions that the world evokes in them.

But Maslow could not have foreseen the enormous impact of the cognitive revolution, and it is up to contemporary humanists to develp responses to it. One promising effort has been launched by Ron Miller (1990) and others in the area of humanistic education. Miller believes that educators can counter the scientific, technological worldview by articulating and promoting a *holistic* paradigm, a paradigm that recognizes the full range of human potential. "Children," Miller says, "do not simply learn through their minds, but through their feelings and concerns, their imaginations and their bodies" (1990, p. 153). When educators focus only on one aspect of experience—the rational, calculating intellect—they do children a great disservice; they deny children opportunities to develop the organic, subjective, artistic, spiritual dimensions of their lives (1990, p. 153).

To develop his holistic paradigm, Miller does something that has been all too rare in humanistic theory: He explicitly draws upon historical writings and gives special attention to writers in the developmental tradition. Rousseau, Miller observes, was the first theorist to point out that the child's full development is governed by an inner energy or force, and that it is our task to respect and nurture this force. Miller then shows how a concern for this self-guiding force has been central to a wide range of thinkers, including Pestalozzi, Montessori, Emerson, Thoreau, Quaker educators, anarchists, Rudolf Steiner, and some of the followers of Dewey, as well as contemporary writers such as John Holt and Theodore Roszak. All these writers, Miller points out, have charged that mainstream education has been too concerned with meeting society's needs (e.g., the need for more scientists and technicians). As a result, educational systems have forced children into narrow channels, depriving them of the chance to develop their full personalities. If we want to help children develop, these writers say, we need to take our cues from the children themselves. We need to pay special attention to their spontaneous interests and creative energies, for these are expressions of the inner force that guides their full and healthy development.

In Miller's view, this self-guiding force is something that all humans share with one another and with Nature as well. Ultimately, Miller believes, it is a spiritual force—a force that comes from the transcendent source of our being. Miller recognizes that others prefer to think of this force in nonreligious terms, such as "intrinsic growth forces," "maturation," and the drive toward "self-actualization." But these differences, he says, are not as important as the common respect writers have for it (1990, p. 154).

On a practical level, Miller and his colleagues are attempting to build a coalition of humanists and educators who share the holistic worldview. The alliance would include Montessori, Waldorf, progressive, open-education, and various child-centered educators, many of whom see their work as directly rooted in the Rousseauist, developmental tradition. Whether anyone can unite these groups into a single movement is, of course, an open question. But if these educators can regularly meet to exchange observations and insights and compare practices, the outcome could be fruitful. A great deal might be learned about children's spontaneous development and methods of fostering it. In any event, it is encouraging to see Miller and others advancing the humanistic viewpoint by drawing upon writers in the developmental tradition.

References

Aber, J. L., and **Slade, A.** (1987). Attachment theory and research: A framework for clinical interventions. Paper presented at the Regional Scientific Meeting of the Childhood and Adolescence Division of the American Psychological Association, New York.

Abraham, K. (1924a). A short study of the development of the libido viewed in light of mental disorders. *Selected Papers of Karl Abraham.* New York: Basic Books, 1927.

——— (1924b). The influence of oral eroticism on character formation. *Selected Papers of Karl Abraham.* New York: Basic Books, 1927.

Ainsworth, M. D. S. (1962). The effects of maternal deprivation: A review of findings and controversy in the context of research and strategy. *Public Health Papers, 14.* Geneva: World Health Organization.

——— (1967). *Infancy in Uganda: Infant Care and the Growth of Love.* Baltimore: Johns Hopkins University Press.

——— (1973). The development of infant and mother attachment. In B. M. Caldwell and H. M. Ricciuti (Eds.), *Review of Child Development Research* (Vol. III). Chicago: University of Chicago Press.

——— (1982). Attachment: Retrospect and prospect. In C. M. Parkes and J. Stevenson-Hinde (Eds.), *The Place of Attachment in Human Behavior.* New York: Basic Books.

———, **Bell, S. M.,** and **Stanton, D. S.** (1971). Individual differences in strange-situation behavior of one-year-olds. In H. R. Schaffer (Ed.), *The Origins of Human Social Relations.* New York: Academic Press.

———, **Blehar, M. C., Waters, E.,** and **Wall, S.** (1978). *Patterns of Attachment.* Hillsdale, NJ: Erlbaum.

Aitchison, J. (1976). *The Articulate Mammal: An Introduction to Psycholinguistics.* New York: University Books.

Almy, M., Chittenden, E., and **Miller, P.** (1966). *Young Children's Thinking.* New York: Columbia Teachers' College Press.

Als, H. (1978). Assessing an assessment: Conceptual considerations, methodological issues, and a perspective on the future of the Neonatal Behavioral Assessment Scale. In A. J.

Sameroff (Ed.), Organization and Stability of Newborn Behavior: A Commentary on the Brazelton Neonatal Behavior Assessment Scale. *Monographs of the Society for Research in Child Development, 43*, Serial No. 177.

Ames, L. B. (1971). Don't push your preschooler. *Family Circle Magazine, 79*, 60.

Appleton, T., Clifton, R., and **Goldberg, S.** (1975). The development of behavioral competence in infancy. In F. D. Horowitz (Ed.), *Review of Child Development Research* (Vol. IV). Chicago: University of Chicago Press.

Ariès, P. (1960). *Centuries of Childhood: A Social History of Family Life* (R. Baldick, trans.). New York: Knopf, 1962.

Arnheim, R. (1954). *Art and Visual Perception.* Berkeley: University of California Press.

Ausubel, D. P. (1958). *Theories and Problems in Child Development.* New York: Grune & Stratton.

Baerends, G., Beer, C., and **Manning, A.** (1975). *Function and Evolution in Behavior.* Oxford: Clarendon Press.

Baldwin, A. L. (1980). *Theories of Child Development* (2nd ed.). New York: John Wiley.

Balinsky, B. I. (1981). *An Introduction to Embryology* (5th ed.). Philadelphia: Saunders.

Bandura, A. (1962). Social learning through imitation. In M. R. Jones (Ed.), *Nebraska Symposium on Motivation.* Lincoln: University of Nebraska Press.

———— (1965a). Vicarious processes. A case of no-trial learning. In L. Berkowitz (Ed.), *Advances in Experimental Social Psychology* (Vol. II). New York: Academic Press.

———— (1965b). Influence of model's reinforcement contingencies on the acquisition of imitative responses. *Journal of Personality and Social Psychology, 1*, 589–95.

———— (1967). The role of modeling processes in personality development. In W. W. Hartup and W. L. Smothergill (Eds.), *The Young Child: Reviews of Research.* Washington, DC: National Association for the Education of Young Children.

———— (1969). Social-learning theory of identificatory processes. In D. A. Goslin (Ed.), *Handbook of Socialization Theory and Research.* Chicago: Rand McNally.

———— (1971). Analysis of modeling processes. In A. Bandura (Ed.), *Psychological Modeling.* Chicago: Atherton, Aldine.

———— (1977). *Social Learning Theory.* Englewood Cliffs, NJ: Prentice Hall.

———— (1986). *Social Foundations of Thought and Action: A Social Cognitive Theory.* Englewood Cliffs, NJ: Prentice Hall.

———— (1989). Social cognitive theory. In R. Vasta (Ed.), *Annals of Child Development, 6*, 1–60.

————, **Grusec, J. E.,** and **Menlove, F. L.** (1967). Vicarious extinction of avoidance behavior. *Journal of Personality and Social Psychology, 5*, 16–23.

————, and **Huston, A. C.** (1961). Identification as a process of incidental learning. *Journal of Abnormal and Social Psychology, 63*, 311–18.

————, and **Kupers, C. J.** (1964). The transmission of patterns of self-reinforcement through modeling. *Journal of Abnormal and Social Psychology, 69*, 1–9.

————, and **McDonald, F. J.** (1963). Influence of social reinforcement and the behavior of models in shaping children's moral judgments. *Journal of Abnormal and Social Psychology, 67*, 274–81.

————, **Ross, D.,** and **Ross, S. A.** (1963). A comparative test of the status envy, social power, and secondary reinforcement theories of identificatory learning. *Journal of Abnormal and Social Psychology, 67*, 527–34.

————, and **Walters, R. H.** (1963). *Social Learning and Personality Development.* New York: Holt, Rinehart & Winston.

Barten, S. S., and **Franklin, M. B.** (Eds.) (1978). *Developmental Processes: Heinz Werner's Selected Writings* (Vols. I and II). New York: International Universities Press.

Bartlett, E. J. (1972). Selecting preschool language programs. In C. B. Cazden (Ed.), *Language in Early Childhood Education.* Washington, DC: National Association for the Education of Young Children.

Bateson, P. P. G. (1966). The characteristics and context of imprinting. *Biological Reviews, 41*, 177–220.

Baumrind, D. (1967). Child care practices anteceding three patterns of preschool behavior. *Genetic Psychology Monographs, 75*, 43–88.

Bell, S. M. (1970). The development of the concept of object as related to infant-mother attachment. *Child Development, 41*, 291–311.

————, and **Ainsworth, M. D. S.** (1972). Infant crying and maternal responsiveness. *Child Development, 43*, 1171–90.

Bellugi-Klima, U. (1968). Linguistic mechanisms underlying child speech. In E. M. Zale (Ed.), *Proceedings of the Conference on Language and Language Behavior.* Englewood Cliffs, NJ: Prentice Hall.

Belsky, J. (1988). The "effects" of infant day care reconsidered. *Early Childhood Research Quarterly, 3,* 235–72.

Benedek, T. (1938). Adaptation to reality in early infancy. *Psychoanalytic Quarterly, 7,* 200–15.

Beres, D. (1971). Ego autonomy and ego pathology. *Psychoanalytic Study of the Child, 26,* 3–24.

Bergman, I. (1957). *Wild Strawberries* (filmscript) (L. Malmstrom and D. Kushner, trans.). New York: Simon & Schuster.

Berkowitz, M. W., and **Gibbs, J. C.** (1985). The process of moral conflict resolution and moral development. In M. W. Berkowitz (Ed.), *Peer Conflict and Psychological Growth.* San Francisco: Jossey-Bass.

Berlin, I. (1956). *The Age of Enlightenment: The Eighteenth Century Philosophers.* New York: Mentor.

Bernstein, R. (1990, November 4). Accusations of abuse haunt the legacy of Dr. Bruno Bettelheim. *The New York Times,* Week in Review.

Bettelheim, B. (1960). *The Informed Heart: Autonomy in a Mass Age.* New York: Free Press.

_____ (1967). *The Empty Fortress: Infantile Autism and the Birth of the Self.* New York: Free Press.

_____ (1974). *A Home for the Heart.* New York: Knopf.

_____ (1976). *The Uses of Enchantment: The Meaning and Importance of Fairy Tales.* New York: Knopf.

_____ (1987). *A Good Enough Parent.* New York: Vintage (Random House).

_____, and **Zelan, K.** (1981). *On Learning to Read.* New York: Random House.

Bijou, S. W. (1976). *Child Development: The Basic Stage of Early Childhood.* Englewood Cliffs, NJ: Prentice Hall.

_____, and **Baer, D. M.** (1961). *Child Development* (Vol. I). Englewood Cliffs, NJ: Prentice Hall.

Blasi, A. (1980). Bridging moral cognition and moral action: A critical review of the literature. *Psychological Bulletin, 88,* 593–637.

Blatt, M. M., and **Kohlberg, L.** (1975). The effects of classroom moral discussion upon children's level of moral judgment. *Journal of Moral Education, 4,* 129–61.

Blos, P. (1962). *On Adolescence.* New York: Free Press.

Borke, H. (1975). Piaget's mountains revisited: Changes in the egocentric landscape. *Developmental Psychology, 11,* 240–43.

Bower, T. G. R. (1977). Competent newborns. In E. M. Hetherington and R. D. Parke (Eds.), *Contemporary Reading in Child Psychology.* New York: McGraw-Hill.

_____ (1982). *Development in Infancy* (2nd ed.). San Francisco: W. H. Freeman.

_____ (1989). *The Rational Infant.* New York: W. H. Freeman.

Bowlby, J. (1953). *Child Care and the Growth of Love.* Baltimore: Penguin Books.

_____ (1973). *Attachment and Loss* (Vol. II). *Separation.* New York: Basic Books.

_____ (1982). *Attachment and Loss* (Vol. I). *Attachment* (2nd ed.). New York: Basic Books.

_____ (1988). *A Secure Base.* New York: Basic Books.

Brackbill, Y. (1958). Extinction of the smiling response in infants as a function of reinforcement schedule. *Child Development, 29,* 115–24.

Bretherton, I. (1985). Attachment theory: Retrospect and prospect. In I. Bretherton and E. Waters (Eds.), Growing points of attachment theory and research. *Monographs of the Society for Research in Child Development, 50,* Serial No. 209.

_____, **Ridgeway, D.,** and **Cassidy, J.** (1990). Assessing internal working models of the attachment relationship: An attachment story completion task for 3-year-olds. In M. T. Greenberg, D. Cicchetti, and E. Mark Cummings (Eds.), *Attachment in the Preschool Years.* Chicago: University of Chicago Press.

Breuer, J., and **Freud, S.** (1895). *Studies on Hysteria* (A. A. Brill, trans.). New York: Nervous and Mental Disease Publishing Co., 1936.

Brown, A. L., and **Ferrara, R.** (1985). Diagnosing zones of proximal development. In J. Wertsch (Ed.), *Culture, Communication, and Cognition: Vygotskian Perspectives.* New York: Cambridge University Press.

Brown, J. F. (1940). *The Psychodynamics of Abnormal Behavior.* New York: McGraw-Hill.

Brown, P., and **Elliott, R.** (1965).   Control of aggression in a nursery school class.   *Journal of Experimental Child Psychology, 2,* 103–7.

Brown, R. (1965).   *Social Psychology.*   New York: Free Press.

———— (1973).   *A First Language: The Early Stages.*   Cambridge, MA: Harvard University Press.

————, and **Bellugi, U.** (1964).   Three processes in the child's acquisition of syntax.   *Harvard Educational Review, 34,* 133–51.

————, **Cazden, C.,** and **Bellugi-Klima, U.** (1969).   The child's grammar from I to III.   In J. P. Hill (Ed.), *Minnesota Symposia on Child Psychology* (Vol. II).   Minneapolis: University of Minnesota Press.

————, and **Hanlon, C.** (1970).   Derivational complexity and order of acquisition in child speech.   In Brown, R., *Psycholinguistics: Selected Papers.*   New York: Free Press.

————, and **Herrnstein, R. J.** (1975).   *Psychology.*   Boston: Little, Brown.

Bruner, J. (1984).   Vygotsky's zone of proximal development: The hidden agenda.   In B. Rogoff and J. Wertsch (Eds.), *Children's Learning in the "Zone of Proximal Development."*   San Francisco: Jossey-Bass.

Bryan, J. H. (1975).   Children's cooperation and helping behaviors.   In E. M. Hetherington (Ed.), *Review of Child Development Research* (Vol. 5).   Chicago: University of Chicago Press.

————, and **Walbek, N.** (1970).   Preaching and practicing generosity: Children's action, and reactions.   *Child Development, 41,* 329–53.

Bryant, P. E. (1974).   *Perception and Understanding in Young Children: An Experimental Approach.*   New York: Basic Books.

Butler, R. N. (1963).   The life review: An interpretation of reminiscence in the aged.   *Psychiatry, 26,* 65–76.

Cairns, H. S., and **Cairns, C. E.** (1976).   *Psycholinguistics: A Cognitive View of Language.*   New York: Holt, Rinehart & Winston.

Caldwell, B. M. (1964).   The effects of infant care.   In M. L. and L. W. Hoffman (Eds.), *Review of Child Development Research* (Vol. I).   New York: Russell Sage Foundation.

Chattin-McNichols, J. (1992).   *The Montessori Controversy.*   Albany, NY: Delmar.

Chomsky, C. (1969).   *The Acquisition of Syntax in Children from 5 to 10.*   Cambridge, MA: MIT Press.

Chomsky, N. (1957).   *Syntactic Structures.*   The Hague: Moulton.

———— (1959).   A review of *Verbal Behavior* by B. F. Skinner, *Language, 35,* 26–58.

———— (1962).   Explanatory models in linguistics.   In E. Nagel, P. Suppes, and A. Tarshi (Eds.), *Logic, Methodology and Philosophy of Science.*   Stanford: Stanford University Press.

———— (1965).   *Aspects of the Theory of Syntax.*   Cambridge, MA: The MIT Press.

———— (1968).   Recent contributions to the theory of innate ideas.   In R. S. Cohen and M. W. Wartofsky (Eds.), *Boston Studies on the Philosophy of Science* (Vol. III).   Dordrecht, Holland: D. Reidel.

———— (1972).   *Language and Mind.*   New York: Harcourt Brace Jovanovich.

———— (1975).   *Reflections on Language.*   San Diego, CA: Pantheon.

———— (1977).   Interview.   In Cohen, D., *Psychologists on Psychology.*   New York: Taplinger.

———— (1980).   *Rules and Representations.*   New York: Columbia University Press.

———— (1983).   Interview.   In R. W. Reiber and G. Voyat (Eds.), *Dialogues on the Psychology of Language and Thought.*   New York: Plenum.

———— (1986).   *Knowledge of Language: Its Nature, Origin, and Use.*   New York: Praeger.

Clarke-Stewart, K. A. (1989).   Infant day care: Maligned or malignant?   *American Psychologist, 44,* 266–73.

Coates, B., and **Hartup, W. W.** (1969).   Age and verbalization in observational learning.   *Developmental Psychology, 1,* 556–62.

Colby, A., Kohlberg, L., Gibbs, J., and **Lieberman, M.** (1983).   A longitudinal study of moral judgment.   *Monographs of the Society for Research in Child Development,* Serial No. 200.

————, **Kohlberg, L.,** and **Kauffman, K.** (1987a).   Theoretical introduction to the measurement of moral judgment.   In A. Colby and L. Kohlberg, *The Measurement of Moral Judgment* (Vol. I).   Cambridge, England: Cambridge University Press.

————, **Kohlberg, L.** and **Kauffman, K.** (1987b).   Instructions for moral judgment interviewing.   In A. Colby and L. Kohlberg, *The Measurement of Moral Judgment* (Vol. I).   Cambridge, England: Cambridge University Press.

————, **Kohlberg, L., Speicher, B., Hewer, A., Candee, D., Gibbs, J.,** and **Power, C.** (1987c).   *The Measurement of Moral Judgment* (Vol. II).   Cambridge, England: Cambridge University Press.

Cole, M., and **Cole, S.R.** (1989). *The Development of Children.* New York: Scientific.

———, and **Scribner, S.** (1978). Introduction. In M. Cole, V. John-Steiner, S. Scribner, and E. Souberman (Eds.), *L. S. Vygotsky: Mind in Society.* Cambridge, MA: Harvard University Press.

Coles, R. (1970). *Erik H. Erikson: The Growth of His Work.* Boston: Little, Brown.

Condon, W. S., and **Sander, L. W.** (1974). Neonate movement is synchronized with adult speech: Interactional participation and language acquisition. *Science, 183,* 99–101.

Corman, H. H., and **Escalona, S. K.** (1969). Stages of sensori-motor development: A replication study. *Merrill-Palmer Quarterly, 15,* 351–61.

Costa, A. L. (1985). *Developing Minds.* Alexandria, VA: Association for Supervision and Curriculum Development.

Cowan, P. A., Langer, J., Heavenrich, J., and **Nathanson, J.** (1969). Social learning and Piaget's theory of moral development. *Journal of Personality and Social Psychology, 11,* 261–74.

Crain, S., and **Nakayama, M.** (1987). Structure dependence in children's language. *Language, 63,* 522–43.

Crain, W., and **Crain, E. F.** (1987). Can humanistic psychology contribute to our understanding of medical problem-solving? *Psychological Reports, 61,* 779–88.

Cromer, R. F. (1970). "Children are nice to understand." Surface structure clues for the recovery of deep structure. *British Journal of Psychology, 61,* 397–408.

Dale, P. S. (1972). *Language Development: Structure and Function.* Hinsdale, IL: The Dryden Press.

Damon, W. (1983). *Social and Personality Development.* New York: W. W. Norton & Co.

Darwin, C. (1859). *The Origin of Species.* New York: Modern Library.

——— (1871). *The Descent of Man.* New York: Modern Library.

——— (1887). *The Autobiography of Charles Darwin.* New York: W. W. Norton & Co., 1958.

Dasen, P. R. (1972). Cross-cultural Piagetian research: A summary. *Journal of Cross-Cultural Psychology, 3,* 23–39.

DeVries, R., and **Kohlberg, L.** (1987). *Constructivist Early Education: Overview and Comparison with Other Programs.* Washington, DC: National Association for the Education of Young Children.

Dewey, J. (1916). *Democracy and Education.* New York: Free Press.

———, and **Dewey, E.** (1915). *Schools for Tomorrow.* New York: Dutton.

Donaldson, M. (1978). *Children's Minds.* New York: W. W. Norton.

Dubos, R. J. (1961). *The Dreams of Reason.* New York: Columbia University Press.

Edwards, C. P. (1981). The comparative study of the development of moral judgment and reasoning. In R. L. Munroe, R. Munroe, and B. B. Whiting (Eds.), *Handbook of Cross-Cultural Development.* New York: Garland Press.

Ehrlich, P. R., and **Holm, K. W.** (1963). *The Process of Evolution.* New York: McGraw-Hill.

Eisenberg, L., and **Kanner, L.** (1956). Early infantile autism, 1943–1955. *American Journal of Orthopsychiatry, 26,* 556–66.

Elkind, D. (1981). *The Hurried Child.* Reading, MA: Addison-Wesley.

——— (1985, May). Formal education and early childhood education: An essential difference. *Phi Delta Kappan.*

Ellenberger, H. F. (1958). A clinical introduction to psychiatric phenomenology and existential analysis. In R. May, E. Angel, and H. F. Ellenberger (Eds.), *Existence: A New Dimension in Psychiatry and Psychology.* New York: Basic Books.

——— (1970). *The Discovery of the Unconscious.* New York: Basic Books.

Ellis, A. (1962). *Reason and Emotion in Psychotherapy.* New York: Lyle Stuart.

Engels, F. (1925). *Dialectics of Nature* (C. Dutt, trans.). Moscow: Foreign Languages Publishing House, 1954.

Erikson, E. H. (1958). *Young Man Luther.* New York: W. W. Norton & Co.

——— (1959). Identity and the life cycle. *Psychological Issues, 1:* 1. New York: International Universities Press.

——— (1963). *Childhood and Society* (2nd ed.). New York: W. W. Norton & Co.

——— (1964). *Insight and Responsibility.* New York: W. W. Norton & Co.

——— (1969). *Gandhi's Truth.* New York: W. W. Norton & Co.

——— (1976). Reflections on Dr. Borg's life cycle. *Daedalus, 105,* 1–28.

——— (1982). *The Life Cycle Completed.* New York: W. W. Norton.

Ervin, S. M. (1964).   Imitation and structural change in children's language.   In E. H. Lenneberg (Ed.), *New Directions in the Study of Language.*   Cambridge, MA: MIT Press.

Estes, W. K. (1944).   An experimental study of punishment.   *Psychological Monographs, 57,* 94–107.

Etzel, B. C., and **Gewirtz, J. L.** (1967).   Experimental modification of care-taking maintained high-rate operant crying in a 6- and 20-week-old infant (*infans tyrannotearus*): Extinction of crying with reinforcement of eye contact and smiling.   *Journal of Experimental Child Psychology, 5,* 303–17.

Evans, E. (1975).   *Contemporary Influences in Early Childhood Education* (2nd ed.).   New York: Holt, Rinehart & Winston.

Evans, R. I. (1969).   *Dialogue with Erik Erikson.*   New York: Dutton.

Fantz, R. L. (1961).   The origin of form perception.   *Scientific American, 204,* 459–63.

Fenichel, O. (1945).   *The Psychoanalytic Theory of Neurosis.*   New York: W. W. Norton & Co.

Flavell, J. H. (1963).   *The Developmental Psychology of Jean Piaget.*   New York: Van Nostrand Reinhold.

———— (1977).   *Cognitive Development.*   Englewood Cliffs, NJ: Prentice Hall.

———— (1985).   *Cognitive Development* (2nd ed.).   Englewood Cliffs, NJ: Prentice Hall.

————, **Botkin, P. T., Fry, C. L., Wright, J. W.,** and **Jarvis, P. E.** (1968).   *The Development of Role-Taking and Communication Skills in Children.*   New York: John Wiley.

Freedman, D. G. (1971).   An evolutionary approach to research on the life cycle.   *Human Development, 14,* 87–99.

———— (1974).   *Human Infancy: An Evolutionary Perspective.*   New York: John Wiley.

Freud, A. (1936).   *The Ego and the Mechanisms of Defense.*   New York: International Universities Press, 1946.

———— (1958).   Adolescence.   *Psychoanalytic Study of the Child, 13,* 255–78.

Freud, S. (1900).   *The Interpretation of Dreams* (J. Strachey, trans.).   New York: Basic Books (Avon), 1965.

———— (1905).   Three contributions to the theory of sex.   *The Basic Writings of Sigmund Freud* (A. A. Brill, trans.).   New York: The Modern Library.

———— (1907).   The sexual enlightenment of children (J. Riviere, trans.).   *Collected Papers* (Vol. II).   New York: Basic Books, 1959.

———— (1908a).   Character and anal eroticism (J. Riviere, trans.).   *Collected Papers* (Vol. II).   New York: Basic Books, 1959.

———— (1908b).   On the sexual theories of children (J. Riviere, trans.).   *Collected Papers* (Vol. II).   New York: Basic Books, 1959.

———— (1909).   Analysis of a phobia in a five-year-old boy (A. and J. Strachey, trans.).   *Collected Papers* (Vol. III).   New York: Basic Books, 1959.

———— (1910).   *The Origin and Development of Psychoanalysis.*   New York: Henry Regnery (Gateway Editions), 1965.

———— (1911).   Formulations regarding the two principles of mental functioning (J. Riviere, trans.).   *Collected Papers* (Vol. IV).   New York: Basic Books, 1959.

———— (1912).   Contributions to the psychology of love: The most prevalent form of degradation in erotic life (J. Riviere, trans.).   *Collected Papers* (Vol. IV).   New York: Basic Books, 1959.

———— (1913).   The excretory functions in psychoanalysis and folklore (J. Strachey, trans.).   *Collected Papers* (Vol. V).   New York: Basic Books, 1959.

———— (1914a).   On the history of the psychoanalytic movement (J. Riviere, trans.).   *Collected Papers* (Vol. I).   New York: Basic Books, 1959.

———— (1914b).   On narcissism: An introduction (J. Riviere, trans.).   *Collected Papers* (Vol. IV).   New York: Basic Books, 1959.

———— (1915a).   Instincts and their vicissitudes (J. Riviere, trans.).   *Collected Papers* (Vol. IV).   New York: Basic Books, 1959.

———— (1915b).   The unconscious (J. Riviere, trans.).   *Collected Papers* (Vol. IV).   New York: Basic Books, 1959.

———— (1916).   Metapsychological supplement to the theory of dreams (J. Riviere, trans.).   *Collected Papers* (Vol. IV).   New York: Basic Books, 1959.

———— (1917).   Mourning and melancholia (J. Riviere, trans.).   *Collected Papers* (Vol. IV).   New York: Basic Books, 1959.

———— (1920).   *A General Introduction to Psychoanalysis* (J. Riviere, trans.).   New York: Washington Square Press, 1965.

—— (1922). Medusa's head (J. Strachey, trans.). *Collected Papers* (Vol. V). New York: Basic Books, 1959.

—— (1923). *The Ego and the Id* (J. Riviere, trans.). New York: W. W. Norton & Co., 1960.

—— (1924). The passing of the Oedipus complex (J. Riviere, trans.). *Collected Papers* (Vol. II). New York: Basic Books, 1959.

—— (1925a). Some psychological consequences of the anatomical distinction between the sexes (J. Strachey, trans.). *Collected Papers* (Vol. V). New York: Basic Books, 1959.

—— (1925b). The resistance to psychoanalysis (J. Strachey, trans.). *Collected Papers* (Vol. V). New York: Basic Books, 1959.

—— (1931). Female sexuality (J. Strachey, trans.). *Collected Papers* (Vol. V). New York: Basic Books, 1959.

—— (1933). *New Introductory Lectures on Psychoanalysis* (J. Strachey, trans.). New York: W. W. Norton & Co., 1965.

—— (1936a). *The Problem of Anxiety* (H. A. Bunker, trans.). New York: The Psychoanalytic Press and W. W. Norton & Co.

—— (1936b). A disturbance in memory on the Acropolis (J. Strachey, trans.). *Collected Papers* (Vol. V). New York: Basic Books, 1959.

—— (1940). *An Outline of Psychoanalysis* (J. Strachey, trans.). New York: W. W. Norton & Co., 1949.

Fromm, E. (1967). Introduction. In E. Fromm (Ed.), *Socialist Humanism.* London: Allen Page, The Penguin Press.

Gardner, H. (1973). *The Arts and Human Development.* New York: John Wiley.

—— (1980). *Artful Scribbles.* New York: Basic Books.

—— (1982). *Developmental Psychology: An Introduction* (2nd ed.). Boston: Little, Brown.

Gay, P. (1988). *Freud: A Life for Our Time.* New York: W. W. Norton.

Gelfand, D. M. (1969). *Social Learning in Childhood.* Belmont, CA: Brooks/Cole.

Gelman, R. (1969). Conservation acquisition: A problem of learning to attend to relevant attributes. *Journal of Experimental Child Psychology, 7,* 167–87.

—— (1972). The nature and development of early number concepts. In H. Reese (Ed.), *Advances in Child Development and Behavior* (Vol. 7). New York: Academic Press.

—— (1979). Preschool thought. *American Psychologist, 34,* 900–905.

——, and **Baillargeon, R.** (1983). A review of some Piagetian concepts. In P. H. Mussen (Ed.), *Handbook of Child Psychology* (4th ed.) (Vol. III, *Cognitive Development,* J. H. Flavell and E. M. Markman, Eds.). New York: John Wiley.

Gesell, A. (1945). *The Embryology of Behavior.* New York: Harper & Row, Pub.

—— (1946). The ontogenesis of infant behavior. In L. Carmichael (Ed.), *Manual of Child Psychology* (2nd ed.). New York: John Wiley, 1954.

—— (1952a). Autobiography. In E. G. Boring, H. Werner, R. M. Yerkes, and H. Langfield (Eds.), *A History of Psychology in Autobiography* (Vol. IV). Worcester, MA: Clark University Press.

—— (1952b). *Infant Development: The Embryology of Early Human Behavior.* Westport, CT: Greenwood Press, 1972.

——, and **Amatruda, C. S.** (1941). *Developmental Diagnosis: Normal and Abnormal Child Development.* New York: Hoeber.

——, and **Ilg, F. L.** (1943). *Infant and Child in the Culture of Today.* In A. Gesell and F. L. Ilg, *Child Development.* New York: Harper & Row, Pub., 1949.

——, and **Ilg, F. L.** (1946). *The Child from Five to Ten.* In A. Gesell, and F. L. Ilg, *Child Development.* New York: Harper & Row, Pub., 1949.

——, **Ilg, F. L.,** and **Ames, L. B.** (1956). *Youth: The Years Ten to Sixteen.* New York: Harper.

——, and **Thompson, H.** (1929). Learning and growth in identical infant twins: An experimental study by the method of co-twin control. *Genetic Psychology Monographs, 6,* 1–124.

Gilbert, S. F. (1988). *Developmental Biology* (2nd ed.). Sunderland, MA: Sinauer.

Gilligan, C. (1982). *In a Different Voice.* Cambridge, MA: Harvard University Press.

Ginsburg, H., and **Opper, S.** (1988). *Piaget's Theory of Intellectual Development* (3rd ed.). Englewood Cliffs, NJ: Prentice Hall.

Gitelson, M. (1975). The emotional problems of elderly people. In W. C. Sze (Ed.), *Human Life Cycle.* New York: Jason Aronson.

Gleitman, L. R., and **Gleitman, H.** (1986a). Language. In H. Gleitman, *Psychology* (2nd ed.). New York: W. W. Norton.

―――― (1986b). Cognitive development: Language. In H. Gleitman, *Psychology* (2nd ed.). New York: W. W. Norton.

Glick, J. (1983). Piaget, Vygotsky, and Werner. In S. Wapner and B. Kaplan (Eds.), *Toward a Holistic Developmental Psychology.* Hillsdale, NJ: Lawrence Erlbaum Associates.

Goldberg, S. (1983). Parent-infant bonding: Another look. *Child Development, 54,* 1355–82.

Goldstein, K. (1939). *The Organism: A Holistic Approach to Biology Derived From Pathological Data in Man.* New York: American Book.

Goleman, D. (1990, March 14). Bruno Bettelheim dies at 86; Psychoanalyst of vast impact. *New York Times,* p. D25.

Gouin-Décarie, T. (1965). *Intelligence and Affectivity in Early Childhood.* New York: International Universities Press.

Griffin, P., and **Cole, M.** (1984). Current activity for the future: The Zo-ped. In B. Rogoff and J. Wertsch (Eds.), *Children's Learning in the Zone of Proximal Development.* San Francisco: Jossey-Bass.

Grimm, The Brothers (1972). *The Complete Grimm's Fairy Tales.* New York: Random House.

Gruber, H. E., (1981). *Darwin on Man* (2nd ed.). Chicago: University of Chicago Press.

Grusec, J. E., and **Brinker, D. B.** (1972). Reinforcement for imitation as a social learning determinant with implications for sex-role development. *Journal of Personality and Social Psychology, 21,* 149–58.

Grusec, J. E., and **Abramovitch, R.** (1982). Imitation of peers and adults in a natural setting: A functional analysis. *Child Development, 53,* 636–42.

Haan, N., Smith, M. B., and **Block, J.** (1968). Moral reasoning of young adults: Political-social behavior, family background, and personality correlates. *Journal of Personality and Social Psychology, 10,* 183–201.

Haber, R. N. (1969). Eidetic images. *Scientific American,* April, *220,* 36–44.

Hall, C. (1954). *A Primer of Freudian Psychology.* New York: Mentor Books (New American Library).

――――, and **Lindzey, G.** (1975). *Theories of Personality* (2nd ed.). New York: John Wiley.

Harris, J. R., and **Liebert, R. M.** (1984). *The Child.* Englewood Cliffs, NJ: Prentice Hall.

Hartmann, H. (1939). *Ego Psychology and the Problem of Adaptation.* New York: International Universities Press, 1958.

―――― (1950). Comments on the psychoanalytic theory of the ego. In H. Hartmann, *Essays on Ego Psychology.* New York: International Universities Press, 1964.

―――― (1956). The development of the ego concept in Freud's work. *International Journal of Psychoanalysis, 37,* 425–38.

――――, **Kris, E.,** and **Lowenstein, R. M.** (1946). Comments on the formation of psychic structure. *Psychoanalytic Study of the Child, 2,* 11–38.

Hass, W. R. (1975). Pragmatic structures of language: Historical, formal, and developmental issues. In K. F. Riegel and G. C. Rosenwald (Eds.), *Structure and Transformation.* New York: John Wiley.

Havighurst, R. J. (1952). *Developmental Tasks and Education.* New York: David McKay.

―――― (1968). A social-psychological perspective on aging. *The Gerontologist, 8,* 67–71.

――――, **Neugarten, B. L.,** and **Tobin, S. S.** (1968). Disengagement and patterns of aging. In B. L. Neugarten (Ed.), *Middle Age and Aging.* Chicago: University of Chicago Press.

Hawton, H. (1961). Humanism versus authoritarianism. In M. Knight (Ed.), *Humanist Anthology.* Bungay, Suffolk (Great Britain): Barrie & Rockliff.

Hess, E. H. (1962). Ethology: An approach toward the complete analysis of behavior. In *New Directions in Psychology* (Vol. I). New York: Holt, Rinehart & Winston.

―――― (1973). *Imprinting: Early Experience and the Developmental Psychology of Attachment.* New York: Van Nostrand Reinhold.

Hetherington, E. M., and **Parke, R. D.** (1977). *Contemporary Readings in Child Psychology.* New York: McGraw-Hill.

Hofer, M. A. (1981). *The Roots of Human Behavior: An Introduction to the Psychobiology of Early Development.* San Francisco: W. H. Freeman.

Hoffman, M. L. (1970). Moral development. In P. H. Mussen (Ed.), *Carmichael's Manual of Child Psychology* (3rd ed.) (Vol. II). New York: John Wiley.

Hogan, R. (1973). Moral conduct and moral character: A psychological perspective. *Psychological Bulletin, 79,* 217–32.

―――― (1975). Theoretical egocentrism and the problem of compliance. *American Psychologist, 30,* 533–40.

Holstein, C. B. (1973).   Irreversible, stepwise sequence in the development of moral judgment: A longitudinal evaluation.   Paper presented at the biannual meeting of the Society for Research in Child Development, March 1973.

Holt, J. (1964).   *How Children Fail.*   New York: Dell Pub. Co., Inc.

Homme, L. E., and **Totsi, D. T.** (1969).   Contingency management and motivation.   In D. M. Gelfand (Ed.), *Social Learning in Childhood: Readings in Theory and Application.*   Belmont, CA: Brooks/Cole.

Honigmann, J. J. (1967).   *Personality in Culture.*   New York: Harper & Row, Pub.

Huston, A. C., Watkins, B. A., and **Kunkel, D.** (1989).   Public policy and children's television.   *American Psychologist, 44,* 424–33.

Hyams, N. M. (1986).   *Language Acquisition and the Theory of Parameters.*   Dordrecht, Holland: D. Reider Publishing Co.

Ingram, D. (1975).   If and when transformations are acquired.   In D. P. Dato (Ed.), *Developmental Psycholinguistics.*   Washington, DC: Georgetown University Press.

Inhelder, B. (1971).   The criteria of the stages of mental development.   In J. M. Tanner and B. Inhelder (Eds.), *Discussions on Child Development.*   New York: International Universities Press.

_____, and **Piaget, J.** (1955).   *The Growth of Logical Thinking from Childhood to Adolescence.*   (A. Parsons and S. Milgram, trans.).   New York: Basic Books, 1958.

Jacobi, J. (1965).   *The Way of Individuation* (R. F. C. Hull, trans.).   San Diego, CA: Harcourt Brace Jovanovich, 1967.

Jacobson, E. (1954).   The self and the object world.   *Psychoanalytic Study of the Child, 9,* 75–127.

Jatich, A. M. (1990, October).   Repudiating Bettelheim.   *University of Chicago Magazine, 83.*

John-Steiner, V., and **Souberman, E.** (1978).   Afterword.   In M. Cole, V. John-Steiner, S. Scribner, and E. Souberman (Eds.), *L. S. Vygotsky: Mind in Society.*   Cambridge, MA: Harvard University Press.

Jones, E. (1918).   Anal-erotic character traits.   *Journal of Abnormal Psychology, 13,* 261–84.

_____ (1961).   *The Life and Work of Sigmund Freud* (ed. and abridged by J. Trilling and S. Marcus).   New York: Basic Books.

Jones, M. C. (1924).   A laboratory study of fear: The case of Peter.   *Pedagogical Seminary, 31,* 308–15.

Jung, C. G. (1931).   Marriage as a psychological relationship (R. F. C. Hull, trans.).   In C. G. Jung, *Collected Works* (Vol. XX).   *The Development of Personality.*   Princeton: Princeton University Press, 1953.

_____ (1933).   *Modern Man in Search of a Soul* (W. S. Dell and C. F. Baynes, trans.).   New York: Harvest Book.

_____ (1945).   The relations between the ego and the unconscious (R. F. C. Hull, trans.).   *The Collected Works of C. G. Jung* (Vol. VII).   *Two Essays in Analytic Psychology.*   Princeton: Princeton University Press, 1953.

_____ (1961).   *Memories, Dreams, Reflections* (A. Jaffe, Ed., R. and C. Winston, trans.).   New York: Vintage Books.

_____ (1964).   Approaching the unconscious.   In C. G. Jung (Ed.), *Man and His Symbols.*   New York: Dell Pub. Co., Inc.

Kagan, J. (1984).   *The Nature of the Child.*   New York: Basic Books.

Kamii, C. K. (1973).   Piaget's interactionism and the process of teaching young children.   In M. Schwebel and J. Raph (Eds.), *Piaget in the Classroom.*   New York: Basic Books.

_____ (1980).   Why use group games?   In C. Kamii and R. DeVries (Eds.), *Group Games in Early Education.*   Washington, DC: National Association for the Education of Young Children.

_____ (1985).   *Young Children Reinvent Arithmetic.*   New York: Teachers College Press.

Kamii, C., and **De Vries, R.** (1977).   Piaget for education.   In M. C. Day and R. K. Parker (Eds.), *The Preschool in Action* (2nd ed.).   Boston: Allyn & Bacon.

Kanner, L. (1943).   Austistic disturbances of affective contact.   *Nervous Child, 2,* 217–50.

Kant, I. (1788).   *The Critique of Practical Reason* (L. W. Beck, trans.).   New York: Liberal Arts Press, 1956.

Kardiner, A. (1945).   *The Psychological Frontiers of Society.*   New York: Columbia University Press.

Karen, R. (1990, February). Becoming attached. *Atlantic Monthly, 265.*

Kegan, R. (1985). The loss of Pete's Dragon: Developments of the self in the years five to seven. In R. L. Leahy (Ed.), *The Development of the Self.* New York: Academic Press.

Keniston, K. (1971). The perils of principle. In Keniston, K., *Youth and Dissent.* San Diego, CA: Harcourt Brace Jovanovich.

Kessen, W. (1965). *The Child.* New York: John Wiley.

Klahr, D. (1989). Information-processing approaches. *Annals of Child Development, 6,* 133–85.

Klaus, M. H., and **Kennell, J. H.** (1970). Mothers separated from their newborn infants. *Pediatric Clinics of North America, 17,* 1015–37.

——— (1983). *Parent-infant Bonding* (2nd ed.). St. Louis: The C. V. Mosby Co.

Klima, E. S., and **Bellugi, U.** (1966). Syntactic regularities in the speech of children. In J. Lyons and R. J. Wales (Eds.), *Psycholinguistics Papers.* Edinburgh: Edinburgh University Press.

Kohlberg, L. (1958a). *The Development of Modes of Thinking and Choice in the Years 10 to 16.* Unpublished doctoral dissertation, the University of Chicago.

——— (1958b). *Global Rating Guide with New Materials.* School of Education, Harvard University.

——— (1963). The development of children's orientations toward a moral order: I. Sequence in the development of moral thought. *Human Development, 6,* 11–33.

——— (1964). Development of moral character and moral ideology. In M. L. Hoffman and L. W. Hoffman (Eds.), *Review of Child Development Research* (Vol. I). New York: Russell Sage Foundation.

——— (1966a). Cognitive stages and preschool education. *Human Development, 9,* 5–17.

——— (1966b). A cognitive-developmental analysis of children's sex-role concepts and attitudes. In E. E. Maccoby (Ed.), *The Development of Sex Differences.* Stanford: Stanford University Press.

——— (1968). Early education: A cognitive-developmental approach. *Child Development, 39,* 1013–62.

——— (1969a). Stage and sequence. A cognitive-developmental approach to socialization. In D. A. Goslin (Ed.), *Handbook of Socialization Theory and Research.* Chicago: Rand McNally.

——— (1969b). The relations between moral judgment and moral action. Colloquium presented at the Institute of Human Development. Berkeley: University of California Press.

——— (1970). The child as a moral philosopher. *Readings in Developmental Psychology Today.* Del Mar, CA: CRM Books.

——— (1976). Moral stages and moralization: The cognitive-developmental approach. In T. Lickona (Ed.), *Moral Development and Behavior: Theory, Research, and Social Issues.* New York: Holt, Rinehart & Winston.

——— (1981). *Essays on Moral Development* (Vol. I). New York: Harper & Row.

———, and **Candee, D.** (1984). The relationship of moral judgment to moral action. In W. Kurtines and S. Gewirtz (Eds.), *Morality, Moral Behavior, and Moral Development.* New York: Wiley.

———, and **Elfenbein, D.** (1975). The development of moral judgments concerning capital punishment. *American Journal of Orthopsychiatry, 45,* 614–40.

———, and **Gilligan, C.** (1971). The adolescent as philosopher. *Daedalus, 100,* 1051–86.

———, **Kauffman, K., Scharf, P.,** and **Hickey, J.** (1975). The just community approach to corrections: A theory. *Journal of Moral Education, 4,* 243–60.

———, and **Kramer, R.** (1969). Continuities and discontinuities in childhood and adult moral development. *Human Development, 12,* 93–120.

———, **Yaeger, J.,** and **Hjertholm, E.** (1968). The development of private speech: Four studies and a review of theories. *Child Development, 39,* 691–736.

Kohler, W. (1925). *The Mentality of Apes.* London: Routledge & Kegan Paul.

Kozulin, A. (Ed.). (1986). Vygotsky in context. Introductory chapter to L. S. Vygotsky's *Thought and Language.* Cambridge, MA: MIT Press.

Kramer, R. (1976). *Maria Montessori: A Biography.* New York: Putnam's.

Krashen, S. D. (1975). The development of cerebral dominance and language learning: More new evidence. In D. P. Dato (Ed.), *Developmental Psycholinguistics: Theory and Applications.* Washington, DC: Georgetown University Press.

Kris, E. (1952). *Psychoanalytic Explorations in Art.* New York: International Universities Press.

Kuhn, D. (1974). Inducing development experimentally: Comments on a research paradigm. *Developmental Psychology, 10,* 590–600.

_____, **Langer, J., Kohlberg, L.,** and **Haan, N.** (1977). The development of formal operations in logical and moral judgment. *Genetic Psychology Monographs, 95,* 97–188.

Labov, W. (1970). The logic of nonstandard English. In F. Williams (Ed.), *Language and Poverty: Perspectives on a Theme.* Chicago: Markham.

Laing, R. D. (1965). *The Divided Self: An Existential Study in Sanity and Madness.* Middlesex, England: Penguin.

_____ (1967). *The Politics of Experience.* New York: Ballantine Books.

Lamb, M. E., and **Campos, J. J.** (1982). *Development in Infancy.* New York: Random House.

Lee, D. (1959). *Freedom and Culture.* Englewood Cliffs, NJ: Spectrum (Prentice Hall).

Levinson, D. (1977). The mid-life transition. *Psychiatry, 40,* 99–112.

_____ (1978). *The Seasons of a Man's Life.* New York: Ballantine.

Liebert, R. M., Odom, R. D., Hill, J. H., and **Huff, R. L.** (1969). Effects of age and rule familiarity on the production of modeled language constructions. *Developmental Psychology, 1,* 108–12.

Liebert, R. M., Poulos, R. W., and **Marmor, G. S.** (1977). *Developmental Psychology* (2nd ed.). Englewood Cliffs, NJ: Prentice Hall.

Lightfoot, D. (1982). *The Language Lottery: Toward a Biology of Grammars.* Cambridge, MA: The MIT Press.

Lillard, P. P. (1972). *Montessori: A Modern Approach.* New York: Shocken Books.

Lipsitt, L. P. (1971). Babies: They're a lot smarter than they look. *Psychology Today,* December, 5.

_____ (1975). The synchrony of respiration, heart rate, and sucking behavior in the newborn. *Biologic and Clinical Aspects of Brain Development,* Mead Johnson Symposium on Prenatal and Developmental Medicine, No. 6. Reprinted in Smart, R. C. and Smart, M. S. (Eds.), *Readings in Child Development and Relations* (2nd ed.). New York: Macmillan, 1977.

Locke, J. (1689). *Two Treatises on Government,* P. Laslett, (Ed.). Cambridge, England: Cambridge University Press, 1960.

_____ (1690). *Essay Concerning Human Understanding* (Vol. I, J. W. Yolton, Ed.). London: J. M. Dent and Sons Ltd., 1961.

_____ (1693). *Some Thoughts Concerning Education.* P. Gay (Ed.), *John Locke on Education.* New York: Bureau of Publications, Teacher's College, Columbia University, 1964.

Looft, W. R., and **Bartz, W. H.** (1969). Animisim revived. *Psychological Bulletin, 71,* 1–19.

Lorenz, K. (1935). Companions as factors in the bird's environment. In Lorenz, K. *Studies in Animal and Human Behavior* (Vol. I) (R. Martin, trans.). Cambridge, MA: Harvard University Press, 1971.

_____ (1937). The establishment of the instinct concept. In Lorenz, K. *Studies in Animal and Human Behavior* (Vol. I) (R. Martin, trans.). Cambridge, MA: Harvard University Press, 1971.

_____ (1952a). The past twelve years in the comparative study of behavior. In C. H. Schiller (Ed.), *Instinctive Behavior.* New York: International Universities Press, 1957.

_____ (1952b). *King Solomon's Ring* (M. K. Wilson, trans.). New York: Thomas Y. Crowell.

_____ (1963). *On Agression.* San Diego, CA: Harcourt Brace Jovanovich.

_____ (1965). *Evolution and Modification of Behavior.* Chicago: University of Chicago Press.

_____ (1981). *The Foundations of Ethology.* New York: Touchstone Book (Simon & Schuster).

Lovaas, O. I. (1969). *Behavior Modification: Teaching Language to Autistic Children.* Instructional film, 45 min., 16mm-sound. New York: Appleton-Century-Crofts.

_____ (1973). *Behavioral Treatment of Autistic Children.* University Programs Modular Studies. Morristown, NJ: General Learning Press.

_____ (1977). *The Autistic Child.* New York: Halstead Press.

_____, **Simmons, J. Q., Koegel, R. L.,** and **Stevens, J.** (1973). Some generalization and follow-up measures on autistic children in behavior therapy. *Journal of Applied Behavior Analysis, 6,* 131–66.

Lovell, K. (1968). Piaget in perspective: The experimental foundations. Paper presented to the conference of the University of Sussex. Sussex, England, April 5 and 6, 1968.

Lozoff, B., Brittenham, G. M., Trause, M. A., Kennell, J. H., and **Klaus, M. H.** (1977). The mother-newborn relationship: Limits of adaptability. *The Journal of Pediatrics, 91,* 1–12.

Luria, A. R. (1960).   Verbal regulation of behavior.   In M. A. B. Brazier (Ed.), *The Central Nervous System and Behavior.*   New York: Josiah Macy Jr. Foundation.

―――― (1961).   *The Role of Speech in the Regulation of Normal and Abnormal Behavior.*   New York: Liveright Publishing Corp.

―――― (1976).   *Cognitive Development: Its Cultural and Social Foundations* (M. Lopez-Morillas and L. Solotaroff, trans.).   Cambridge, MA: Harvard University Press.

―――― (1981).   *Language and Cognition* (J. Wertsch, ed.).   New York: Wiley.

Lyons, J. (1970).   *Noam Chomsky.*   New York: Viking Press.

Maccoby, E. E., and **Wilson, W. C.** (1957).   Identification and observational learning from films.   *Journal of Abnormal and Social Psychology, 55*, 76–87.

――――, and **Jacklin, C. N.** (1974).   *The Psychology of Sex Differences.*   Stanford, CA: Stanford University Press.

MacFarlane, A. (1981).   What a baby knows.   In H. E. Fitzgerald (Ed.), *Human Development 81/82.*   Annual Editions, Guilford, CT: Dushkin Publishing Group.

McNeill, D. (1966).   Developmental psycholinguistics.   In F. Smith and G. A. Miller (Eds.), *The Genesis of Language: A Psycholinguistic Approach.*   Cambridge, MA: MIT Press.

―――― (1971).   The capacity for the ontogenesis of grammar.   In D. Slobin (Ed.), *The Ontogenesis of Grammar.*   New York: Academic Press.

Main, M., and **Goldwyn, R.** (1987).   Interview-based adult attachment classifications: Related to infant-mother and infant-father attachment. Unpublished manuscript, Department of Psychology, University of California, Berkeley.

――――, **Kaplan, N.,** and **Cassidy, J.** (1985).   Security in infancy, childhood, and adulthood: A move to the level of representation.   In I. Bretherton and E. Waters (Eds.), Growing points of attachment theory and research.   *Monographs of the Society for Research in Child Development, 50*, Serial No. 209.

Malinowski, B. (1927).   *Sex and Repression in Savage Society.*   San Diego, CA: Harcourt Brace Jovanovich.

Marcia, J. E. (1966).   Development and validation of ego identity status.   *Journal of Personality and Social Psychology, 3*, 551–58.

Marks, L. (1975).   On colored-hearing synesthesia.   *Psychological Bulletin, 82*, 303–331.

Marler, P., and **Tamura, M.** (1964).   Culturally transmitted patterns of vocal behavior in sparrows.   *Science, 146*, 1483–86.

Marx, K. (1844).   *Economic and philosophical manuscripts* (M. Milligan, trans.).   In R. C. Tucker (Ed.), *The Marx-Engels Reader.*   New York: W. W. Norton, 1972

―――― (1845).   Theses on Feuerbach.   In R. C. Tucker (Ed.), *The Marx-Engels Reader.*   New York: W. W. Norton, 1972.

―――― (1859).   Preface to *A Contribution to the Critique of Political Economy.*   In R. C. Tucker (Ed.), *The Marx-Engels Reader.*   New York: W. W. Norton, 1972.

――――, and **Engels, F.** (1846).   *The German Ideology* (S. Ryazanskaya and W. Lough, trans.).   In R. C. Tucker (Ed.), *The Marx-Engels Reader.*   New York: W. W. Norton, 1972.

――――, and **Engels, F.** (1872).   *Manifesto of the Communist Party.*   In R. C. Tucker (Ed.), *The Marx-Engels Reader.*   New York: W. W. Norton, 1972.

Maslow, A. (1943).   A dynamic theory of human motivation.   *Psychological Review, 50*, 370–96.

―――― (1954).   *Motivation and Personality* (2nd ed.).   New York: Harper & Row, Pub., 1970.

―――― (1962).   *Toward a Psychology of Being* (2nd ed.).   New York: Van Nostrand Reinhold, 1968.

―――― (1966).   *The Psychology of Science: A Reconnaissance.*   Chicago: Henry Regnery (Gateway), 1969.

―――― (1971).   *The Farther Reaches of Human Nature.*   New York: Viking.

Mead, M. (1964).   *Continuities in Cultural Evolution.*   New Haven: Yale University Press.

Meichenbaum, D. H., and **Goodman, J.** (1971).   Training impulsive children to talk to themselves: A means of developing self-control.   *Journal of Abnormal Psychology, 77*, 115–26.

Meltzoff, A. N., and **Moore, M. K.** (1977).   Imitation of facial and manual gestures by human neonates.   *Science, 198*, 75–78.

―――― (1989).   Imitation in newborn infants: Exploring the range of gestures imitated and the underlying mechanisms.   *Developmental Psychology, 25*, 954–62.

Miller, L. B., and **Dyer, J. L.** (1975).   Four preschool programs: Their dimensions and effects.   *Monographs of the Society for Research in Child Development, 40*, Serial No. 162.

Miller, P. H. (1989). *Theories of Developmental Psychology* (2nd ed.). New York: W. H. Freeman

Miller, R. (1990). *What Are Schools For? Holistic Education in American Culture.* Brandon, VT: Holistic Education Press.

Mills, C. W. (1962). *The Marxists.* New York: Dell.

Mischel, W. (1970). Sex-typing and socialization. In P. H. Mussen (Ed.), *Carmichael's Manual of Child Psychology* (3rd ed., Vol. II). New York: John Wiley.

Misiak, H., and **Sexton, V. S.** (1973). *Phenomenological, Existential, and Humanistic Psychologies: A Historical Survey.* New York: Grune & Stratton.

Montessori, M. (1917). *The Advanced Montessori Method* (Vol. I). *Spontaneous Activity in Education* (F. Simmonds, trans.). Cambridge, MA: Robert Bentley, Inc., 1964.

_____ (1936a). *The Child in the Family* (N. R. Cirillo, trans.). Chicago: Henry Regnery Co., 1970.

_____ (1936b). *The Secret of Childhood* (M. J. Costelloe, trans.). New York: Ballatine Books, 1966.

_____ (1948). *The Discovery of the Child* (M. J. Costelloe, trans.). Notre Dame, IN: Fides Publishers, 1967.

_____ (1949). *The Absorbent Mind* (C. A. Claremont, trans.). New York: Holt, Rinehart & Winston, 1967.

_____ (1970). *Maria Montessori: A Centenary Anthology, 1870–1970.* Koninginneweg, Amsterdam: Association Montessori Internationale.

Munn, N. L. (1946). *Psychology.* Boston: Houghton Mifflin.

_____ (1974). *The Growth of Human Behavior* (3rd ed.). Boston: Houghton Mifflin.

_____, **Fernald, L. D.,** and **Fernald, P. S.** (1974). *Introduction to Psychology* (3rd ed.). Boston: Houghton Mifflin.

Munroe, R. (1955). *Schools of Psychoanalytic Thought.* New York: Henry Holt and Co., Inc.

Mussen, P. H., and **Eisenberg-Berg, N.** (1977). *Roots of Caring, Sharing, and Helping.* San Francisco: W. H. Freeman.

Muuss, R. E. (1975). *Theories of Adolescence* (3rd ed.). New York: Random House.

Needham, J. (1959). *A History of Embryology* (2nd ed.). Cambridge, England: Cambridge University Press.

Neill, A. S. (1960). *Summerhill: A Radical Approach to Child Rearing.* New York: Hart Publishing Co.

Neimark, E. D. (1975). Longitudinal development of formal operations thought. *Genetic Psychology Monographs, 91,* 171–225.

Neugarten, B. L. (1964). A developmental view of adult personality. In J. E. Birren (Ed.), *Relations of Development and Aging.* Springfield, IL: Charles C Thomas.

_____ (1968). Adult personality: Toward a psychology of the life cycle. In Neugarten, B. L. (Ed.), *Middle Age and Aging.* Chicago: University of Chicago Press.

Nisan, M., and **Kohlberg, L.** (1982). Universality and variation in moral judgment: A longitudinal and cross-sectional study in Turkey. *Child Development, 52,* 865–76.

Parkes, C. M. (1982). Attachment and the prevention of mental disorders. In C. M. Parkes and J. Stevenson-Hinde (Eds.), *The Place of Attachment in Human Behavior.* New York: Basic Books.

Parsons, A. (1964). Is the Oedipus complex universal? In W. Muensterberger and S. Axelrad (Eds.), *The Psychoanalytic Study of Society* (Vol. III). New York: International Universities Press.

Pavlov, I. P. (1927). *Conditioned Reflexes* (G. V. Anrep, trans.). London: Oxford University Press.

_____ (1928). *Lectures on Conditioned Reflexes* (Vol. I, W. H. Gantt, trans.). New York: International Publishers.

Peill, E. J. (1975). *Invention and Discovery of Reality.* London: John Wiley.

Peiper, A. (1963). *Cerebral Function in Infancy and Childhood* (3rd ed., trans. B. and H. Nagler). New York: Consultants Bureau.

Piaget, J. (1923). *The Language and Thought of the Child* (M. Gabain, trans.). London: Routledge and Kegan Paul, Ltd., 1959.

_____ (1924). *Judgment and Reasoning in the Child* (M. Warden, trans.). Savage, MD: Littlefield, Adams and Co., 1972.

_____ (1926). *The Child's Conception of the World* (J. and A. Tomlinson, trans.). Savage, MD: Littlefield, Adams and Co., 1963.

—— (1932). *The Moral Judgment of the Child* (M. Gabain, trans.). New York: Free Press, 1965.

—— (1936a). *The Origins of Intelligence in Children* (M. Cook, trans.). New York: International Universities Press, 1974.

—— (1936b). *The Construction of Reality in the Child* (M. Cook, trans.). New York: Ballantine Books, 1954.

—— (1946). *Play, Dreams and Imitation in Childhood* (C. Gattegno and F. M. Hodgson, trans.). New York: W. W. Norton & Co., 1962.

—— (1947). *The Psychology of Intelligence* (M. Piercy and D. E. Berlyne, trans.). Savage, MD: Littlefield, Adams and Co., 1973.

—— (1952). Autobiography. In E. Boring, H. S. Langfeld, H. Werner, and R. M. Yerkes, *A History of Psychology in Autobiography* (Vol. IV). Worcester, MA: Clark University Press.

—— (1964a). *Six Psychological Studies* (A. Tenzer and D. Elkind, trans.). New York: Vintage Books, 1968.

—— (1964b). Development and learning. In R. Ripple and V. Rockcastle (Eds.), *Piaget Rediscovered*. Ithaca, NY: Cornell University Press, 1969.

—— (1969). *Science of Education and the Psychology of the Child* (D. Coltman, trans.). New York: Viking, 1970.

—— (1970). Piaget's theory. In P. H. Mussen (Ed.), *Handbook of Child Psychology* (4th ed.) (Vol. I, W. Kessen, Ed.). New York: John Wiley, 1983.

—— (1972). Intellectual evolution from adolescence to adulthood. *Human Development, 15*, 1–12.

——, and **Inhelder, B.** (1948). *The Child's Conception of Space* (F. J. Langdor and J. L. Lunzer, trans.). London: Routledge & Kegan Paul Ltd., 1956.

——, and **Inhelder, B.** (1966). *The Psychology of the Child* (H. Weaver, trans.). New York: Basic Books, 1969.

——, and **Szeminska, A.** (1941). *The Child's Conception of Number* (C. Cattegno and F. M. Hodgson, trans.). New York: W. W. Norton & Co.

Piatelli-Palmarini, M., Ed. (1979). *Language and Learning: The Debate between Jean Piaget and Noam Chomsky.* Cambridge, MA: Harvard University Press, 1980.

Pierce, A. (1989). *On the Emergence of Syntax: A Cross-linguistic Study.* Doctoral Dissertation, MIT.

Pinker, S. (1989). Language acquisition. In D. N. Osherson and H. Lasnik (Eds.), *Language: An Invitation to Cognitive Science* (Vol. I). Cambridge, MA: MIT Press.

Podd, M. (1972). Ego identity status and morality. *Developmental Psychology, 6*, 497–507.

Pollock, L. (1983). *Forgotten Children.* Cambridge, England: Cambridge University Press.

Power, C., and **Reimer, J.** (1979). Moral atmosphere: An educational bridge between moral judgment and action. In W. Damon (Ed.), *New Directions for Child Development*, No. 2, San Francisco: Jossey-Bass.

Power, F. C., Higgins, A., and **Kohlberg, L.** (1989). *Lawrence Kohlberg's Approach to Moral Education.* New York: Columbia University Press.

Premack, D. (1961). Predicting instrumental performance from the independent rate of the contingent response. *Journal of Experimental Psychology, 61*, 161–71.

Rawls, J. (1971). *A Theory of Justice.* Cambridge, MA: Harvard University Press.

Reiber, R. W., and **Voyat, G.** (1983). *Dialogues on the Psychology of Language and Thought.* New York: Plenum Press.

Reimer, J., Paolitto, D. P., and **Hersh, R. H.** (1983). *Promoting Moral Growth* (2nd ed.). New York: Longman.

Redl, F., and **Wineman, D.** (1951). *Children Who Hate.* New York: The Free Press.

Rest, J. (1973). The hierarchical nature of moral judgment: The study of patterns of preference and comprehension of moral judgments made by others. *Journal of Personality, 41*, 86–109.

—— (1983). Morality. In P. H. Mussen (Ed.), *Handbook of Child Psychology* (4th ed.) (Vol. III, J. H. Flavell and E. M. Markman, Eds.). New York: John Wiley.

——, **Turiel, E.,** and **Kohlberg, L.** (1969). Relations between level of moral judgments and preference and comprehension of the moral judgment of others. *Journal of Personality, 37*, 225–52.

Reynolds, C. S. (1968). *A Primer of Operant Conditioning.* Glenview, IL: Scott, Foresman and Co.

Rheingold, H. L., Gewirtz, J. L., and **Ross, H. W.** (1959). Social conditioning of vocalizations in the infant. *Journal of Comparative and Physiological Psychology, 52,* 68–73.

Riegel, K. F. (1975). Toward a dialectical theory of development. *Human Development, 18,* 50–64.

Riess, B. F. (1954). Effect of altered environment and of age on the mother-young relationships among animals. *Annals of the New York Academy of Science, 57,* 606–10.

Rimland, B. (1964). *Infantile Autism: The Syndrome and Its Implications for a Neural Theory of Behavior.* Englewood Cliffs, NJ: Prentice Hall.

Robertson, J. (1952). *A Two Year Old Goes to Hospital,* 16 mm., B & W film. London: Tavistock Clinic. New York: New York University Film Library.

Rogoff, B., Malkin, C., and **Gilbride, K.** (1984). Interaction with babies as guidance and development. In B. Rogoff and J. Wertsch (Eds.), *Children's Learning in the "Zone of Proximal Development."* San Francisco: Jossey-Bass.

Rosenthal, T. L. (1976). Modeling therapies. In M. Herson, R. M. Eisler, and P. M. Miller (Eds.), *Progress in Behavior Modification* (Vol. II). New York: Academic Press.

———, and **Zimmerman, B. J.** (1972). Modeling by exemplification and instruction in training conservation. *Developmental Psychology, 6,* 392–401.

Roszak, T. (1972). *Where the Wasteland Ends.* Garden City, NY: Anchor (Doubleday), 1973.

Rousseau, J. J. (1750). Discourse on the Sciences and Arts. In R. D. Masters (Ed.), *The First and Second Discourses* (R. D. and J. R. Masters, trans.). New York: St. Martin's Press, 1964.

——— (1755). Discourse on the Origin and Foundations of Inequality. In R. D. Masters (Ed.), *The First and Second Discourses* (R. D. and J. R. Masters, trans.). New York: St. Martin's Press, 1964.

——— (1762a). *The Social Contract* (G. Hopkins, trans.). New York: Oxford University Press, 1962.

——— (1762b). *Emile, Or Education* (B. Foxley, trans.). London: J. M. Dent and Sons Ltd., 1948.

——— (1788). *The Confessions of Jean Jacques Rousseau.* New York: The Modern Library, 1945.

Rushton, J. P. (1975). Generosity in children: Immediate and long term effects of modeling, preaching, and moral judgment. *Journal of Personality and Social Psychology, 31,* 459–66.

Russell, B. (1945). *A History of Western Philosophy.* New York: Simon & Schuster.

——— (1971). *Education and the Social Order.* London: George Allen and Unwin, Ltd.

Sachs, J. S. (1976). Development of speech. In E. C. Carterette and M. P. Friedman (Eds.), *Handbook of Perception* (Vol. VII). New York: Academic Press.

Sagi, A., Van Idzendoorn, M. H., and **Koren-Karie, N.** (1991). Primary appraisal of the strange situation: A cross-cultural analysis of preparation eposides. *Developmental Psychology, 27,* 587–96.

Sahakian, W. S., and **Sahakian, M. L.** (1975). *John Locke.* Boston: Twayne Publishers.

Sameroff, A. J., and **Cavanaugh, P. J.** (1979). Learning in infancy: A developmental perspective. In J. D. Osofsky (Ed.), *Handbook of Infant Development.* New York: John Wiley.

de Santiallana, G. (Ed.) (1956). *The Age of Adventure: The Renaissance Philosophers.* New York: Mentor.

Schachtel, E. G. (1959). *Metamorphosis.* New York: Basic Books.

Schneirla, T. C. (1960). Instinctive behavior, maturation-experience, and development. In B. Kaplan and S. Wapner (Eds.), *Perspectives in Psychological Theory.* New York: International Universities Press.

Schwartz, B. (1984). *Psychology of Learning and Behavior* (2nd ed.). New York: W. W. Norton.

Scribner, S., and **Cole, M.** (1981). *The Psychology of Literacy.* Cambridge, MA: Harvard University Press.

Searles, H. F. (1965). *Collected Papers on Schizophrenia and Related Subjects.* New York: International Universities Press.

Seligman, M. E. P. (1972). Phobias and preparedness. In M. E. P. Seligman and J. L. Hager (Eds.), *Biological Boundaries of Learning.* New York: Appleton-Century-Crofts.

Selman, R. K. (1976). Social-cognitive understanding: A guide to educational and clinical practice. In T. Lickona (Ed.), *Moral Development and Behavior.* New York: Holt, Rinehart & Winston.

Sheehy, G. (1976). *Passages: Predictable Crises of Adult Life.* New York: Dutton.

Sigel, I. E. (1968). Reflections. In I. E. Sigel and F. H. Hooper (Eds.), *Logical Thinking in Children: Research Based on Piaget's Theory.* New York: Holt, Rinehart & Winston.

———— (1986).   Mechanism. A metaphor for cognitive development?   A review of Sternberg's "Mechanisms of Cognitive Development."   *Merrill-Palmer Quarterly, 32,* 93–101.

Simpson, E. L. (1974).   Moral development research: A case study of scientific cultural bias.   *Human Development, 17,* 81–106.

Sinclair, H. (1971).   Sensorimotor action patterns as a condition for the acquisition of syntax.   In R. Huxley and E. Ingram (Eds.), *Language Acquisition: Methods and Models.*   New York: Academic Press.

Singer, J. L., and **Singer, D. G.** (1979).   Come back, Mr. Rogers, come back.   *Psychology Today, 12,* 56–60.

Skinner, B. F. (1938).   *The Behavior of Organisms.*   Englewood Cliffs, NJ: Prentice Hall.

———— (1948).   *Walden Two.*   New York: Macmillan.

———— (1953).   *Science and Human Behavior.*   New York: Macmillan.

———— (1957).   *Verbal Behavior.*   Englewood Cliffs, NJ: Prentice Hall.

———— (1959).   *Cumulative Record.*   Englewood Cliffs, NJ: Prentice Hall.

———— (1967).   Autobiography.   In E. G. Boring and G. Lindzey (Eds.), *A History of Psychology in Autobiography* (Vol. V).   Englewood Cliffs, NJ: Prentice Hall.

———— (1968).   *The Technology of Teaching.*   Englewood Cliffs, NJ: Prentice Hall.

———— (1969).   *Contingencies of Reinforcement.*   Englewood Cliffs, NJ: Prentice Hall.

———— (1971).   *Beyond Freedom and Dignity.*   New York: Bantam.

———— (1974).   *About Behaviorism.*   New York: Knopf.

Slobin, D. I. (1966).   Soviet psycholinguistics.   In N. O'Connor (Ed.), *Present-Day Russian Psychology: A Symposium by Seven Authors.*   Oxford: Pergamon Press.

———— (1972).   They learn the same way all around the world.   *Psychology Today, 6,* 71–82.

———— (1973).   Cognitive prerequisites for the development of grammar.   In C. A. Ferguson and D. I. Slobin (Eds.), *Studies of Child Language Development.*   New York: Holt, Rinehart & Winston.

———— (1979).   *Psycholinguistics* (2nd ed.).   Glenview, IL: Scott, Foresman.

Smart, M. S., and **Smart, R. C.** (1978).   *Preschool Children* (2nd ed.).   New York: Macmillan.

Snow, C. E. (1979).   Conversations with children.   In P. Fletcher and M. Garman (Eds.), *Language Acquisition.*   Cambridge, England: Cambridge University Press.

Spock, B. (1945).   *Baby and Child Care.*   New York: Pocket Books, 1968.

Sroufe, L. A. (1983).   Attachment and adaptation in preschool.   In M. Perlmutter (Ed.), *Development and Policy Concerning Children with Special Needs. Minnesota Symposium on Child Development, 16.*   Hillsdale, NJ: Erlbaum.

————, and **Cooper, R. G.** (1988).   *Child Development: Its Nature and Course.*   New York: Knopf.

Sternberg, R. S. (1984).   *Mechanisms of Cognitive Development.*   San Francisco: Freeman.

Sullivan, H. S. (1953).   *The Inerpersonal Theory of Psychiatry.*   New York: W. W. Norton & Co.

Sze, W. C. (Ed.) (1975).   *Human Life Cycle.*   New York: Jason Aronson.

Tanner, J. M., and **Inhelder, B.** (Eds.) (1971).   *Discussions on Child Development.*   The Proceedings of the Meetings of the World Health Organization Study Group on the Psychological Development of the Child, Geneva, 1953–56.   New York: International Universities Press.

Thompson, C. (1950).   Cultural pressures in the psychology of women.   In P. Mullahy (Ed.), *A Study of Interpersonal Relations.*   New York: Hermitage Press.

Thorndike, E. L. (1905).   *The Elements of Psychology.*   New York: Seiler.

Tinbergen, N. (1951).   *The Study of Instinct.*   Oxford: Clarendon Press.

———— (1965).   The shell menace.   In T. E. McGill (Ed.), *Readings in Animal Behavior.*   New York: Holt, Rinehart & Winston.

———— (1977).   Interview.   In Cohen, D., *Psychologists on Psychology.*   New York: Taplinger.

Tolman, E. C. (1948).   Cognitive maps in rats and man.   *Psychological Review, 55,* 189–208.

Treffert, D. A. (1970).   Epidemiology of infantile autism.   *Archives of General Psychiatry, 22,* 431–38.

Tulkin, S. R., and **Konner, M. J.** (1973).   Alternative conceptions of intellectual functioning.   *Human Development, 16,* 33–52.

Turiel, E. (1966).   An experimental test of the sequentiality of developmental stages in the child's moral judgments.   *Journal of Personality and Social Psychology, 3,* 611–18.

Turner, E. W., and **Rommetveit, R.** (1967).   Experimental manipulation of the production of active and passive voice in children.   *Language and Speech, 10,* 169–80.

Uzgiris, I. C. (1964).   Situational generality of conservation. *Child Development, 35*, 831–41.

Valsiner, J. (1984).   Construction of the zone of proximal development in adult-child joint action: The socialization of meals.   In B. Rogoff and J. Wertsch (Eds.), *Children's Learning in the "Zone of Proximal Development."*   San Francisco: Jossey-Bass.

Von Franz, M. L. (1964).   The process of individuation.   In C. G. Jung (Ed.), *Man and His Symbols.*   New York: Dell Pub. Co., Inc.

Vygotsky, L. S. (1930).   Tool and symbol in children's development (A. R. Luria and M. Cole, trans.).   In M. Cole, V. John-Steiner, S. Scribner, and E. Souberman (Eds.), *L. S. Vygotsky: Mind in Society.*   Cambridge, MA: Harvard University Press, 1978, chs. 1–4.

_____ (1931a).   *Development of higher mental functions.*   In *Psychological Research in the U.S.S.R.*   Moscow: Progress Publishers, 1966.

_____ (1931b).   The history of the development of the higher mental functions (M. Cole, trans.).   Excerpt in M. Cole, V. John-Steiner, S. Scribner, and E. Souberman (Eds.), *L. S. Vygotsky: Mind in Society.*   Cambridge, MA: Harvard University Press, 1978, Ch. 5.

_____ (1932).   The problem of will and its development in childhood.   In R. W. Rieber and A. S. Carton (Eds.), *The Collected Works of L. S. Vygotsky* (Vol. I, N. Minick, trans.).   New York: Plenum Press, 1987.

_____ (1933).   The role of play in development (M. Lopez-Morillas, trans.).   In M. Cole, V. John-Steiner, S. Scribner, and E. Souberman (Eds.), *L. S. Vygotsky: Mind in Society.*   Cambridge, MA: Harvard University Press, 1978.

_____ (1934).   *Thought and Language* (A. Kozulin, trans.).   Cambridge, MA: MIT Press, 1986.

_____ (1935).   Mental development of children and the process of learning (M. Lopez Morillas, trans.).   In M. Cole, V. John-Steiner, S. Scribner, and E. Souberman (Eds.), *L. S. Vygotsky: Mind in Society.*   Cambridge, MA: Harvard University Press, 1978, chs. 7–8.

Waddington, C. H. (1962).   *Biology for the Modern World.*   New York: Barnes & Noble.

Wapner, S., Kaplan, B., and **Cohen, S. B.** (1973).   An organismic-developmental perspective for understanding transactions of men and environments.   *Environment and Behavior, 5*, 255–89.

Watson, J. B. (1913).   Psychology as the behaviorist views it.   *Psychological Review, 20*, 158–77.

_____ (1924).   *Behaviorism.*   New York: W. W. Norton & Co., 1970.

_____ (1928).   *Psychological Care of Infant and Child.*   New York: W. W. Norton & Co.

_____ (1936).   Autobiography.   In C. Murchison (Ed.), *A History of Psychology in Autobiography* (Vol. III).   Worcester, MA: Clark University Press.

Watson, R. I. (1968).   *The Great Psychologists from Aristotle to Freud* (2nd ed.).   Philadelphia: Lippincott.

Weiss, R. S. (1982).   Attachment in adult life.   In C. M. Parkes and J. Stevenson-Hinde (Eds.), *The Place of Attachment in Human Behavior.*   New York: Basic Books.

Wells, G. (1985).   *Language Development in the Preschool Years.*   Cambridge, England: Cambridge University Press.

Werner, H. (1934).   The unity of the senses.   In S. S. Barten and M. B. Franklin (Eds.), *Developmental Processes: Heinz Werner's Selected Writings* (Vol. I).   New York: International Universities Press, 1978.

_____ (1948).   *Comparative Psychology of Mental Development* (2nd ed.).   New York: Science Editions.

_____ (1956).   On physiognomic perception.   In G. Kepes (Ed.), *The New Landscape.*   Chicago: Theobald.

_____ (1957).   The concept of development from a comparative and organismic point of view.   In D. B. Harris (Ed.), *The Concept of Development.*   Minneapolis: University of Minnesota Press.

_____, and **Kaplan, B.** (1956).   The developmental approach to cognition: Its relevance to the psychological interpretation of anthropological and ethnolinguistic data.   *American Anthropologist, 58*, 866–80.

_____, and **Kaplan, B.** (1963).   *Symbol Formation.*   New York: John Wiley.

Wertsch, J. V. (1985).   *Vygotsky and the Social Formation of Mind.*   Cambridge, MA: Harvard University Press.

White, G. M. (1972).   Immediate and deferred effects of model observation and guided and unguided rehearsal on donating and stealing.   *Journal of Personality and Social Psychology, 21*, 139–48.

White, R. W. (1960).   Competence and the psychosexual stages of development.   In M. Jones (Ed.), *Nebraska Symposium on Motivation.*   Lincoln: University of Nebraska Press.

———— (1963).   Sense of interpersonal competence: Two case studies and some reflections on origins.   In R. R. White (Ed.), *The Study of Lives.*   New York: Atherton Press.

————, and **Watt, N. F.** (1973).   *The Abnormal Personality* (4th ed.).   New York: Ronald Press.

————, and **Watt, N. F.** (1981).   *The Abnormal Personality* (5th ed.).   New York: Wiley.

White, S. (1965).   Evidence for a hierarchical arrangement of learning processes.   In L. P. Lipsitt and C. C. Spiker (Eds.), *Advances in Child Development and Behavior* (Vol. II).   New York: Academic Press.

———— (1970).   Some general outlines of the matrix of developmental changes between five and seven years.   *Bulletin of the Orton Society, 20,* 41–57.

Whitehead, A. N. (1929).   *Science and the Modern World.*   New York: Macmillan.

Whitehurst, G. J., Ironsmith, M., and **Goldman, M.** (1974).   Selective imitation of the passive construction through modeling.   *Journal of Experimental Child Psychology, 17,* 288–302.

Whitehurst, G. J., Falco, F. L., Lonigan, C. J., Fischel, J. E., DeBaryshe, B. D., Valdez-Menchaca, M. C., and **Calufield, M.** (1988).   Accelerating language development through picture book reading.   *Developmental Psychology, 24,* 552–59.

Whiting, J. W. M., and **Child, I. L.** (1953).   *Child Training and Personality: A Cross-cultural Study.*   New Haven, CT: Yale University Press.

Whitmont, E. C. (1969).   *The Symbolic Quest: Basic Concepts of Analytical Psychology.*   New York: Putnam's.

————, and **Kaufmann, Y.** (1973).   Analytic psychotherapy.   In R. Corsini (Ed.), *Current Psychotherapies.*   Ithaca, IL: F. E. Peacock Publishers.

Williams, C. D. (1959).   The elimination of tantrum behavior by extinction procedures.   *Journal of Abnormal and Social Psychology, 5,* 269.

Wilner, W. (1975).   Schachtel: A life.   *William Alanson White Newsletter,* Winter, 3–4.

Wilson, C. (1972).   *New Pathways in Psychology: Maslow and the Post-Freudian Revolution.*   New York: Mentor Books.

Witkin, H. (1965).   Heinz Werner.   *Child Development, 30,* 307–28.

Wohlwill, J. F. (1984).   Martha Muchow and the life-space of the urban child.   Paper presented to the Society for Research in Child Development, Ann Arbor, Mich.

Wolpe, J. (1969).   *The Practice of Behavior Therapy.*   New York: Pergamon Press.

Zelazo, P. R., Zelazo, N. A., and **Kolb, S.** (1972).   "Walking" in the newborn.   *Science, 176,* 314–15.

Zimmerman, B. J., and **Rosenthal, T. L.** (1974).   Conserving and retaining equalities and inequalities through observation and correction.   *Developmental Psychology, 10,* 260–68.

Name Index

Aber, J. L., 49, 50
Abraham, K., 227–29
Abramovitch, R., 190
Adler, A., 225
Ainsworth, M. D. S., 26, 47, 48–55
Aitchison, J., 304
Allport, G., 261
Almy, M., 127
Als, H., 26
Amatruda, C., 17
Ames, L. B., 23, 24, 337
Appleton, T., 26
Ariès, P., 1–3
Arnheim, R., 87, 292
Ausubel, D., 2

Baer, D. M., 164, 166, 168
Baerends, G., 32
Baillargeon, 127, 130
Baldwin, A. L., 83, 97, 175
Baldwin, J. M., 135
Balinsky, B. I., 2
Balzac, H., 90
Bandura, A., 102, 133, 175–80,
    181–92, 217, 311, 314
Barten, S., 96
Bartlett, E. J., 315
Bartz, W. H., 127
Bateson, P. P. G., 37
Baumrind, D., 27
Beer, C., 331
Bell, S. M., 26, 331
Bellugi, U., 307, 308, 311, 315
Bellugi-Klima, U., 308, 333
Belsky, J., 54
Benedek, T., 242, 250
Benedict, R., 263
Beres, D., 238
Bergman, I., 261
Berkowitz, M. W., 150
Berlin, I., 318
Bernstein, R., 272
Bettelheim, B., 26, 74, 96, 170, 227,
    243, 271–80, 281

Bijou, S. W., 164, 166, 168, 174
Blasi, A., 148
Blatt, M. M., 149–50
Blehar, M. C., 331
Blos, P., 235
Borke, H., 130
Bower, T. G. R., 25, 26
Bowlby, J., 33, 37–56, 160, 250
Brackbill, Y., 163
Bretherton, I., 50, 51
Breuer, J., 223, 224
Brinker, D. B., 181
Brittenham, G. M., 341
Brown, A. L., 215
Brown, J. F., 229
Brown, P., 167
Brown, R., 110, 148, 245, 300, 301,
    307, 307n., 309–11, 315
Brückner, G. H., 32
Bruner, J., 220
Bryan, J. H., 182
Bryant, P. E., 130
Burlingham, D., 248
Butler, R. N., 260, 269

Cairns, C. E., 306n., 309
Cairns, H. S., 306n., 309
Caldwell, B. M., 26
Calufield, M., 347
Campos, J. J., 213
Candee, D., 148, 334
Cassidy, J., 333, 342
Cavanaugh, P. J., 160, 174
Cazden, C., 333
Charcot, J. M., 223
Chattin-McNichols, J., 72
Châtenay, V., 101
Child, I. L., 228
Chittenden, E., 331
Chomsky, C., 309
Chomsky, N., 73, 133, 286, 299–316,
    326, 328
Clifton, R., 331
Coates, B., 177

Cohen, S. B., 347
Colby, A., 136n., 137–41, 143, 144,
    145 (fig.), 149
Cole, M., 18, 128, 147, 195, 200, 212,
    215, 218, 220, 315
Cole, S. R., 18, 128, 147, 315
Coles, R., 247
Collins, J. L., 184
Condon, W. S., 306
Cooper, R. G., 18, 50, 54, 311, 312
Corman, H. H., 127
Costa, A. L., 329
Cowan, P. A., 187, 190
Crain, E. F., 97
Crain, S., 299, 304
Crain, W., 97
Cromer, R. F., 313

Dale, P. S., 308, 315
Damon, W., 127
Darwin, C., 28–31, 130, 264n.
Darwin, E., 28
Dasen, P. R., 128
De Baryshe, B. D., 347
Descartes, R., 4
DeVries, 125, 126
Dewey, E., 73
Dewey, J., 73, 96, 135, 192, 220
Donaldson, M., 216
Dubos, R. J., 80
Dyer, J. L., 72

Edwards, C. P., 147
Ehrlich, P. R., 30
Eisenberg, L., 273
Eisenberg-Berg, N., 182
Elkind, D., 125
Ellenberger, H., 243, 278
Elliot, P., 167
Ellis, A., 217
Engels, F., 195–97
Erasmus, D., 317
Erikson, E. H., 235, 247–70, 281,
    286, 287, 323
Ervin, S. M., 307
Escalona, S. K., 127
Estes, W. K., 167
Etzel, B. C., 163
Evans, E., 72, 127, 129
Evans, R., 259

Falco, F. L., 347
Fantz, R. L., 39
Fenichel, O., 228, 232, 233
Fernald, L. D., 170n., 343
Fernald, P. S., 170n., 343
Ferrara, R., 215
Fischel, J. E., 347
Flavell, J. H., 102, 121, 124, 127,
    129, 201, 266
Franklin, M. B., 77, 96
Freedman, D. G., 33, 37, 39, 40
Freud, A., 235–36, 241, 248, 256
Freud, S., 205–6, 222–46, 248–49,
    251–54, 256, 258, 268–70,
    281–83, 286–88, 295,
    323–24
Froebel, F., 57
Fromm, E., 317

Gandhi, M. K., 140, 153
Gardner, H., 25, 93, 132, 188, 189,
    307
Gay, P., 224
Gelfand, D. M., 176
Gelman, R., 127, 129–31
Gesell, A., xvi, 1, 16–27, 52, 174,
    193, 199, 217, 268–69, 279,
    322–23, 326
Gewirtz, J. L., 163
Gibbs, J., 150, 334
Gilbert, S. F., 18
Gilligan, C., 124, 146, 152–53, 266n.
Ginsburg, H., 101–3, 104n., 106, 114
Gitelson, M., 260
Gleitman, H., 310, 316
Gleitman, L. R., 310, 316
Glick, J., 77, 98
Goethe, J. H., 212
Goldberg, S., 54, 331
Goldman, M., 347
Goldstein, K., 320
Goldwyn, R., 51
Goleman, D., 271
Goodman, M., 216
Griffin, P., 215, 220
Grimm, The Brothers, 227
Gruber, H., 29, 130
Grusec, J. E., 181, 190, 332

Haan, N., 148, 340
Haber, R. N., 84

Haeckel, E. H., 30, 82
Hall, C., 229, 239, 246
Hanlon, C., 310
Harlow, H., 320
Harris, J. R., 160
Harris, Z., 299
Hartmann, H., 238, 241–42, 269n.
Hartsoeker, N., 2 (fig.)
Hartup, W. W., 177
Hass, W., 316
Havighurst, R. J., 260, 298
Hawton, H., 317
Heavenrich, J., 334
Hegel, G. W. F., 196
Herrnstein, R. J., 148, 300–301,
        307n., 309
Hersh, R. H., 344
Hess, E. H., 36–37
Hetherington, E. M., 179
Hewer, A., 334
Hickey, J., 340
Higgins, A., 344
Hill, J. H., 341
Hjertholm, E., 340
Hofer, M. A., 26, 78
Hogan, R., 152
Holm, K. W., 30
Holstein, C., 143
Holt, J., 65, 330
Homme, L. E., 169
Honigmann, J. J., 176
Huff, R. L., 341
Huston, A. C., 189, 191
Hyams, N. M., 302

Ilg, F. L., 16–19, 22–24, 337
Ingram, D., 313
Inhelder, B., 31, 38, 110, 112, 113
        (fig.), 114n., 119, 122, 122n.,
        267
Ironsmith, M., 347
Itard, J. M. G., 57

Jacobi, J., 290, 293, 295
Jacobson, E., 226–27
Jatich, A. M., 272
Jirari, C., 39
John-Steiner, V., 199
Jones, E., 222–23, 225, 229
Jones, M. C., 159, 189
Jung, C. G., 153, 225, 287–98, 232

Kagan, J., 51
Kamii, C. K., 125, 129, 191
Kandinsky, W., 88
Kanner, L., 271, 273
Kant, I., 75, 140, 153
Kaplan, B., 77, 88–91, 96–97, 347
Kaplan, N., 342
Kardiner, A., 245
Karen, R., 55
Karen-Karie, N., 345
Katz, D., 79
Katz, R., 79
Kauffman, K., 334
Kaufman, Y., 290, 291, 294, 297
Kegan, R., 128
Keniston, K., 147, 148
Kenell, J. H., 53–54, 341
Kessen, W., 7
King, M. L., 140, 153
Klahr, D., 329
Klaus, M. H., 53–54, 341
Klima, E. S., 308
Koegel, R. L., 341
Koffka, K., 76
Kohlberg, L., 15, 103, 117–18, 121,
        124–25, 127, 134–53, 174,
        185, 187–88, 191, 203–4,
        262, 264, 266n., 269, 323,
        325, 334, 340, 344
Kohler, W., 76, 201–2
Konner, M. J., 128
Kozulin, A., 195, 200
Kramer, R., 143
Kramer, Rita, 57–58, 73
Krashen, S. D., 316
Kris, E., 240, 338
Kuhn, D., 128, 185
Kunkel, D., 338
Kupers, C. J., 183

Labov, W., 315
Laing, R. D., 27, 297
de Lamarck, C., 29
Lamb, M. E., 160
Langer, J., 92, 334, 340
Lee, D., 86
Levinson, D., 297–98
Lieberman, M., 334
Liebert, R. M., 129, 160, 167, 180,
        192
Lightfoot, D., 312
Lillard, P. P., 58, 65, 69

Lindzey, G., 246
Lipsitt, L. P., 25, 163
Locke, J., 1, 2–7, 15, 37, 156, 318
Lonigan, C. J., 347
Looft, W. R., 127
Lorenz, K., 30n., 31–36, 80
Lovaas, O. I., 165, 170, 272, 279,
    309–10
Lovell, K., 127
Lowenstein, R. M., 338
Lozoff, B., 53–54
Luria, A. R., 194, 199, 200, 204,
    206–8
Lyons, J., 244

Maccoby, E. E., 181
McDonald, F. J., 102, 187
MacFarlane, A., 25, 26
McNeill, D., 306, 307
Main, M., 51
Malinowski, B., 244
Mandelstam, O., 210
Manning, A., 331
Marcia, J. E., 269
Marks, L., 88
Marler, J. E., 36
Marmor, G. S., 341
Martin, P. C., 20
Marx, K., 195–96
Maslow, A., 192, 319–24, 327–29
Mead, M., 181
Meichenbaum, D. H., 216
Meltzoff, A. N., 25
Mendel, G., 31
Menlove, F. L., 332
Miller, A., 258
Miller, L. B., 72
Miller, P., 331
Miller, P. H., 328
Miller, R., 329–30
Mills, C. W., 196
Mischel, W., 180
Misiak, H., 319, 320
Montessori, Maria, xvi, 1, 57–74, 96,
    125–26, 172, 191–92, 218,
    220, 285, 299, 316, 323,
    325–26, 330
Montessori, Mario, 58
Moore, M. K., 25
More, T., 317
Muchow, M., 95, 326
Munn, N. L., 19 (fig.), 162, 165,
    170n., 206

Munroe, R., 230, 233
Mussen, P. H., 182
Muuss, R. E., 8n.

Nakayama, M., 304
Nathanson, J., 334
Needham, J., 2, 2 (fig.)
Neill, A. S., 243
Neimark, E. D., 127, 128
Neugarten, B. L., 298
Nisan, M., 147

Odom, R. D., 341
Opper, S., 101–3, 104n., 106, 114

Paolitto, D. P., 344
Parke, R. D., 179
Parkes, C. M., 50
Parsons, A., 245
Pavlov, I. P., 1, 37, 154–57, 164, 171
Peill, E. J., 112
Peiper, A., 78
Pestalozzi, J. H., 330
Piaget, J., xvi, 1, 78, 97, 100–33,
    134–36, 185–88, 191–93,
    199, 204–5, 205 (fig.), 210–
    11, 217–18, 220, 258, 262,
    265–67, 313–14, 323, 325,
    328
Piatelli-Palmarini, M., 313
Pierce, A., 308
Pinker, S., 316
Plato, 4
Podd, M., 270
Pollock, L. A., 1
Poulos, R. W., 341
Power, C., 150, 151
Premack, D., 169

Rawls, J., 140
Raynor, R., 157
Redl, F., 238, 242
Reimer, J., 150, 151, 153
Rest, J., 146, 148, 153
Reynolds, C. S., 165
Rheingold, H. L., 163
Ricks, D. F., 134
Ridgeway, D., 333

Riess, B. F., 37
Rimland, B., 273
Robertson, J., 47, 48
Rogers, C., 319
Rogoff, B., 212, 215, 220
Rommetveit, R., 309
Rosenthal, T. L., 188, 190
Ross, D., 332
Ross, H. W., 344
Ross, S. A., 332
Roszak, T., 98, 330
Rousseau, J. J., xv, xvi, 1, 8–15, 57–
    59, 65, 82, 92, 96, 125, 132,
    135, 218, 269, 279, 285–86,
    322, 324–25
Rushton, J. P., 182
Russell, B., 4, 7, 243

Sachs, J. S., 306, 309
Sagi, A., 51
Sahakian, M. L., 4
Sahakian, W. S., 4
Sameroff, A. J., 160, 174
Sander, F., 76
Sander, L. W., 306
de Santiallana, G., 318
Schachtel, E., 281–86, 324, 326
Scharf, P., 340
Schneirla, T. C., 37
Schultz, D., 175, 222
Schwartz, B., 155, 165, 170
Scribner, S., 195, 200, 212, 218
Searles, H. F., 95
Sears, R. R., 175
Seguin, E., 57
Seligman, M. E. P., 160
Selman, R. K., 148
Sexton, V. S., 319, 320
Sheehy, G., 297
Sigel, I. E., 328
Simmons, J. Q., 341
Simpson, E. L., 152
Sinclair, H., 313
Singer, D. G., 74n.
Singer, J. L., 74n.
Skinner, B. F., 1, 37, 161–74, 175,
    200, 309, 313
Slade, A., 49, 50
Slobin, D. I., 207, 282, 307–9, 311
Smart, M. S., 79
Smart, R. C., 79
Snow, C. E., 311

Socrates, 153
Souberman, E., 199
Speicher, B., 334
Spock, B., 17, 160, 251
Sroufe, L. A., 18, 50, 54, 311, 312
Stanton, D. S, 331
Steiner, R., 330
Stern, W., 75
Sternberg, R. S., 346
Stevens, J., 341
Strauss, A., 96
Sullivan, H. S., 250
Sullivan, M. W., 172
Sze, W. C., 260
Szeminska, A., 110, 112, 114, 132

Tamura, M., 36
Tanner, J. M., 31, 38
Thompson, C., 245
Thompson, H., 18
Thorndike, E. L., 162, 320
Thoreau, H. D., 330
Tinbergen, N., 31–33, 80
Tiutcheve, F., 210
Tobin, S. S., 338
Tolman, E. C., 178
Totsi, D. T., 169
Trabasso, T., 131
Trause, M. A., 341
Treffert, D. A., 272
Tulkin, S. R., 128
Turiel, E., 149
Turner, E. W., 309

Uspenksky, G., 210
Uzgiris, I. C., 127

Valdez-Menchaca, M. C., 347
Valsiner, J., 215
VanIJzendoorn, M. H., 345
Vincent, E. L., 20
Voltaire, 318
Von Franz, M. L., 290
Von Frisch, K., 32
Von Uexkull, J., 75, 95
Vygotsky, L. S., xvi, 133, 177, 193–
    95, 197–207, 209–21, 315

Waddington, C. H., 31
Walbeck, N., 182

Wall, S., 331
Wallace, A. R., 29
Walters, R. H., 176, 180, 186–87,
        189
Wapner, S., 81
Waters, E., 331
Watkins, B. A., 334
Watson, J. B., 157–61
Watson, R. I., 155, 292
Watt, N. F., 96, 228, 243, 245
Weiss, R. S., 55
Wells, G., 315
Werner, H., xvi, 1, 75–85, 87–92,
        94–99, 116–17, 132, 153,
        193, 240, 316, 324–25, 326
Wertheimer, M., 76
Wertsch, J., 194–95, 218
White, G. M., 182, 189
White, R. W., 26, 96, 228, 243, 245,
        269
White, S., 127–28, 174

Whitehead, A. N., 79
Whitehurst, G. J., 315
Whiting, J. W. M., 228
Whitmont, E. C., 290–91, 294–95,
        297
Williams, C. D., 163
Wilner, W., 281
Wilson, C., 320
Wilson, W. C., 181
Wineman, D., 238, 242
Witkin, H., 77
Wohlwill, J. F., 95
Wolpe, J., 160
Wundt, W., 318

Yaeger, J., 340

Zelan, K., 96, 272
Zimmerman, B. J., 188

Subject Index

Abilities (*see* Individual differences)

Abstract thinking, 79, 83–84, 92,
(*fig.*, 92), 96–97, (*fig.*, 102),
119, 124–25, 198–200,
211–13

Accommodation, 103, 104, 107
defined, 103

Achievement:
vs. development, 25, 72–73
standards, 24
modeling effects on, 182–83

Acquisition vs. performance in
learning, 178, 180

Activism, 148, 189

Adjustment, 279, 284, 286, 293, 298

Adolescence:
Erikson's stage, 256–58, 266–67,
268
Freud, A. and S., on, 235–36, 243
Kohlberg's stages, 135, 138–41
Piaget's stage, 119–21, 267
Werner on, 78

Adult development:
Erikson, 258–62, 269
Jung, 287, 293–98, 323
Maslow, 322–24

Affection in child-rearing, 53–54,
160, 268

Affectionless characters, 46–47

Afterlife, archetype, 296

Age vs. sequence, 17, 102 (*see also*
Rate of development)

Agencies of the mind (Freud),
236–42

Aggression:
in adolescents, 11, 236, 256
in adults, 294, 295
in autistic children, 272, 276
in children, 227–28, 229–30, 231,
235, 250 (*see also* Negativistic
phase)
and classical conditioning, 158
and competition (*see* Oedipus
complex)

and operant conditioning, 136, 167
in parents, 189, 268
socialization and modeling of, 179–
80, 189
and television, 180, 189

Aggressive drive, 237, 323

Albert B. (Watson's case), 159

Allocentric attitude, 284

Allocentric senses, 283

Amnesia, 223
infantile, 282

Anal-compulsive character, 230

Anal-expulsive character, 230

Anal stage, 229–30, 245–46, (*table*,
252), 252–53, 283

Anima, 291 (*fig.*, 292), 294

Animism, 116–17

Animus, 291, (*fig.*, 292)

Anxiety:
adolescent, 236
castration, 231, 233, 234
early, 227
moral, 240
neurotic, 240
realistic, 240
separation, 43, 47, 227, 250
stranger, 43, 46, 47

Appeasement gestures, 30n.

Archetypes, 291, (*fig.*, 292), 295

Art:
in children, 92–93, 132
and physiognomic perception, 88,
90
and synesthesia, 88–89

Assimilation, 103, 104
defined, 103

Associations, 4, 7, 158–59, 162–63,
177 (*see also* Conditioning,
classical; Stimulus,
contiguity)

Associativity (logical concept), 108

Attachment:
defined, 38
as imprinting, 46

Attachment (continued)
 patterns (Ainsworth), 48–51
  in adults (Main), 51
 phases, 39–46
 Rousseau on, 15
Attention-getting, 163, 167, 267
Autism:
 causes, 273–74
 operant conditioning, 170
 psychoanalytic treatment, 274–80
 symptoms, 272–73
Autocentric senses, 283–84
Autonomy:
 Bettelheim's view, 275–77, 278–79
 of language, 303, 313, 316
 and object permanence, 265–66
 (*see also* Negativistic phase)
Autonomy vs. shame, doubt, 252–53,
  (*table*, 252), 262, 263, 264

Babbling, 41, 306
Baby box, 161
Baby talk, 90
Bandura's theory compared with:
 Chomsky's theory, 313–14
 Piaget's theory
  conservation, 188
  moral judgment, 187–88
  (*see also* Developmental change;
   Stages)
 Skinner's theory (*see* Observational
  learning, and operant
  conditioning)
Base from which to explore, 45, 48–
  50, 52–53
Beginning of thought, 106–7
Behaviorism, 157, 161, 318–19,
  328
Behavior modification:
 cognitive behavioral therapy,
  216–17
 modeling, 189
 operant, 163, 166, 167, 169–70
  with autistic children, 170
  compared with Bettelheim,
   170, 279
 systematic desensitization, 159–60
Black English (African-American
  dialects), 215
Bonding in newborns, 53–54
Brain injury, 84, 96, 195, 316
 and self-regulation, 208

Care, (*table*, 252), 259
Castration anxiety (*see* Anxiety)
Cell, 18, (*fig.*, 19)
Centration, 110, 119
Cephalocaudal trend, 17
Cerebral dominancy of reflexes, 21,
  24, 41, 78
Chains of behavior, 165
Child-proofing a home, 12, 285
Child-rearing recommendations:
 child-centered, 15, 22–24, 26–27,
  51–52, 321–22
 Erikson, 251, 268
 ethologists, 51–53
 Freud, 243
 Gesell, 22–25, 26–27
 Locke, 5–7
 Maslow, 321–22
 Montessori, 62–63
 Rousseau, 12–14
 Schachtel, 285–86
 sixteenth century, 2–3
 social-learning theory, 188–89
 talking to children, 314–15
 Watson, 160
Children:
 as blank slates, 3–4
 different from adults, 6–7 (*see also*
  Qualitative differences in
  development)
 immoral, 2–3
 innocents, 2–3
 miniature adults, 1–2, 25–26, 132,
  316 (*see also*
  Preformationism)
Children's House (Casa dei Bambini),
  38, 63
Chomsky's theory compared with
 others (*see* Language
 development)
Circular reactions, 104–6, 301
 primary, 104–5, 160
 secondary, 105, 174
 tertiary, 106, 123
Civil disobedience, 141, 148
Class, logical concept, 109
Classification, 114
Clinging in babies, 41, 43, (*fig.*, 43)
Clinical interview (Piaget's), 101
Cognitive conflict, 110–11, 123–24,
  142, 149–50, 210
Cognitive development:
 ego development, 241–42, 249–
  52, 255, 260–62

Kohlberg's stages, 136–41
Montessori's sensitive periods,
     58–62
Piaget's stages, 102–21
Rousseau's stages, 10–11
Schachtel's stages, 282–85
Vygotsky, 197–203, 210–21
Werner's levels, 78–79
Cognitive events in learning theories,
     155, 157, 167, 173, 176–77
Cognitive operations, 112–14
Cognitive schemes, 104
Cognitive science, 328
Collective monologues, 115, 203
Commands, 6 (*see also* Preaching vs.
     practicing)
Comparative approach and studies
     (Werner), 71–72, 81–89
Compensation, concept, 110, 113,
     114
Competence, (*table*, 252), 256
Competence motivation (White), 269
Competence vs. performance
     (grammatical), 302
Competition, problems with, 233–34
Computer models of cognition, 98,
     128, 328–29
Concentration, 63, 102
Concrete operations, (*table*, 102),
     110–19, 123–24, 128, 266
Concrete thinking, 10, 84
Conditioning, classical:
  basic paradigm, 155
  of emotions, 158–59
  of infants' responses, 159–60
  range of responses, 160–61
Conditioning, operant:
  and achievement, 183–84
  and aggression, 167–68, 179–80
  basic model, 161–62
  compared with classical, 161–62,
     (*fig.*, 162)
  of emotions, 168
  of language, 164–65, 170, 309–11
  and programmed instruction,
     170–73
  range of responses, 160, 161–62
  and self-efficacy, 184
  and sensori-motor activity, 174
  and sex roles, 180
  and species specific behavior, 169
Confidence:
  children in parents, 242, 250
  parents', 12, 23–24, 250, 268, 322

Conformity, 8, 9, 11, 15, 279, 293,
     320–23
  and modeling experiments, 190
Conscience (*see* Superego)
Consciousness:
  Freud, (*fig.*, 239), 239–40
  Jung, 290, (*fig.*, 292)
  Vygotsky, 211–13, 216
  Wundt, 318
  (*see also* Metacognition)
Conservation, 110–14
  continuous quantities, 110–12,
     (*fig.*, 111)
  and egocentrism, 119
  number, 112–13, (*fig.*, 113)
  sequences, 114n., 127
  training studies, 129–30
  modeling, 188
Constraints (innate):
  on classical conditioning, 160
  linguistic, 303–5, 306, 309
  on operant conditioning, 169
Constructivism, 103–5, 115, 123–24,
     125–26, 129, 174, 185, 210–
     11
Control of error, 66, 69
Conventional morality, 138–39, 141,
     269
Coordination of body schemes, 105,
     160
Coordination of secondary schemes,
     105–6
Crawling, 23, 43
Creative function of grammatical
     rules, 165, 185, 300, 301,
     309–11
Creativity, 80–81 (*see also* Art;
     Microgenetic mobility)
Cries, as signals and calls, 23, 24, 26,
     39, 41, 47, 48, 52, 55
Critical period, 34, 47, 315–16
Cross-cultural research:
  Kohlberg's stages, 147
  literacy, 199–200, 212
  Piaget's stages, 117–18, 128
  Vygotsky's work, 199–200
  (*see also* Cultural factors;
     Universals)
Cross-sectional studies, 143
Cues, taking from child, 23, 24, 26,
     48, 52, 62, 65, 72, 125, 277,
     279, 321–22
Cultural factors:
  Bandura's theory, 181

Cultural factors (continued)
  Erikson's theory, 248, 251, 253,
    256, 257
  Freud's theory, 244–45
  Gesell's theory, 18, 22, 24–25
  Kohlberg's theory, 146–47, 152
  Maslow's theory, 320–22
  Piaget's theory, 117–18, 122, 128
  Schachtel's theory, 284–86
  Vygotsky's theory, 194, 197–201,
    210–12, 217
Curiosity (*see* Interest, spontaneous)
Cylinders, 63–64, (*fig.*, 64), 66, 73

Day care, 54–55
Death, 260–61, 291, 296
Decalage, 122, 124
Decentering, 115, 116, 119, 121, 125,
    126, 139, 148
Deep structures, 305–6, 308
Defense mechanisms (*see* Ego)
Degenerate data base for children's
    language, 302, 311
Delay of gratification, 106, 238, 242
Dependency, 8, 11, 65, 73, 115, 227,
    235, 236, 268, 273
Depression, 168, 229, 260–62, 294
Detour behavior in infancy, 108, 266
Development, Werner's definition,
    77–78
Developmental change:
  Erikson, 263, 264, 269, 323
    compared with Piaget, 265, 323
  Freud, 222, 226, 323
  Piaget, 102–3, 115, 122–24, 126,
    129–30, 323
    compared with Bandura, 185–
      86, 191–92
    compared with Chomsky,
      313–14
    compared with Gesell, 102–3, 322
    compared with Skinner, 174
    compared with Vygotsky, 199,
      210–11, 219–20
  (*see also* Maturation; Learning
    theory)
Developmentalist position, xv, xvi, 8,
    14–15, 154, 170–74, 190–
    92, 218–19, 221, 279–80,
    281, 286, 322–23, 325–27,
    329–30
Dialectic, 123, 150, 196, 200, 217–18

Differentiation:
  defined, 77–78
  and egocentrism, 114–15
  Kohlberg's stages, 146
  lack of
    in children, 78, 81–90
    in infants, 78, 107–8
    in preliterate thinking, 82–84,
      85–89
    in schizophrenic thinking, 84, 85,
      87, 88, 95
  and sensori-motor intelligence,
    105, 107–8
  and symbolic activity, 89, 316
Discontinuity issue, 91–94 (*see also*
    Qualitative differences;
    Stage, rigorous definitions)
Discrimination learning, 156, 164–65
Disequilibrium in development, 20,
    123, 150 (*see also* Cognitive
    conflict)
Disinhibitory effects, 180
Displacements (Piaget), 108
Distress calls, 32, 39, 41, 55
Dreams:
  Freud on, 241, 244
  Jung on, 295
    compared with Freud, 295
  Piaget, children's conceptions,
    117–18
Drive:
  component of instinct, 33
  Freud, 237
  general drive vs. instinct, 34
  Skinner, 168–69

Early stimulation and maturation, 18
Educational recommendations:
  Chomsky, 314–15
  Freud, 243–44
  Gesell, 24–25
  holistic educators, 329–30
  Kamii's constructivism, 125–26
  Kohlberg, 149–51
  Locke, 5–7
  Montessori, xvi, 52–58, 63–74,
    323
  Piaget, 124–25
    compared with Montessori,
      124–25
    compared with Rousseau,
      124–25

programmed instruction (Skinner),
170–73
compared with Montessori,
172–73
Rousseau, 12–15
Schachtel, 285–86
sixteenth century, 23
Vygotsky, 210–16
compared with Piaget, 210–12
Rousseauist (developmentalist)
critique, 218–21
Werner, 96–97
Ego:
Erikson, 249–62, 269
Freud's concept
defined, 238
defenses, 241
in adolescence, 236
and delay, 238, 242
development, 241–42
harmonizing role, 240
levels of awareness, 239–40,
(*fig.*, 239)
Hartmann, 241–42, 269n.
Jung, (*fig.*, 290), 292
regression in service of, 240, 325
Egocentric speech, 115
Vygotsky vs. Piaget, 203–5
Egocentric thought:
adult egocentrism, 2, 10, 81, 124
and attachment, 45
Piaget's concept, 114–15
criticized, 130
defined, 114
at each period, 120–21
and Kohlberg's stages 1 and 2,
148
and other forms of
preoperational thought,
188–89
overcoming, 115
Ego ideal, 239
Ego identity (*see* Identity vs. role
confusion)
Ego integrity vs. despair, (*table*, 252),
260–62, 296
Eidetic imagery, 84
Electra complex, 234
Elizabeth von R. (Freud's case), 223
Embryology:
early views, 2
and evolution, 30–31
modern, 17–18, 263, 302

Emile's education, 12–14
Environment of adaptedness, 38,
53
Equilibration, 123, 150
Equilibrium, 20, 22, 120
Erikson's theory compared with:
Gesell's theory, 269 (*see also*
Maturation)
Freud's theory, 247–49, 251, 252–
58, 323
Piaget's theory (*see* Developmental
change; Stages)
Rousseau's theory, 269
Maslow's theory, 323–24, 326
Erogenous zones, 226, 229, 230
and modes, 249, 251, 252, 253,
269
Evolution (*see* Natural selection)
Exercises of daily living, 65, (*fig.*,
67), 69
Exhibitionism, 225, 230
Explosion of language, 61
Explosion of reading, 69
Explosion of writing, 69
Extinction:
classical conditioning, 155–56,
159–60
operant conditioning, 163, 166,
169, 170
Extraversion/introversion:
Gesell, 20
Jung, 292–93

Fairy tales:
Bettelheim on, 74, 227–28
Montessori on, 71, 73–74
Fantasy:
Montessori on, 71–72, 73–74
neurotics, 224
phallic stage child, 230–31, 254,
266
Fear:
conditioning, 158–59
eliminating, 159–60
of strangers, 43, 46, 47
Feeding infants, 21–23, 249–50,
321–22
Fidelity, (*table*, 252), 258
Five-to-seven shift, 128
Fixation, 228–29
Fixed action pattern, 33
Formal operations, (*table*, 102), 119–
21, 125, 135, 192, 267

Formal operations (continued)
in tribal societies, 128
Free association, 223
Free choice, 64–65
Freud's theory compared with:
Erikson's theory, 247–49, 251,
252–58, 323
Maslow's theory, 232–36
Schachtel's theory, 282, 286
Jung's theory (*see* Dreams)
Functional asymmetry, 20–21

Generalization:
response, 165, 310
teaching Piagetian concepts, 129
(*see also* Stimulus, generalization)
Generativity vs. self-absorption,
stagnation, (*table*, 252),
259–60
Genes, 18, (*fig.*, 18)
Genetic epistemology, 101
Geometric-technical perception, 85,
87
Gesell's theory compared with:
Bettelheim's theory, 277
Bowlby's child-rearing advice, 52
learning theory, 25
Maslow's theory, 322, 326
Piaget's theory (*see* Developmental
change)
(*see also* Maturation)
Gestalt psychology, 72, 292
Goal-corrected following, 33, 44–45,
56
Good interpersonal relationships
(Kohlberg's stage), 138, 141,
147, 152
Grades, 7, 65, 191
Graduate preparation, 66
Grammar:
competence vs. performance, 302
growth of, 60–62, 306–9
rules, 60, 300–302
creative function, 300
universal grammar, 302–3
Grasping, 19, (*fig.*, 20), 104, 123,
249–51
Greeting, babies', 43–48
Group, mathematical, 108
Guilt, 223, 227, 231, 233, 239, 254
(*see also* Superego)

Habits, 4
Hallucinations, 237, 238, 241
Hand-eye coordination, 19, (*fig.*, 19),
68, 78, 103, 105
Hans (Freud's case), 231
Hearing, 249, 283, 284
intersensory (synesthetic), 88–89,
90
Heteronomy, moral, 116, 135
Hierarchic integration, 77–78, 79,
80, 122, 145–46, 264
defined, 77–78
Higher order conditioning, 156, 158
Holding on:
anal stage, 229, 252, 267
reflexes, 41, (*fig.*, 43)
(*see also* Grasping)
Holistic approach, 76, 329–30
Hope, 251–52, (*table*, 252)
Humanistic philosophy, 317–18
Humanistic psychology, xvi, 319–30
and developmentalists, xvi, 322–
27, 329–30
and learning theorists, 318, 327
Hypnosis, 223
Hypothetical thinking, (*table*, 102),
119–20, 122, 267
Hysteria, 223, 224, 242

Id, 237, 238, 239, (*fig.*, 239), 240,
241
Idealism in adolescence, 120, 218
Identification:
in Erikson's case of Peter, 267
and identity, 257
and Oedipus complex, 231, 234
Identity concept (Piaget), 110, 113
Identity vs. role confusion, (*table*,
252), 256–58, 264, 266
and formal operations, 266–67
identity foreclosure, 258
identity formation, 257
and Kohlberg's stages, 269
psychosocial moratorium, 247, 257
Imitation, 4, 6, 175–92
deferred, 107, 177
exact copying vs. abstract
modeling, 185, 311
expanded, 311–12, 315
and language development, 89–90,
300, 311–12, 315
motoric basis (Piaget), 107, 109

and reinforcement, 178, 180–81
Imprinting, 34–37, (*fig.*, 35), 39, 46, 47
and language development, 61, 303
and songs, 36
Impulses, trusting, 26–27, 321–22
Impulsivity, 237–38, 242
Incest taboo, 231, 244
Incestuous wishes, 230–31, 254
Independence:
adolescent quest, 236
defensive, 49, 50
Jung, 295
Kamii, 125–26
Kohlberg, 15, 139, 149–51
Maslow, 320–21
Montessori, xvi, 62, 63, 65–66, 72, 73
and responsiveness to babies' cues, 26, 52, 55
Piaget, 103, 106, 115, 124, 129, 211
Rousseau, 8, 11–15
U.S. value, 260, 263
Vygotsky, 211, 220
(*see also* Autonomy vs. shame, doubt; Conformity)
Individual differences:
abilities, 22, 23, 24, 84, 128, 214, 256, 321, 327
attachment, 48–51
developmental rates, 17, 21, 25, 102, 128, 147
and temperament, 22
interests, 128
microgenetic mobility, 80, 96–97
(*see also* Multilinear development)
Individualism and exchange morality, 137, 141, 142, 143, 148, 151
Individuation, 295
Industry vs. inferiority, (*table*, 252), 254–56
and concrete operations, 266
Infantile amnesia, 282, 283
Inhibitory effects of models, 180
Inhibitory effects of speech, 207
Initiative vs. guilt, (*table*, 252), 254, 262, 266, 267
and preoperational thought, 266
Innate constraints (*see* Constraints)
Innate ideas, 4
Inner speech, 202, 203, 209–10
and microgenesis, 209–10

Instinct, 32–34, 37–38, 39, 56, 292, 297, 321
defined, 32–33
Institutional deprivation, 46–47, 53–54
Intelligence tests, 101, 195, 214, 326
Interest, spontaneous, xv, xvi, 7, 10, 12, 18, 58–62, 64, 71, 72, 106, 123, 125, 126, 150, 174, 185–86, 191–92, 229, 230, 254, 265, 285, 326, 330 (*see also* Moderate novelty)
Internalization, 202, 203, 206, 207–8
Intimacy vs. isolation, 258–59, (*table*, 252)
Intrinsic growth forces, xv, xvi, 8, 12, 14, 154, 193, 199, 222, 279, 298, 322–24, 327, 329–30 (*see also* Maturation; Developmental change)
Intrinsic motivation, 65–66, 72, 105, 123
Bandura vs. Piaget, 185–86 (*see also* Interest, spontaneous)
Introversion (*see* Extraversion/introversion)
Invariant sequence:
Bandura, 186, 187
Erikson, 262–63
Freud, 226
Gesell, 17, 18
Kohlberg, 143–44
Piaget, 102, 114, 118, 121, 127
Rousseau, 11
Inversion, concept, 112, 113
Irradiation, 156

Justice, 140–41, 149, 153

Laboratory research:
and ethology, 32, 36–37
social learning, 190
Language:
and cognition
Piaget, 108–10, 112, 313–14
Vygotsky, 201–2, 203–5, 209
conventional labeling
Schachtel, 282–87
Werner, 89–90
instruction, 310, 311–12, 315
and microgenesis, 90–91, 209–10
teaching apes, 310

Language (continued)
  verbal coding and imitation, 177
  verbal coding and memory, 177,
    282–83
  verbal regulation of behavior, 205–
    10, 216
Language development:
  abstract modeling, 185
  Chomsky, 299–316
    compared with Bandura, 311–12
    compared with Montessori, 73,
      299, 316
    compared with Piaget, 313
    compared with Skinner, 309–11
    compared with Werner, 316
  ego function, 241
  imitation, 185, 300, 311–12
  Montessori, 60–62, 73, 299, 316
  operant conditioning, 165, 170,
    309–11
  psycholinguistic research, 306–9
  Rousseau, 10
  Werner, 89–91
Latency stage, 235, (*table*, 252), 254–
    56, 266
Law and order morality, 138–39
Learning curve, (*fig.*, 163)
Learning problems, psychoanalytic
    view, 243–44
Learning theory, xv, xvi, 3–7,
    154–92
Libido, 226
Life review, 260, 269
Locke's theory compared with:
  preformationism, 3
  Rousseau's theory, 8
Logic, Piaget's theory, 108, 110, 112,
    120, 132
Longitudinal studies, 143
Love:
  Borg (Erikson's case), 161
  conditioning of, 158
  Erikson, adulthood, (*table*, 252),
    259
  growth of (ethological studies), 42,
    43, 46–47
  loss of, 234, 245, 267
  parental, 40–41, 53–54, 259
  in therapeutic environment
    (Bettelheim), 274–75, 278,
    279, 324

Making interesting sights last, 105, 174
Mandala, 288, (*fig.*, 289), 292

Marital difficulties, 258–60, 295
Masculinity complex, 324
Maslow's theory compared with
    various developmentalists,
    321–27
Maturation:
  of attachment phases, 39–45, 56
  Chomsky, 306
  defined, 17–18
  Erikson, 249, 251, 253, 263, 264,
    265, 269, 323
  Freud, 222, 226
  Gesell, 17–27, 322
  guide for child-rearing, 15, 22–24,
    26–27, 52, 62–63, 268, 285,
    321, 322, 330
  Hartmann, 241–42, 269
  and imprinting, 37
  Kohlberg, 142, 146, 323
  Maslow and humanists, 321–22,
    330
  Montessori, 58–59
  Piaget, 102–3, 122–23, 265, 323
  recapitulation in embryology,
    30–31
  Rousseau, 14
  Schachtel, 284
  Skinner, 174
  Vygotsky, 193, 199, 214–15, 217
  Werner, 97
Mediated behavior (Vygotsky), 198
Member-of-society moral perspective,
    139
Memory:
  aids, 177, 197, 200–201
  deferred imitation, 107, 177
  metamemory, 177, 201, 216
  photographic (eidetic), 84
  verbal and preverbal, 282–83
Metacognition, 212 (*see also* Memory,
    metamemory)
Metamorphoses, 92
Microgenesis, 80, 90–91, 209–10
Microgenetic mobility, 80–81, 97
Mid-life crisis, 293–96
Misbehavior in school, 70
Mistakes, xv, xvi, 10, 13, 24, 62, 66,
    69, 72, 101, 126, 172, 307–8
Modeling, xv, 175–92
  abstract modeling, 185–88
    of conservation, 188
    of language, 185, 311–12
    of moral judgment, 149, 187–88
  of aggression, 179–80, 189

developmentalist view, 185–86,
190–91
Locke, 4, 6
of prosocial behavior, 181–82
of self-efficacy, 184
of self-regulation, 183
of sex roles, 180–81
Models, symbolic and verbal, 176,
182, 189
televised, 189
Moderate novelty, 105, 123, 186, 191
Modes (Erikson's):
biting and grasping, 249
incorporation, 249
intrusion, 254
retention and elimination, 252
Montessori's theory compared with:
Chomsky's theory, 73, 299, 316
Kamii's theory, 126
Maslow's theory, 322–23
Piaget's theory (*see* Educational
recommendations)
Programmed instruction (*see*
Educational
recommendations)
Rousseau's theory, xvi, 58–59,
124–25
Moral judgment:
Kohlberg's stages, 136–53
and behavior, 147–48
compared with Piaget's stages,
135, 136, 138, 187–88
Gilligan's critique, 152–53
and other forms of cognition,
148–49
Piaget's stages
autonomy and heteronomy,
115–16, 135
consequences vs. intentions,
135–37
and egocentrism, 116, 118–19
modeling effects on, 187–88
Moratorium (*see* Identity vs. role
confusion)
Motherese, 311–12
Motor development, 16–21, 25, 26,
41–44, 59–60, 78, 238,
241–42, 249, 252–53, 254
(*see also* Sensori-motor
intelligence)
prenatal, 17, 77–78
Moveable alphabet, 69
Movement through stages (*see*
Developmental change)

Multilinear development, 91, (*fig.*,
92)
Myths, 227, 244, 291

Narcissism, 226–27, 229
Naturalistic observation, 32
Natural selection, 29–31
Need for order, xv, 29–31
Needs, hierarchical order, 320
Negative education, 14
Negatives in speech, 308
Negativistic phase, 23, 218, 252, 262,
269
Nervous system, 17, 18, 20, 78
Neurosis, 224, 226 (*see also* Hysteria)
Newborns' capacities, 19, 25–26, 39,
53, 306
Newborns in hospital, 53–54
"New math," 124
Normalization, 64
Norms (Gesell's), 22, 25
No-trial learning, 176
Noun-phrase units, 304–5, 307

Obedience and punishment moral
orientation, 136–37
Object permanence, 78, 107–8, 226,
265
Object relations, 242
Observational learning:
attentional processes, 177, 181
motor reproduction processes, 178
and operant conditioning (direct
rewards and punishments),
176, 178, 180, 181, 183, 184
reinforcement and motivational
processes, 178, 184
retention processes, 177
(*see also* Imitation; Modeling)
Oedipus complex, 224, 230–34, 254,
256
in adolescents, 235–36
in adults, 232, 234
cultural critique, 244–45
Old age:
Erikson, (*table*, 252), 260–62, 269
Jung, 296
One-word utterances, 306
Operant conditioning (*see*
Conditioning)
Operation (Piaget), 112
Oral stage, 226–29, 242, 249–52,
(*table*, 252), 262, 265

Oral stage (continued)
  and delay of gratification, 242
Organismic orientation, 76, 81, 89
  and symbol formation, 89
Organization (Piaget's concept), 103
Orthogenic principle, 77–78, 82
Orthogenic School, 271, 274
Overregularizations, 307–8, 309,
  311, 311n.

Palmar grasp, 19, (*fig.*, 20)
Partnership behavior in attachment,
  45–46
Passive voice, 305, 309, 311, 313
Patterns of growth (Gesell), 19–20
Peak experiences, 321n.
Peer interaction:
  Erikson, 255
  Piaget, 115, 116, 123, 125, 126
Penis envy, 233
  critique, 245
Perception:
  child's fresh, 284–85, 321, 324
  vs. conceptual thought (Werner),
    79
  of details, 59
  infants', 25, 39, 53, 78, 306
  vs. logic (Piaget), 110, 113, 131
  of order, 59
  organismic approach, 81
  "pct.-cs.", Freud, 239, (*table*, 239)
  physiognomic, 85–88, 90, 91, 92,
    99, 116–17, 326
  pictorial imagery, 84–85
  synesthetic, 88
  and specific senses, 282–83
  tied to action/emotion, 10, 79, 81,
    83, 92
  of words, 61, 89–90, 306 (*see also*
    Microgenesis)
Periods, Piaget's, (*table*, 102)
Permissiveness, 24, 26, 51–52, 160
Perseveration, 207–8
Persona, 290, (*fig.*, 292)
Perversions, 225
Peter (Erikson's case), 267
Peter (M. C. Jones's case), 159, 189
Phallic stage, 230–33, (*table*, 252),
  253, 263, 266, 267
Phenomenology, 94–95, 278, 286,
  319, 321, 325–26
Phrase structure units, 304, 305,
  307

Piaget's theory compared with:
  Bandura's theory
    conservation, 188
    moral judgment, 187–88
    (*see also* Developmental change;
      Stages)
  Chomsky's theory (*see*
    Developmental change)
  Erikson's theory (*see* Developmental
    change; Stages)
  Gesell's theory (*see* Developmental
    change)
  Kohlberg's theory, 141–42 (*see also*
    Moral judgment)
  Maslow's theory, 323, 325, 326
  Montessori's theory, 323 (*see also*
    Educational
    recommendations)
  Rousseau's theory, 131–32 (*see also*
    Educational
    recommendations)
  Skinner's theory, 173 (*see also*
    Developmental change)
  Vygotsky's theory (*see*
    Developmental change;
    Egocentric speech)
Pincer grasp, 19, (*fig.*, 20)
Play, make-believe, 92, 109, 132, 219,
  219n.
Pleasure principle, 237, 283
Postconventional morality, 139–41,
  146, 149, 153, 269
Practice in learning, 4, 6
Praise, 5, 65, 167, 179, 187
Preaching vs. practicing, 182, 189
Preconcepts, 109
Preconscious, 239–40, (*fig.*, 239)
Preconventional morality, 136
Preformationism, 1–2, (*fig.*, 2), 25,
  316
Prenatal growth, 17, 263, 302
Preoperational thought, (*table*, 102),
  108–19, 132, 266, 325
  criticized, 130–31
Preverbal experience, 278, 282–83
  (*see also* Sensori-motor
    intelligence)
Primitive thought, 79–80, 82, 88–89,
  99
Principles, moral, 140–41, 148, 149,
  152
Prior-to-society moral perspective,
  139

Programmed instruction (*see*
    Educational
    recommendations)
Projection, 290–91
Protest-despair-detachment, 47
Psychoanalytic theory, xvi, 222–98
Psychological predicate of sentence,
    209
Psychological subject of sentence,
    209
Psychosis, 227, 288, 297 (*see also*
    Autism; Schizophrenia)
Puberty (*see* Adolescence)
Punishment in operant conditioning,
    166–67 (*see also* Rewards
    and punishments)
Purpose, (*table*, 252), 254
Puzzle box, 162, 175

Qualitative differences in
    development:
    Bettelheim, 278, 281
    developmentalists, 325
    Erikson, 262, 281
    Kohlberg, 142
    in language, 60–61, 306, 308, 312,
        316
    Locke, 7
    Montessori, 59–61
    Piaget, 101, 121, 152
    Rousseau, 10, 14, 131
    Werner, 92–93, 132

Rage, conditioned, 158 (*see also*
    Aggression)
Rate of development:
    and age, 17, 22, 102
    and temperament, 22
Rate of responding, 162
    Premack principle, 169
Reading, 66–69, 72, 199–200 (*see
    also* Writing)
Reality principle, 238
Recapitulation, 11, 30–31, 82
Reciprocal interweaving, 20
Reflexes:
    grasp, 41, (*fig.*, 43)
    id, 237
    Moro, 41, (*fig.*, 42)
    in Piaget's theory, 103, 104
    rooting, 41

sucking, 41
tonic neck, 21, (*fig.*, 21)
unconditioned, 155, 155n.
walking, 25, 26
Regression:
    Erikson, 267
    Freud, 228
    Gesell, 21
    Kohlberg, 143, 153, 325
    in service of ego, 240, 325
    Werner, 80 (*see also* Microgenesis)
Rehearsal in modeling, 177
Reinforcement:
    and attention to models, 178, 181
    continuous, 166
    and drive, 168–69
    immediacy, 164
    negative, 166
    as probability of response, 169
    in programmed instruction, 172
    and punishment, 167
    schedules, 165–66
    self-reinforcement, 178, 182–83,
        191
    vicarious, 178, 179–80
    (*see also* Conditioning, operant;
        Observational learning)
Reinforcer, primary and secondary,
    163
Reinforcing stimuli, 162, (*fig.*, 162)
Relativistic moral thought, 116, 135,
    137, 141, 148
Releaser, 32–33, 39, 41, 46, 56
    filled in in imprinting, 34, 39, 46
Reliability of ratings, 136, 136n., 279
Religion, 251, 268, 287–88, 291, 292,
    296, 297
Repetitions, Montessori's, 63, 65, 301
Repression, 223, 224, 231, 233, 234,
    241, 242, 244, 266, 291, 294
Rescuing behavior in animals, 30, 32,
    41
Resistance, 324
Respondent, 161, (*fig.*, 162)
Response generalization (*see*
    Generalization)
Retardation, mental, 57, 310
Retentive mode, 252, 267
Reversibility (Piaget), 108, 112
Rewards and punishments:
    Locke, 4–5, 7
    Montessori, 65–66
    Rousseau, 14

Rewards and punishments (continued)
  vicarious, 176, 178–79
  (*see also* Conditioning, operant)
Rights, individual (moral judgment),
    139–41
Role-taking and moral judgment,
    142, 148–49
Romanticism, 8, 98, 324–25, 327
Rousseau's theory compared with:
  Bettelheim, 279, 324
  Erikson, 269, 323
  Gesell, 16
  holistic paradigm, 329
  Locke, 8
  Maslow, 322–27
  Montessori, xvi, 58–59 (*see also*
      Educational
      recommendations)
  Piaget (*see* Educational
      recommendations)
  preformationism, 8
  Werner, 92, 324–25
Rousseauian critique:
  of Chomsky, 316
  of Piaget, 131–32
  of Vygotsky (*see* Educational
      recommendations)
Rules, as commands, 6 (*see also*
      Preaching vs. practicing)
Rules, grammatical, 300

Sandpaper letters, (*fig.*, 68), 69, 72,
    96
Scheme (Piaget), defined, 104
Schizophrenia, 26–27, 80, 84, 87, 95,
    229
Scientific concepts (Vygotsky),
    211–13
Secondary process thinking, 238
Self:
  archetype, 292, (*fig.*, 292)
  differentiated from external world,
      38, 85, 89, 226–27, 229, 295
Self-actualization, 320–22, 330
Self-analysis, Freud's, 224
Self-control, 5, 238–39
Self-demand feeding, sleeping, 21,
    23, 321, 322
Self-efficacy, 183–85
Self-image, vs. ego, 238
Self-regulation:
  Bandura, 182–83, 191–92
  Gesell, 21, 23

  verbal
    Luria, 206–9
    Vygotsky, 198, 201–6
  Vygotsky, 197–206, 212–13
Self-reinforcement, Bandura, 178
Semantic categories, 307
Semantic vs. excitatory function of
    speech, 207
Sensitive periods:
  bonding, 53–54
  Montessori's
    defined, 59
    details, 59, (*fig.*, 61)
    hands, 60, (*fig.*, 61)
    language, 60–62, (*fig.*, 61)
    order, 59, (*fig.*, 61)
    walking, 60, (*fig.*, 61)
Sensori-motor-affective level
    (Werner), 78
Sensori-motor intelligence, (*table*,
    102), 103–8
  in kittens, 130
  and language, 313
  and operant conditioning, 174
Separation anxiety (*see* Anxiety)
Separations from parents, 38, 47–48,
    53, 267 (*see also* Strange
    Situation)
Sequences (*see* Invariant sequences)
Sex:
  adolescents, 11, 235–36, 243,
      256–57
  adults
    inhibitions, 168, 223–24, 226
    "utopia of genitality," 259
  childhood, 138, 225–35, (*fig.*,
      232), 245, 249–54, 263
  drive, 235, 237, 254, 256, 323 (*see
      also* Libido)
  education, 243
  Freud's definition, 225
Sex (gender) differences, 180–81,
    291
Sex roles, 180–81, 291, 293, 295
Shadow, 290–91, (*fig.*, 292), 294
Shaping, 165, 169, 170, 171, 176
Shoe-tying, 66, (*fig.*, 67)
Siblings and Oedipus complex, 233,
    234n.
Signals (*see* Cues; Cries)
Signs and sign systems, Vygotsky,
    197–221
  defined, 197

Skinner box, 162, (*fig.*, 163), 175
Smell, 282–83, 285
Smiling in infants, 39–41, (*fig.*, 40), 55
Social contract and individual rights (moral judgment), 139–41
Social order (moral judgment), 138–39, 141, 142, 146, 147
Socialization:
　Bandura, 178–85, 187–88, 189, 192
　Bettelheim, 279
　defined, 178–79
　Erikson, 253, 254, 263, 265
　Freud, 222, 226, 229, 231
　Gesell, 18, 24–25
　Jung, 291, 293, 295, 298
　Kohlberg, 142, 146
　Locke, 7
　Maslow and humanists, 320–23, 330
　Rousseau, 8, 14, 322
　Schachtel, 283, 285, 286
　Vygotsky, 199–200, 202, 205–8, 211, 216, 217, 239, 243
Socialization, social-learning studies:
　aggression, 179–80
　conservation, 188
　moral judgment, 187
　prosocial behavior, 181–82
　self-efficacy, 184
　self-regulation (achievement) standards, 182–83
　sex-roles, 180–81
Socialization and technical skills, 179, 330
Socratic teaching, 150
Space:
　infant's sense, 106, 108
　young child's sense, 83
Species-specific behavior, 33, 169, 303, 310
Spoiling, 24, 52
Spontaneous concepts (Vygotsky), 211–13
Spontaneous recovery, 156, 163
Stage, rigorous definitions, 121–22, 142–46, 262–64
Stages:
　attachment, 39–46
　Erikson's, 248–62
　　compared with Piaget's, 265–67
　Freud's, 225–36
　grammar development, 306–9

Kohlberg's, 136–41
Piaget's, 103–21
　Bandura's critique, 186, 187, 192
Rousseau's, 10–11
Schachtel's, 282–85
Skinner's view, 173–74
Stages, generality of:
　Erikson's stages, 262
　　compared with Freud's, 248–49
　Kohlberg's stages, 143, 188
　Piaget's stages, 103–22, 127–28, 186
Stimulus:
　conditioned, 155, 158, 159, 160
　contiguity, 177
　discrimination, 156
　discriminative, 164
　eliciting, 161, (*fig.*, 162)
　generalization, 156, 159, 164
　unconditioned, 155
Stimulus-bound behavior, 96, 197–98, 201–2, 208
Strange Situation, 48, 51, 55
Sublimation, 221, 241
Sucking, non-nutritive, 104, 225
Superego, 168, 205–6, 238–39, (*fig.*, 239), 240, 241
Surface and deep structures, 305–6, 308
Survival value:
　of attachment, 38–39, 48–49, 55
　of imprinting, 37
　of instincts, 33–34
　of smile, 41
Symbol formation:
　Piaget, (*table*, 102), 109, 313
　Werner, 89–91
Symptoms, 223, 224
　Bettelheim on, 277, 278, 279–80
Syncretic thinking, 82–83
Synesthesia, 88–89, 92
Syntactic categories, 307–8

Tabula rasa, 3
Tag questions, 301, 304, 305
Taoistic letting be, 321
Taoists, 291
Taste, 282, 284
Teacher's attitude in Montessori school, 65, 66, 72, 73
Temporal order, classical conditioning, 155

Therapy, psychoanalytic, 207, 223–24, 242–43, 274–80, 297, 322, 324 (*see also* Behavior modification)
Thermal sense, 282
Thinking skills, 127–28, 186, 329
Time:
  infant's sense, 106
  young child's sense, 83
Toilet-training, 27, 229–30, 253, 263, 276, 283
Tool-use and technology, 98, 195–97, 255, 264, 328–30
  and human evolution, 30, 196–97
  psychological tools, 197–221
Topography of behavior, 169, 174
Training studies, conservation, 129–30
Transductive reasoning, 109
Transformational rules, 300–301, 303–7, 308
  and concrete operations, 313
Transition through stages (*see* Developmental change)
Trial-and-error learning, 106, 107, 160–61, 176
Trust vs. mistrust, 249–52, (*table*, 252), 262, 263, 264–65
  and object permanence, 265
Trust in Bettelheim's approach, 275, 278
Twin studies, 18
Two-word utterances, 306–7, (*table*, 307)
Tying frame, 60, (*fig.*, 67)

Unconscious:
  Freud, 223, 225, 237, (*fig.*, 238), 240, 241
  Jung
    collective unconscious, 291, (*fig.*, 292)
    personal unconscious, 291, (*fig.*, 292)
Unconscious grasp of language, 60–61, (*fig.*, 61), 301–2
Universal moral principles, 140–41

Universals:
  developmentalists' search, 326–27
  stages as
    Erikson, 263–64
    Kohlberg, 143–45
    language development, 309
    Piaget, 122

Verbal coding (*see* Language)
Vision, infants', 19, 25, 39–40, 283–84
Vygotsky's theory compared with:
  Gesell's theory, 193–94, 199, 217
  Piaget's theory (*see* Developmental change; Educational recommendations; Egocentric speech)
  Rousseau's theory (*see* Educational recommendations)

Walking, 18, 24, 60, 62
  and parental attitudes, 62
Warning calls, 33
Weaning, 246, 250, 263
Wernerian critique of Chomsky, 316
Werner's theory compared with:
  Rousseau's theory on discontinuity, 92, 132
  Maslow's theory, 324–25
Will, (*table*, 252), 253
Will-power (and verbal self-regulation), 206
Wisdom:
  infants', 23, 321
  older people's, (*table*, 252), 260, 262
Wish-fulfillment, 237
Work (*see* Generativity vs. self-absorption, stagnation)
Working models, attachment, 45, 51
Writing, 66–69, 72, 198, 199–200, 210, 212, 219

Zone of proximal development, 214–15, 218–20
Zones (*see* Erogenous zones)